The Flatbush Journal of Jewish Law and Thought

Volume 15 / Summer 2013

A publication of
Hakirah, Inc.
www.Hakirah.org

Ḥakirah

The Flatbush Journal of Jewish Law and Thought

Volume 15 / Summer 2013

MINHAG

הלכה

תלמוד תורה

Introduction

In this volume of *Ḥakirah* we reflect upon the challenges the people of Israel have faced in their long *galut* amongst the nations of the world.

In our opening essay "A Yeshiva Curriculum in Western Literature," a prominent columnist and thinker suggests an approach to Western literature that allows Torah students to consider both what they can learn from the Western world of our exile and what the Torah has to teach the modern world. In a review essay of Gerald J. Blidstein's "Society and Self: On the Writings of Rabbi Joseph B. Soloveitchik," we engage the writings of the twentieth-century Torah giant who willingly confronted the outside world, embracing that which is consistent with the Torah while distancing himself and his many followers from ideas and movements which are not.

Two articles deal with *kiddush ha-Shem*, the obligation of a Jew to place his commitment to his faith above his life—an obligation that many have been called upon to fulfill over the last two thousand years. "Jewish GIs and Their Dog-Tags" looks at how, historically, the Jewish American soldier's dog-tag was a source of danger to him and analyzes whether there was a halakhic prohibition against altering it to disguise his religion. Another essay, "Kiddush HaShem: Israel's Mission," contrasts Rambam's understanding of this mitzvah with that of others and looks at recent applications of the principle of *kiddush ha-Shem* in light of his understanding.

Two articles deal with how medieval scholars maintained adherence to halakha in their day and even enhanced the study of Torah in the medieval Diaspora. "Concise and Succinct: Sixteenth Century Editions of Medieval Halakhic Compendiums" demonstrates how the Rishonim responded to the needs of their time by compiling practical halakhic guides. "The Emergence and Development of Tosafot on the Talmud" shows how a small group of scholars in Northern France and Germany plumbed the depths of Torah and recorded their attempts to resolve all the apparent contradictions in the Babylonian Talmud. "The Gaon of Rogatchov: A Study in Abstraction" shows how the creative process of Talmud study continues to expand even in recent years, with an exploration of the methodology of the Rogatchover Gaon.

The joyful return of the Jewish People to the Land of Israel after two thousand years and the emergence of the democratic State of Israel brought new challenges to halakhic Jews. Israel's fourth Chief Rabbi, Shlomo Goren, faced the task of trying to implement the principles of the Torah under the critical eyes of both gentiles and Jews who were committed to the principles of western democracy. Some of his more controversial halakhic decisions are discussed in a Hebrew article. "The Propriety of a Civil Will" deals with an issue that is common when Jews live in foreign lands and analyzes whether a will written under secular law can be viewed as binding in halakha.

Other essays look at common customs and discuss their origins. "Should Visiting the Cemetery be Encouraged or Discouraged?" examines whether frequent visits to graves and prayer at gravesites are halakhicly sound practices. "The History of Pointing to the Torah and other Hagbaha Customs" suggests that what has now become widespread practice originated as recently as fifty years ago.

A final Hebrew essay suggests that Rabbi Yehuda HaNasi, author of the Mishnah, did not consider the thirty-nine prohibited *melakhot* of Shabbos to be based solely on the work done in the Mishkan.

Special thanks to all those who worked hard to make this edition of *Ḥakirah* a reality, including Ari Bornstein, Nina Ackerman Indig and Pearl Lam who helped proofread and copyedit the articles; and Heshy Roz for participating in the review process of many of the submitted manuscripts. Thanks also to Ronny Hersh for his constant encouragement and support; Tuvia Ganz for cover design and production; and Chaim Lam for the design and maintenance of our Web page, www.Hakirah.org.

It is our continuing hope that the articles in this journal will stimulate thought, study and discussion, and inspire other members of the public to contribute their own insights. The articles we print thus reflect a wide range of opinion and do not necessarily reflect the view of our Editorial Board. ☙

Instructions for Contributors

Ḥakirah, The Flatbush Journal of Jewish Law and Thought, publishes original, interesting, well-researched and well-organized manuscripts that provide new or profound insights into areas of Jewish *halakhah* and *hashkafah.*

Manuscripts should be in Microsoft Word format and sent as an email attachment to HakirahFlatbush@msn.com. Short references—for example, to a Biblical verse or to a page within the Talmud—should be embedded directly into the text of the manuscript. Longer references should be inserted electronically as footnotes, rather than endnotes.

The author's name should not appear on the manuscript, as it is the Journal's policy to forward the articles for evaluation without disclosing the author's identity. On a separate cover sheet include your name, a short bio, an abstract of your article, your telephone number, fax number, and e-mail address.

After reviewing and accepting your manuscript, we are likely to request clarification of certain points. A revised electronic copy of your manuscript will then be required.

To encourage a wide variety of contributors, the Journal accepts articles employing the Hebrew transliteration style of either *Encyclopedia Judaica* or *ArtScroll.* If you have no preference we suggest you follow the pronunciation rules used by the *Encyclopedia Judaica.* Words in languages other than English should always be italicized, unless the foreign words have become part of the English language.

For more information about writing an article for *Ḥakirah* see <www.Hakirah.org\HakirahGuideToWriting.pdf>.

Letters to the Editor

The Eruvin in Brooklyn

RABBI ADAM MINTZ'S important historical review of the *eruvin* in Brooklyn omits mention of the *eruv* established by the Sephardic Rabbinical Council. This *eruv* has since obtained the public endorsement of Rav Ovadia Yosef and other Sephardic *gedolei Torah*, copies of which are now to be found on the Sephardic Erub web site www. erub.org.

However, in 1983 it was not clear if Rav Menashe Klein's *heter* was appropriate only for Ashkenazim, or whether Sephardim too might rely on it. I therefore wrote to Rav Klein asking him for clarification. His response, dated the 4th night of Hanukka 5744 (1983), follows with my free translation. *Inter alia*, it reflects the acrimonious debate surrounding the *eruv* which Rabbi Mintz mentioned.

הנה ימחול נא לעיין בספרי משנה הלכות ח"ח סי' ק"ב דברוקלין מוקף מחיצות עשוי בידי אדם וכה"ג כ"ע מודים ועיין עוד שם סי' קמ"א ועוד בכמה מקומות האמנם לעדה הקדושה של אחינו בני ישראל הספרדים בכאן באמת שאין צריכין לסמוך על פסקי שלי כי לפני כמה שבועות בקרתי פה אצל הרב הגאון עובדיה יוסף שליט"א (מלפנים הרב הראשון לציון) ושהה פה ונתפגשנו אחר ושוחחנו בד"ת והי' שם נוכח גם אחד מחשובי וגדולי הרבנים דעדה הספרדית בפלעדבוש ושאל אותו אודות העירוב בפלעטבוש מה דעתו ועכ"פ לנשים וקטנים והשיב לו שלא זאת[1] נשים וקטנים מותרים לטלטל על סמך עירוב אלא אפילו הוא בעצמו מותר לטלטל והרב הנ"ל בקש ממנו שיתן לו הדבר בכתב והשיב לו שמפחד מליכנס בדבר מפני החולקין (ואוי לנו שכך עלתה בימינו שגדולי הדור מפחדים מלהגיד דעתם אבל המציאות הוא מציאות) ובעזה"י ראינו ושמע הדברים ד' רבנים חשובים וגדולי התורה שהיו שם וכלנו חיים תהלה לא-ל ואין החי מכחיש את החי וא"כ יש להם לעדה הספרדית הקדושה בפלעטבוש פסק ברור מגדול הפוסקים שלהם וכדאי הוא לסמוך עליו אפילו שלא בשעת הדחק.

Please be good enough to see my *Mishane Halakhot*, vol. 8, *siman* 103. Brooklyn is surrounded by man-made *meḥiẓot*, and in such a situation all agree to the possibility of establishing an *eruv*. But our Sephardic brethren do not have to rely on my *psak*. A few weeks ago I visited *HaRav HaGaon* Ovadia Yosef, *Shalit"a*, the former *Rishon leTzion*, and was able

---

[1] Unclear in original. Perhaps instead of זאת, read רק, ed.

to exchange *divrei Torah* with him. Present there too was one of the important rabbis of the Flatbush Sephardic community who asked his opinion regarding the Flatbush *eruv:* Could at least women and small children rely on it? He responded that not only could women and children rely on it, but he too could. When the rabbi asked him to put it in writing, he replied that he feared getting involved in the fighting regarding the *eruv*. (Woe to us that we have reached a point where *gedolei haDor* fear to say publicly their position, but such is the case.) With God's help, four important rabbis and *gedolei hora'a* were there and heard this and, thank God, we are all alive, and what was said cannot be contradicted. Therefore, the Holy Sephardic Community in Flatbush has a definitive *psak* from one of its major *poskim*, and it can be relied upon even in non-emergency situations.

Joel B. Wolowelsky
Brooklyn, NY

Dating the Exodus

JUDAH LANDA HAS provided us with an erudite discussion of the various chronologies of the Exodus (*Ḥakirah* 14). However, he does not give sufficient weight to the possibility that Yosef's rise to power coincided with Hyksos rule, rather than preceded it. Here the internal evidence of the Torah is conclusive, in my opinion. No fewer than six passages of the Yosef story are best or solely explained by reference to Hyksos rule:

1) "Yosef was taken down to Egypt, and Potiphar, minister of executions, *an Egyptian*, purchased him" (*Bereishit* 39:1). One would hardly need to identify a high official in Egypt as "an Egyptian"—what else would he be?—were it not that, under Hyksos rule, a native-born minister was an anomaly. We choose to translate *sar ha-tabaḥim* as "minister of executions" rather than chief cook, because the prison system was within his purview (40:3-4, 41:10). Why, then, appoint an Egyptian as chief executioner? So that the hatred of the people be focused on him rather than on his Hyksos overlords. Much the same consideration prompted Polish landowners to appoint Jews as tax collectors.

2) "He gave him Asnat the daughter of Poti Phera, priest of On, as a wife" (41:45). The

Egyptians could not even eat together with the Hebrews "because it was an abomination to the Egyptians" (43:32), so how could they marry them? Rather, Asnat was not an Egyptian but a daughter of the Hyksos ruling class, which had no taboos against foreigners.

3) "Yosef recognized his brothers, but they did not recognize him" (42:8). Were Yosef a foreigner in an otherwise Egyptian court, the brothers would have made a special effort to note just who was this official with singularly Semitic features. As it was, as a minister in a quasi-Semitic Hyksos government his origins attracted no attention.

4) "The news reached Pharaoh's house that Yosef's brothers had come, and it was welcomed by Pharaoh and his servants" (45:16). The non-Egyptian rulers welcomed the arrival of more Semites, as reinforcements.

5) "So that you dwell in the land of Goshen, for all shepherds are an abomination to the Egyptians" (46:34). Goshen was "the best part of the country" (47:6), and why would the Egyptians give it to those they abominated? Rather, the Hyksos, themselves shepherds, ruled the country, and they took the best parts for themselves and their allies.

6) "A new king arose in Egypt who knew not Yosef" (*Shemot* 1:8). A new, Egyptian dynasty arose that threw out the Hyksos. Following standard practice, it blotted out all memory of the previous rulers and administration.

Much of the above, particularly 1) and 6), has already been remarked upon by modern commentators. We will introduce, however, an additional hypothesis: Potifar, Yosef's master, was an Egyptian, but his *wife was a Hyksos.*[2] Perhaps, as with Yosef and Asnat, the practice was to give new ministers a wife from the ruling circles—if only to keep watch over them.[3]

This explains the astonishing latitude Potifar's wife gave herself in speaking about, and to, her husband. "She called the men of her house (*anshei beitah*[4]) and

---

[2] This casts her infatuation with Yosef in a new light, both being non-Egyptian.

[3] Another possibility is that he married her as a means of gaining access to the ruling circles. In either case, Potifar ignored his own people's taboos.

[4] Not to be confused with *anshei ha-bayit*, "men of the house" (servants) in v. 11, and see my *Ḥibah*

told them, 'See, he brought us a Hebrew (*ish ivri*) to ridicule us'" (*Bereishit* 39:14). When Potifar returned, "She spoke to him in the same way: 'The Hebrew slave you brought us came to ridicule [or: have relations with] me.'" It is remarkable for a high official's wife to express such disdain for her husband, let alone to her servants, and inconceivable that she class herself together with the latter, "he brought *us*...." Rather, "men of her house" means men of her *family.* She called in her Hyksos relatives to complain to them about her Egyptian husband.

This is the sting in her accusation: "He brought us an *ish ivri* to ridicule us." *Ivri* means one who came from over (*me-eiver*) the Euphrates River, and can refer to any Semite. Potifar, the Egyptian, had made a point of buying a Semitic slave in order to ridicule and denigrate the part-Semitic Hyksos in whose government he served!

Potifar was furious, but not at Yosef. Had he entertained the possibility that his wife was telling the truth, he would have executed Yosef, and certainly not have placed him in the highest-quality prison (39:20) and continued to look after his welfare (40:4). But as a lone Egyptian in a Hyksos court, his hands were tied. He could not free Yosef without further incurring the wrath of his wife's family, who were closer to the center of power than he was. Yosef knew this and so did not ask the chief cup-bearer to intercede with Potifar on his behalf, but only with Pharaoh (40:14).

The wider significance of the Hyksos connection is that it reveals the intrinsic fragility of Israel's foothold in Egypt: the Hyksos were a foreign graft in Egypt destined to be rejected, and with their overthrow, the reaction against Israel was only a matter of time. The rise to power of Yosef under a Hyksos regime contained within it the seeds of Israel's enslavement.

Rabbi Yehudah Henkin
Jerusalem

Yeteirah to *Bereishit* 15:3.

I WOULD LIKE to commend you for publishing Judah Landa's article on the dating of the Exodus. I have also written an article on this topic (*The Date of the Exodus: A Guide to the Orthodox Perplexed*). I use largely the same sources, but come to a different conclusion. I defend the view that Ramesses II (1279–1213) and Merneptah (1213–1203) were the relevant Pharaohs. My article, written in April 2011, can be found at seforim.blogspot.com.

Mr. Landa and myself are in agreement on two key issues:

1. We both agree that the date that the First Temple was built was approximately 966 BCE.

2. We both agree that the next issue is how Orthodox Jews, in attempting to date the Exodus, understand I Kings 6:1. This verse states clearly that 480 years elapsed from the Exodus to the building of the First Temple. In being willing to look at all the archaeological evidence and concluding that the Exodus occurred around 1600 BCE, Mr. Landa is willing to overlook (or perhaps adopt a difficult interpretation of) this verse. This verse points clearly to an Exodus date of approximately 1446 B.C.E.

Where Mr. Landa and I disagree is as follows. Mr. Landa focuses on the evidence for the destruction of Jericho around 1560 BCE, and suggests that this was the period that the Israelites entered the land of Israel. I argue that the late 13th century BCE was the period of the Exodus and the start of the invasion, since archaeology is now documenting that the late 13th – early 12th century BCE is the period that Israelite settlements begin to appear in the land. (Mr. Landa is aware of this difficulty and attempts solutions to it. See pp. 228–230 of his article.) Moreover, the Philistines appear as a major enemy of Israel during the period of the Judges, appearing in chapters 3, 10 and 11 of the book. But they only arrived in the land of Canaan around the 8th year of Ramesses III (=1177 BCE). Thus, the period of the Judges seems to be the 12th century BCE, not centuries earlier. Finally, Egypt is never mentioned as one of the oppressors against whom Joshua or a leader in the book of Judges fought. This would be very strange for a conquest commencing around 1560 BCE. Egypt exerted strong control over the land of Canaan at this time and in the following centuries until c. 1200 BCE.

Most likely, the relevant Pharaohs are Ramesses II (1279–1213) and Merneptah (1213–1203). Exodus 1:11 tells us that the Israelites built a store city called רעמסס. Since this is an exact match to the name of a Pharaoh, this suggests that the Pharaoh who ordered this work (=the Pharaoh of the Oppression) bore this name. No Pharaoh bore this name until the 13th century BCE. The first to do so was Ramesses I. But he only reigned sixteen months (1295-94). Thereafter, after the reign of Seti I, Ramesses II reigned for over **six decades**. In all probability, he is the Ramesses that we should be focusing upon. Moreover, archaeology has shown that Ramesses II was responsible for building a vast city called Pi-Ramesse, which would have required vast amounts of laborers and brick.

Exodus 2:23 tells us that the Pharaoh of the Oppression died. If we take this verse literally (compare Exodus Rabbah 1:34), the Pharaoh of the Exodus would be Merneptah, who was the successor to Ramesses II. (But then the Merneptah Stele comes into play and raises issues of its own. I discuss all this in my article. See also the comments of Rabbi J. H. Hertz, *The Pentateuch and Haftorahs*, 2d. ed. 1975, p. 395, Exodus-Additional Notes.)

Just as the lack of evidence for Israelite settlement in Israel prior to the late 13th century BCE is difficult for Mr. Landa, the 1560 BCE destruction date of Jericho is difficult for me. (I rely on the solution mentioned by Mr. Landa on p. 205.) But it is preferable to rely on evidence from many regions in Israel (the evidence that Israelite settlement began in the late 13th and early 12th centuries BCE) than to build a theory based mainly on evidence from one specific location only. On the whole, a 13th century BCE Exodus date presents fewer difficulties and requires less far-reaching reconstructions than does a 1600 BCE date.

(Aside from my own article at seforim.blogspot.com, I would recommend all readers interested in this topic to the following article available on line: James K. Hoffmeier, "What is the Biblical Date for the Exodus? A Response to Bryant Wood," *Journal of the Evangelical Theological Society* 50/2 June 2007, pp. 225–47.)

Mitchell First
Teaneck, N.J.

Judah Landa Responds:

I wish to thank both Rabbi Yehuda Henkin and Mr. Mitchell First for the time and effort they evidently devoted to the complicated and much-debated chronology of the Exodus. Both present what appear to be sound arguments in favor of alternative scenarios to the one I presented in *Ḥakirah* (vol. 14), and that differ from each other. R. Henkin's placement of the Yosef story in the Hyksos period (ca. 1650–1550 BCE) indirectly moves the exodus to around 1400 BCE, and First places the exodus in the low 1200s BCE. Both of these scenarios are contradicted by the three independent lines of scientific evidence that place the destruction of Jericho at about 1560 BCE, and by the other evidence I presented in support of ca. 1600 as the time frame for the exodus. These significant divergences, in turn, affect all of the history of ancient Israel.

Since only one of these dates can be correct, for the exodus in the Torah happens only once (contrary to some scholarly speculation), it is incumbent upon us to probe deeply into the veracity of the presented arguments.

Let us begin with R. Henkin's first point, based on the apparently superfluous phrase *ish mitzri* (an Egyptian man) in Gen 39:1. The question he raises, as to why the Torah finds it necessary to inform us that Yosef was sold to 'an Egyptian man,' when we already know that the event takes place in Egypt, is a good one. R. Henkin's solution is that we need to be informed of this detail because it was an anomaly. The Hyksos foreigners who ruled Egypt at the time appointed a native Egyptian man (to whom Yosef was sold) as minister of executions, so that the hatred of the people would be focused on him, rather than on his Hyksos overlords.

None of this, of course, is in the text and other, at least as plausible, explanations exist. While the Hebrew *tabaḥim* does mean 'slaughterers,' many commentators translate the word here as 'butchers'—that is, of animals, not humans (see *Rashi, ad loc.*). Just as Pharaoh had a minister for baking bread and one for preparing drinks (40:2), so he had a minister for preparing meat. Nor is it at all clear that Yosef's master, Potiphar, was a prison warden, as R. Henkin asserts. Verses 39:21–23 refer three times to an anonymous prison warden, deliberately avoiding identifying him, when the Torah could have saved a few words by simply referring to him as 'Potiphar,' who has already been named. Later, Pharaoh puts the ministers of bread and drink, who sinned against him, in the custody (*mishmar*) of their colleague, the minister of butchers, Potiphar, who in turn placed them in the prison where Yosef was imprisoned (40:1–3), a prison that was not necessarily under his direct jurisdiction. Nor is there any basis in the text or historic justification for assuming that, at this time, executions were taking place in Egypt on a grand scale, to justify the title of 'slaughterer.' Ancient Egypt, we know, generally had a court system with an appeals process, with the vizier as the final arbiter of disputes and punishment.

The difficulties with R. Henkin's theory, however, run deeper than all this. The Hyksos did not take over Egypt in one quick step. Egypt's twelfth and thirteenth dynasties, in the decades preceding the Hyksos era, maintained a policy of tolerating, even encouraging, mass immigration from, and trade with, the east (Canaan). Egypt was teeming with foreigners, primarily Canaanites, before the Hyksos takeover. Many of these foreigners, we know, rose to positions of influence in (lower, northern) Egypt at this time. Eventually, as their numbers and influence grew, and the power of the pharaohs waned during the so-called Second Intermediate period, the foreigners took over the northern portion of the country **from within**. In this they probably had some help from their fellow Canaanites back home.

In this context (the 1800s BCE) the Torah needs to inform us that Yosef's master was not a Canaanite 'landsman' whose ethnicity he was familiar with, but a strange and alien native Egyptian, who would be expected to oppress him. And that despite this, "Yosef found favor in his eyes" (39:4) because "God was with Yosef" (39:2). Looking at it this way, the specification of *ish mitzri* is directly connected to what the Torah says immediately afterward. This is not all that different from the Torah's informing us, also apparently unnecessarily, that God came to Laban 'the Aramean' (Gen 31:24) when we well know by then that Laban was an Aramean (31:20). The point is to emphasize that to protect Yaakov, God would communicate even with the likes of Laban, the Aramean (the deceptive, oppressive idol worshipper that we know he was).

In his next point, R. Henkin argues that in marrying Yosef, Asnat, the daughter of Poti-Phera, the priest of On, could not have been a native Egyptian, since we are told that Egyptians would not even eat with the Hebrews, as it was an abomination to them (Gen 43:32). Asnat must therefore have been, claims R. Henkin, a daughter of the Hyksos ruling class.

This is incorrect on multiple grounds. First, the word *ivri* in the Torah, in this context, cannot refer to 'Hebrews.' The Egyptians would not have adopted a custom not to associate with 'Hebrews' at a time when the Hebrews constituted one small family (Yaakov and his descendants) in a distant land. The Hebrews would not even have been on the 'radar screen,' so to speak, of the Egyptians.

Nor is it correct to say, as R. Henkin later asserts, that *ivri* here refers to the inhabitants of the other side of the Euphrates River, or to all Semites, as R. Henkin's third definition would have it. Rather, *ivri* here is cognate with the widely used term in the ancient Mideast, *hibaru*, a term applied by the urbane, settled and relatively well-to-do folk in reference to the nomadic 'riff-raff' out there struggling to eke out a living, such as the shepherd under-class that Yosef's brothers appeared to belong to. It was a condescending, derogatory appellation, not associated with a particular ethnic group but with an economic class of people.

Second, the priest of On is certainly to be identified with Heliopolis, known to the ancient Egyptians as *Iunu.* This ancient town housed the temple dedicated to the native Egyptian (as opposed to the Hyksos foreigners) sun-god (thus the 'Helio') known as *Ra.* This is reflected in the priest's name Poti-Phera, from the Egyptian *pa-di-pe-ra*, meaning 'gift of the house of (the sun-god) Ra.' While the Hyksos allowed the native Egyptians to maintain their priestly class and religious practices, they would be highly unlikely to honor their newly crowned vizier, Yosef, by giving him a wife associated with a priesthood they did not revere.

It was the native Egyptian reigning Pharaoh, not a Hyksos ruler, who orchestrated the marriage of Asnat to Yosef, as the Torah informs us in 41:45. This renders mute all speculation as to his or her preferences in this regard. In marrying a woman associated with the elite and influential native Egyptian—not Hyksos—priesthood, Yosef was elevated from his former lowly status as a *hibaru* to a member of the upper class of Egypt. This was precisely what Pharaoh intended. When Yosef's brothers later arrived in Egypt, they appeared as the *hibaru* that they were and did not disguise (bearded shepherds, in contrast to the clean-shaven Egyptians), and the Egyptians of Yosef's household preferred not to associate with these *ivrim* (Gen 43:32).

R. Henkin's next point, that since the brothers did not recognize Yosef it must be concluded that he blended in with the Semitic Hyksos rulers, is not persuasive. For as stated above, Egypt during the twelfth dynasty, preceding the Hyksos era, was teeming with foreigners, many of them Semites, many of them achieving prominence. Yosef could easily have blended in with them. Also, as vizier over Egypt, Yosef's clean-shaven face (see Gen 41:14) was likely masked, in whole or in part, as was the custom of the highest Egyptian officials in ancient times while performing their official duties. This would make it additionally difficult for the brothers to recognize the once bearded Yosef they saw twenty-two years earlier. (Unfortunately, this reverses the beard/no beard dynamic presented by *Rashi* on verse 42:8 from the Talmud and Midrash.)

R. Henkin's remaining arguments are similarly addressed by the above considerations. The speculation pertaining to the interaction between Potiphar's wife and Yosef, while interesting, is obviously debatable. Alternative interpretations abound.

Many of Mitchell First's points were addressed in my article, as he himself notes. I am, however, animated to make the following observations.

The appearance of the name Ramesses in Ex 1:11 pertaining to the store cities the Israelites built 'for Pharaoh' does not establish that the pharaoh's name at the time these store cities were built was Ramesses, just as the appearance of the name Ramesses in Gen 47:11 in the context of the Yosef story does not establish that the pharaoh in Yosef's time was named Ramesses (something no one supports). The only thing these names establish is that the land (in the case of Gen 47:11) and the city (in the case of Ex 1:11) became known, at some point, by the name of Ramesses.

Consider the Torah's words in Ex 1:11. "And it (Israel) built store cities for Pharaoh, *et* Pithom ***vi-et*** Ramesses." This may mean that they built store cities **at** Pithom **and at** Ramesses. The Hebrew *et* is notoriously challenging to translate, as it is often not apparent what meaning it imparts to the text. It is clear, however, that it sometimes means 'at,' as it does, for example, in Gen 33:18. Now, the Hyksos capital at Avaris, known at the time as Hat-Waret, was located in the same place where the city Pi-Ramesse ('house of Ramesses') was later established during the reign of Pharaoh Ramesses. So the Israelites built Hat-Waret 'for (the Hyksos) Pharaoh' **at** (what later came to be known as) Ramesses (Pi-Ramesse).

The argument based upon the Philistines and the Book of Judges (*Shoftim*) is flawed on two grounds. One, the era of the Judges spans about six hundred years, from after Joshua to King Saul, and the Philistines appear only toward the end of that time span (despite all the attention paid to them in the book). Two, Jephthah's message with its 'three hundred years' comment (Judges 11:26) makes no sense if, as First contends, Joshua was active ca. 1200 and King Solomon built the temple at about 970 BCE, as discussed at length in section VI-d of my article.

Contrary to First's assertion, the archaeological data I presented in favor of ca. 1600 BCE as the date of the exodus were not based "mainly on evidence from one specific location (Jericho) only." Section VII of my article presents quite a range of other avenues of archaeological evidence, in addition to the overarching web of biblical and historical considerations. And the evidence pertaining to Jericho, approached from three independent scientific directions, is in my view mighty indeed. *Ḥahut ha-mishulash lo bimhaira yinataik.* And Jericho's destruction must come after the exodus. That is a foundational aspect of the Torah's chronology; it is not a matter of interpreting a word here or a phrase there.

By contrast, the so-called 'solution' I present on page 205 of the article to conceivably negate the evidence from Jericho, upon which Mr. First says he relies, is quite anemic. It assumes a small, imaginary replacement city to the large but destroyed MBA Jericho, a city for which no evidence exists where we would expect to find at least some supporting data. This city exists only in the inventive minds of those who need it to rescue their hypothesis. And the counter-evidence from the new Israelite settlements in the central highlands of ca. 1200 BCE, the centerpiece of Mr. First's position, is not persuasive. It demonstrates merely that the Israelites built new settlements at that time, in that area; it does not demonstrate that the Israelites were nowhere in the country in the decades prior to that period.

Mr. First recognizes that the Merneptah Stele of ca. 1210, in which the 'people Israel' appear in a list of that pharaoh's claimed conquests, poses serious difficulties for his position that Merneptah was the pharaoh of the exodus. Indeed it does. But the difficulty runs even deeper than Mr. First seems to realize. Up to very recently it was widely assumed that the Merneptah Stele represents the earliest extra-biblical reference to 'Israel,' thereby compelling the exodus to occur (more than four decades) before 1210 BCE (to allow for the Israelites' wandering in the wilderness of Sinai). In recent years, however, a previously ignored Egyptian stone inscription, resting unobtrusively in the Egyptian Museum in Berlin, has gained much attention in the world of Egyptology. It almost certainly contains a reference to 'Israel,' and it is to be dated epigraphically to as early as ca. 1400 BCE (Van der Veen, Theis and Gorg, in *The Journal of Ancient Egyptian Interconnections*, vol. 2:4, 2010, p. 15–25). If this is correct, the earliest extrabiblical reference of 'Israel' as a people or state occurs some two centuries earlier than anyone previously thought. (This came to my attention after I wrote the article.) This, of course, moves the exodus to a date **much** earlier than the thirteenth century and Merneptah. Why not, in light of all the evidence, move it a bit further to ca. 1600 BCE?

Shemoneh Esreh ca. 250

I ENJOYED AND LEARNED much from Heshey Zelcer's article on the early *Amidah* ("Shemoneh Esreh in Eretz Yisrael ca. 220–250 CE"). There are, however, a number of points that merit further discussion.

The article's thesis is that (a) Yerushalmi Berkahot 2:4, 4d ("*Shemoneh Esreh Text One*" in the article) preserves the language of an early version of the *Amidah*'s petitionary (middle) blessings, (b) the first two words of *Shemoneh Esreh Text One*'s description of each of those blessings constituted the entirety of the pre-*ḥatima* part of that blessing in this early version and (c) the Cairo Genizah texts cited by Mr. Zelcer (and, in particular, the text cited on pp. 94-95) is strong evidence for proposition (b).

To substantiate propositions (b) and (c), Mr. Zelcer must demonstrate that (i) there was an early, very brief, form of *Shemoneh Esreh* and (ii) the Cairo Genizah's brief version preserves that early form. If I understand Mr. Zelcer correctly, he relies heavily on the (ninth century or later) Cairo Genizah version of the *Shemoneh Esreh* he brings on pp. 94-95 for that proof. That is, he assumes that this Cairo Genizah text is a version of (an early third century) text reflected in *Shemoneh Esreh Text One*—and is thus proof that *Shemoneh Esreh Text One* embodies the entirety of the pre-*ḥatima* portions of the middle blessings. Apparently, the reason for this assumption is a supposition that the simpler a liturgical text, the older the version it preserves. If this supposition is true, goes the reasoning, the very brevity of the ninth century (or later) Genizah text is (i) proof that it is a preserved version of an ancient—perhaps 600+ year-old—tradition and thus (ii) evidence that the comparably brief (two word) opening parts of the intermediate blessings found in the third-century *Shemoneh Esreh Text One* represent the entirety of the pre-*ḥatimah* portion of those blessings. Conversely, the more verbose versions of the middle blessings found in the Genizah preserve later traditions—and the longer the version, the later the tradition.

This assumption that the *Amidah* developed linearly from the simple to the more complex is, however, not in accord with most modern scholarship or with other evidence as to the early *Amidah*'s text. Having examined the evidence closely, most modern scholars conclude that while in some cases a given prayer or *Amidah* blessing followed the simple-to-more-complex (or shorter-to-longer) route, in other cases the opposite was true, while in yet other cases the text changed over time while the length did not change materially. See, for example, Menachem Kister's summary, "It is difficult to see the development of prayer as a simple linear one, from the simple to the complex, from the short to the long, from one *nusach* to that which developed from it." *Liturgical Formulae in the Light of Fragments from the Judaean Desert, Tarbiz* 77 (2009), p. 336.

An excellent illustration of these points can be found in, among other places, another recent article in *Tarbiz* by Shulamit Elizur, *The Chains of Verses in the* Qedushta *and the Ancient Benediction*. That article focuses on the *Amidah* as it existed in the immediate post-Yavneh period and the centuries thereafter—in other words, approximately the same time period that Mr. Zelcer focuses on. In addition to examining many of the sources that Mr. Zelcer looks to, she examines perhaps the principal body of evidence that sheds light on the *Amidah*'s text in the approximately 700-year period between the end of R. Gamliel deYavneh's era and the Cairo Genizah—the earliest *piyutim*.

Professor Elizur concludes that "[s]everal ancient rabbinical sources indicate that a longer and more complex version of the *Amidah* was ... recited [in the post-Yavneh period], and it included biblical verses ... The *Amidah* prayer evidently underwent processes of change and abbreviation." She does hypothesize that there may have been an early, brief version that coexisted with the longer and more complex version, and that this version could be an 'ancestor' of the modern *Shemoneh Esreh*. However, she sees (i) that 'ancestral' version as the *mei'ein Shemoneh Esreh* (*Havineinu*) of Rav that incorporated the *ḥatima* of each intermediate blessing, rather than, for example, Shemuel's version cited by Zelcer on p. 87 as a possible 'cousin' of *Shemoneh Esreh Text One* and (ii) the commonality of the two (Rav's *Havineinu* and the modern *Amidah*) as rooted in the structure each shares rather than in their specific language.

Other scholars (in particular Prof. Uri Ehrlich, several of whose articles are cited by Mr. Zelcer) reconstruct early (post-Yavneh/pre-Cairo Genizah) versions of several of the *Amidah*'s blessings—including of the intermediate blessings—that are longer and more complex than the laconic early versions hypothesized by Mr. Zelcer.

The conclusions and observations above are not flatly at odds with Mr. Zelcer's thesis. He acknowledges that "[w]e are implying not that this was the only version of *Shemoneh Esreh* that was recited at that time but rather that it was a version." It is thus *possible* that (a) there was an early, abbreviated version of the *Amidah*'s petitionary blessings, (b) *Shemoneh Esreh Text One* preserves much of that version and (c) the Cairo Genizah text from at least six centuries later is a 'fossilized' representation of that early, abbreviated *Amidah*. However, in the absence of any evidence that bridges that (at least) six-hundred-year chasm, and given the existence of evidence to the contrary, the article's thesis is most properly characterized as intriguing speculation.

What Mr. Zelcer *does* demonstrate very nicely is that the first two words of *Shemoneh Esreh Text One*'s description of each middle blessing are two key words that were likely present in many early formulations of those blessings. In fact, Mr. Zelcer arguably 'undersells' the proof that *Shemoneh Esreh Text One* provides of the early presence of the two key words. He states that the Mahara Fulda's explanation of that text is that it is "a sequential list of asking something of G-d, and then after acknowledging that the request was granted asking Him to fulfill our next request."

An alternative description of the Mahara Fulda's explanation that both accords with the Mahara Fulda's words and (better) supports Mr. Zelcer's thesis would be as follows: the Yerushalmi is explaining that there is a logical and necessary relationship between each blessing, such that blessing #2 cannot be granted until we have been granted blessing #1, blessing #3 cannot be granted until we have been granted blessing #2, etc. Thus, the Yerushalmi should be read as stating that "we utter 'ḥoneinu dei'ah'; once G-d has granted this prayer by giving us 'dei'ah,' we have the knowledge to know that we should ask for forgiveness by uttering 'retzeh be-teshuvateinu'" etc. This seems to be the plain reading of the Yerushalmi and would produce precisely one of the conclusions that Mr. Zelcer reaches: that the first two words of each four-word description of a given blessing in *Shemoneh Esreh Text One* are (at least part of) the actual words of the blessing while the last two words are not part of the blessing, but merely a way of explaining why blessing #2 follows blessing #1, #3 follows #2, etc.

Finally, readers of *Ḥakirah* should know that, in addition to the articles and books cited by Mr. Zelcer, there is a plethora of recent scholarship on the early history of both Jewish prayer in general and the *Amidah* in particular. That scholarship should be read by anyone who wants to better understand the *tefilot* we recite every day. In particular, I refer readers to the sources noted in my article on the twelve words that open every *Shemoneh Esreh*—"*The* Amida's *Biblical and Historical Roots: Some New Perspectives.*" The article can be found in the Fall 2012 issue of *Tradition.*

Again, Mr. Zelcer deserves our gratitude for a very interesting and thought-provoking article and for introducing readers to modern scholarship on Jewish liturgy.

Allen Friedman
Teaneck, NJ

Heshey Zelcer Responds:

I thank Allen Friedman for his careful reading of my article and for his detailed and worthy comments.

For the benefit of the reader I will limit my response to Mr. Friedman's main critique of my thesis, which I believe is summarized by his statement that "This assumption that the *Amidah* developed linearly from the simple to the more complex is, however, not in accord with most modern scholarship..."

A careful analysis of the tables in my appendix (pp. 109 – 121) shows that the different versions of each blessing are not arranged linearly from shortest (simple) to longest (more complex) but rather are usually arranged by their two main branches: the so-called Palestinian versions first, and afterwards the so-called Babylonian versions. It is only within each of these branches that the different versions are arranged—for visual ease—from shortest to longest.

My thesis is not that *Shemoneh Esreh* developed from the simple to the complex but that "*Shemoneh Esreh Text One*" contains "core phrases" that seem to be the "fathers" of the intermediate blessings (p. 96). Regardless of the length of the intermediate blessings recited in different geographic areas across different generations, the version of *Shemoneh Esreh* recited usually contained these core phrases.

Take, for example, the first intermediate blessing we colloquially refer to as אתה חונן. Two very different branches of this blessing are shown in our table (p. 109). In the first branch (Palestinian, lines 2 - 9) the blessing begins with a phrase similar to חנינו דעה and then expands to the left. The second branch (Babylonian, lines 14 – 36) also contain some form of חנינו דעה but its versions expand to the right. The two branches are very different but they both share the core phrase חנינו דעה.

This overlapping of core phrases in different branches is also obvious for סלח לנו (p. 111) where lines 5 – 10 show one branch and lines 14 – 26 show a very different branch; for גאלינו (p. 112); and perhaps others.

Mr. Friedman acknowledges that I argue only that "*Shemoneh Esreh Text One*" represents an early version but not necessarily the only early version. In fact, in footnotes 22 and 42 I go much further and state that I find R. Heinemann convincing when he argues that many versions of *Shemoneh Esreh* were recited at that time—some very long, others very short. *Berakhot* 34a, *Mekhilta* and various other sources mentioned in the above footnotes seem to confirm this.

In conclusion, it is my hope that others who try to recreate the core phrases of *Shemoneh Esreh* will be motivated to give due consideration to "*Shemoneh Esreh Text One*," a text that has been mostly overlooked by modern scholars studying the *Shemoneh Esreh*.

Sefer ha-Mitzvot

THANK YOU for the insightful article by Rabbi Buchman about the order of the *mitzvoth in Sefer ha-Mitzvot le-ha-Rambam.*

It is interesting to note that in 1945 a book by the name *Seder ha-Mitzvot le-ha-Rambam*, by Rabbi Jacob Moinester, was printed in New York, addressing this issue. See <http://www.hebrewbooks.org/pdfpager.aspx?req=15291&st=&pgnum=2>.

Thank you.

Dovid Olidort
Brooklyn, NY

Learning Mathematics

THE ARTICLE *"Learning" Mathematics* concludes with suggestions on how and when mathematics is to be taught.

I am surprised that the authors do not recommend the GRA's *sefer, Ayil Me'Shulash*. In my article "The Case for Secular Studies in Yeshivas" **The Jewish Press**, November 19, 2004 p. 1 I wrote:

> In most "right-wing" yeshivas students take three years of mathematics consisting primarily of selections from topics in algebra, geometry, trigonometry, probability, logic, and statistics. In New York, passing the math Regents is the goal, while in other states, the state guidelines for public school curricula are adhered to. Often there is no mathematics taught in the twelfth grade. I do not understand why the yeshivas do not gear their mathematics courses to the goal of having their students study selections from the GRA's *sefer, Ayil Me'Shulash,* in the twelfth grade.
>
> The sefer *Ayil Me'Shulash HaMevuar HaGRA*, volume 1, by Rabbi Avinoam Solimani was published not long ago in Eretz Yisrael. It contains the text of the first three sections of the GRA's original *sefer* as well as modern-day diagrams and Hebrew explanations of these sections. If yeshiva students were to study this *sefer* they would not only learn some of the mathematics that the Vilna Gaon thought was important, but they would also have the benefit of studying these topics in Hebrew, something that would no doubt improve their mastery of the language.

These comments are, of course, geared to American high schools that teach secular subjects. However, I fail to understand why Israeli yeshivas, even the Chareidi ones, do not teach enough mathematics so that their *talmidim* can study the *sefer Ayil Me'Shulash* and incorporate its study into their curriculum. Clearly the GRA felt that the study of these topics in mathematics is important.

You may wonder why I focused only on the GRA's sefer rather than on the "many available *sheilos u-teshuvos seforim, m'forshei ha shas* and journal articles that discuss a wide variety of Talmudic sources from a mathematical perspective" mentioned in the article. There are two reasons for this.

1. The GRA's *sefer* is readily

available and hence implementation would be easy, assuming there are yeshivos that would be interested in doing this.

2. My suggestion to use this *sefer* rather than others was an attempt to make the study of mathematics important in the eyes of Chareidi high school boys. Today there is a far-too-prevalent attitude in many yeshivas that the study of secular subjects is a waste of time and *bitul Torah*. There was a time some years ago that I did a good deal of tutoring of high school mathematics and most of my students were from Chareidi yeshivos. Time and time again I heard a boy who came to me for help say, "I don't want to study this, it is waste of time, but my mother (or father) wants me to." Given the esteemed position of the GRA in Chareidi circles, I think that using the GRA's sefer in yeshivos would go a long way to dispel this negative attitude at least towards mathematics.

Professor Yitzchok Levine
Dept. of Mathematical Sciences
Stevens Institute of Technology
Hoboken, NJ

The authors respond:

Thank you for your comments. Your suggestion to include the Gra's *sefer* as part of a high school level curriculum is certainly well taken. However to limit the curriculum to just this one *sefer* in order "to learn some of the mathematics that the Vilna Gaon in the 18th Century thought was important" we feel is too narrowly focused and insufficient. We prefer to include interesting "*lamdesha*" pieces from the Rashash, Chavas Yair, Maharam Shiff, etc. that tackle various types of geometric, algebraic and probabilistic problems. Expanding the range of topics and the accepted gedolim who demonstrate mathematical sophistication should dissuade anyone from saying that it is only someone like the Gra who would do mathematics.

Learning Mathematics (2)

IN THEIR RECENT article in *Ḥakirah*, "'Learning' Mathematics," Vol. 14, Winter 2012, Epstein, Wilamowsky and Dickman describe some of the efforts in the Talmud to solve certain halakchic problems that rely on mathematical concepts and methods. This article represents one of many studies in this area, but is distinguished by its suggestions concerning mathematics education in Yeshivot. In the current paper, we consider a topic in the Talmud that was not analyzed from a mathematical point of view, and demonstrate its analysis using a classical result in mathematical probability theory far removed from the halakhic context.

The Mishna in *Yevamot* 98b states: Five women gave birth to five sons who, just after birth, were "mixed up" so that the true mother-son relationships were unknown. Each of the mothers also has a son known to be hers, either born prior to these five or born subsequently to this incident. Each of the first five unattributed sons marries and dies without children, so that their five widows are subject to *yibum* by the surviving brothers. However, since the identity of the actual deceased brother of a surviving brother is unknown, the *yibum* ties between the widows and the surviving brothers are also unknown. Under these conditions, it appears at first sight that the only way to allow the widows to remarry—albeit not to any of the brothers—would be to have each surviving brother give *ḥalitza* to each of the widows.

The Mishnah proposes another solution that allows each widow a possibility of *yibum* (or marriage) with one of the surviving brothers—possibly her true *yavam*. One brother selects a particular widow for marriage, then each of the other four brothers gives her *ḥalitza*, and then the first brother marries the selected widow. This is permissible because this brother is either the true *yavam* or, if not, then the true *yavam* has already given *ḥalitza*. A second brother then selects one of the remaining four widows and marries her after each of the other four brothers gives her *ḥalitza*. This is repeated for each of remaining three widows until they are all married to one of the brothers.

The Gemara notes that another solution would be for one brother to marry all five widows after the other four brothers have given *ḥalitza* to each of the five widows. However, the solution in the Mishna is considered preferable because, *by chance alone*, one or more of the widows might marry her true *yavam* (in addition to the fact that it is not necessarily practical for one man to have five wives). This raises the question: how many of the five widows are likely to marry their true brothers-in-law under the protocol stated in the Mishna? More exactly, the possible number of correct matches of widows and their true brothers-in-law is one of the numbers 0, 1, 2, 3, 5. (4 is not a possible number because four matches necessarily imply a fifth match.) A mathematical question is: what are the probabilities of 0, 1,

2, 3, 5, matches?

This is a special case of the following classical problem in probability theory known as the problem of "coincidences." It was solved in 1708 by P. R. Montmort. Consider two decks of cards, each numbered 1 through n, where n is the number of cards in each deck. The cards in one deck are placed on a table with the numbers facing up. The other deck is shuffled at random and each card is placed face-down next to a card from the first deck. This produces a set of n pairs of cards, where each pair has a card facing up and a card facing down, so that the card number is visible on only one card of the pair. We say that there is a "coincidence" or a "match" if the numbers on each of the pair of cards are the same. Question: What is the probability distribution of the number of matches among the n pairs? That is, what are the probabilities of 0, 1, 2, ... matches? The solution to this problem depends on some basic but elementary concepts in probability theory, and is described in several elementary textbooks. See, for example, W. Feller, *An Introduction to Probability Theory and its Applications*, Vol. Third Edition, 1968; S. Ross, *A First Course in Probability*, Seventh Edition, 2006. The solution is summarized by a formula for calculating the probability of getting a specified number of matches for a specified number of cards in each deck. In particular, for the case discussed in the Mishna, which is equivalent to five cards to be matched, the probabilities are as follows:

# of Matches:	0	1	2	3	5
Probability:	0.367	0.375	0.167	0.083	0.008

These probabilities are calculated under the assumption that the matching of the cards is purely random, that is, every card has the same likelihood of a match with every other card. This may be applied to the *yibum*-matching problem because it is likely that the mix-up described in the Mishna was purely random.

The mathematical theory of coincidences also provides the following striking result: The *expected number of matches* for a card deck (or widow set) of any size is always equal to 1. This implies that if the matching procedure is repeated many times for a card deck of any fixed size then the *average number of matches approaches 1 as the number of repetitions gets larger.* See, for example, K. L. Chung and F. AitSahlia, *Elementary Probability Theory*, Fourth Edition, 2003.

The probability calculations also illuminate the implications of the differences between the protocol of the Mishna and that proposed in the Gemara. Under the former, there is probability 0.367 that there will be no matches; however, the probability is 0.167 + 0.083 + 0.008 = 0.258 of two or more matches. Under the latter protocol there will be exactly one correct match. The preference of the Mishna for the first procedure, stated in the Gemara as based on "chance," can be analyzed in terms of these probabilities. Under the protocol of the Mishna there is at least a positive probability—though possibly small—that the mitzvah of *yibum* will performed one or two or three or five times. By contrast, under the alternative protocol mentioned in the Gemara the mitzvah of *yibum* will be performed exactly once—no more and no less.

Simeon M. Berman
Emeritus Professor of Mathematics at the Courant Institute of Mathematical Sciences
New York University

Pinchas Willig
Ph.D. in Mathematics
New York University

The authors respond:

We would like to thank Drs. Berman and Willig for their thoughtful insights into *Yevamos* 98b and use their analysis to further demonstrate the thrust of our paper. We are not offering "suggestions concerning mathematics education in Yeshivos" for the sake of mathematics. Rather, we are suggesting that a full appreciation of many Gemaras is not possible without a sophisticated appreciation of the relevant mathematics. Towards this end, we would suggest that their analysis of the Gemara in *Yevamos* may explain an issue touched on by the classical Mishnaic commentators (e.g., Tosfos Yom Tov, Tifferes Yisrael etc.): Why did the Mishna present the halacha in the case of 5 brothers? Would the Mishna's preference of having each brother marry one woman also apply in cases involving less than 5 brothers? Yam Shel Shlomo suggests that in the case of only 2 brothers, the Gemara's alternate approach of having one brother marry all of the women is better and Aruch LaNer extends it to the cases of 3 and 4 as well. Below is a chart of probabilities of all possible matches in cases involving 2 to 5 brothers. These probabilities may explain the Yam Shel Shlomo's position in the case of 2 brothers (i.e., 50% chance of having no *yebum* marriage using the Mishna's approach vs. 100% chance of getting one match using Gemara's approach).

Probability Table

	Number of Brothers			
Matches	2	3	4	5
0	0.50000	0.33333	0.37500	0.36667
1	0	0.50000	0.33333	0.37500
2	0.50000	0	0.25000	0.16667
3		0.1667	0	0.08333
4			0.04167	0
5				0.00833

Do these numbers, however, justify the Aruch LaNer's extension (i.e., the difference in probability for not getting a single match in cases 3 to 5 are almost identical)?

ೲ

A Yeshiva Curriculum in Western Literature*

By: DAVID P. GOLDMAN

Why should observant Jews learn the literature of the West? It seems a reasonable question. First, the greatest cultural achievements of the Christian West cannot be appreciated in isolation from their religious inspiration. Second, secular notion of a Western high culture has its origins in a sort of idolatry, namely, to make out of art a substitute for religion, starting with the German Classic at the end of the 18th century and continuing through the efforts of Matthew Arnold late in the 19th. Third, the project itself has failed: in his 1995 book *The Western Canon,* the critic Harold Bloom complains that Western literature no longer can be taught to undergraduates who do not have sufficient background to understand the dialogue among writers of different generations. If the Christian West no longer cares about its high culture, why should Jews?

Judaism has its own autonomous high literature in *Tanakh*, Talmud, rabbinic commentaries and Hebrew poetry. It is argued that the elevated literature of the West embodies the best of the universal human experience. Judaism, though, looks less toward the universal human experience, and rather to the exceptional experi-

* This essay incorporates some material previously published in *First Things*, *The Tablet*, and *Asia Times Online.*

David P. Goldman writes the Spengler column at *Asia Times Online* and blogs at PJ Media. He has written on Jewish topics for numerous publications including *First Things*, where he was a senior editor during 2009–2011, as well as *Tablet, The American Interest,* and *Commentary.* He is also a Fellow at the Jewish Institute for National Security Affairs. His book *How Civilizations Die (and Why Islam is Dying, Too)* was published in 2011 by Regnery. A book of essays, *It's Not the End of the World—It's Just the End of You* (Van Praag) also appeared in 2011.

ence of a people apart. Dante and Shakespeare require a longer attention span and finer interpretative skills than romance novels or detective stories, but scholarship in traditional Jewish sources demands such capacities more rigorously than any kind of secular literary criticism.

Orthodox students who plan to apply to universities, to be sure, study the standard English literature curriculum to pass the usual examinations. The literature curriculum at Orthodox day schools preparing students for university cannot vary much from that of secular schools. Yeshiva students, however, have no such requirement. But should they study Western literature? There are compelling reasons in favor. The most obvious is to master the arts of persuasion—what the classical Greeks and Romans called "liberal arts," that is, the arts of free citizens: grammar, rhetoric and logic. Prosperity and political survival demand the capacity to use the language of the Diaspora with skill. Mastery of language is something to be learned from the great masters. Modern language is inherited from the great literature of the past; those who are ignorant of the language of Shakespeare, the King James Bible translation, Milton and Keats never will fully command English usage and cadence.

There are yet more important reasons, though, to study Western literature. Although Jewish religious culture may be thought of as autonomous from Western culture, the Diaspora Jew lives in Western culture and cannot extricate himself from its influence, except by sealing himself off in an alternative culture. Some Hassidim have created an alternative culture in Yiddish, including teen fiction and musical comedies. To isolate ourselves from the Christian culture of the West, though, blinds us to a basic fact of Jewish existence: Western democracy as embodied in the United States and its political institutions have given the Jewish people a unique degree of security as well as honor in the Diaspora. In its best manifestations, the political culture of the West draws deeply on Torah sources, as Rabbi Lord Jonathan Sacks argued forcefully in his 2007 book *The Home We Build Together*. We cannot understand the West without engaging its high culture, any more than gentiles can understand their own history without engaging the Jewish people and the distinct and separate culture of Torah. And without understanding it, we cannot act effectively on behalf of our interests as well as the universal principles that the Torah embodies.

Great literature typically is taught as a "Western Canon," as a continuing, consistent corpus of thought. The survey courses that form part of the core curriculum at some secular liberal arts colleges dilute the original idea of a "Great Books" reading list, formulated at the University of Chicago during the 1930s. In this canonical view, Greek and Latin thought segue into Christian civilization; Hebrew sacred literature is a byway. The concept of a "Western Canon" as such constitutes an implicit form of Christian apologetics, with a distinctly Christian bias towards Hellenic rather than Hebrew sources. Students read Homer, Virgil, Dante, and Shakespeare as if they constituted an unbroken chain of genius within Western Civilization. The curriculum is supposed to edify, uplift and acculturate students in the great apologetic project of the West. The "Western Canon" approach emerged as a secular, cultural response to the declining authority of religion in Western thought, with the aim of substituting artistic and philosophical sources for religion. Inevitably it was abandoned except for a few surviving pockets in academia. The "Western Canon" had no inherent authority except for custom and habit by which to determine what belonged to the canon and what did not. It is not surprising that this "canon" has for the most part failed to defend itself against multicultural incursions (ethnic studies, women's studies, and so forth): it has no claim to be authoritative except for the aesthetic taste of a cultural elite and its claims to exclusiveness are easily challenged as arbitrary and subjective.

The beauty of moral truth is foremost in Jewish thinking. But the beauty of artifice has a place as well, from the construction of the *mishkan* to the verse of Yehudah HaLevi. The classical curriculum in Western literature justified itself on aesthetic grounds alone. The modern curriculum sacrifices aesthetic criteria on putatively moral grounds, but these moral grounds stem from multicultural concern for the self-esteem of minorities, for example. The literature curriculum at major universities is increasingly Balkanized to meet the demands of various constituencies. Secular Jewish literature is taught under the rubric of Jewish studies as one more minority contribution to the multicultural mix. According to the multicultural criterion, Philip Roth is as Jewish as Maimonides.

There is an alternative to learning Western literature uncritically in the same fashion as secular schools. That alternative exists in large measure because Jews made enormous contributions to the literature of the West. Some of these contributions came from forced converts. Jews have been in the West but never of it. Although Christian civilization ultimately rests on its Jewish antecedents, it has often sought to suppress or even expunge Jewish influence. We do not accept the presumption of apologists for Western Civilization, namely, Christianity blended Greek Reason and Hebrew Religion into a harmonious synthesis. From the Jewish vantage point, Western Civilization embodies great achievements as well as great flaws. Both are mirrored in its literature. Modern literature arose as a critique of the failings of Christian civilization. Some of the foundational works of modern literature were a covert cry of protest on the part of Jews compelled to convert to Christianity. For Jews to engage the literature of the West is to come to grips not only with the achievements of the West, but also with its flaws. We should not attempt to stand the "Western Canon" approach on its head, and turn the study of literature into Jewish apologetics in place of Christian apologetics. Critical learning of Western literature can help religious students to understand the worthy contributions of Christian civilization as well as its failures, without compromising the autonomy of Jewish religious culture.

And there is something more: Jews do not have a monopoly on insights into Jewish sources. During the 19th and 20th centuries, Orthodox religious authorities drew insights about *Tanakh* from the great literature of their time, especially in Germany. Sometimes there is a great deal to learn from gentile thinkers. Some of the high literature of the West proceeds from *Tanakh*—Goethe's great drama *Faust* among others—and great rabbis of the past did not hesitate to glean insight from this literature.[1]

---

1 See for example R. Isaac Rosenberg (1860–1940), "*Koheleth* and Goethe's *Faust*" <http://jbq.jewishbible.org/assets/Uploads/372/372_goethe1.pdf>. Also R. Marc Angell, "Rabbi Samson Raphael Hirsch and Friedrich von Schiller," online lecture <http://www.yutorah.org/lectures/lecture.cfm

Some of the works selected in the rough sketch of a literature curriculum below would seem out of place in a conventional university curriculum, for two reasons. First, no pride of place is assigned to works written in English. My concern is not English literature, but the literary engagement of Jews with the West throughout our history. Second, I have chosen works that embody a Jewish response to Christian civilization. Some of these works, such as Fernando de Rojas' *Celestina* and Tirso de Molina's *Don Juan* play, have a minor role in the literary canon today. In their own century, though, they were the equivalent of blockbuster bestsellers, the most widely read and influential fiction of their age. The subject of this curriculum is not literary aesthetics, but the conflict of great ideas through the history of the West, in which Jews and Jewish thinking played a decisive, if underappreciated, role. Rather than array the sources according to period or genre, in the conventional way, I suggest three great themes: Time, Love and Evil.

I. Time: Homer *vs. Tanakh*
II. Love: Medieval Romance *vs. La Celestina*
III. Evil: *Don Juan* and the Paradox of Christian Salvation

Topic I: Time: Homer *vs. Tanakh*

Readings:

1. Homer, *The Odyssey*
2. Etienne Gilson, *God and Philosophy* (Yale University Press 2002), chapter one ("God and Greek Philosophy")
3. Erich Auerbach, *Mimesis*, "Odysseus' Scar"

/745805>. For a discussion of the influence of Goethe's *Faust* on Rav Michael Friedländer's translation of *Kohelet*, see David P. Goldman, "Faustian Bargains," in *The Tablet*, December 14, 2010 <http://www.tabletmag.com/jewish-news-and-politics/53221/faustian-bargains>. See also David P. Goldman, "Hast Thou Considered My Servant Faust?" (First Things, Aug/Sept. 2009) for a discussion of *Faust* and the Book of Job.

Dizzily it bears you along on restless streaming waves;
Behind and in front you only see heaven and sea.

—Friedrich Schiller, "The Epic Hexameter"

Revelation is the first thing to set its mark firmly into the middle of time; only after Revelation do we have an immovable Before and Afterward. Then there is a reckoning of time independent of the reckoner and the place of reckoning, valid for all the places of the world.

—Franz Rosenzweig, "The Star of Redemption"

The poetry of Homer is supremely beautiful, but it is beautiful in a specific way. As the Schiller epigram above states, there is an eternal sameness to Homer's heroic verse that stems from the world outlook of pagan Greece. The concept of beauty itself has a different meaning for Greeks than for Jews. Judaism does not accept the Greek concept of beauty as it was carried over into Christianity. For Plato, beauty is the perception of harmonious order. Plato's concept embedded in Christianity makes beauty into an attribute of God. That is alien to Jewish thinking. Rabbi Meir Soloveichik observes that not once does the *Tanakh* call God "beautiful" (*yafeh*). God is called *adir* (splendid), and his voice is called *hadar* (majestic). As Rav Aharon Lichtenstein wrote:

> The verse says (*Tehillim* 29:4), "*Kol Hashem ba-koaḥ*; *kol Hashem be-hadar*—The voice of God is power; the voice of God is splendor." We perceive God in one sense as boundless, unbridled power. In another sense, we perceive Him in terms of values, of truth and goodness. ... Hadar is presumably some kind of objective beauty, a moral beauty, a beauty of truth.

But that is moral beauty, not visual or sonorous beauty as in the Christian definition. In all of the *Tanakh* we find God and beauty mentioned only once in the same verse: "I have observed the task which God has given the sons of man to be concerned with: He made everything beautiful in its time; He also put an enigma [*ha-Olam*] into their mind [*b-libam*] so that man cannot comprehend what God has done from beginning to end" (*Kohelet* 3:11, ArtScroll translation). What ArtScroll translates (following the *Targum*) as "enigma" and Koren as "mystery," *ha-Olam*, is rendered in its more common usage as "eternity" in other translations. Ibn Ezra supports the latter reading, noting that in the whole of the *Tanakh*, the word *olam* is used only in the sense of time and eternity. Perhaps the ambiguity sheds light on the implicit Jewish understanding of beauty.

Kohelet tells us that beauty comes from God. We are obligated to say the blessing "*shekakha lo be-olamo*" when we see beautiful things. But God made things beautiful *in their time*. Creation is contingent; even the world itself will wear out like a suit of clothes, and God will replace it (*Tehillim* 102:26). Beauty is not an eternal characteristic of nature in its recondite essence, accessible to the adept through special knowledge, as Plato taught; much less is it an attribute of God. Beauty, rather, is temporal and *hevel*, or "fleeting" (rather than "vain" as *Kohelet* is usually rendered).

Next to this terse statement about beauty we find a statement about man, namely that God has put an enigma (eternity) into the minds of humans such that we seek after eternity, even if we cannot fully comprehend it. This reading of *Kohelet* 3:11 gains clarity if we read *Kohelet* 3:15 in the Koren translation by the 19th-century *rosh yeshiva* Rabbi Michael Friedländer: "That which is, already has been; and that which is to be has already been; and only God can find the fleeting moment." As I wrote in another context for *Tablet Magazine*, Rabbi Friedländer might have had in mind the celebrated wager that Faust offered the Devil in Goethe's tragedy. Faust would lose his soul and will if he attempted to hold onto the passing moment, that is, to try to grasp what only God can find.[2] Goethe's

---

2 The devil Mephistopheles offers Faust his usual bargain:
"Then Faustus, here,
Here do I bind myself to be thy servant,
And at thy nod forsake repose and ease:
When in another place we meet hereafter,
Thou'lt do the like for me."
Faust rejects this: "What can'st thou give,
Thou miserable fiend?" He proposes a wager instead. If ever he should say to the passing moment
""Linger, still linger, beautiful illusions,"
Then throw me into fetters; then I'll sink,
And willingly, to ruin. Ring my death-knell."
(Translation S. T. Coleridge)

drama in turn drew inspiration from *Kohelet*, according to a monograph by the German Orthodox Rabbi Isaac Rosenberg. Time belongs to God, and the time of human existence stretches between the memory of promise and the hope of redemption. The impulse to seize the moment and hold onto it is in a sense idolatrous; it is an attempt to make ourselves immortal by our own force of will, to cheat eternity, to wrest control of time away from God. As we will see below, the narrative style of the ancient Greeks attempts to fix the moment in time, while Biblical narrative proceeds in the light of eternity. The distinction between pagan and biblical time will become clearer by example below. Rashi comments that the day of our death is unknown, so that a man says, "Perhaps my death is far off," and builds a house or plants a vineyard. Because the time of our death is concealed from us, we should rejoice with our portion and follow God's law while we yet live. But rejoicing in our portion throughout the days of our lives is never quite enough, for eternity is set in our hearts, which is to say that our hearts are set on eternity. St. Augustine paraphrased *Kohelet* in the opening words of the Confessions: "You have made us for Yourself, Lord, and our hearts are restless until we come to You." We might think of beauty as an intimation of the eternity that God has set in our hearts. God has planted in our hearts the enigma of eternity, which is the same as the mystery of human mortality, and beauty is an intimation of that eternity. We do not say that God is beautiful, for we have never seen His form. For Jews, unlike Christians, beauty is not an attribute of God, but rather a fleeting human perception of God's action in the world.

The perception of beauty from the Jewish standpoint therefore is a human act that occurs in time. To distinguish between Jewish and Greek concepts of beauty, we must first consider the differences in their perception of time. Literature is first of all narrative, and narrative proceeds in time. In the "god-infested world" (Etienne Gilson) of the Greek pagans, time is simply the demarcation of movement, ultimately of the indifferent, perpetual motion of the heavenly bodies. Past and present, as Friedrich Schiller wrote in the above-cited epigram on the heroic meter of Greek poetry, appear the same. By contrast, time is an illusion to Jews ("That which is, already has been; and that which is to be has already been; and only

God can find the fleeting moment," *Kohelet* 3:15 [Koren]). This concept of time permeates Jewish practice. "All you who cling to Hashem are alive today" (*Dev.* 4:4). Every Jew who left Egypt stood before Mount Sinai. Creation is guided not by the perpetual sameness of time but by its suspension, namely Shabbat. *Teshuvah* literally changes the past, for the Jew who does *teshuvah* becomes a different person, and that different person would not have committed the sin in question; retrospectively the sin becomes a *shogeg* rather than a sin of intent (R. Jonathan Sacks).

This distinction is stamped on literary style from the beginning of written memory. The philologist Erich Auerbach, a Jewish refugee from Nazi Germany, contrasted Greek and Hebrew modes of thought in a classic essay comparing two stories: the binding of Isaac in Genesis 22, and the story of Odysseus' scar told in flashback (*Odyssey*, Book 19).[3] Auerbach's essay is justly one of the most celebrated exercises in literary criticism of the past century.

Homer's hero has returned incognito to his home on the island of Ithaca, fearful that prospective usurpers will murder him. An elderly serving woman washes his feet and sees a scar he had received on a boar hunt two decades earlier, before leaving for the Trojan War, and recognizes him. Homer then provides a detailed account of the boar hunt before returning to his narrative. The story stops for several hundred lines while Homer recounts the origin of the scar. Homer places everything on the surface, Auerbach explained:

> The separate elements of a phenomenon are most clearly placed in relation to one another; a large number of conjunctions, adverbs, particles, and other syntactical tools, all clearly circumscribed and delicately differentiated in meaning, delimit persons, things, and portions of incidents in respect to one another, and at the same time bring them together in a continuous and ever flexible connection; like the separate phenomena themselves, their relationships—their temporal, local, causal, final, consecutive, comparative, concessive, antithetical, and conditional limitations—are brought to light in perfect fullness; so that a continuous rhythmic procession of phenomena

3 Erich Auerbach, *Mimesis: The Representation of Reality in Western Literature*, trans. Willard R. Trask. Princeton, 1953, repr. 1974, chapter one.

> passes by, and never is there a form left fragmentary or half-illuminated, never a lacuna, never a gap, never a glimpse of unplumbed depths.

Auerbach adds, "And this procession of phenomena takes place in the foreground—that is, in a local and temporal present which is absolute. One might think that the many interpolations, the frequent moving back and forth, would create a sort of perspective in time and place; but the Homeric style never gives any such impression." The "local and temporal present is absolute," in Auerbach's words. Biblical time, as Auerbach explains, transcends the present; each moment is lived in the memory of past promise and the expectation of future redemption. The self-evident, simple present of Homer does not exist for biblical man; in its place, past and future join together in his consciousness. In place of the meticulously decorated moment—for example the hundreds of lines of background to the discovery of Odysseus' scar—biblical narrative implies and evokes the presence of God in the world and the human response to Him with an infinite subtlety and depth. A different mode of writing pertains to Hebrews and Greeks.

Stark and spare, by contrast, is the story of God's summons to Abraham to sacrifice his beloved son Isaac. Where Homer tells us everything, the Bible tells us very little. God speaks to Abraham, and Abraham says, "Here I am." Auerbach observes, "Where are the two speakers? We are not told. The reader, however, knows that they are not normally to be found together in one place on earth, that one of them, God, in order to speak to Abraham, must come from somewhere, must enter the earthly realm from some unknown heights or depths. Whence does He come, whence does He call to Abraham? We are not told."

Abraham and Isaac journey together. Auerbach writes, "Thus the journey is like a silent progress through the indeterminate and the contingent, a holding of the breath, a process which has no present, which is inserted, like a blank duration, between what has passed and what lies ahead, and which yet is measured: three days!" In contrast to the "local and temporal present" in Greek narrative, the narration of the Aqedah "has no present."

Auerbach concludes:

> On the one hand, externalized, uniformly illuminated phenomena, at a definite time and in a definite place, connected together without lacunae in a perpetual foreground; thoughts and feeling completely expressed; events taking place in leisurely fashion and with very little of suspense. On the other hand, the externalization of only so much of the phenomena as is necessary for the purpose of the narrative, all else left in obscurity; the decisive points of the narrative alone are emphasized, what lies between is nonexistent; time and place are undefined and call for interpretation; thoughts and feeling remain unexpressed, are only suggested by the silence and the fragmentary speeches; the whole, permeated with the most unrelieved suspense and directed toward a single goal (and to that extent far more of a unity), remains mysterious and "fraught with background."

The radical difference between the Hebrew and Greek concept of divinity, Auerbach adds, implies a radically different concept of character:

> God is always so represented in the Bible, for he is not comprehensible in his presence, as is Zeus; it is always only "something" of him that appears, he always extends into depths. But even the human beings in the Biblical stories have greater depths of time, fate, and consciousness than do the human beings in Homer; although they are nearly always caught up in an event engaging all their faculties, they are not so entirely immersed in its present that they do not remain continually conscious of what has happened to them earlier and elsewhere; their thoughts and feelings have more layers, are more entangled. Abraham's actions are explained not only by what is happening to him at the moment, nor yet only by his character (as Achilles' actions by his courage and his pride, and Odysseus' by his versatility and foresightedness), but by his previous history; he remembers, he is constantly conscious of, what God has promised him and what God has already accomplished for him—his soul is torn between desperate rebellion and hopeful expectation; his silent obedience is multilayered, has background. Such a problematic psychological situation as this is impossible for any of the Homeric heroes, whose desti-

ny is clearly defined and who wake every morning as if it were the first day of their lives: their emotions, though strong, are simple and find expression instantly.

The Jewish and Greek vision of God, man and time itself are fundamentally incompatible. The aesthetic character of Homeric and biblical narrative is radically different.

Topic II: Christian Love and Its Paradoxes

World of nightingales, how fair!
Where instead of worship rendered
To the true God, Love, the false god,
And the muses were adored.

Clergy, crowned with wreaths of roses
On their tonsures, sung the psalms
In the happy Languedoc,
And the laity, good knights.

Proudly ambled on their chargers,
Conning rhymes and amorous verses
To the glory of the lady
Whom their heart was happy serving.

For with love there must be ladies,
And the lady was as needful
To the tuneful minnesinger
As, to bread and butter, butter.

And the hero whom we sing of,
Our Jehuda Halevy,
Had his heart's beloved lady.
But a strange one he had chosen.

For the lady was no Laura,
She whose eyes, sweet mortal stars,
In the minster on Good Friday
Lit the fire for ever famous —

Was no chatelaine who, radiant
In the bloom of youthful beauty,
O'er the tourneying presided.
And bestowed the wreath of laurel —

Was no casuist who lectured
On the law concerning kisses,
In the college of a court of
Love, a learned doctrinaire.

She, beloved of the Rabbi,
Was most sorrowful and wretched,
Piteous spectacle of ruin,
And was called Jerusalem.

—Heinrich Heine

Readings:

1. Dante Alighieri, *La Vita Nuova*; *The Divine Comedy* (*Inferno*; Selections from *Purgatorio* and *Paradiso*)
2. Petrarch, *Selected Sonnets*
3. Yehudah HaLevi, *Selected Poems*
4. Fernando de Rojas, *La Celestina*
5. Miguel de Cervantes, *Don Quixote* (Book I)

6. William Shakespeare, *Romeo and Juliet* and *Othello*

In the fragment quoted above, the German-Jewish poet Heinrich Heine gently ridicules Romantic love as portrayed in Christian medieval literature, contrasting it to Yehudah Halevi's love for Jerusalem. If love is the great theme of literature, the critique of the Christian concept of love is the great contribution of Jews to Western literature. Judaism and Christianity understand love in very different ways. Rabbi Meir Soloveichik observes:

> Over the years, many Christian theologians have expressed abhorrence at the idea of God's preferential love. The twentieth-century Swedish theologian Anders Nygren, for example, contrasts the different depictions of divine love found in Jewish and Christian Scripture: "In Judaism love is exclusive and particularistic," while Christian love "overleaps all such limits; it is universal and all-embracing." God's love stands in stark contradistinction to human love, absolutely "unmotivated." It expects nothing back, no return on the emotional investment.
>
> [The Orthodox theologian Michael] Wyschogrod takes issue with just this sort of understanding. The Hebrew Bible does not depict such a radical distinction between divine and human love. Humanity was created in the image of God; our love is a reflection of his. God can desire to enter into a relationship with us; He can be drawn to some aspect of our identity. In the Hebrew Bible, writes Wyschogrod, God's love is "a love very much aware of a human response. God has thereby made himself vulnerable: He asks for man's response and is hurt when it is not forthcoming." Further, because "God's love is directed toward who we are ... there are those whom God loves especially, with whom he has fallen in love."[4]

The Christian concept of love informs the crowning achievement of European medieval literature, Dante Alighieri's *Commedia Divina*. Dante's guide to Heaven is the spirit of Beatrice, a young Florentine woman whom Dante had met twice during her brief life, and whom he loved from a distance with absolute devotion. Dante's

4 Rabbi Meir Soloveichik, "God's First Love: The Theology of Michael Wyschogrod," in *First Things*, November 2009.

love for Beatrice, which had no possibility of consummation, follows in the tradition of so-called courtly love, which considered love to be pure only when the object of love was unattainable.

From the medieval Christian standpoint, only unrequited love might be considered "unmotivated," unselfish, asking nothing in return, corresponding to the "*agapic*" love of the man-become-God who sacrificed himself to take away the sins of the world. The term "Romantic" was coined at the end of the 18th century to describe a literary movement that sought to restore the Christian medieval concept of love. The German poet and critic Friedrich Schlegel wrote in 1790, "I seek and find the romantic among the older moderns, in Shakespeare, in Cervantes, in Italian poetry, in that age of chivalry, love and fable, from which the phenomenon and the word itself are derived."

The father of all Western poets, and perhaps still the greatest, was the 14th-century Florentine poet-diplomat Dante Alighieri. He remains the Christian poet par excellence, folding the experience of human love into a great division of Christian order: *The Divine Comedy*. Dante's collection of reminiscences and poems, *La Vita Nuova* ("The New Life"), reports his first meeting with Beatrice at the age of nine with these enraptured words:

> Nine times already since my birth the heaven of light had almost revolved to the self-same point when my mind's glorious lady first appeared to my eyes, she who was called by many Beatrice ('she who confers blessing'), by those who did not know what it meant to so name her. At that moment I say truly that the vital spirit, that which lives in the most secret chamber of the heart began to tremble so violently that I felt it fiercely in the least pulsation, and, trembling, it uttered these words: 'Ecce deus fortior me, qui veniens dominabitur michi: Behold a god more powerful than I, who, coming, will rule over me.' At that moment the animal spirit, that which lives in the high chamber to which all the spirits of the senses carry their perceptions, began to wonder deeply at it, and, speaking especially to the spirit of sight, spoke these words: 'Apparuit iam beatitude vestra: Now your blessedness appears.'

Beatrice reappears in Dante's *Commedia*. In crisis "at the midpoint of our life," Dante envisions a journey through hell, with colorful depictions of his contemporaries in torments that fit their sins. His guide through the Inferno is the Roman poet Virgil. He then passes through Purgatory and Paradise, for which he requires a more elevated guide, the spirit of Beatrice. The poet's unsullied, unselfish love for the girl he worshipped as a young man lifts him into Heaven. A similar concept of love is elaborated a generation after Dante by his countryman Petrarch in love sonnets inspired by the vision of an unattainable woman he called Laura. Petrarch struggles with the Christian concept of courtly love and desires of the flesh, and elaborated this contest in the form of sonnets that defined the poetic form.

At the conclusion of the Purgatory episode of the *Commedia*, Virgil—the noble pagan—can no longer guide Dante, and hands the poet over to the spirit of Beatrice. Dante sees the spirit of the erstwhile object of his earthly love, and compares himself to the disciples of Jesus who watched his transfiguration into a figure of light on the mountaintop (Matthew 17:1–9).

Beatrice tells Dante:

"Here you shall be–awhile–a visitor;
but you shall be with me–and without end–
Rome's citizen, the Rome in which Christ is
Roman.
(*Purgatory Canto 32,* translated by Allen Mandelbaum)

Dante's pure love for the mortal Beatrice has a salvific character in Dante's story, for her spirit becomes his angelic guide through Heaven where he achieves a beatific vision beyond description:

Then my mind was struck by light that flashed
and, with this light, received what it had asked.
Here force failed my high fantasy; but my
desire and will were moved already–like
a wheel revolving uniformly–by
the Love that moves the sun and the other stars.
(*Paradiso Canto 33*)

That is the pinnacle of Christian literature, the participation of unrequited, unselfish human love in Divine love. It is a love untainted by the body and its desires. And it is radically different from covenantal love, which is a partnership between God and His people. "The carnal election of Israel is not unconnected with Judaism's view of the body. God chose to embrace a people in the fullness of its humanity. But this had to include the bodyness of this people alongside its national soul. God therefore loves the spirit and body of the people of Israel and it is for this reason that both are holy," Michael Wyschogrod wrote.[5]

Christianity, by contrast, does not proclaim God's love for a particular people, but invites the nations of the world to become children of Abraham of the spirit (Paul, Galatians 3:7) while keeping their gentile, ethnic identity. Christians (to cite Wyschogrod again) maintain a sort of dual nationality, with a spiritual membership in God's People, a sort of spiritualized Israel, and a fleshly membership in their *gens*, the nation of their birth. In Christian self-understanding, the flesh is always in some way sinful, tainted by its gentile origin. In its purest form, Christian love must be spiritual rather than carnal. No Christian nation can see its flesh as a vessel for the *Shekhinah*, for that would exclude all other Christian nations. Thus the Christian concept of love that gives but asks nothing in return—the Greek neologism of the New Testament for this is *agape*—is integral Christian self-understanding. From the Gothic invasion of Italy in A.D. 401 to the defeat of the Magyars at Lech in 955 and the conversion of St. Vladimir in 1015, the Church brought the barbarians into Christian life not as individuals joining a self-styled new People of God, but as tribes brought into Christendom through conquest or alliance. As pagan tribes, the newly converted Christians had no claim on a special, covenantal love such as God showed to Israel. The pagans could not make themselves holy through the *Mitzvoth*, and love God by cleaving to His will. They could only become the passive receptors of an ineffable grace, the *agapic* love that led the Christian God to sacrifice himself on the cross. Jews consider the body of the people of Israel to be holy, and honor its holiness in marital relations. Christianity from the beginning tended to separate body and soul, and considered sexual abstinence preferable to marriage.[6]

---

5 *The Body of Faith*, p. 177.

6 "It is good for a man not to marry... Now to the unmarried and the widows I say: It is good for them to stay unmarried, as I am. But if they can-

Western civilization was the Catholic Church during its first thousand years, from the fall of Rome in 476 to Luther's rupture in 1517. Not until the end of the Thirty Years War in 1648 did the Church accept the sovereignty of non-Catholic rulers, and not until the Second Vatican Council half a century ago did the Church abandon the concept of a state religion. The civilization in which the Church was embedded existed only because a single Church rose above the welter of Roman remnants and barbarian invaders who inhabited Europe in the wake of Rome's fall. That is the nub of Hillaire Belloc's celebrated phrase "Europe is the faith, the faith is Europe."

The Church's concept of unmotivated, *agapic* love had a dark side. As R. Joseph Dov Soloveitchik wrote (in *And From There You Shall Seek*):

> Pragmatically, fearing God precedes loving Him. Western metaphysical religious philosophy, born out of the union of the Greek eros and the Christian agape, says much about the plenitude of love for the spiritual and higher realms. But all its statements remain hollow utterances devoid of reality, because it has never understood fear in all its terrible essence. It therefore has often turned apostate and brought chaos to the world. From time to time, Satan has taken control over the realm of Western religiosity, and the forces of destruction have overcome the creative consciousness and defiled it.

It was scandalous, the Church thought, for the Jews to insist on a special relationship to God after the Catholic Church had come to offer salvation to all the nations equally. God's promises to Abraham, the Church insisted, had passed instead to the descendants of Abraham "of the spirit," namely Christians. Not until 1982 did Pope John Paul II speak of "the old covenant, never revoked" in recognition of God's special relationship to the Jewish people. To hate the Jews in the spirit of *agapic* love was a monstrous anomaly in Christian doctrine. The anti-Judaism of the Church, moreover, incubated ethnic ambitions on the part of its constituent nations.

---

not control themselves, for it is better to marry than to burn with lust" (I Corinthians 7).

As Franz Rosenzweig observed, once the gentile nations embraced Christianity, they abandoned their ancient fatalism regarding the inevitable extinction of their tribe. It is the God of Israel who first offers eternal life to humankind, and Christianity extended Israel's promise to all. But the nations that adhered to Christendom as tribes rather than as individuals never forswore their love for their own ethnicity. On the contrary, they longed for eternal life in their own gentile skin rather than in the Kingdom of God promised by Jesus. After Christianity taught them the election of Israel, the gentiles coveted election for themselves and each gentile nation strove to be the chosen nation, at the expense of Israel as well as every other gentile nation.

Christianity proposes absolutely unselfish love, a love of the spirit rather than a body, a love that asks nothing of the beloved. But the Christians too often preferred the old carnal love of tribe and nation to the insubstantial spiritualized love that Paul called *agape*. And this atavistic tribal love too often turned into a motive for the persecution of God's people Israel.

In an important way, modern literature begins as a response to this anomaly—the great gulf fixed between the *agape* preached by the Church and the Christians' residual love of their gentile flesh. The first great modern work was a distinctly Jewish critique of Christian hypocrisy, written just after the 1492 expulsion from Spain. It presented a withering critique of the Christian concept of Romantic love, and, by extension, of the flaws at the foundation of Christian society. *The Tragicomedy of Calixto and Melibea*, known simply as *La Celestina*, appeared in 1499; by 1506 it had been translated into Hebrew by a prominent Jewish poet. Its 23-year-old author, Fernando de Rojas, was a converso whose family had been persecuted by the Inquisition:

> In 1485, when Rojas was only nine, some of his family living in Toledo (Rojas's aunts, uncles, and cousins surnamed Franco) appear to have been permanently dishonored as Judaizers by the Toledo Inquisition... an early captive of these procedures was a man named Alvaro de Montalban, who would later become Rojas's father-in-law... Alvaro was accused and found guilty of observing certain Jewish rituals, and also of violating the Catholic fast of Lent. At the same time as Alvaro's sentenc-

> ing, his deceased parents were also found guilty of Judaizing. Their bodies were exhumed and burned... His father-in-law, who had been charged almost forty years earlier with breaking Lent, was brought before the Inquisition again in 1525, at almost seventy-five years of age. In this case he was charged with denying basic Christian doctrines... he named [as attorney] his son-in-law—"the Bachiller Fernando de Rojas, who is a converso," as his choice.[7]

La Celestina became the runaway bestseller of the 16th century, read by the entire literate world in every major language:

> Rojas's work *Celestina* was so rapidly popular that numerous editions were produced almost immediately—the first edition was published in Burgos in 1499, with the second following in Toledo in 1500, the third in Seville in 1501, and the fourth in Salamanca in 1502. By the end of the sixteenth century, at least thirty editions had been published, with possibly as many as eighty. *Celestina's* popularity was not confined to Spain alone. Translations were produced in Italian (1505), Hebrew (1507), German (1520), English (1525), and French (1527) during the lifetime of the author. Others followed after his death—Flemish (1550) and Latin (1624). By the mid seventeenth century the work had received at least fifty-eight translations (one into Latin, one into Hebrew, four into German, four into English, five into Flemish, nineteen into Italian, and twenty-four into French).[8]

Why did *La Celestina* fascinate the literate world for a century after its publication? The simple answer is that it told the truth about the character of Christian society at the threshold of modernity. A gentler (and ultimately more popular) critique came at the turn of the 17th century from Miguel Cervantes in *Don Quixote*. But nothing in modern literature had the cultural impact of de Rojas' work.

---

7 Shon Hopkins, "Joseph ben Samuel Tsarfati and Fernado de Rojas," doctoral dissertation (University of Texas at Austin, 2011).

8 Hopkins.

Celestina is perhaps the most frightful character ever to walk the Western stage. She is as courageous as she is evil, and brilliantly manipulative. Next to her, Shakespeare's Iago, or even Goethe's Mephistopheles, are mischievous schoolboys. Hired to help a young man seduce the socially superior girl he desires, Celestina sets events in motion that cause the death of the entire cast. As a genre, tragicomedy has its roots in antiquity, but in the modern world, the juxtaposition of comedic and horrific elements begins with De Rojas' gallows humor under the shadow of the Inquisition.

De Rojas created his anti-heroine in the image of the Spain that persecuted his family. The world he portrays is the opposite of Dante's harmonious order permeated by Divine love. It is at war with itself:

> "It is the saying of that great and wise philosopher Heraclitus," he begins his introduction, that all things are created in manner of a contention or battle ... The stars encounter one another in the whirling firmament of heaven; your contrary elements wage war each with other; the earth, that trembles and quakes as if it were at odds with itself; the sea, that swells and rages, breaking its billows one against another; the air, that darteth arrows of lightning and is moved this way and that way; the flames, they crack, and sparkle forth their fury; the winds are at perpetual enmity with themselves; times with times do contend; one thing against another, and all against us... the very life of men, if we consider them from their first and tender age till they grow grey-headed, is nothing else but a battle. Children with their sports, boys with their books, young men with their pleasures, old men with a thousand sorts of infirmities, skirmish and war continually.[9]

The corrosive element that turns the world into a cockpit of perpetual strife, de Rojas argues, is romantic love. He has pulled Dante and the courtly poets inside out, turning the Christian ideal of love into an agency of destruction rather than (as in the *Commedia*) salvation. "Our country," he wrote by way of introduction, "needs the present work because of its multitude of young men in

---

9 From James Mabbe's 1631 translation.

love." In a series of prefatory poems, de Rojas warns against romantic love. "You who love, take this example to heart, this piece of armor with which you may defend yourselves...forget the vices which have taken hold of us; do not trust in frivolous hopes...Ladies, matrons, young men, husbands, note well what happened to [Calixto and Melibea], and keep as a mirror the end to which they came. Clean your eyes which have erred so blindly...Do not let Cupid's golden arrows pierce you."

By 1506, Joseph ben Samuel Tsarfati, a prominent Hebrew poet, physician to the pope and leader of the Italian Jewish community, translated *La Celestina* into Hebrew. The translation itself is lost but an introductory poem survives. It begins by reiterating de Rojas' warnings to lovers and then shifts suddenly to its true subject: the despoliation of the Spanish Jews fourteen years earlier by Isabella of Spain:

How all the wise leaders of the people, like Calcol,
Sit ashamed robbed by the hand of a woman.
Destitute and barefoot they go by the thousands,
Scattered on every corner, they wander to and fro;
I will tell their tales, their vagabond ways, and their travails
As they suffer a heavy load, like that of thousands of mules,
When they stumble, wither, and perish
With burdens too heavy for them.[10]

Tsarfati does not mention the Spanish queen by name, but Jews could have read these lines in no other way. The great Jewish tragedy of the time preoccupied the poet-physician. He addressed another poem "to the exiles of Spain who descended to Rome," warning them to "go forth from the midst of the Amelekites," and instructing them to "loathe the people of anger and decadence in every region of Rome and Italy before you are destroyed in their sin."

De Rojas' drama is a window into the soul of Amelek. The young nobleman Calixto is obsessed with Melibea, a young girl just past adolescence, to the point of idolatry; as he tells a servant, his religion is "Melibeism." Both are from noble families, although it is clear from context that Melibea's social status is more elevated. His

10 Translation by Hopkins.

first attempt to approach her in open country leads to a harsh rebuff. Despondent, Calixto takes the advice of a servant to seek the help of Celestina, who keeps a brothel, mixes love potions, and performs various unsavory functions. Celestina has access to Melibea's home as a purveyor of needles, thread and other sundries. She will have one chance to approach the young girl, at great personal risk, for if Melibea denounces her, the family will have her killed as a procuress. The old woman knows that Melibea is wary of Calixto and prepared for just such an approach, and that she is staking her life on the outcome. She is afraid, but her pride in her powers and native courage overcome her trepidation.

Celestina gains Melibea's confidence and sympathy by making the girl pity her age and poverty, and then tells her that she has come on behalf of Calixto. Melibea is about to denounce the old woman. But Celestina is prepared for her. She has come not as a lover's emissary but in a mission of mercy, to borrow from Melibea a relic that will help cure Calixto of a toothache. Her story seems so harmless, and so credible, that the girl falls for it, and lends her belt to the old woman to assuage Calixto's toothache. By appealing to the girl's kindness and religious faith, she plants a thought that soon will turn into passionate love. Disasters ensue that kill off the whole dramatis personae, including Celestina, who is killed by her servants when she tries to cheat them. After Calixto's death Melibea throws herself from a high window and dies before the eyes of her despairing father.

Spanish society with its illusions and hypocrisy is no match for Celestina, who has more intelligence and presence of mind than her social superiors. She manipulates the young girl's innocent emotions, and molds them into a violent and self-destructive passion. In the narrow sense, De Rojas' drama deals with emotions at the intimate level of personal encounter. In the broader sense, though, we should read it precisely as did Tsarfati, as a work of social criticism. The unselfish *agapic* love that Christianity proposes does not suffice; its complement is the carnal love of tribe and nation that erupted again and again through the history of the West, and repeatedly took the form of Jew-hatred. Unrequited, selfless courtly love expressed in the intimate sphere what agape expressed in the social realm. By the same token, carnal passion corresponds to the brutal love of each nation for its own ethnicity. When Tsarfati writes in his introduction to *La Celestina*, "How all the wise leaders of the people, like Calcol/Sit ashamed robbed by the hand of a woman," it seems clear that he is referring to Isabella of Spain. But the drama is not simply an allegory, a work of political criticism disguised as theater. It is a work of great art, in which weakness in the face of malevolent evil stems from the inner flaws of the characters.

A century later, Shakespeare invented similar characters. Othello's nemesis Iago bears more than a passing resemblance to Celestina, while Romeo and Juliet recall Calixto and Melibea. Students should read the two Shakespeare plays in contrast to *La Celestina*. As a poet, Shakespeare's sublime expressiveness is of an entirely different order, and the richness of his language transcends anything found in de Rojas. Shakespeare is a Christian; his world presumes an inherent order, in which disturbances (Othello's jealousy, Romeo and Juliet's passion) do their damage and then dissipate. De Rojas, by contrast, presents a diseased and disordered world in which a disturbance like the intervention of Celestina lays everything to waste.

Topic III. Evil and the Paradox of Salvation

Readings:

Tirso de Molina, *The Trickster of Seville*
Voltaire, *Candide*

Celestina's literary grandson is Don Juan, the invention of Tirso de Molina, a Spanish monk from a family of converted Jews. If the 48 translations of *La Celestina* establish de Rojas' tragicomedy as the great bestseller of the 17th century, Tirso's drama and its imitators dominate the 17th and 18th centuries. One scholar lists 1,720 published variants on the theme since Tirso de Molina printed *The Trickster of Seville* in 1630. No other character in literary history has inspired so many versions. Like *Celestina*, it is also a tale of love, manipulation and violence that links the most intimate failings of its characters to the grand failings of society. Concealed in its puppet-theater plot is a Jewish joke: Don Juan exists to prove by construction that a devout Christian can be a sociopath, and by extension, that the Christian world can be ruled by sociopaths. For the two centuries between Tirso and Byron's eponymous epic poem, Don Juan dominated the literary imagination like no other personage in history.

In a post-Christian world that has lost interest in the problem of sin and salvation, Don Juan is passé. By 1821, when Juan appears in Byron's eponymous masterwork, Juan was on his farewell tour. E.T.A. Hoffman's and Kierkegaard's fascination with the subject is a response to Mozart's astonishing music, not to the literary theme. Baudelaire's poem "Don Juan in Hell" and Shaw's intermezzo of the same title make Juan into a defiant hero. Juan held the audience of the 17th and 18th centuries in thrall, because he personified the Christian world's foreboding about its own vulnerability. Tirso's trickster poses an impossible paradox for the Christian concept of salvation: The story is not about eros, but evil. Christian society is founded on the premise that it requires "only one precept," as St. Augustine put it: "Love, and do as you will." Once humankind accepts the utterly unselfish love of Jesus Christ, Christianity asserts, the elaborate body of Jewish law becomes redundant, for Christian love will elicit the right behavior spontaneously.

The trouble, Tirso demonstrates, is that society that depends on conscience has no defense against a sociopath who has none. Don Juan is a predator inside the Christian world with no natural enemies. Juan enjoys murdering the male relatives of his female victims almost as much he enjoys seducing the women. To the extent that we can speak of Juan's descendants in today's fiction, they are not so much lovers as serial killers.

Tirso's theological mousetrap had more than hypothetical importance for the audience of 1630, a dozen years into the Thirty Years War that would ruin the Spanish Empire and kill not quite half of central Europe's population. His world was infested with sociopaths in positions of power, including Spain's King Philip IV, one of whose illegitimate sons would eventually stage a coup against the legitimate heir to the Spanish throne. Philip makes an appearance in *The Trickster of Seville*, lightly disguised as the 14th-century king Alfonso XI, who also peopled the Spanish royal line with bastards. Alfonso's bastard son, Henry of Trastámara, incited Jew-hatred to overthrow his more tolerant half-brother, the legitimate heir Pedro I of Castile. Henry led the massacre of 12,000 Spanish

Jews in Toledo on May 7, 1335. The Jews had fought alongside Pedro in a prolonged civil war and suffered horribly after Henry won and beheaded his brother with the words: "Where is that son-of-a-whore Jew who calls himself King of Castile?"[11]

Tirso drives the paradox still deeper. The original Don Juan of the Spanish Golden Age is a believing Catholic, who has no doubt that repentance and forgiveness through the Church can save his soul: For that reason he can devote his youth to evil and repent sometime later. "You're giving me plenty of time to pay up!" ("que largo me lo fíais"), he mocks whomever urges him to repent and save his soul. (A variant of *The Trickster of Seville* was published under the title *Que largo me fíais*, making clear that the play hinges on Juan's twisted but orthodox theology.)

Juan's servant Catalinón (Leporello in Mozart's opera) warns him that even a long life is short, and sin will be punished. "If you give me so much time to pay up," Juan replies brightly, "let the tricks continue!" Besides, he adds, his father is the king's favorite. Christianity, as Tirso observes, can produce a monster who does nothing but evil precisely because he believes in Heaven, hell, and the sacraments of the Church. Tirso might have had *Kohelet* 8:11 in mind: "Because the sentence against an evil work is not executed speedily, therefore the heart of the sons of men is fully set in them to do evil." But Christian reliance on the Attribute of Mercy at the expense of the Attribute of Justice, as the theologian Michael Wyschogrod puts it, frees Juan to formulate a sociopath's theory of salvation.

Tirso's critique of Christianity follows the rabbinic reading. As Rav Joseph Dov Soloveitchik puts it, "Subjective faith, lacking commands and laws, faith of the sort that Saul of Tarsus spoke about—even if it dresses itself up as the love of God and man—cannot stand fast if it contains no explicit commands to do good deeds, to fulfill specific commandments not always approved by rationality and culture." In Don Juan, the Christian world saw its own susceptibility to chaos. That is why the European audience could not take its eyes off him for 200 years.

---

11 "Historia social, política y religiosa de los judíos de España," by José Amador de los Ríos (T. Fortanet, 1876), p. 254

No writer portrayed this chaos and its theological sources more vividly than Tirso. The usual account of Don Juan and his 1,719 literary imitations reduces Tirso's brilliant and complex play to a simple-minded morality lesson. Christian critics do not seem to grasp how great and enduring was the pain of the Spanish Jews; even worse, they evince a deaf ear for Jewish irony. *The Trickster* is a Jewish joke, and the critics don't get it. The theologian David Bentley Hart, for example, wrote recently that "Juan was the greatest immoralist of European literature precisely because he served as the negative image of the moral convictions and capacities of his time and place, the exemplary contradiction of an entire and coherent vision of the good, whose story magically combined a certain nostalgia for fading cultural certitudes with a certain cynicism toward them."

Tirso drew on folk tales in which a living person invites a dead man to dinner and perishes when the invitation is returned. But Juan is not an archetype of legend: He is a metaphysical construct unique to his time, and to the tragedy of the Spanish Jews. He is a devout believer who has figured out that the system entitles him to be thoroughly evil for the interim. His existence points up the hypocrisy around him; because the Christian world cannot deal with this monster, it must accommodate him. Both Celestina and Don Juan haunted the literary imagination with the same message: Your world is badly made, and it will come to a horrible end.

Don Juan fascinated a Europe with the paradox of Christian faith. A century later, the 18th-century skeptic Voltaire fascinated a world that had lost its faith. After Tirso's work and its many imitators, the next story that the whole literary world read was his 1769 novel *Candide*. The eponymous hero wanders through sundry disasters of mid-18th-century Europe, under the tutelage of "Dr. Pangloss," a lampoon of the philosopher-mathematician Gottfried Wilhelm Leibniz, who reassures him after each mishap that this is "the best of all possible worlds." This is a caricature of Leibniz's views, but in general Voltaire's critique is accurate.

Candide finds himself in Lisbon during the 1755 earthquake that leveled the city, killing up to 100,000 people. Untold thousands more perished along the Mediterranean coast. No matter, Dr. Pangloss explains after their narrow escape: If we hadn't gone through the earthquake, we wouldn't be sitting here now eating strawberries. Voltaire taunted the theologians with this question: How could a benevolent and omnipotent God slaughter so many innocents at random? If this is the best of all possible worlds (as Leibniz maintained), because a good God would not create a worse one, why do such awful things happen? That is one trouble with the so-called clockmaker's argument, one of the five classic proofs for the existence of God cited by St. Thomas Aquinas. The workings of nature are so complex and perfect, the argument states, that they bespeak a design, and a design must have a designer. The trouble is that the same clock seems to set off a bomb at random intervals.

But there is another way of thinking about man's relationship to nature, emphasized in rabbinic Judaism and espoused eloquently by Rabbi Joseph Dov Soloveitchik: God made an imperfect world and gave the task of improving it to his junior partner in Creation, humankind. As Rabbi Soloveitchik observed, the final perfection of nature is a messianic vision: In the prayers for the New Moon, for example, Jews look to the day when God will restore the moon to parity with the sun. But there is a great deal to do in the meantime. Man is not the passive victim of earthquake, flood, famine or disease. We can build defenses against natural disasters, cure disease, and eliminate hunger. Whatever harm might befall us today we can change our destiny in the future. God does not reveal his infinite mind to us, except through an infinite procession of discoveries, to which we are led by intuition, or, if you will, inspiration.

We are not the passive victims of nature. We strive to establish human dignity by mastering nature. We are neither gods who can grasp the infinite mind of the God of Creation, nor mere animals for whom evolution is destiny. We do not need to worry whether there is an Intelligent Design, nor whether we might grasp such a design if it indeed exists: As creative beings, we are part of the design. We do not know the full scope of the design, because we do not know what we have yet to accomplish. God does not need us to justify His position as creator; our task is nobler, and incomparably more challenging, namely, actually to advance His work of Creation.

The Christian concept of *agapic* love cannot account for evil, either in the form of human malevolence or natural disaster. Western literature comes into being as an allegorical representation of Divine order founded on *agapic* love (Dante). Modern literature begins as a critique of romantic love (de Rojas) and the susceptibility of the Christian order to evil (Tirso de Molina). The literature of the Enlightenment is a weapon turned against faith itself. **For Jews, the point is not to admire the accomplishments of the West, but to assess their contributions and failures from the autonomous vantage point of Judaism's own high culture of Torah.** ☙

Review Essay
Exposition as High Art

Society and Self: On the Writings of Rabbi Joseph B. Soloveitchik. By Gerald J. (Ya'akov) Blidstein. OU Press, New York, 2012.

By: Lawrence Kaplan

I

Rabbi Professor Gerald J. (Ya'akov) Blidstein, Professor Emeritus of Jewish Thought at Ben-Gurion University and a recipient of the Israel Prize in Jewish Thought, was one of the most distinguished students of the Rav, Rabbi Joseph B. Soloveitchik, and over the past twenty-five years—in particular since the Rav's death in 1993—has written many essays about the writings of his teacher. These have now been collected and have appeared under the title *Society and Self: On the Writings of Rabbi Joseph B. Soloveitchik*, the volume under review.

Blidstein begins his Introduction with the following remarks:

> The materials presented in this book reflect, by and large, my thoughts regarding the writings of the Rav, Rabbi Joseph B. Soloveitchik, over the last decades. As I look at these essays, I realize that I engaged mostly in exposition, which is perhaps a natural stance for a former student to adopt. By and large, I address the question: What does the Rav say? (p. 11)[1]

---

1 All page numbers in parentheses refer to Gerald J. (Ya'akov) Blidstein, *Society and Self: On the Writings of Rabbi Joseph B. Soloveitchik*, OU Press, New York, 2012.

Lawrence J. Kaplan received his BA from Yeshiva College, his MA and PhD from Harvard University, and his rabbinical ordination from Rabbi Isaac Elchanan Theological Seminary. He has taught at McGill University since 1972, and is currently Professor of Rabbinics and Jewish Philosophy in its Department of Jewish Studies. In 2011-12 he was a Tikvah Fellow at the Tikvah Center for Law and Jewish Civilization of the New York University Law School.

These remarks, of course, reflect Blidstein's genuine modesty and integrity. In truth, however, these very lucid and incisive essays, devoted primarily to exposition and consisting in large measure of penetrating readings of key texts of the Rav, reflect the unique blend of thematic discussion and commentary form, scholarly synthesis and textual exegesis, literary sensitivity and conceptual rigor, found in all of Blidstein's writings. One thing is clear: if what we have in these essays is "mostly ... exposition," it is exposition as a high art.

First, even when the points he makes are well known, Blidstein phrases them with his customary elegance and insight. Thus in speaking of "the priority generally attached to the halakhic over the aggadic," Blidstein notes that this priority "reflects the central role of the community. For halakhah is normative, obliging all members of the community equally..., as against the often individualistic, idiosyncratic, and moderately non-normative quality of the *Aggadah*. Put another way: the language of halakhah, its basic forms are often communal" (p. 95). The point itself is not new, but rarely has it been expressed with such deftness. I particularly like the exactness and nuance of Blidstein's description of the *Aggadah* as "moderately non-normative." This seems to me to get it just right.

One more example: In discussing the Rav's claim that, in Blidstein's words, "the identity of the Jewish people moves on two levels..., both covenantal..., the Covenant of Fate (*brit goral*) and the Covenant of Destiny (*brit ye'ud*)," Blidstein remarks that this is "a maneuver that is characteristic of R. Soloveitchik's midrashic method—we shall encounter it in *The Lonely Man of Faith* [=*LMF*]—but that may have been borrowed from his halakhic method. Simply put, R. Soloveitchik frequently discovers contrasting characteristics in ostensibly unitary or homogeneous topics (p. 65)." Again, the point has been made before,[2] but rarely with such concision and precision. Indeed, "contrasting characteristics in ostensibly unitary

[2] See, for example, Reuven Ziegler, *Majesty and Humility: The Thought of Rabbi Joseph B. Soloveitchik* (Jerusalem: Urim, 2012), pp. 27-28. This important recent work is perhaps the most thorough examination of the Rav's thought.

or homogeneous topics" is about as neat a definition of the Brisker method of "*tzvai dinim*" as I have come across.

But praiseworthy as Blidstein's style may be, what ultimately counts is the substance of his "exposition." Precisely here, however, he has a special contribution to make. As is well known, the Rav was both a rabbinic figure of the first rank—indeed, he is considered by many to have been the outstanding traditional rabbinic scholar and jurist of the second half of the twentieth century—and also a creative theologian and philosopher who mastered the entire western tradition of philosophical and scientific thought. The dazzling scope of his writings, ranging from the most complex and technical halakhic discussions to the most complex and technical philosophical discussions and incorporating between these two poles *Aggadah*, *Derush*, Biblical interpretation, phenomenological analysis, autobiographical reflection, and much else, is also well known. Consequently, as has often been pointed out, very few of the Rav's students are qualified to explore that full range, and they either, to oversimplify somewhat, focus more on the Rav's philosophical writings or more on his halakhic writings. Blidstein, as someone who is equally expert and at home in the fields of Halakhah, Midrash, and Jewish thought, is one of the Rav's few students qualified to examine the broad spectrum of his writings in their rich and colorful variety, though I would note that he does not engage in the analysis of the Rav's more technical philosophical writings.

Any division of the essays in *Society and Self* is, to a certain extent, arbitrary. Thus Blidstein's essay "Letters on Public Affairs," an extended review and discussion of *Community, Covenant, and Commitment: Selected Letters and Communications*, deals, as the essay's title indicates, with what one may term the Rav's public thought broadly speaking; at the same time a major section of the essay consists of a penetrating examination of three English responsa of the Rav, and thus deals with his more strictly halakhic writings. That said, we may, nevertheless, divide the essays into four categories: the essays "A Religious-Zionist Thinker?" "Letters on Public Affairs," "The Jewish People," and "'Fate' and 'Destiny'" focus on the Rav's public thought, the "Society" in the title; the essays "The Covenant of Marriage" and "Death" focus on the more personal existential side of the Rav's thought, the "Self" in the title; the essay "The Norms and Nature of Mourning" deals with the Rav's halakhic writings; and the essay "Biblical Models" deals with the Rav's hermeneutics, his phenomenological readings of biblical texts. Of course, as indicated above, this division is very rough, and there is much overlap between these categories. As we saw, "Letters on Public Affairs" deals both with the Rav's public thought and with his halakhic writings; "Biblical Models" deals not only with the Rav's hermeneutics, but, treating, as it does, both "Kol Dodi Dofek" and *LMF*, touches on both the Rav's public thought and his more personal, existential thought; the essay "The Norms and Nature of Mourning" focusing, as it does, on the Rav's treatment of "grief—the internalization of mourning—as a norm, not as a natural emotion" (p.134), raises existential issues; and, finally, "The Covenant of Marriage," insofar as it shows how the Rav uses "Scripture as his source of guidance" and that for him "the creation of Adam and Eve in the book of Genesis is a formative narrative" (p. 117), raises the issue of hermeneutics. Nevertheless, in my discussion of Blidstein's essays I will try to keep as much as possible to my fourfold division, moving from Blidstein's discussion of the Rav's public thought to his discussions of the Rav's personal existential thought, his halakhic writings, and, finally, his hermeneutics.

II

Blidstein, as is well known, has written widely and deeply about the various institutional frameworks in which the Jewish collective has expressed itself in Talmudic, medieval, and modern times, whether rabbinical, political, or communal, their modes of operation and claims to authority. It should not be surprising, then, that half the book's essays deal with the Rav's public thought. To be sure, as Blidstein points out in his essay "The Jewish People," "the individual is at the heart of Rabbi...Soloveitchik's writings" (p. 77). Indeed, in his essay "A Religious-Zionist Thinker?" Blidstein goes so far as question whether the Rav can be considered a Religious-Zionist thinker, inasmuch as that "the discussion of the Zionist or Religious-Zionist problem constitutes only a small portion of his work. The great majority of his articles deal with other issues: the nature of the spiritual experience, the nature of the halakhic experience, the standing of the individual vis-à-vis the community, and the like" (p. 21).[3] Still, as Blidstein observes, "the focus on the person ... should not obscure the fact that the community, and specifically the Jewish community of course, has also been a central concern of the Rav" (p. 77).

Blidstein notes the Rav's subtle balancing act in adjudging which has priority, the individual or the community. On the one hand, "the community transcends the person and bestows upon him the forms of spiritual life and the possibility of God's forgiveness and acceptance"; on the other, "the community is constituted by virtue of the ontological loneliness of the individual" (p. 83). Indeed, Blidstein points out, "Immediately after describing *Knesset Israel* as a 'metaphysical entity,' the Rav asserts that 'the personalistic unity and reality of a community, such as *Knesset Israel*, is due to the philosophy of existential complementarity of the individuals belonging to *Knesset Israel*'" (p. 83).[4]

Of course, to revert to an earlier point, the Rav "discovers contrasting characteristics in [the] ostensibly unitary or homogeneous topic..." of the community, as he does elsewhere. Here Blidstein discusses, as is to be expected, the majestic community of Adam the first and the covenantal community of Adam the second, as developed in *LMF*, as well as the people of the covenant of fate and the nation of covenant of destiny, as developed in "Kol Dodi Dofek" and other essays of the Rav.[5] I will return to Blidstein's discussion of the majestic and covenantal communities

---

3 In his Introduction Blidstein modifies his contention. "In one of the essays of this volume, I argued that the Rav was not a Zionist thinker. This may have been a hasty superficial judgment. But I would still assert that Israel and the Zionist enterprise are not at the center of the Rav's thought" (p. 12).

4 Citing "Community," *Tradition* 17:2 (1978): 9-10.

5 See "Brit Avot" in *Ḥamesh Derashot*, edited and translated from the Yiddish by D. Telsner (Jerusalem, 1974), pp. 87–97 [= "The Covenant of the Fathers," *The Rav Speaks: Five Addresses* (Jerusalem, 1983), pp. 135–152]; and "'Iyyunim be-Malkhuyot, Zikhronot, ve-Shofarot," *Yemei Zikkaron*, ed. M. Krone (Jerusalem, 1986), pp. 155–164.

later. Here let me say a few words about his discussion of the two covenants, particularly the covenant of fate.

Blidstein maintains that "even one who argues that the creation of the concepts of 'covenant of fate' and 'covenant of destiny' was directed primarily at the Zionist reality, to the problematic attitude toward religiously non-observant Jews in the context of the return to Zion and the establishment of a state" (p. 23) must agree that that "is not the real topic of the piece.... For the State of Israel is, primarily, a secular reality, and it graphically represents the secularization of Jewish peoplehood in the modern world.... The true topic of 'Kol Dodi Dofek,' then, is the character of the modern Jewish people, or more precisely the integration of this reality into the world view of the believing Jew.... It is likely, then, that the existence of the secular Jew and his community provided the problematic that R. Soloveitchik undertook to confront in 'Kol Dodi Dofek'" (pp. 64, 66).

This point is well taken; still as one of those who argued "that the creation of the concepts of 'covenant of fate' and 'covenant of destiny' was directed primarily at the Zionist reality, to the problematic attitude toward religiously non-observant Jews in the context of the return to Zion and the establishment of a state," I believe that Blidstein underplays the Zionist setting. In my essay "Rabbi Abraham Isaac Kook, Rabbi Joseph B. Soloveitchik, and Dr. Isaac Breuer on Jewish Identity and the Jewish National Revival,"[6] I showed how as late as 1944 the Rav, in a major published discourse,[7] used many of the motifs later found in "Kol Dodi Dofek," but without any mention of a covenant of fate. The 1944 discourse sets forth an unambiguous indictment of modern secular Jewry, which is seen in a wholly negative light, and leaves no room, no ground for cooperation, between religious and secular Jewry. What then led to the shift in the Rav's view?

---

6 "Rabbi Abraham Isaac Kook, Rabbi Joseph B. Soloveitchik, and Dr. Isaac Breuer on Jewish Identity and the Jewish National Revival," *Jewish Identity and the Postmodern Age: Scholarly and Personal Reflections*, Charles Selengut ed. (St. Paul, Minnesota: Paragon, 1999), pp. 51–55.

7 "Kuntrus Halakhah ve-Aggadah," *Musaf Ha-Pardes* 17:1 (1944): 22–44.

In my essay I showed how the Rav in that discourse combined his indictment of modern secular Jewry with a call for a Jewish national revival, a revival set against the background of the destruction of European Jewry in the Holocaust. But, I suggested, such a combination proved to be unstable and untenable. For how can one laud the Jewish national revival without according at least some measure of religious credit to the major group promoting that revival, namely, the secular Zionists? Moreover, the Rav was very well aware that the religious Zionists could not promote the national revival on their own. Thus, to come to "Kol Dodi Dofek," the Rav there sets a great task before religious Jewry: to transform the covenant of fate into a covenant of destiny, the people into a nation; while, at the same time, he criticizes it sharply for what he perceived to be its failure to respond to the voice of the Beloved knocking, to the call of the historic moment, to the divine act of *Ḥesed* expressed in the establishment of the State of Israel. There is no doubt that he realized that, for the meanwhile, religious Jewry would be a junior partner in the task of national renewal.

Moreover, as Blidstein himself concedes in another context—a point to which I shall return soon—there are places in his writing where the Rav does not seem to have absorbed the full dimensions of the secularization of the Jewish people. In sum, without denying Blidstein's argument that "Kol Dodi Dofek" grapples with the secular character of large segments of the Jewish people in the modern era, it still seems to me that it is the Zionist context which constitutes the primary framework for the Rav's discussion of this secularization and for his creation of the concepts of covenants of fate and destiny.

Regarding the moral content of the covenant of fate, Blidstein appears to waver. In the brief essay "'Fate' and 'Destiny,'" Blidstein incisively compares and contrasts the Rav's view of the covenants of fate and destiny with the very similar view of Martin Buber in his 1936 essay "On Nationalism." In that essay, Buber, like the Rav, distinguishes between the people of Israel fashioned by "fate," and the Israelite nation created by "a great inner transformation." For both Buber and the Rav, the nation was created by the revelation at Mt. Sinai, though, as Blidstein points out, for the Rav that revelation was first and foremost a revelation of the Law, while for

Buber it refers to a personal divine address calling for "a living relationship" with God.[8] The more significant difference between the two though, Blidstein notes, is that, "for Buber the decisive fateful moment [in the fashioning of the people] was the exodus from Egypt, whereas R. Soloveitchik focuses on the Egyptian bondage itself" (p.107). As a result, Blidstein argues, "According to Buber, the people fashioned by 'fate' forms for itself a cultural mold and way of life .... This activity also exists for the Rav, with respect to the solidarity established among the slaves and the like, but nevertheless the difference is clear. According to Buber, the struggle with fate is active, whereas according to R. Soloveitchik, the people formed by way of the covenant of fate is fundamentally passive" (pp. 106-107). Blidstein continues to elaborate on this difference between Buber and the Rav, concluding that for the Rav "the covenant of fate is defined ... in an almost minimalist fashion from a moral perspective, almost like preserving the body until the soul is returned to it" (p. 108).

However, in his primary discussion of "Kol Dodi Dofek" in his essay "The Jewish People," Blidstein strikes a different tone. To be sure, he correctly insists there that for the Rav "Egypt and Sinai, the Jew of fate and the Jew of destiny and purpose clearly reflect a hierarchical order" (p. 90). But he goes on to note—and how could he not?—that the Rav in describing the covenant of fate "tells us about the values that emerge in a people that must struggle to ensure its physical survival: mutuality, sympathy, self-sacrifice, *ḥesed*. These are functional values of the collective, to be sure, but they also require the individual to transcend his own selfish concerns, and as *ḥesed* resonate deeply in the Jewish consciousness" (p. 91). We have come very far in this "moral perspective" from a mere concern with "solidarity," from a minimalist definition of the covenant of fate. Indeed, the values of *Ḥesed*, loving-kindness, and *Kedushah*, holiness, which, for the Rav, exemplify the covenants of fate and destiny re-

8 Buber, Martin, *Moses: The Revelation and the Covenant* (Oxford and London: East and West Library, 1946), pp. 130-131.

spectively, constitute the primary ways whereby the individual, as the Rav always emphasized, imitates God.[9]

This emphasis on *Ḥesed* as constituting the leading moral virtue of the covenant of fate again needs to be understood within the essay's Zionist setting. In the section of "Kol Dodi Dofek," "The Obligation of Torah Jewry to the Land of Israel,"[10] the Rav calls on Orthodox American Jews to increase what he views as their inadequate financial support for the state and, in particular, for religious institutions in the state, to "establish more religious kibbutzim, build more houses for religious immigrants, [and] create an elaborate and extended system of schools."[11] In this context he launches the following remarkable accusation. "We Orthodox Jews suffer from a unique illness that is not found among non-religious Jews (with a few exceptions); we are all misers! In comparison with other American Jews, we do not excel in the attribute of *Ḥesed*."[12] This section precedes the sections on the covenants of fate and destiny.[13] But in retrospect it becomes evident that in terms of financial support of the State of Israel and its institutions secular American Jews, in the view of the Rav, turn out to be more committed to the covenant of fate than Orthodox American Jews.

Another major theme of the Rav's public thought discussed by Blidstein is the Jewish people as a source of authority. This, putting together different discussions of Blidstein, takes place on three levels. First, as Blidstein notes in speaking of the Rav's religious Zionism, though the Rav "bases the standing of the state on its halakhic significance" (p. 28), "this does not mean that his attitude toward [both the land and state] exhausted itself solely in halakhic terms" (p. 28). Blidstein proceeds to eloquently elaborate:

---

9 I would like to thank my friend and former student Jason Kalman for reminding me of this point.

10 *Fate and Destiny: From the Holocaust to the State of Israel*, translated by Lawrence Kaplan (Hoboken, NJ: Ktav Publishing House, 2000), pp. 35–41.

11 Ibid, p. 39. I have paraphrased here very slightly.

12 Ibid, p. 39.

13 Ibid, pp. 42–63.

> Zionism obligates every Jew, inasmuch as he harbors "yearnings of the generations."[14] In other words, a Jew who has an organic, natural, healthy, and normal connection to his people, its fate and destiny, its memories, hardships, and hopes, will want to participate in the building of the land and the establishment of the state, and return to Zion. The voices of the generations denied this are clearly heard; they resonate in his soul. The Rav does not see in the fact that essential elements of the state are secular something to prevent the "yearnings of the generations" from identifying with it. The main thing is the craving for the collective return to the Land of Israel, which includes an independent political foundation.... Regarding the Land of Israel and the state, as in other matters the Rav did not seek analytic or even halakhic support in the strict sense of the term; he listened to the generations speaking in his blood. (p. 28)

Second, Blidstein notes, the Rav extends Maimonides' view that "one of the bases of Talmudic authority as a whole is the consent of the people" by arguing that "popular consent is given an institutional concretization—the great Sanhedrin. The Sanhedrin is thus understood as having a dual function, for it expresses the will of the people Israel as well as pronouncing opinions and decisions in its role as the major organ of Oral Law" (pp. 95-96). Here Blidstein discusses the Rav's famous *ḥiddush* that the Great Court's authority to constitute the Jewish calendar derives from its being the representative of the Jewish people. This enables the Rav to solve the problem as to how the calendar can continue to function authoritatively if the Great Court no longer exists, the answer being that in the absence of the Great Court this power reverts to the people. As Blidstein points out, the Rav offers two variants of this solution. In an earlier variant "what is really crucial are the calculations done by

---

14 The citation is from "Al Ahvat ha-Torah u-Geulat Nefesh ha-Dor," in P. Peli, ed., *Be-Sod ha-Yaḥid ve-ha-Yaḥad* (Jerusalem: Orot, 1976), p. 418.

'the Jews of the land of Israel,'"[15] while in a later one what is crucial is "the practice of Jewry as a whole"[16] (p. 96).

This later variant, however, Blidstein indicates, raises an intriguing problem. The Rav writes, "Now *Knesset Israel* sanctifies... the holidays and New Moons by its ritual practice.... The entire people fix the calendar through the calculations, and the celebrations of the holidays and New Moons according to these calculations function to set the calendar."[17] But, as Blidstein notes, "we all know—and so does Rabbi Soloveitchik—that the 'entire people' no longer celebrates the holidays" (p. 97), certainly not in a halakhic mode. We need not enter into Blidstein's insightful discussion of this conundrum, except to note three things. First, Blidstein confronts here the issue I raised earlier, namely, to what extent the Rav absorbed the full dimensions of the secularization of the Jewish people. But second—and here we arrive at the very heart and soul of the Rav's faith—Blidstein suggests that if the Rav's halakhic theory simply refuses to accept the reality of the secularization of the Jewish people, it may be because

> Halakhic theory, in this case at least, is more than analytic description. It is also a statement of faith. Here (and elsewhere) the Rav asserts that the Jewish people, which is incomprehensible to him outside its covenantal commitment, will return to its vocation of holiness. Messianic faith, he declares, is "faith in the Jewish people." (p. 98)

Yet—and this is the third point—Blidstein soberly concludes:

> Ironically it is precisely the description of the authority immanent in the Jewish people that suggests how far contemporary Jewish life actually is from its sacred vocation, and the argument for the indispensability of this authority, which suggests how fragile the sacred existence of this people is today. The calendar—at least on the theory developed by the Rav—is living on borrowed time, and not the calendar alone. (p. 98)

15 *Kovetz Ḥiddushei Torah* (Jerusalem, n. d.), pp. 47–65.

16 *Shi'urim le-Zekher Abba Mari*, I (Jerusalem: Mossad ha-Rav Kook, 2002), pp. 147–152.

17 Ibid, p. 148.

The third level on which the authority of the people operates relates to the people's practice more broadly conceived. In his well-known halakhic essay, "Shenei Sugei Massoret" ("Two Types of Tradition"), the Rav writes:

> There are two traditions: 1) One tradition relates entirely to a tradition of study, debate, give and take, and halakhic rulings based on intellectual considerations. This sage offers a reason for his view, and another sage offer a reason for his competing view, and they take a vote, as the Torah pictures it for us in the periscope regarding the rebellious elder (Deut. 17:8-13); 2) the tradition of practice constituted by the behavior of the entire Jewish people regarding the performance of commandments. This tradition is based on the verse "Ask your father, and he will show you; your elders, and they will tell you." (Deut. 32:7)[18]

The Rav, as his wont, elaborates brilliantly on the nature of these two traditions and the differences between them. In particular, he uses the concept of a tradition of practice to answer the well-known problem as to why the *Amoraim* can't disagree with the *Tannaim* or for that matter why the *Geonim* can't disagree with the *Amoraim*, given Maimonides' ruling (*Laws of Rebels* 2:1) that in matters of exegesis and reasoning a later court can controvert the law proclaimed by an earlier court and "judge in accordance with what appears to them to be the law" even if the later court is not as great as the earlier one in wisdom and numbers. To enter into an examination of the Rav's answer here would, however, take us too far afield.[19]

---

18 Ibid, p. 249.

19 Ibid, pp. 256–259. It is surprising that the Rav does not mention that this question was raised by the *Kesef Mishneh* in connection with the authority of the *Mishnah* in the latter's commentary on *Laws of Rebels* 2:1 and does not explain how his answer differs from the *Kesef Mishneh*'s. Again this is not the place to elaborate, but it seems to me that the Rav's answer is superior to the *Kesef Mishneh*'s, insofar as the Rav's answer, unlike the *Kesef Mishneh*'s, does not require any explicit acceptance on the part of "the later generations ... not to disagree with the earlier ones." The discussion of the *Kesef Mishneh*, in turn, became the starting point for the famous de-

Blidstein, unfortunately, does not have that much to say about "these two forms of traditional authority" (p. 103). He does, however, make the challenging claim that the Rav's analysis of these two types of tradition, "that of scholarly analysis and decision and that of life lived by the people itself" (p. 103), "dovetails perfectly" with his famous description of two other types of tradition, the tradition of the fathers and that of the mothers. It would follow that the tradition of the fathers is one of "scholarly analysis and decision," while the tradition of the mothers refers to the "life lived by the people itself." I cannot agree.

In his very well-known essay "A Tribute to the Rebbetzin of Talne" the Rav writes:

> We have two massorot, two traditions, two communities...— the massorah community of the fathers and that of the mothers. Father teaches the son the discipline of thought as well as the discipline of action. Father's tradition is an intellectual-moral one.... Mother [teaches]... that Judaism expresses itself not only in formal compliance with the law but also in a living experience...that there is a flavor, a scent and warmth to the *mitzvot*.[20]

I would suggest, then, contra Blidstein, that far from the traditions of the fathers and of the mothers "dovetail[ing] perfectly" with the traditions "of scholarly analysis and decision and ... of life lived by the people itself," the latter traditions are two subcategories, two aspects of the tradition of the fathers.

---

bate between the Ḥazon Ish and Rav Elḥanan Wasserman on this issue. The exchange between Rav Elhanan and the Ḥazon Ish can be found in the former's *Kovets 'Inyanim*, 3, ed. R. Zalman Drori (Jerusalem, 1983), pp. 191–216. For further discussion, see Benjamin Brown, *The Ḥazon Ish: Halakhist, Believer, and Leader of the Ḥaredi Revolution* (Jerusalem: Magnes Press, 2011), pp. 405-406; idem, *He-Ḥazon Ish: Halakhah, Emunah, ve-Ḥevrah* (Doctoral thesis, Hebrew University, 2003), Excursus 12; Chanah Kehat, "Bittzur Ma'amadah shel ha-Torah be-Mishnat he-Ḥazon Ish," *Yeshivot u-Batei Midrashoth*, ed. E. Etkes (Jerusalem, 2007), pp. 330–337, and my forthcoming essay, "The Ethos of Submission, Union with the Spirit of the Torah, and Confronting the Challenges of the Times: The Ḥazon Ish."

20 "Tribute to the Rebbetzin of Talne," *Tradition* 17:2 (1978): 75.

In truth, the Rav's multiple and varying analyses of the concept of tradition serve as a perfect illustration of his ability to "frequently discover contrasting characteristics in ostensibly unitary or homogeneous topics." First, in "A Tribute to the Rebbetzin of Talne" the Rav differentiates between the tradition of the fathers and that of the mothers. The tradition of the fathers is intellectual-practical, while the tradition of the mothers is experiential. Then *within* the intellectual- practical tradition of the fathers the Rav in "Shenei Sugei Massoret" differentiates between the intellectual tradition "of scholarly analysis and decision" and the practical tradition "of life lived by the people itself." Finally, within the intellectual tradition itself the Rav in his essay "Kevi'at Mo'adim 'al pi ha-Re'iyah ve-'al pi ha-Ḥeshbon,"[21] *further* differentiates between an intellectual tradition handed down through a process of teaching and study from teacher to student and an intellectual tradition where the oral Law, *aside* from being handed down through the standard process of teaching and study from teacher to student (*limmud*), is formally *transmitted* (*mesirah*) as a theoretical-intellectual discipline. That is, here the teacher, who himself is one of the *Ḥakhmei ha-Massorah*, one the those Sages who are part of and constitute the ongoing chain of tradition, does not only teach his students, but formally transmits the oral Law to those very few students of his who are worthy so that they in turn become yet another link in that chain of tradition. And, as the Rav emphasizes, "This act of transmission ... constitutes a process and an institution by itself."

The analysis contained in the above paragraph may perhaps best be presented in the form of the following chart:[22]

---

21 "Kevi'at Mo'adim 'al pi ha-Re'iyah ve-'al pi ha-Ḥeshbon," *Kovetz Ḥiddushei Torah* (Jerusalem: Makhon Yerushalayyim, n.d,), pp. 60–62. Cf. the Rav's oral discourse, "Seguliyyuto shel Sefer Mishneh Torah," ed. Rabbi Zev Gotthold, *Mahanayyim* 4:2 (1992): 8–29.

22 I will discuss this at greater length and with full documentation in my forthcoming study "The Rav on the Multi-Functional and Multi-Faceted Nature of the Massorah."

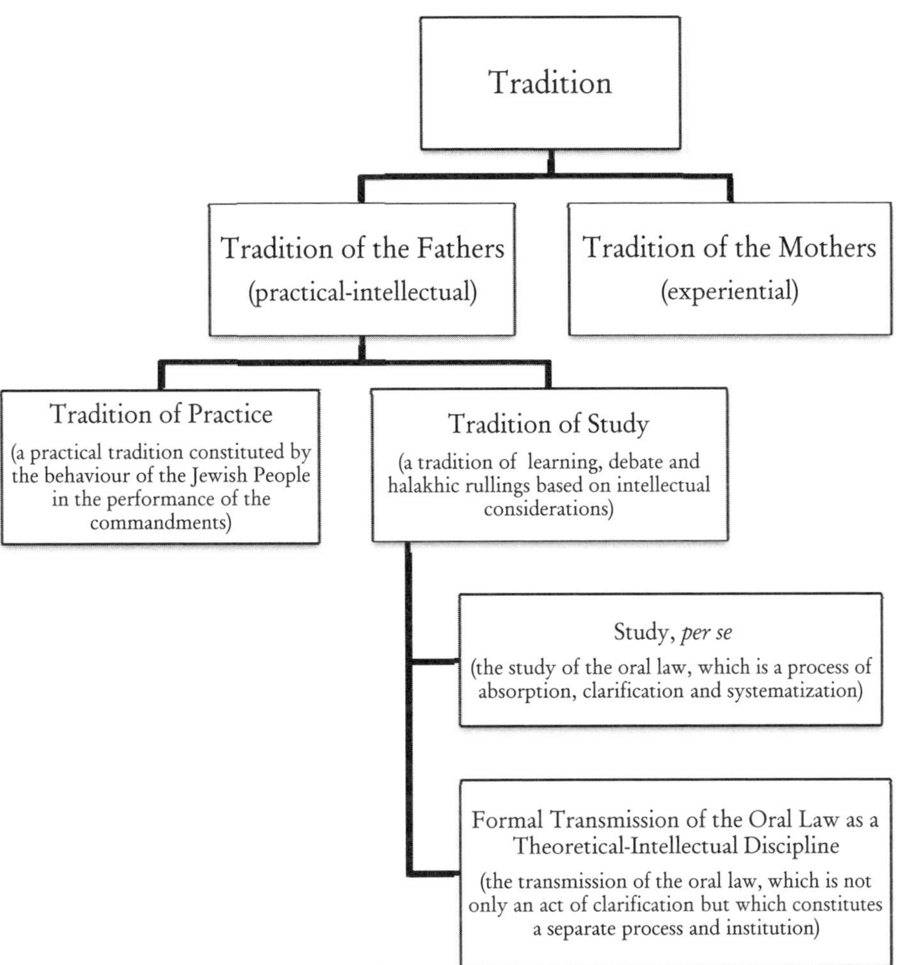

Blidstein's review-essay of *Community, Covenant, and Commitment* contains much rich discussion of the Rav's public thought. He provocatively claims that one ought to group together the Rav's discussions of "interreligious dialogue and contact with the Catholic Church before the issuance of the Vatican Declaration on the Jews, Orthodoxy's relationship with the Conservative movement and its rabbis, and (even!) the relations between Orthodox rabbis and non-rabbinic Orthodox agencies" (pp. 46-47).

He admits that "On the face of it these groupings seem quite different from one another: What does the Pope have in common with the leader of Mizrachi" (p. 47)? Yet he convincingly argues that "the Rav sees in each of these contexts the need to strike a balance (that will differ from case to case, of course) between drawing closer and keeping one's distance, thereby setting the boundaries of cooperation and estrangement" (p. 47). Here we will concentrate on Blidstein's analysis of the Rav's view regarding interreligious dialogue and contact with the Catholic Church.

As Blidstein indicates, the philosophical foundation "the Rav posited ... for rejecting [Interfaith] dialogue" in his famous essay "Confrontation" "had already been set into place in his 1950 letter to [Professor Milton Konvitz of Cornell University and intended to be read by] Cornell's President" (p. 49) regarding the "Depiction of Human Images on Stained Glass Windows in an Interfaith Chapel." In that letter, the Rav expresses his opposition to the very idea of an interfaith chapel, though, interestingly enough, he had been informed that the decision to build it had already been made and was not on the table, arguing, to cite Blidstein's paraphrase, that "every faith community has its own structure, forms of expression, and content, and that these cannot coexist within a single architectonic space" (50).[23] It is particularly noteworthy, Blidstein stresses, "that the Rav manages to deny legitimacy of a shared house of worship for Jews and Christians without ever hinting at the possibly that Christianity has the status of idolatry" (pp. 42-43).

Actually, this letter and others from the early 1950s anticipate the Rav's position as set forth in "Confrontation" even more fully than indicated by Blidstein. For, as is well known or should be well known, the Rav's rejection of interfaith theological dialogue is only one side of the theological coin he mints in that essay. In the essay the Rav speaks of a *double* confrontation, "a universal human and an exclusively covenantal confrontation."[24] The "universal human

---

23 *Community, Covenant, and Commitment: Selected Letters and Communications of Rabbi Joseph B. Soloveitchik*, ed. Nathaniel Helfgot (Jersey City, N.J. Ktav Publishing House for the Toras HoRav Foundation, 2005), pp. 8-9. Actually, Rabbi Helfgot already anticipated Blidstein's point. See p. xvii.

24 "Confrontation," *Tradition* 6:2 (1964):17.

confrontation" is the confrontation of humankind and the cosmos. Here Jews "stand with civilized society shoulder to shoulder over against the great [natural] order that defies us all."[25] The "exclusively covenantal confrontation" comes into play in connection with the "personal confrontation of two faith communities,"[26] and it is in this connection that the Rav rejects interfaith theological dialogue on the ground of the uniqueness and incommensurability of different faith commitments.

Both in his letter of 1950 to Professor Konvitz and in his letter of 1953 to Rabbi Theodore Adams regarding Orthodox participation in Communal Tercentenary Celebrations, the Rav clearly adumbrates this theme of a double confrontation. Thus in his letter of 1950 he writes:

> We identify ourselves with our gentile neighbors in all matters of collective endeavor—social, political, and cultural activities. There should be no retreat on the part of the Jew from full participation in all phases of national life and we are committed to all of America's institutions. However, the worship of God is not a social or collective gesture, but is a genuinely individual, most personal, intimate and tender relationship which cannot be shared with anyone else.[27]

The same note is struck in his letter of 1953:

> As to interfaith celebrations we are ready and willing to encourage such projects as long as they are held within the confines of secular activities. No joint worship, however, can be encouraged. We are loyal citizens of our great country and are committed to all its institutions, political, economic, and educational without any reservation or qualification, as are all other Americans. Hence joint action and common effort are commendable in all areas of mundane endeavor. Yet one's relationship to, worship and dialogue with God, is an inner experience most intimate, most personal, most unique. Each com-

25 Ibid, p. 20.

26 Ibid, p. 21.

27 *Community, Covenant, and Commitment*, pp. 8-9.

munity worships God in its singular way. "*Gleichschaltung*" distorts the very essence of the religious experience.[28]

I have treated this point at some length because, as David Shatz has noted,[29] many people in discussing "Confrontation" focus only on the Rav's emphasis on the importance of the "exclusively covenantal confrontation" and his consequent rejection of interfaith dialogue, ignoring his emphasis on the equal importance of "universal human confrontation" and his consequent affirmation of the need for Jews to "stand with civilized society shoulder to shoulder over against the great [natural] order that defies us all."[30] It is important then to show that not just the Rav's rejection of interfaith dialogue had its philosophical roots in his letters from the 1950s, but his broader theme of the need for Jews to perform a double confrontation also had its roots in those letters.

---

28 Ibid, pp. 113-114.

29 David Shatz, "The Rav's Philosophical Legacy," in *Memories of a Giant: Eulogies in Memory of Rabbi Dr. Joseph B. Soloveitchik*, ed. Michael A. Bierman (Jerusalem: Urim Publications, 2003), p. 315.

30 In this connection it is revealing to contrast the Rav's view regarding the typological meaning that the presents that Jacob sent Esau had for the "unprotected, helpless, abandoned ... and despised" Jews "during a long Diaspora night," with the typological meaning that they have for Western, particularly American Jews living in free and open societies. During the long Diaspora night, the "Jew would try to contend with the cruelty of his enemies and oppressors simply by appeals and pleading, through bribery and gifts. 'And he took of that which he had in hand as a present for Esau his brother' (Gen. 32:4). In truth, the Jews successfully annulled many cruel edicts by these means." See "The Everlasting Ḥanukah," in *Days of Deliverance: Essays on Purim and Ḥanukah*, eds. E. Clark, J. Wolowelsky, and R. Ziegler (Jersey City, N.J.: Ktav Publishing House for the Toras HoRav Foundation, 2007), p. 135. [This essay is a translation—significantly abridged in places—of "Ḥanukah, 1951," *Yiddish Drashos and Writings*, ed. David Fishman (Jersey City, N.J. Ktav Publishing House for the Toras HoRav Foundation, 2009).] For Jews living in free and open societies the presents that Jacob sent Esau signify that "We are determined to participate in every civic, scientific, and political endeavor. We feel obligated to enrich society with our creative talents and to be constructive and useful citizens" ("Confrontation," pp. 28-29).

III

As noted earlier, the two essays in Blidstein's collection that focus on the more personal existential side of the Rav's thought are "The Covenant of Marriage" and "Death." Indeed, love, sexuality, and marriage, on the one hand, and suffering, evil, and death, on the other, form the two poles around which much of the Rav's personal thought revolves. If the Rav, thus, as Avi Ravitzky has maintained,[31] is the philosopher of the Song of Songs,[32] he is also the philosopher of Koheleth. Again, there is much of great interest in Blidstein's analysis, and I will focus only on a few select points related to his essay "The Covenant of Marriage."

In this essay, a wide ranging survey and analysis of *Family Redeemed: Essays on Family Relationships*,[33] Blidstein emphasizes the uniqueness of the work.

> The six essays in this volume are dedicated to marital and parental relationships as a Jewish and human phenomenon. It

31 Aviezer Ravitzky, "Kinyan Ha-Da'at be-Haguto: Beyn ha-Rambam le-Neo-Kantianism," *Sefer ha-Yovel li-Khvod ha-Gaon Rav Yosef Dov Soloveitchik*, eds., Shaul Yisraeli, Nachum Lamm, and Yitzhak Raphael (Jerusalem: Mossad ha-Rav Kook, 1984), Vol. 1, p. 125, and throughout the article. Note how in the English version of Ravitzky's article, "Rabbi Joseph B. Soloveitchik on Human Knowledge: Between Maimonidean and neo-Kantian Philosophy," *Modern Judaism* 6:2 (1956): 157 and throughout, the phrase "pilosof shel Shir ha-Shirim" is translated either as "the philosopher of the religious personality" or as "the philosopher of the dialectical religious personality." In general, a comparison of the article's Hebrew and English versions indicates that Ravitzky's richly allusive Hebrew style has been greatly attenuated in the English translation.

32 Of course, I am using this phrase metaphorically. As is well known, for the Rav the Song of Songs may not be interpreted according to its literal, but only according to its allegorical meaning. See *And From There You Shall Seek* (Jersey City, N.J.: Ktav Publishing House for the Toras HoRav Foundation, 2008), note 1 (pp. 151–153).

33 *Family Redeemed: Essays on Family Relationships* eds. David Shatz and Joel Wolowelsky (Jersey City, N.J.: Ktav Publishing House for the Toras HoRav Foundation, 2000). I wrote a review of this work in *Judaism* 50 (Fall 2001): 491–499. While there is some slight overlap between my review and Blidstein's, we generally focus on different aspects of the essays; our reviews thus nicely complement one another.

> seems to me that the very writing of these essays during the late 1950s, the surprising decision to devote so much attention to the problems and challenges of marriage and family life, is in itself of great significance for understanding the Rav's world and personality. There is even a certain daring to this choice, as the Rav does not refrain from relating to the erotic component of marital union. I am not familiar with another Jewish treatment of the issue similar to the one found in this book: a gaping divide stands between it and contemporary religious writing dealing with marriage. (pp. 111-112)[34]

In addition to his discussion of the Rav's views on "the erotic component of marital union," Blidstein also touches on the Rav's views regarding the issue of gender, which on the whole he finds to be rather traditional. One point, however, he singles out for particular attention.[35]

> In light of this traditional attitude to gender, I found great interest in the section the volume's editors named "The Tragedy in Motherhood." Indeed, the Rav himself uses the term "tragedy" in this context....This assessment is based on the fact that Abraham (who sits "in front of the tent") responds to the angels' question "Where is Sarah, your wife," with the answer, "Behold in the tent," inside, concealed,... despite the im-

[34] But see now Rav Shagar, "Ahavah, Romantikah, u-Berit," *Nehalekh be-Regesh: Mivḥar Ma'amarim Yotse le-'Or Likrat Yom ha-Shanah ha-Rishon le-Histalkuto* (Efratah: Makhon Kitve ha-Rav Shagar, 2007), pp. 271–286. Note that on pp. 281-282, Rav Shagar praises the novelty and, to use Blidstein's adjective, "daring" of the Rav's approach to marriage, family life, and sexuality and proceeds to build his own approach to these sensitive issues, in large measure, on that of the Rav, while, at the same time, modifying the Rav's approach in light of his, Rav Shagar's, own well-known post-modernist commitments. I suspect that the Rav would have been unhappy both with the praise and with the modifications. A full comparison of the approaches of these two major figures regarding these critical issues is an important desideratum.

[35] Indeed, as Blidstein noted in a "Letter to the Editor" he wrote to *Judaism* Magazine in response to my own review of *Family Redeemed*, "the point ... is brief, but it exceeds in originality and daring much of the other more lengthy discussion." See "Communications," *Judaism* 51:4 (Summer 2002): 380-381.

> portance of her work. The woman is found deep inside the tent, hidden, and her presence is passed on through her husband. Sarah's concealment—and that of all women—is not interpreted here in a favorable light. According to the Rav's homiletical reading of the passage, the dialogue between Abraham and the angels embodies the price that a woman must pay. The Rav reminds us that Abraham's historic role came to an end with Sarah's death...The message is clear. "Why do people not know the truth" that Abraham's work was in large measure the work of Sarah? "And yet... we say [in our prayers] 'God of Abraham, God of Isaac, and God of Jacob,' but not 'God of Sarah, God of Rebecca, and God of Leah and Rachel,' even though they had an equal share in the Creator of the World."[36] According to the Rav, it is here that "the tragedy manifests itself with all its impact."[37] The term "tragedy" is significant. The tragic is inherent, almost unpreventable, in reality—the human-social reality or the religious-halakhic reality, as in our case. ...It is interesting to see how the Rav leads the homily to the halakhic realm, and in this realm—to prayer and its formulations, issues that were so close to his heart. (pp. 118-119)

While the Rav, in this section cited by Blidstein, states that the Matriarchs "had an equal share in the Creator of the World" with the Patriarchs, he, of course, does not mean that their shares were identical. How did their shares differ, and how were they equal? I would suggest the following.

This section is from the essay "Parenthood: Natural and Redeemed." In this essay the Rav distinguishes between the mother's and father's missions in the covenantal community, the father's mission or teaching role being intellectual in nature, the mother's experiential. This distinction, of course, is almost identical with that drawn in "A Tribute to the Rebbetzin of Talne" between the intellectual-practical tradition of the fathers and the experiential tradition of the mothers. However in "Parenthood" the Rav takes the theme of the two missions or the two traditions one step further than he does in "A Tribute to the Rebbetzin of Talne." In

36 Family Redeemed, p. 120.

37 Ibid, p. 120.

"Parenthood" the Rav makes the additional point that "in normal times, when routine decisions are reached," the father takes the lead.[38] However, in times of crisis, "when the situation ... requires instantaneous action that flows from the depths of a sensitive personality," it is the mother "who steps to the fore and takes command."[39] It follows, then, as the Rav states, that it was the biblical Matriarchs who, in times of crisis, had the primary responsibility for transmitting the covenant.

In light of the above, we may say that the phrase in the liturgy: "God of Abraham, God of Isaac, and God of Jacob," refers to the fact that in normal times it was the Patriarchs who had the primary responsibility for transmitting the covenant; but in times of crisis it was the Matriarchs—Sarah, Rebecca, Leah, and Rachel—who bore that responsibility. Of course, I hasten to add, all this does not diminish in the slightest the "tragedy" inherent in Sarah's reality, a tragedy manifested, as the Rav notes, in our saying "God of Abraham, God of Isaac, and God of Jacob," and not "God of Sarah, God of Rebecca, and God of Leah and Rachel," even though "they had an equal share in the Creator of the World." All it does is to clarify the Rav's view as to differing but equal shares the Patriarchs and Matriarchs had in the Creator of the World.

Blidstein, along with many others, notes that sacrifice, retreat, defeat, and submission "are central values in the Rav's thought," (pp. 145-146), and that they particularly come into play in connection with marriage and sexuality. He sums up the Rav's position thus.

> Marriage requires, first and foremost, mutual sacrifice. The reference, of course, is to the creation of an existential space in which the couple can both live together and as separate individuals. But marriage involves sacrifice in another sense as well. The two parties sacrifice sexual freedom...in marital life itself, where total abstinence is demanded at the time of the woman's monthly period.... According to the Rav, at issue is simple and painful abstinence that leads to catharsis. (p. 114)

---

38 Ibid, p. 116.

39 Ibid, pp. 116-117.

Blidstein elaborates on this point in his essay "On Death." There he notes that "retreat, sacrifice, and failure in the Rav's teaching are almost always found in dialectical movement... Almost without exception, man falls solely in order to rise again with increased strength. He falls only so that he may know how to achieve true ascent" (p. 147). In this connection Blidstein returns to the role of sacrifice and retreat in marriage and sexuality.

> David Hartman correctly noted that the Rav's use of the motif of falling in Eve's formation from the body of Adam in his sleep also comes to teach the interpersonal and moral lesson that man is asked to make room for the existence of the other, which translates into the sacrifice of the personal ego.[40] This is also the story of the bride and bridegroom who sacrifice their happiness on the altar of halakhah: "Sex, if unredeemed, may turn into a brutal ugly performance.... Sex, therefore, is in need of redemption.... What action did Judaism recommend to man in order to achieve this purpose? The movement of withdrawal and defeat."[41] Retreat comes in the midst of life so that the continuation should be more delicate, more human. (pp. 147-148)

Blidstein in these two passages has put his finger on something very important about the Rav's conception of sacrifice; however, it requires spelling out. Indeed, here we may yet again "discover contrasting characteristics in ostensibly unitary or homogeneous topics." For, as I have argued elsewhere,[42] the Rav operates with two conceptions of sacrifice, one found primarily in *LMF* and "The Community," the other in "Majesty and Humility" and "Catharsis."

---

40 Blidstein refers here to David Hartman, "Love and Terror in the God Encounter: The Theological Legacy of Rabbi Joseph Soloveitchik" (Woodstock, Vermont, 2001), pp.108–111.

41 Blidstein cites here "Majesty and Humility, *Tradition* 17:2 (Spring 1978): 36.

42 Lawrence Kaplan, "Rav Soloveitchik's The Lonely Man of Faith in Contemporary Modern Orthodox Jewish Thought" (in Hebrew), Rabbi in the New World: The Influence of Rabbi J. B. Soloveitchik on Culture, Education, and Jewish Thought, eds. Avinoam Rosenak and Naftali Rothenberg (Jerusalem: Magnes Press and Van Leer Institute, 2011), pp. 147–176.

In *LMF* sacrifice is essentially connected with withdrawal in order to recognize and make room for the other, both human and divine. Limiting ourselves to the human other, it means that Adam the second must withdraw in order to make room for the other, in order to listen to and hear what the other has to say in his or her otherness, for only thereby is true communication and consequently true community possible. In "The Community," in like manner, the recognition of another's existence is "*eo ipso*, a sacrificial act, since the mere admission that a Thou exists in addition to the I is tantamount to *tzimtzum*, self-limitation and self-contraction."[43]

In "Majesty and Humility" and "Catharsis," by contrast, sacrifice means that "at every level of [one's] total existential experience"[44] the individual gives up, withdraws from, if only temporarily, whatever he "desires the most."[45] This act of withdrawal, of self-defeat is, for the Rav, the true heroic act. Man, whenever "victory is within reach ...stop[s], turn[s] around, and retreats."[46] Defeat here is an intra-psychic category, one basically unconnected with the presence of an other, whether human or divine. It is an *akedah* experience in the precise sense of the term, as man sacrifices that which is most precious to him only to re-acquire it once again.

To return, then, to Blidstein's two passages about the Rav's view on marriage cited above, it is clear that in both passages he begins with *LMF* and "The Community" type of sacrifice where one withdraws in order to make room for the other, and then moves to the "Majesty and Humility" and "Catharsis" type of sacrifice where defeat is an intra-psychic category.

I still believe that my claim that the Rav operates with two different conceptions of sacrifice is fundamentally correct. However, in light of both Blidstein's discussion and further reflection on my own, it seems to me now that I failed to properly discern the link between the two. In truth, both conceptions of sacrifice are linked to interpersonal ethics. However, in the conception of sacrifice found in *LMF* and "The Community," the connection between sac-

---

43 "The Community" (above, n. 4), p. 15.

44 "Catharsis," p. 44.

45 Ibid, p. 46.

46 Ibid, p. 43.

rifice and interpersonal ethics is clear and immediate, for by sacrifice the Rav means withdrawal precisely for the purpose of recognition of the other and of the other's needs. The conception of sacrifice as self-defeat found in ''Majesty and Humility'' and ''Catharsis'' is also connected to interpersonal ethics, but given the intra-psychic nature of this type of sacrifice, the connection is indirect. The Rav argues that such self-defeat is a heroic, cathartic act, a "divine dialectical discipline,"[47] whereby man purges himself of pride and arrogance and develops a sense of humility and critical self-awareness. Presumably, such refinement of character can have only positive ethical consequences on the interpersonal level. Thus we may say that the intra-psychic type of sacrifice found in ''Majesty and Humility'' and ''Catharsis'' refines and purges an individual's personality so that he is sensitized to the existence and needs of the other and is thus better able to withdraw in order to make room for him or her, thereby performing the *LMF* and "The Community" type of sacrifice. It is this link, I believe, Blidstein has in mind when at the end of the second passage cited he first quotes the Rav's assertion that through withdrawal and defeat—the ''Majesty and Humility'' and ''Catharsis'' type of sacrifice—man redeems sex and purges it of any possible brutal and ugly aspects, and then comments, "Retreat comes in the midst of life so that the continuation should be more delicate, more human"—the *LMF* and "The Community" type of sacrifice.

IV

As noted earlier, Blidstein deals with the Rav's halakhic writings both in his review-essay of *Community, Covenant, and Commitment* and in his essay "The Norms and Nature of Mourning."

The first section of Blidstein's review essay (pp. 39–46) is devoted to a penetrating examination of three English responsa of the Rav: 1) the aforementioned letter "On the Depiction of Human Images on Stained Glass Windows in an Interfaith Chapel"; 2) "On Directing Foundlings to Jewish Welfare Agencies"; and 3) "On Drafting Rabbis and Rabbinical Students for the U.S. Armed Forces

47 Ibid, p. 46.

Chaplaincy." As Blidstein notes in the introductory section of his essay, these responsa are of particular importance in shedding light on the Rav's conception of halakhah and providing a corrective to the impression one might receive from his more theoretical writings. Blidstein comments, "the Rav's essay *Ish ha-Halakhah* often is cited as proof that he viewed the halakhah as the realm of the a priori, impervious to social reality, and as subject to a method partaking more of mathematics than of the human sciences.... But that reading of *Ish ha-Halakhah*, taken alone, can afford a one-sided picture" (p. 38).

Of special relevance to this issue, Blidstein points out, is the Rav's "methodological pronouncement" introducing his responsum on "Drafting Rabbis and Rabbinical Students for the U.S. Armed Forces Chaplaincy." Blidstein explains:

> [This] methodological pronouncement included a two-fold statement of reservations about the "objective" model of halakhic decision-making. First, every intellectual activity (including even aspects of natural science) combines formal components and human intuitive components; in our case he declared his intuition was to approve the project... Second, one must distinguish between but ultimately combine "pure halakhic formalism which... places the problem on an ahistorical conceptual level... [and] applied halakhah which transposes abstractions into central realities.... Under this aspect I gave thought not only to halakhic speculation but also to the concrete situation." It is likely—though not certain—that the intuitive component of the project pertained primarily to the practical decision. In any event, it is clear that the Rav was not about to adopt the "mathematical" model of the halakhic process so admired within certain segments of Modern Orthodoxy—a model envisioned as automatically spitting out halakhic solutions solely on the basis of objective expertise. (pp. 44-45)[48]

I would like to take a closer look at the Rav's responsum "On the Depiction of Human Images on Stained Glass Windows in an

---

[48] It is, of course, not too hard to discern from Blidstein's use of the metaphor "spitting out" his own view of this model.

Interfaith Chapel," which, I believe, sheds clearer light on the interplay of halakhic and extra-halakhic in his responsa. Blidstein first presents the Rav's basic argument:

> The Rav begins by declaring that he cannot base his response on formal halakhah, but must look as well "to central historical realities with their deep-seated philosophical meaning."...That leads him to a passage in Tractate *Avodah Zarah*, from which one can only conclude that the greatest of the *amora'im* permitted the presence of a non-cultic human statue in the synagogue and that this teaching can be seen as normative.... But the Rav then goes on to find that Judaism historically did not act in accordance with this view and, as a practical matter, forbade the presence of images in the Synagogue. This approach ...was consistently followed in synagogues built in Christian Europe, and remains the practice to this day.
>
> Here the impact of Christianity proves decisive. In the Christian milieu, the Rav argues with outstanding cultural sensitivity, every human figure found in a cultic site instantly becomes a cultic figure—a consequence of the basic Christian belief in Jesus as man-god .... These circumstances are quite different, then, from those of Babylonian synagogues in Talmudic times. (p. 40)

To cite the Rav, "To what our sages in a non-Christian Babylonia did not object, our forefathers in Christian counties were quite susceptible."

Blidstein, after this summary, goes on to argue that the Rav's "treatment here of the halakhic sources ... provides ...an illustration of his comment that when he decides a halakhic issue, he has 'always been guided by a dim intuitive feeling which pointed out to me the true path,' and that 'my inquiry consisted only in translating vague intuitive feeling into fixed terms of halakhic discursive thinking.' That is so even though the argumentation here is far from halakhic, as the Rav himself acknowledges" (p. 41).

But, we may ask, is the argumentation in this responsum "far from halakhic," and does the Rav acknowledge this? Indeed, immediately after making the observation cited above that "To what our sages in a non-Christian Babylonia did not object, our forefathers in Christian counties were quite susceptible," the Rav goes on to say,

"I wish to emphasize that this [unequivocal iconoclastic attitude of Judaism toward the display of human images in houses of worship in Christian countries] was not merely a medieval addendum to the law but it expresses its very spirit."

I believe that Blidstein himself in the contrast he implicitly draws between the permissible "presence of a *non-cultic* human statue in the [Babylonian] synagogue" and forbidden presence of "a human figure" in synagogues in a "Christian milieu," inasmuch as it instantly "becomes a cultic figure," has provided us with the key for understanding the Rav's *halakhic* argument, but again the point needs to be spelled out.

The Rav in his brief presentation of the "formal halakhic viewpoint" regarding images first notes: "There are two fundamental prohibitions against the making of images. One deals with the making or possessing of idols ... and is not limited to a specific design.... The second ... applies to the making of [certain] images even if it not be for cultic but artistic purposes."

He then adds—and this serves as the basis of his entire argument—"It is also prohibited to create or possess any design which is usually associated with a cultic or religious motif, though the objective meaning of this design is purely artistic."

It is this *halakhic* principle which enables the Rav to combine here a formal-halakhic analysis with the taking into account of "central historical realities." For if we are speaking of a design "the objective meaning of [which] is purely artistic," what is it that determines whether or not this design "is usually associated with a cultic or religious motif," if not "central historical realities?" Here then sensitivity and responsiveness to historical and cultural change are built into the *very fabric* of the halakhic principle. Thus the Rav's main point is that in "non-Christian Babylonia" a human image in a synagogue was *not* "associated with a cultic or religious motif," while in Christian Europe it was. Indeed, after emphasizing that "the unequivocal iconoclastic attitude of Judaism toward the display of human images ... in Christian countries ... was not merely a medieval addendum to the law but it expresses its very spirit," the Rav goes on to explain, "As I have emphasized before, the law prohibits the representation of any figure or form which ... alludes to a cultic motif, and the human figure in the synagogue"—and here we may add in Christian Europe though not in non-Christian Babylonia—"though its objective meaning be of an artistic nature, comes under this category."

One can also raise the broader question as to how extensive a light these three responsa shed on the Rav's conception of halakhah, particularly halakhic *pesak*. One must remember that these responsa, which indeed make use of "axiological premises" and "philosophico-historical" considerations, were all written in the space of five months from December 1950 through April 1951, and, at least on the basis of current information, appear to be unique. Moreover, as is well known and as Blidstein surely knows, the Rav when describing the halakhah in *Ish ha-Halakhah* "as the realm of the a priori, impervious to social reality, and as subject to a method partaking more of mathematics than of the human sciences" is speaking of the halakhah as an ideal system, and *not* of halakhic pesak. It is only with his essay "Mah Dodekh mi-Dod," written in 1961, that we find the view of halakhah as a formal, abstract, self-contained system extended, albeit not entirely, to the realm of pesak. Certainly the need to combine, when engaging in pesak, "axiological premises" and "philosophico-historical" considerations with a formal-halakhic analysis, though not absent entirely in "Mah Dodekh mi-Dod," plays a peripheral role. One could then maintain that the Rav shifted from a more values-oriented approach to *pesak* in the 1950s to a more formalistic approach in the 60s. I put forward this possibility very tentatively, for our current knowledge of the Rav's halakhic activity qua *posek* is incomplete, but it serves to remind us that while these three responsa indeed possess great intrinsic interest, it is not clear whether they are truly representative of that activity over a period of forty years.

Blidstein's essay "The Norms and Nature of Mourning" begins with the observation that while "a not insignificant body of analysis, interpretation, and commentary to ... the Rav's view ... of the nature and ends of halakhah, his descriptions of the halakhic process, and 'how' one does halakhah,... nevertheless little has been done ... in actual treatment of the Rav's specific halakhic studies" (p.121).[49] His essay itself consists primarily of a lucid and incisive summary and analysis of two major essays of the Rav found in *Shi'urim le-Zekher Abba Mari* [*SZAM*], "Tum'at ha-Kohanim le-Shiv'at ha-Kerovim" ("Priests Rendering themselves Impure on the Death of one of the Seven Closest Relatives") and "Aveilut" ("Mourning"). "The first... deals with the obligation that priests render themselves impure on the death of one of the seven closest relatives, despite the general ban on priestly impurity.... The [second] ... directly confronts the performative norms of mourning as well as its essential internal correlates and manifestations" (pp. 123, 127).

The question arises to what extent these *shi'urim* and the others in *SZAM* are representative of the Rav's *derekh ha-limmud*, as contained in the bulk of his *shi'urim*. Blidstein does not address this question directly, but touches on it indirectly when considering the issue as to whether these *shi'urim* should be viewed as being in the traditional mode or not. In the body of his essay he asserts:

> The *shi'urim* I shall discuss proceed in the traditional mode. The Rav first assembles a list of textual anomalies and contradictions and then proceeds to solve the series of problems by presenting an overall thesis—analytical, of course, rather than textual or historical—which accounts for the earlier puzzling phenomena. (p.122)

However in the appended note Blidstein expresses second thoughts.

> I would no longer characterize the Rav's *shi'urim*, given in memory of his father and subsequently published, as being in the traditional mode.... Most traditional work is anchored in a

---

[49] For a similar observation in a different context, see Neria Guttel, "On Ways of Teaching Talmud in Our Generation: Preliminary Notes to Rabbi Shagar's *Be-Torato Yehege*" (in Hebrew), *Netuim* 17 (2011): 157-158, particularly note 23 (p. 158). For "actual treatments of the Rav's specific halakhic studies," see Avinoam Rosenak, "Pilosophiyyah u-Maḥshevet ha-Halakhah: Keri'ah be-Shi'urei ha-Talmud shel ha-Rav Soloveitchik le-'or Modelim Neo-Kantianim," *Emunah bi-Zemanim Mishtanim*, ed. Avi Sagi (Jerusalem, 1997), pp. 275–306; and Lawrence Kaplan, "Review Essay: *Worship of the Heart*," *Hakirah* 5 (2007): 79–114.

> specific text, broadening out to other texts only as ramifications (or contradictions) of the initial source. Thus it is hardly true ... that traditional halakhic study assembles a list of anomalies and then proceeds to solve the problems by presenting an overall thesis. Traditional halakhic commentary, rather, tends to focus on single sources, interpreted through an initial hypothetical thesis, which is then refined by the dialectical interpolation of more and more sources.... In these *shi'urim* the Rav, on the contrary, makes an initial presentation of numerous sources that require resolution in the guise of an overall thesis. (p. 122, note 2)[50]

It is somewhat surprising that Blidstein in recording his change of mind does not advert to the already well-known debate between Rabbis Elyakim Krumbein and Avraham Walfish[51] regarding the question I raised earlier as to whether the *shi'urim* in *SZAM* can be viewed as being representative of the bulk of the Rav's *shi'urim*, Krumbein arguing yes, Walfish no, for certainly *those shi'urim* are in the traditional mode. In particular, the argument Walfish presents in support of his position anticipates the distinction Blidstein draws in his note and seeks to account for it as well.

> It is only to be expected that *SZAM* would differ in its rhetorical structure from most *shi'urim* of the Rav, given the unique forum in which it was given: a mass audience, before whom a single lecture would be delivered, as opposed to the bulk of his *shi'urim*, which were delivered before his students, with whom he met on a regular basis for consecutive study of a single text. It is no wonder that such a lecture would focus much more heavily on concept than on text ... [as opposed to] the daily

50 Note the similarity between the Rav's method in *SZAM* and that of Rav Yitzhak Hutner in his multi-volume *Paḥad Yitzḥak*.

51 See the exchange between them in *Lomdus: The Conceptual Approach to Jewish Learning*, ed. Yosef Blau (Jersey City, N.J. Ktav Publishing House for the Orthodox Forum, 2006): Elyakim Krumbein, "From Reb Hayyim and the Rav to Shi'urei ha-Rav Aharon Lichtenstein: The Evolution of a Tradition of Learning," pp. 229–297; Avraham Walfish, "The Brisker Method and Close Reading: A Response to Rav Elyakim Krumbein," pp. 299–321; and Elyakim Krumbein, "Beyond Complexity: A Response to Rav Avraham Walfish," pp. 323–332.

> *shi'urim* [which] focused on the text, on the concepts emerging from the text, and on the methodology the Rav was practicing and teaching.[52]

Whether the two *shi'urim* examined by Blidstein are representative of the bulk of the Rav's *shi'urim* or not, they are both certainly of great intrinsic interest and importance, and, as stated above, his summary and analysis of them both lucid and incisive. Blidstein shows how in both *shi'urim* the Rav "mounts questions that penetrate to the very heart of the topic discussed and molds the myriad particulars of the halakhic discussion into a broad synthetic structure. He deals with details, of course—no authentic halakhic discussion could ever forego that—but details are not trivia." Here I will focus on Blidstein's discussion of the essay on "Aveilut."

As Blidstein notes:

> This essay indicates that both performance and internalization are halakhic components of mourning. To be more specific: mourning requires both patterned ritual activity and individualized emotional activity, that is to say, grief.... Both are equally halakhic. The internalized activity, in other words, is not the "aggadic" correlate of the performed ritual.[53] Rather ritual and emotion are both normative... This, of course, is a claim that the Rav makes frequently. (p. 127)

Blidstein, of course, is referring to one of the best-known innovative insights, *ḥiddushim*, of the Rav, namely, his distinction between the *ma'aseh ha-mitzvah*, the indispensable means whereby one performs a commandment, and the *kiyyum ha-mitzvah*, the actual fulfillment of the commandment. This distinction enables the Rav to incorporate at least part of the realm of subjective religious experience into the inner sanctum of Halakhah.

Normally, the Rav points out, *ma'aseh* and *kiyyum* coincide. Thus, for example, one performs the commandment to eat matzah

---

52 Walfish, "The Brisker Method," pp. 306, 308.

53 This position of the Rav should be contrasted with that of Professor Abraham Joshua Heschel for whom "internalized activity" and subjectivity are always aggadic. I hope to elaborate upon this contrast in a forthcoming article.

by eating matzah, and that very act of eating constitutes the fulfillment of the commandment. The same holds true for most commandments. However, the Rav contends, there are central and fundamental "experiential" commandments—my term—where performance and fulfillment do not coincide, where the performance is an outward act but the fulfillment is an inner experience.

This, of course, as I just stated, is a very famous *ḥiddush* of the Rav, and many scholars, including myself, have discussed it at some length.[54] Examples of such "experiential" commandments are prayer, repentance and (according to some *rishonim*) the recitation of the Shema.[55] What is relevant here, as Blidstein notes, is the Rav's claim that both mourning and rejoicing on festivals are examples of such "experiential" commandments. Indeed, as Blidstein further notes, the halakhic principle that a mourner does not follow his mourning practices on a festival, inasmuch as the positive commandment to "rejoice on thy festival" (Deut. 16:14) overrides the commandment to mourn, the clear implication being that mourning and festival rejoicing are mutually exclusive, serves to indicate that both mourning and festival rejoicing fundamentally require the attainment of an inward emotional experience, mourning that of grief, rejoicing that of joy. To cite Blidstein's paraphrase of the Rav's argument:

---

54 See Yitzhak Gottlieb, "'Al Gishato ha-Hilkhatit shel ha-Rav Y. D. Soloveitchik," *Shanah be-Shanah* (1993-1994): 186–197; Lawrence Kaplan, "The Multi-Faceted Legacy of the Rav: A Critical Analysis of R. Hershel Schachter's *Nefesh Ha-Rav*," *BDD* (*Bekhol Derakhekha Daehu: Journal of Torah and Scholarship*) 7 (1998): 63–65; Shlomo H. Pick, "Le-Darko shel Ha-Grid Soloveitchik, zt"l, be-Limmud ha-Torah," *Mo'adei ha-Rav* (Ramat Gan: Bar-Ilan University, 2003), pp. 24–26; and David Shapiro, "*Ma'aseh ha-Mitzvah* and *Kiyyum ha-Mitzvah*," *Rabbi Joseph B. Soloveitchik on Pesach, Sefirat ha-Omer, and Shavu'ot* (Jerusalem: Urim Publications, 2005), pp. 53–67.

55 With respect to prayer and the recitation of the Shema, see Lawrence Kaplan, "Review Essay: *Worship of the Heart*" (above, n. 49); and with respect to repentance, see idem, "Hermann Cohen and Rabbi Joseph Soloveitchik on Repentance," *Hermann Cohen's Ethics*, edited by Robert Gibbs (Leiden and Boston: Brill, 2006), pp. 213–258.

> Now mourning and holiday ritual do not rule each other out as behavioral norms; it is possible to eat the holiday sacrifices while unshod and unshorn. The point, R. Soloveitchik argues, is that mourning and holiday joy are internalized emotional states before they are performed rituals, and these emotional states are in total conflict. (pp. 127-128)

Of course, one may ask: Granted that grief and joy contradict one another, is it not possible for these contradictory emotions to coexist in the psyche of the mourner? In truth, and this point is not noted by Blidstein, for the Rav there is a deeper inward contradiction between mourning and holiday joy, a contradiction on the level of consciousness. Here the Rav sets forth the following equations: Rejoicing = Standing in the Presence of God (*'amidah lifnei ha-Shem*), while Mourning = Distancing from the Presence of God (*hitrahkut mi-lifnei ha-Shem*). And it is this fundamental contradiction between the *consciousness* of standing in the presence of God and the *consciousness* of exile and separation from Him that is responsible for the commandment of festival rejoicing cancelling the commandment of mourning.[56] (Indeed, also in the other examples

---

[56] "U-Vikashtem mi-Sham," p. 211, n.19 [= *And From There You Shall Seek*, p. 197]; and "Be-'Inyan Avelut," pp. 193–195 [= "The Essential Nature of Mourning," pp. 78, 81-82]. Note, however, the comment of Rashi in *Sukkah* 25a, s.v. *hatam tarid tirda di-reshut*: "For even though a mourner is obligated to practice the rites of mourning and abstain from wearing shoes and washing and anointing himself in order to display honor on behalf of his dead relative (*kevod meito*), he is not obligated to grieve." According to Rashi, then, we may understand the conflict between *avelut* and *simḥat Yom Tov* as the contradiction between the heart's joy, which constitutes the inner *kiyyum* of the holiday rituals of rejoicing, and the display of honor to one's dead relative (*kevod meito*) achieved by means of the rites of mourning. For it is *kevod ha-met* that understandably requires that ordinarily one refrain during *avelut* from acts which cause one to rejoice. To be sure, a mourner on an ordinary day is permitted to eat meat and drink wine, but that is because those activities are not ordinarily seen as expressions of joy. However, on Yom Tov, the whole point of eating meat and drinking wine is to thereby attain the inward experience of joy. I discuss this view of Rashi at much greater length in a forthcoming article, "Can the Halakhah Suspend One's Emotions? Rabbi Joseph Soloveitchik, Rashi, and Maimonides on the Laws of Mourning."

cited previously—prayer, repentance, and the recitation of the Shema—the inner fulfillment is not just an emotional experience, but involves an awareness of a special type of relationship with God.)

Be this last point as it may, Blidstein succinctly shows how the Rav's claim that the commandment of mourning refers first and foremost to the internalized emotional state of grief enables him to account for otherwise perplexing and problematic halakhic phenomena. In response to those who "may view the Rav's assertion that mourning is both behavioral and internalized ... [as] reflect[ing] a modernizing Protestant bent," Blidstein correctly notes that "despite the modern terminology the halakhic analysis seems to be autonomous" (p. 132). Indeed, as Blidstein points out, the Rav, as is to be expected, invokes in support of his thesis a number of *rishonim*, particularly the anonymous disciple of R. Yeḥiel of Paris "for whom this internalization is a consistent motif." Somewhat surprisingly, particularly in light of his great interest in and extensive and illuminating writings on Maimonidean Halakhah, Blidstein does not mention that the Rav devotes considerable energy and ingenuity to arguing that the view that the commandment of mourning refers to the internalized emotional state of grief is also espoused by Maimonides, though in none of his works does Maimonides make the point explicitly.[57]

Blidstein emphasizes that while he has "summarized and occasionally interpreted," he has "not evaluated or attempted a critique" (p. 133). Therefore I do not feel it is appropriate to present here my own critique of the Rav's views, which, in any event, I will present in a forthcoming article of mine.[58] But I would like to take issue here with a point that Blidstein raises in *support* of the Rav's thesis. He argues that "the claim that grief itself possesses normative status

---

57 Indeed, in my forthcoming article referred to in the previous note, I argue that it is preferable to understand Maimonides' view regarding the essence of mourning as reflecting the *kevod ha-met* approach of Rashi as opposed to the inner grief approach of the anonymous disciple of R. Yeḥiel of Paris. For the meanwhile, note that Maimonides in *Hilkhot Aveilut* uses the term grief (*tza'ar*) only in connection with *sheloshim* and not *shiv'a*.

58 See my previous two notes.

ought to come as no surprise. A significant component of the mourning process is, after all, *niḥum aveilim.... Niḥum* presumes, clearly, that grief—to which consolation responds—is normatively present" (p. 121). I cannot agree. The reality of the mourner's grief as a natural emotion is, indeed, normatively present in the sense that it imposes upon *others* the obligation of *niḥum*. But I do not see how this means that the mourner himself is normatively obligated to experience grief, much less that this inner experience of grief constitutes the fulfillment of the commandment to mourn.

Despite this minor caveat, I again wish to commend Blidstein for the skill and deftness with which he summarizes and analyzes the Rav's halakhic thought as contained in these two *shi'urim* from *SZAM*. It is Blidstein's confrontation with the *substance* of the Rav's halakhic thought, with the "it" and not just the "about it," that lends particular weight to his more general reflections on that halakhic thought in the last section of his essay. In that section Blidstein convincingly suggests that the Rav isn't so much presenting a philosophy of halakhah, as he is presenting an interpretation, a hermeneutic of halakhah, which, Blidstein notes, is a hermeneutic in a dual sense. Not only does the Rav attempt to "provide... a coherent 'text,'" but he also attempts "to 'interpret' halakhic ritual behavior, to render [it] coherent and meaningful" (135-136). We have here, Blidstein observes, "A hermeneutic of halakhic behavior—a hermeneutic that draws upon halakhic concepts, values, and, in our case, psychological and emotional facts" (p. 136).[59] Above all,

[59] I find it hard, however, to agree with Blidstein's claim that this hermeneutic led the Rav beyond the famed Brisker focus on the "what" to raise questions of "why." Thus Blidstein maintains that "especially as regards the priest's impurity, the Rav was not only concerned with how priest behaved, but with why he behaved in that way, that is to say, with the meaning of his behavior; it was an act of mourning" (p. 136). It seems to me that that this is still in the realm of "what," particularly in light of Maimonides' view in *Sefer ha-Mitzvot*, Positive Commandment # 37 (cited by Blidstein on p. 124, n. 5) that this mandated impurity is simply identified with the imperative of mourning. I admit, though, that this is a complex matter. See in this regard the differing emphases of Walfish, "The Brisker Method," pp. 313-314, and Krumbein, "Beyond Complexity," pp. 331-332. While Walfish argues that "the boundary between 'understand-

Blidstein concludes, in the Rav's work, as in "certain facets of the work of people like [Peter] Berger, [Clifford] Geertz, [Charles] Taylor, [Michael] Walzer, and others..., norms are taken ... as tools of world-building and world-perceiving" (p. 138).[60] This extremely important observation deserves careful analysis, but such an analysis would take us beyond the bounds of this already greatly distended review-essay.

V

As noted already, the essay "Biblical Models" deals with the Rav's hermeneutics, that is, his phenomenological readings of biblical texts, focusing on "Kol Dodi Dofek" and *LMF*. Blidstein argues, I believe correctly, that *LMF* "works much more closely with the biblical narrative" than does "Kol Dodi Dofek," and that while the latter is more of a homily, "one could describe [the former] as genuine hermeneutic" (p. 69). A major component of Blidstein's essay is his comparison of the Rav's reading of the "exodus experience—bondage, release, Sinai"— in "Kol Dodi Dofek" with that of Martin Buber as found in his 1936 essay "On Nationalism" (pp. 64–69), and of his reading of the two creation stories in *LMF* with that of Karl Barth, as contained in the (almost 300 page!) forty-first section of *Church Dogmatics*. I have already discussed Blidstein's "Kol Dodi Dofek"/"On Nationalism" comparison. It would be worthwhile to analyze as well his *LMF*/*Church Dogmatics* comparison, but I must leave that elaborate task for another occasion. Here I will focus on Blidstein's discussion of the Rav's reading of the two creation stories in *LMF*.[61]

---

ing' and 'teleology,'" that is, between "what" and "why," "is not ironclad" (p. 312) and, like Blidstein, he sees the Rav as, at least in his "experiential" *shi'urim*, moving precisely in this direction, Krumbein maintains that "the Rav's innovation in the realm of *Oraḥ Ḥayyim* is that experience is in fact the 'what' of Halakhah" (p. 332).

60 Blidstein graciously acknowledges that I made a similar point in my (wrongly entitled?) essay, "Rabbi Joseph B. Soloveitchik's Philosophy of Halakhah," *Jewish Law Annual* 7 (1988): 162.

61 See, however, notes 67 and 68, for some brief remarks about Barth's readings.

Blidstein notes that the Rav, as is well known, "rather than harmonizing away the distinctions between these [stories],...pushes them to the limit,...mak[ing] a sharp distinction between First Adam and Second Adam, between the person created in Genesis 1 and the person created in Genesis 2. First Adam may be majestic and dignified, but covenantal dialogical existence is bestowed on Second Adam" (pp. 69, 74).

He explains:

> Jewish tradition ... is not committed to any single understanding of the "image of God" in man, which leaves R. Soloveitchik fairly free to cast the net of his imagination or alternatively to exploit this motif for his own purposes. Moreover ... he tends to read materials—even biblical materials—in a mode that suggests contrasts ... at least as much as continuities, a habit of mind possibly deriving from halakhic studies. In this particular case, he pursues his own agenda, which has as a dual focus the ... affirmation of technological man and the painful awareness of the gap between utilitarian fulfillment and true covenantal existence" (p. 74).

All this is certainly true. But we need to dig deeper. For the Rav, First Adam's relationship with God in Genesis 1 is set within a cosmic framework. Man's image of God in the first creation account refers, for the Rav, to his "inner charismatic endowment as a creative being"[62] that enables him to dominate his environment and thereby achieve dignity and majesty. Most important, "In doing all this Adam the first is trying to carry out the mandate of God.... [The striving for majesty and dignity] is a manifestation of obedience to rather than rebellion against God."[63] Particularly, man in *LMF*, both Adam the first and Adam the second, has a religious awareness of God mediated through the cosmos. Adam the first has a "pure rational religious awareness," which is a product of his creative cultural consciousness that picks out elements that point to the infinite.[64] Adam the second as well, *prior* to his revelational cove-

62 *The Lonely Man of Faith* (Jerusalem: Maggid, OU Press, 2012), p. 8.

63 Ibid, pp. 12-13.

64 Ibid, p. 66.

nantal experience, has an "aboriginal," cosmic religious experience.[65] This is a genuine living experience, receptive in nature and distinct from man's creative cultural consciousness, where the individual searches for the mysterious fascinating personal God hidden within the qualitative sense world. (Indeed, there is a cross-over here, going in the direction from Adam the second to Adam the first, for Adam the first constructs his "pure rational religious awareness" by borrowing "some component parts" from the transcendental, "aboriginal," cosmic religious experience of Adam the second and "translating" them into cultural religious categories.[66]) In a somewhat similar vein, the Rav in *And From There You Will Seek* speaks of the significance and necessity of the rational religious experience. This, like the "aboriginal," cosmic religious experience of Adam the second, is a genuine living experience where God is sought out as the Hidden Intellect standing behind the qualitative sense world, but, unlike the "aboriginal," cosmic religious experience of Adam the second which is receptive in nature and distinct from man's creative cultural consciousness, the rational religious experience is active in nature and part of the individual's creative cultural consciousness. To be sure, the Rav is critical, to a greater or lesser degree, of all these forms of a cosmic approach to God, viewing them all as insufficient and staunchly, indeed passionately, maintaining that the covenantal revelational religious experience is absolutely fundamental and indispensable. Still, while all these cosmic approaches to God are inadequate, none are illegitimate. Given all this, one can understand the contrast the Rav draws between cosmic Adam the first of Genesis 1 and covenantal Adam the second of Genesis 2, privileging the latter but still valuing the former.[67]

Blidstein comments as well on the Rav's understanding of God's relationship with Adam and Eve.

> God [for R. Soloveitchik] is a covenantal partner *with* Adam and Eve.... On the level of human dynamics R. Soloveitchik

---

65 Ibid, pp. 15–17, 35–38, 67–69.

66 Ibid, pp. 66-67.

67 It is, by contrast, not surprising that for Barth, who strongly rejects any natural theology, any approach to God via the cosmos, both Adams are covenantal figures.

> argues that it is the presence of God—a commanding presence that demands mutual commitment to the goals He sets down—which introduces substantive content and value to the human relationship. Yet, by entering into the covenantal relationship, God also commits Himself to the human pair. Both this commitment and the intimacy it implies are adumbrations of God's relationship with His people Israel, a relationship of mutual commitment and intimacy. For R. Soloveitchik ... the covenant between these two humans includes God as a third partner. (pp. 74-75)[68]

Here, of course, we clearly see the Rav's Halakho-centrism. What "introduces substantive content and value to the human relationship" is God's "*commanding* presence" (emphasis added). As Blidstein goes on to say, "R. Soloveitchik ...posits a relationship that is covenantal [only] if it strives toward a normative goal.... Dialogue here has a halakhic character" (p. 75).

In noting the Rav's insistence that it is God's "commanding presence" that "introduces substantive content and value to the human relationship," Blidstein appears to be referring to the following passage from *LMF*:

> Only when God emerged from the transcendent darkness of He-anonymity to the illumined spaces of community knowability *and charged man with an ethical-moral mission* [emphasis added] did Adam *absconditus* and Eve *abscondita*, while revealing themselves to God in prayer and unqualified commitment—also reveal themselves to each other in sympathy and love on the one hand and common action on the other.[69]

But where in Genesis 2 does God charge Adam and Eve "with an ethical-moral mission?" Blidstein suggests that perhaps this reading "responds ... to God's matchmaking role" (p. 72). Indeed, as

---

68 For Barth, on the contrary, as Blidstein notes (p. 74), "the covenant between Adam and Eve prefigures the covenant between Israel and God.... Adam and Eve embody ... the ideal covenant—that which inheres not only in the ideal relationship of man and woman or even Israel and God, but of Jesus and the Church."

69 Ibid, pp. 50-51.

Blidstein notes, the Rav in describing how "Adam the second was introduced to Eve by God"[70] states that "God ... summoned Adam to join Eve in an existential community molded by sacrifice and suffering, and ... Himself became a partner in this community. God is never outside the covenantal community; He joined man and shares in his covenantal existence."[71] As Blidstein comments, "this reading, needless to say, hangs virtually by a hair" (p. 72). Indeed, even with the Rav's midrashic expansion of Adam the second's being introduced to Eve by God, it is still difficult to see where in this "introduction" God charges them "with an ethical-moral mission."

Perhaps the Rav may also have in mind the verse "And the Lord God took the man and placed him the Garden of Eden to cultivate it and keep it" (Gen. 2:15). For the Rav this is a duty with which Adam the second is charged.[72] The Rav understands this duty thus. "God...summoned Adam the second to retreat." Here "humble man makes a movement of recoil, and lets himself be confronted and defeated by a Higher and Truer Being." He thereby achieves redemption, and "a redeemed life is *ipso facto* a disciplined life."[73] Again, this is reading a great deal into the biblical text. Moreover, the verse never actually speaks of a charge to cultivate and keep the Garden. Neither the word "va-yomer," "And He said," much less the word "va-yetzav," "and He commanded," is used. Finally, this "charge" takes place before the creation of Eve.

What is striking and requires further examination is that the Rav in *LMF never* cites the verses forbidding the eating of the tree of knowledge. "And the Lord God commanded the man saying: 'Of every tree in the garden you may freely eat; but of the tree of knowledge of good and evil, you shall not eat of it; for on the day that you eat of it you shall surely die'" (Gen. 2:16-17). These verses play an important role in "Confrontation," and an absolutely critical one in *The Emergence of Ethical Man* [=*EEM*]. In "Confrontation" the Rav cite these verses and comments, "With the birth of the divine norm man becomes aware of his singularly human exist-

70 Ibid, p. 31.
71 Ibid, p. 31.
72 Ibid, p. 8.
73 Ibid, p. 26.

ence."[74] In *EEM* these verses form the key transition from natural man to ethical man. After citing these verses the Rav comments:

> The first ethical norm is disclosed to man.... The Torah [here] used the verb "*va-yetzav,*" "He commanded."... Va-yetzav ... means command. A new law in all its uniqueness was imposed upon [man].... Man suddenly experienced an ethical imperative which was prompted by autonomous, unique interests, unknown to natural man. He suddenly gained insight into a new force, an ethical one. With the *va-yetzav* of divine command, with the dawning of the ethical experience, man began to experience his selfhood, his personalistic existence.[75]

Given this view that "va-yetzav" contains the divine ethical norm, it is difficult to see why the Rav in *LMF* does not appeal to these verses in support of his claim that God "charged man with an ethical-moral mission." To be sure, these verses, like the verse "And the Lord God took the man and placed him in the Garden of Eden to cultivate it and keep it" (Gen. 2:15), take place before the creation of Eve. But the Rav in *EEM*, basing himself on Eve's use of the plural in the verse "God has said, 'You shall not eat (*lo tokhlu*) of [the fruit of the tree]'" (Gen.3:3), argues:

> This ... clearly implies that both Adam and Eve were enjoined from consuming the fruit.... Apparently, the norm given to Adam was binding even with regard to the woman. The unity of the I and the thou, the "and he shall cling to his wife," asserted itself in the common sense of moral duty, ethical solidarity, and also in responsibility... Both are partaking of the same destiny with all its ramifications; coexistence is synonymous with ethical sympathy. What had been a command to Adam became a moral dialogue, an ethical conversation between the I and the thou.[76]

The similarity between the Rav's claim in *LMF* that God's "charging man with an ethical-moral mission" was followed by Ad-

---

74 "Confrontation" (above, n. 24), p. 9.

75 *The Emergence of Ethical Man*, ed. Michael Berger (Jersey City, N.J. Ktav Publishing House for the Toras HoRav Foundation, 2005), pp. 86–88.

76 Ibid, p. 96.

am and Eve's "reveal[ing] themselves to each other in sympathy and love on the one hand and common action on the other" and his claim in *EEM* that "What had been a command to Adam became a moral dialogue, an ethical conversation between the I and the thou" is striking. So the mystery as to why the Rav in *LMF* never cited the verses forbidding the eating of the tree of knowledge remains.[77] One thing though we may state with confidence. The very fact that the Rav's claim in *LMF* that, to cite Blidstein's paraphrase, it is God's "commanding presence ...which introduces substantive content and value to the human relationship" as a reading of the Scriptural text "hangs virtually by a hair" serves only to drive home even more strongly his Halakho-centrism.

---

[77] In correspondence with Prof. David Shatz, I pointed out to him the absence of any citation in *LMF* of the verses forbidding the eating of the tree of knowledge and asked him whether he had any thoughts on the matter. Shatz replied, "I have felt ... that despite the materials about prophets, norms, and revelation, the very concept of divine command in *LMF* is not as conspicuous as one would expect.... [The Rav] stresses (as I see it) friendship and the like, rather than legislation.... Also, since, in the end, the command was disobeyed, and the Rav has things to say about that he did not want to go into in *LMF* (desire, etc.), he left the reference to the norm vague." Shatz's comments are insightful and thought-provoking, though his claim that "the very concept of divine command in *LMF* is not as conspicuous as one would expect" is somewhat at odds with my emphasis on *LMF*'s halakho-centric nature. In his emphasis on the centrality of friendship in the essay, Shatz's approach to *LMF* is similar to that of Shira Wolosky in "The Lonely Woman of Faith," *Judaism* 52:1-2 (2003): 3–18. (I discuss and critique Wolosky's approach in "Rav Soloveitchik's *The Lonely Man of Faith* in Contemporary Modern Orthodox Jewish Thought" [above, n. 42], pp. 152–155.) To pick up on the last sentence of Shatz's comments, I would note that the Rav's portraits of the two Adams in *LMF* are rather static, as contrasted with his more developmental portraits of man in "Confrontation" and *EEM*. The rather static and, indeed, wholly positive portrait of Adam the second might have led the Rav to avoid bringing to the fore in *LMF* Adam the second's failure to obey the divine command and all its negative consequences.

VI

Beyond the specific themes in the Rav's thought that Blidstein treats in *Society and Self*, he raises two broader issues. First, Blidstein in his essay "Letters on Public Affairs" takes note of the "growing dispute over [the Rav's] cultural legacy and personality. The dispute pits those who account for his modernist vision and his openness to general learning as post-facto (*be-di'avad*) submission to the needs of the hour as against those who see these traits as authentic aspects of his identity" (p. 39).[78] While Blidstein does not, except perhaps indirectly, seek to adjudicate this dispute in that essay, he does directly address himself to one critical aspect of it in his essay "The Jewish People." There Blidstein, in speaking of the Rav's depiction of Adam the first in *LMF*, raises the following striking paradox.

> R. Soloveitchik does indeed allow man's technological ability a significant role in the Divine scheme: "majestic" First Adam ... fulfills a godly mandate by subduing the physical world and perfecting it. But this positive appropriation of this major characteristic of Western civilization is not accompanied by a corresponding imperative to appropriate Western culture, its philosophical or literary achievements. This assertion seems improbable or at least paradoxical, with regard to the Rav, whose major writings are suffused with modern Western philosophy and literature, and whose very intellectual world is constructed, at least in part, with materials provided by modern culture. Yet the paradox is a fact; the Rav is a paradigm of the synthesis of Jewish and Western culture, but he nowhere *prescribes* this move or even urges legitimacy. (p. 81)

This "paradox," in turn, leads Blidstein to pose the following disquieting question. "Are we to assume, then, that this silence discloses a measure of ambivalence, as though the Rav is hinting that

---

[78] Blidstein in his footnote to this passage graciously refers the reader to my essay, "Revisionism and the Rav: The Struggle for the Soul of Modern Orthodoxy," *Judaism* 48 (1999): 290–311, describing it as "an overview of the matter (from a particular perspective)." Indeed, my article was written "from a particular perspective," one that I would like to believe is largely shared by Blidstein himself, at least the Blidstein of *Society and Self.*

he cannot fully approve of involvement in Western culture, or even that there is no systematic way to make it part of the spiritual curriculum" (p. 81)?

But how does he answer it? Here, despite Blidstein's assertion in his Introduction that "except for editorial adjustments I have not made changes in the essays I wrote over the years" (p. 11), the answer he provides in the original version of his essay, published in *Tradition* in 1989, differs significantly, certainly in tone and perhaps also in substance, from the one he provides in the version found in *Society and Self*.[79] Here is Blidstein's *Tradition* answer.

> One may explain that technology complements Jewish spirituality, but does not compete with it, as do philosophy, literature, and so on; consequently, only Jewish sources can provide Jewish values. Thus—and this a classic move—the non-Jewish material will be presented simply as Torah insights presented in a different language, as it were.... Put less systematically, the Rav finds the categories and insights of Western philosophy and its literature and psychology to be an accurate description of reality, and as such they need no explicit defense.[80]

And here is Blidstein's *Society and Self* answer.

> Technology is ... concrete and materialistic; it raises the standard of living, but does not necessarily enhance our spiritual or even human quality—nor is that its intention. Technology, then, needs rabbinic approval and even defense. This is, of course, not true of philosophy, literature, music. These, despite their potential dangers, are intrinsically related to the noetic

79 Indeed, Blidstein in the *Society and Self* version of the essay softens the nature of the paradox, as compared with the essay's *Tradition* version. Thus, in the *Tradition* version after the sentence "the Rav is a paradigm of the synthesis of Jewish and Western culture, but he nowhere *prescribes* this move or even urges legitimacy," Blidstein goes on to write, "The Rav constructs his thought within the categories of Western culture, but nowhere explicitly assigns a specific role to this culture." This last sentence in omitted from the *Society and Self* version.

80 "On the Jewish People in the Writings of Rabbi Joseph B. Soloveitchik," *Tradition* 24:3 (1989):20. I am not certain whether the "less systematic" part of Blidstein's answer coheres with the first part of his answer.

> and spiritual component of human existence. It is obvious that they should be cultivated and that the Jew who strives for a fuller spiritual existence will be open to their message and impact. The Rav's silence would derive, then, from the example he provides. How after reading *Ish ha-Halakhah* could one imagine that Max Scheler and William James are not required reading? Indeed, that they would not contribute to one's spiritual formation? (p. 81)

Readers can decide for themselves the distance between First Blidstein and Second Blidstein. Presumably those "who account for [the Rav's] modernist vision and his openness to general learning as post-facto ... submission to the needs of the hour" will prefer Blidstein's first answer, at least its first part,[81] while those—like myself—who "see [the Rav's modernist vision and his openness to general learning] as authentic aspects of his identity" will prefer his second answer.[82]

---

81 See the previous note.

82 Both David Shatz and I have referred in earlier essays to Blidstein's discussion in the original *Tradition* article. Shatz in several of his articles convincingly points to a number of places where the Rav implicitly assigns a positive religious role to Western culture. See Shatz, "The Rav's Philosophical Legacy" (above, n. 29) pp. 312–314; "Practical Endeavor and the Torah U-Madda Debate," *The Torah U-Madda Journal* 3 (1991-1992): 143, n. 62; and above all, "Ha-Madda ve-ha-Toda'ah ha-Datit be-Haguto shel ha-Rav Soloveitchik," *Emunah bi-Zemanim Mishtanim* (above n. 47), pp. 333-334. In my essay, "The Multi-Faceted Legacy of Rabbi Joseph B. Soloveitchik," *BDD* 7 (Summer 1998) [appeared in 1999], p. 60, n. 18, I note that while it is true that nowhere in the Rav's published writings does he "explicitly assign a specific role to [Western] culture," he does, in at least one major public address, explicitly assign it a very positive role, indeed. Thus in a Yiddish address to the Rabbinic Alumni of Yeshiva University on the subject of *Shirah* (Song), the Rav speaks of the two peaks, the two worlds, of Torah and Western culture, and of the individual's need to live on both these peaks, in both these worlds, and to move back and forth between the two. And the Rav adds that though, on the one hand, there is an abyss between these two peaks, and that no one—not even the Rambam—succeeded in building a complete and fully adequate bridge between them, on the other hand, the peaks must be brought into contact, into relationship with one another;

The second broader issue Blidstein raises is that of the Rav's uniqueness. Here Blidstein's answer is unambiguous. As he states in the conclusion of his review of *Family Redeemed*:

> By placing this volume alongside the Rav's halakhic works, we are reminded once again of his uniqueness. Despite recent attempts to blur and even sully his singularity, the written words speak for themselves. (p. 120)

Yet written words rarely "speak for themselves." They require highlighting, exegesis, and interpretation, precisely the skills at which Gerald Blidstein excels. Not the least of the many contributions, then, that *Society and Self*, with its inimitable blend of scholarly precision and literary power, of erudition and insight, makes to our understanding of the Rav's person and his thought is not just to remind us of his and its uniqueness, but to enable us to re-discover and appreciate that uniqueness for ourselves, ever new and ever fresh. ☙

---

they must understand one another. "We want the man who studies Gemara to understand the other peak, the entire physical-mathematical world and the philosophical interpretation of that world differently than the dry mathematical physicist who dwells entirely in the realm of the profane, in the secular work-a-day world; and we also want to bring that experience, that understanding, that depth and exactitude that we acquire while on the other peak, the peak of culture, into the peak of holiness, of Judaism, in order to deepen it and broaden it and gain new insights into it. We must bring the beauty of Yefet into the tents of Shem." An (unfortunately rather poor) Hebrew translation of part of this Yiddish address may be found in "Ramattayim Tzofim," *Ha-Adam ve-'Olamo* (Jerusalem, 1998), pp. 73–83. Compare my English translation, found immediately above, with the Hebrew translation, or rather weak paraphrase, in "Ramattayim Tzofim," p. 83. More recently, a fine English translation, if somewhat paraphrastic in places, of the address appeared. See Avishai David, "Beshalah: Hallel over the Miraculous and the Ordinary," *Darosh Darash Yosef: Discourses of Rabbi Yosef Dov Halevi Soloveitchik on the Weekly Parashah* (Jerusalem and New York: Urim Publications and OU Press, 2011), pp. 146–155. Unfortunately, one of the places R. David chooses to paraphrase is precisely the essay's conclusion where the Rav urges the necessity of bringing the peaks into contact with one another. The full force of that conclusion does not, then, come through in R. David's translation as (I believe) it does in mine.

*Concise and Succinct: Sixteenth Century Editions of Medieval Halakhic Compendiums**

By: MARVIN J. HELLER

> *"Then Joseph commanded to fill their sacks with grain, and to restore every man's money into his sack, and to give them provision for the way (ẓeidah la-derekh); and thus did he to them." (Genesis 42:25)*
>
> *"And the people of Israel did so; and Joseph gave them wagons, according to the commandment of Pharaoh, and gave them provision for the way (ẓeidah la-derekh)." (Genesis 45:21)*
>
> *"And our elders and all the inhabitants of our country spoke to us, saying, Take provisions (ẓeidah la-derekh) with you for the journey, and go to meet them, and say to them, We are your servants; therefore now make a covenant with us." (Joshua 9:11)*

We are accustomed to thinking of concise, succinct, popular *halakhic* digests, such as R. Abraham Danzig's (Danziger, 1748–1820) *Ḥayyei Adam* on *Oraḥ Ḥayyim* with an addendum entitled *Nishmat Adam* (Vilna, 1810) and *Ḥokhmat Adam* with an addendum called *Binat Adam* (1814-15) and R. Solomon ben Joseph Ganzfried's (1801–66) *Kiẓur Shulḥan Arukh* (Uzhgorod, 1864) as a

* I would like to express my appreciation to Eli Genauer for reading this article and for his suggestions.

Marvin J. Heller writes books and articles on Hebrew printing and bibliography. His *Printing the Talmud: A History of the Individual Treatises Printed from 1700 to 1750* (Brill, Leiden, 1999), and *The Sixteenth Century Hebrew Book: An Abridged Thesaurus* (Brill, Leiden, 2004) were, respectively, recipients of the 1999 and 2004 Research and Special Libraries Division Award of the Association of Jewish Libraries for Bibliography.

somewhat modern phenomenon. After the closing of the Talmud, early *halakhic* works that readily come to mind, and there are certainly exceptions, are, more often than not, weighty tomes; for example, R. Jacob ben Asher's (c. 1270–1340) *Arba'ah Turim* (Piove di Sacco, 1475) and R. Moses ben Maimon's (Maimonides, Rambam, 1135–1204) *Mishneh Torah* (Rome, c. 1475) and, of course, albeit somewhat later, R. Joseph Caro's (1488–1575) *Shulḥan Arukh* (Venice, 1564-65), although, in fact, that work too was actually prepared as an abridgement of Caro's *magnum opus*, the *Beit Yosef* on the *Arba'ah Turim*, beginning with *Oraḥ Ḥayyim* (Venice, 1550).[1]

In contrast, R. Menaḥem ben Aaron ibn Zeraḥ's (c. 1310–1385) *Ẓeidah la-Derekh*, aptly named, is a medieval work prepared for Jewish nobles and aristocrats who lacked time to devote to learning in depth; its intent is to provide them with concise *halakhic* provisions for their way. *Ẓeidah la-Derekh* is not widely known today and, when mentioned, may appear to many as a singular work. This certainly is not the case. This article is intended to make clear that succinct *halakhic* works were neither rare nor unusual but, indeed, were a common and widespread phenomenon. The article will describe several such varied works, primarily written in the Middle Ages and all printed in the sixteenth century, thus attesting to their consistent popularity over centuries, although today most are less well known.[2]

The *halakhic* digests described here, despite their many similarities, are not alike, not in style, and not necessarily in content. Furthermore, not only are they dissimilar, but, despite their being de-

---

1 The format and foliation of these editions of the above works are *Ḥayyei Adam* with *Nishmat Adam*, 2°: 3, 68, [1], 42, 13 ff.; *Ḥokhmat Adam* with *Binat Adam*, 2°: [4], 99, [1], 52 ff.; *Kiẓur Shulḥan Arukh*, 8°: [4], 144 ff.; *Arba'ah Turim*, 2°: 138, 108, 70, 155 ff.; *Mishneh Torah*, 2°: [352] ff.; *Shulḥan Arukh*, 4°: 136 [10], 131 [1], 79, 165 [1] ff.; *Beit Yosef, Tur Oraḥ Ḥayyim*, 2°: 24, 494 [1] ff.

2 The core descriptions of the titles mentioned in this article are taken from my *The Sixteenth Century Hebrew Book: An Abridged Thesaurus* (Brill, Leiden, 2004); S. M. Chones, *Toledot ha-Posekim* (Warsaw, 1910, reprint Israel, n.d.) [Hebrew]; Chaim Tchernowitz, *Toledoth ha-Poskim*, (New York, 1946) [Hebrew]; and Solomon Zucrow, *Sifrut ha-Halakhah* (New York, 1932) [Hebrew].

scribed as concise, succinct digests, these works are not overly brief nor of limited content, several being substantial works, albeit not comparable to well-known medieval works such as the *Arba'ah Turim* and the *Mishneh Torah*. The books are varied, some being general *halakhic* compendiums, others enumerations of the *taryag* (613) *miẓvot*, and yet others on specific branches of *halakhah*, such as *issur ve-heter* (dietary laws, prohibited and permitted foods), liturgy, and halakhot specific to women; there are texts in Yiddish (Judeo-German) and Ladino, the last a translation and abridgment of the *Shulḥan Arukh*. Only a small number of these titles are described here, the emphasis being on general *halakhic* rather than specific subject works, space limitations and concern for the readers' patience being limiting factors.[3]

---

3 Among the popular specialized texts, not addressed in this article, are David ben Joseph Abudraham's (14th century) classic work on Jewish liturgy *Sefer Abudraham* (Constantinople, 1513; Fez, 1517, and Venice, 1546, 1566), first printed in Lisbon in 1489; R. Baḥya ben Asher ben Hlava's (13th century) *Shulḥan Shel Arba* (Constantinople and Mantua, 1514, Venice, 1546, Cracow, 1579, and Lublin and in Prague, 1596) on the laws concerning meals; R. Solomon ben Abraham ibn Adret's (Rashba, c. 1235–c. 1310) *Torat ha-Bayit* (*ha-Kaẓer*) compendium on dietary laws (Cremona, 1565); R. Isaac ben Meir of Dueren's (late 13th century) *Sha'arei Dura* on forbidden foods and the kashering process (Cracow, 1534, Venice, 1547, Constantinople, 1553, Venice, 1564, Lublin. 1574, and Basle and Lublin, 1599); R. Moses ben Israel Isserles' (Rema, c. 1530–1572) *Torat ha-Ḥattat* (Cracow, 1569, 1577, and 1590) expanding upon *Sha'arei Dura* with additions according to the customs of Polish and German Jewry, and abbreviated laws of *niddah*; R. Jonah ben Abraham Gerondi's (Rabbenu Yonah, c. 1200–1263; this attribution is uncertain) *Issur ve-Hetter* (Ferrara, 1555); R. Samuel ben Isaac ha-Sardi, *ha-Terumot* (Salonika, 1596), *halakhic* code dealing with monetary matters; [R. Aaron of Barcelona], *Sefer ha-Ḥinnukh* (Venice, 1523), the *taryag* (613) *miẓvot* according to their occurrence in the Torah; R. David ben Solomon Vital, *Keter Torah* (Constantinople, 1536), versified summary of the 613 commandments; R. Eliezer ben Samuel of Metz (c. 1115–c. 1198), *Sefer Yere'im* (Venice, 1566), an enumeration of the *taryag* (613) *miẓvot*, according to the *Halakhot Gedolot*; R. Menaḥem ben Moses ha-Bavli, *Ta'amei Miẓvot* (Lublin, 1570-71), annotations on and explanations of the precepts; and R. Benjamin Aaron ben Abraham Slonik (Solnik, c. 1550 – c. 1619), *Miẓvot*

The books described here, then, are the more general works, mostly, but not always, in chronological order of their printing.[4] The reader should note the recurring emphasis in the introductions on the need for a succinct *halakhic* work for those who, due to the exigencies of daily life, are unable to study a more detailed work. We begin with the *Sefer ha-Rokeaḥ*.

R. Eleazer ben Judah's (Rokeaḥ, c. 1165 - c. 1238) ***Sefer ha-Rokeaḥ*** (Fano, 1505, 2°, 110 ff; reprinted Venice, 1549 and Cremona, 1557), concerned with *minhagim* (customs) and including considerable ethical material, is among the better known general *halakhic* titles. Its author, a member of the renowned Kalonymus family, was a student of his father, R. Judah ben Kalonymus, R. Judah he-Ḥassid, and other prominent halakhists, such as R. Moses ha-Kohen and R. Eliezer of Metz. A scholar and kabbalist, Eleazer was one of the Ḥassidei Ashkenaz, qualities reflected in many of his books. A prolific writer, Eleazer is credited with more than fifty works, including *piyyutim* (liturgical poetry), many of a mystical nature; commentaries on the Torah; Megillot (*Yayin ha-Rekaḥ*); a *Haggadah*; and works of a kabbalisitic nature. Many of Eleazer's writings remain in manuscript.

Eleazer personally suffered from the persecution of the Jews in Germany. While he worked on his Torah commentary, two cru-

---

ha-Nashim (*Ein Schon Frauen Buchlein*, Cracow 1577) compendium in Yiddish on the *miẓvot* specific to women.

4 Among the general *halakhic* compendiums not addressed in this article are R. Asher ben Jeḥiel (Rosh)/ R. Jacob ben Asher (Tur), *Kiẓur Piskei ha-Rosh* (Constantinople, 1515), summary of the *halakhic* rulings in the *Piskei ha-Rosh* prepared by his son, R. Jacob ben Asher (Ba'al ha-Turim); Anonymous, *Kol Bo* (Constantinople, 1519), *halakhic* digest of ritual and civil laws for the entire year; R. Abraham ben Nathan ha-Yarḥi (c. 1155–1215), *Sefer ha-Manhig* (Constantinople, 1519, 4°: 130 ff.) laws and customs on prayers, synagogue, Sabbath, and festivals; Elijah ben Moses Bashyazi (Bashyatchi, c. 1420–90), *Adderet Eliyahu* (Constantinople, 1531), Karaite *halakhic* compendium; R. Ishmael ha-Kohen Tanuji (16th cent.), *Sefer ha-Zikkaron*, (Ferrara, 1555) concise *halakhic* work providing a *précis* of the *halakhah* based on earlier authorities; R. Samson ben Ẓadok (thirteenth century), *Sefer Tashbeẓ* (Cremona, 1556), *halakhic* work based on the customs of R. Meir of Rothenburg (Maharam) by his student R. Samson ben Ẓadok.

saders entered his home on 22 Kislev 4957 (Friday, November 15, 1196), murdered his wife, Dulcina, his daughters, Belat and Hannah, his son Jacob, and his son's teacher. Eleazer was severely wounded. A week later, a perpetrator was apprehended and executed. The condition of Jewish life at the time of the Crusades, emphasized by Eleazer's personal tragedy, is reflected in the somber world-view and manner in which the correct service of the Creator is given in the *Sefer ha-Rokeaḥ*.

The Fano edition of *Sefer ha-Rokeaḥ* was printed by the renowned Gershom Soncino; it is the first Hebrew book with a title page.[5] The text of that title page is spare, really only a title-label, devoid of ornamentation, and providing no more than the most basic information, the title, author, and the name of the editor, R. Judah of Pesaro, who performed his task "with great care." Further information is given in the colophon, that is, the date of completion, *erev Pesaḥ* 265 (Wednesday, March 29, 1505), and the place, Fano. The editor of the third Cremona edition, perhaps to extol his own work, wrote, "The first printer 'has profaned the consecrated thing of the Lord' (Leviticus 19:8) and 'a ruin, a ruin' (Ezekiel 21:32), throughout the land. 'That which is crooked cannot be made straight'" (Ecclesiastes 1: 15).[6]

---

5 The first printed book with a regular title page was a fifty-five-year calendar, 1475–1530, calculated by the German astronomer Johannes Müller of Königsberg (Regiomontanus), printed in simultaneous Latin and Italian editions by Erhard Ratdolt in Venice in 1476 followed by a German edition in 1478. Concerning the development of the title page see E. P. Goldschmidt, *The Printed Book of the Renaissance* (Cambridge, 1950), p. 63; Douglas McMurtie, *The Book, The Story of Printing and Bookmaking* (New York, 1989), pp. 560–62 and Margaret M. Smith, *The Title Page, Its Early Development, 1460–1510* (New Castle & London, 2000), p. 43.

6 The editor of the third Cremona edition's comments should be understood in context. Alfred W. Pollard "Collectors and Collecting," in *Fine Books* (London. 1912, reprint New York, 1964), p. 14, discussing early presses, writes that "editors, an assertive and depreciatory race, always vaunting their own accuracy and zeal and insisting on the incredible blunders by which previous editions had been deformed past recognition."

In the introduction, Eleazer begins by stating his purpose in writing *ha-Rokeaḥ*,

> "I laid to my heart" (Ecclesiastes 9:1) the vanities of this world, which are "vain and false" (*Shevu'ot* 20b); this world is transitory and the days of man limited, "the workmen are indolent" (*Avot* 2:15) due to their many troubles and distress, lacking the heart of a man, for by the gentiles there is no Torah. I said to myself, "not everyone has the privilege" (*Berakhot* 5a) to have (to know) the heart for the study of halakhot, to sift fine flour. I will write a book "so that he who reads it may run" (Habakkuk 2:1) to "find acceptable words" (Ecclesiastes 12:10), to know how to fulfill the *mizvot* as our God, may His name be blessed, commanded.

He continues informing that *ha-Rokeaḥ* is so entitled because the numerical value of Rokeaḥ (רקח = 308, the Perfumer), the family name, equals his personal name, Eleazer (אלעזר = 308).

Sefer ha-Rokeaḥ is not a detailed or casuistic work, but rather gives the *halakhah* in a direct manner, primarily based on Talmudic sources, referencing the Jerusalem as well as the Babylonian Talmud. Use is also made of midrashic sources, and the book reflects the influence of Kabbalah. It is intended for the average person rather than directed to scholars, obvious in its approach, which is practical rather than theoretical. *Sefer ha-Rokeaḥ* begins with a discussion of the love and fear of God, prayer, and humility (*Hilkhot Ḥassidut*), followed by text divided into 497 sections, beginning with a chapter on repentance (29 sections). The remainder of the book deals with the laws encompassing Jewish life, such as prayer, Sabbath, festivals, mourning, and dietary laws. Written in a clear and lucid style, *ha-Rokeaḥ* is a popular and much reprinted work. The ethical portions have also frequently been reprinted apart from the complete *Sefer ha-Rokeaḥ*.

Amudei Golah, or *Sefer Mizvot Katan* (*Semak*) is the concise halakhic compendium of R. Isaac ben Joseph of Corbeil (d. 1280) one of the Ba'alei Tosafot. It was first printed in Constantinople (1510, 4^0: 146 ff.; reprinted in Cremona, 1556; and Cracow, 1596) by [David and Samuel] ibn Nahmias. Isaac ben Joseph, the son-in-law and student of R. Jeḥiel of Paris and pupil of R. Samuel of

Evreux, was known for his outstanding piety. Among Isaac's students are eminent tosafists, who induced him to write an abridgement of R. Moses ben Jacob of Coucy's (13th century) *Sefer Miẓvot Gadol* (*Semag*). *Amudei Golah* is, therefore, also known as *Sefer Miẓvot Katan* (*Semak*) to distinguish it from that work. Indeed, according to the title page, "*Sefer Amudei Golah*, called *Sefer Miẓvot Katan*, is small in quantity and great in value."

In the introduction Isaac states his purpose in writing this book:

> Because of our iniquities the Torah is forgotten. I saw that many do not know well the reasons for the *miẓvot* we are obligated to perform. I wrote those commandments that are incumbent upon us today in seven pillars corresponding to the seven days of the week. I requested every man to read one pillar daily in order that "it may be well for him" (cf. Genesis 12:13) for there are many commandments that a person is not obligated to fulfill until they come to his hand. When one reads and takes to heart to perform them, the Holy One, blessed be He, considers it as if he had fulfilled the precept ... as it says in *Sifrei*, and remember and do them, from here remembering is as doing. At times a *miẓvah* will come to one's hand and he will not know how to fulfill it. Therefore everyone should take to heart for "if not now, when" (*Avot* 1:14)? ...

The seven pillars, each related to at least one of the Ten Commandments, described in the author's introduction, are: 1) service of the heart; 2) matters dependent upon individual action and time; 3) laws related to speech, for example, vows and prayers, 4) laws related to one's hands, that is, manual labor; 5) dietary laws; 6) financial matters, which includes laws of homicide, most often resulting from monetary transactions; and 7) the laws of Shabbat and *milah*. R. Perez ben Elijah of Corbeil (d. c. 1295), a student of Isaac of Corbeil, wrote annotations to the *Amudei Golah*, printed with subsequent editions, here interspersed with the text.

Amudei Golah is built upon the *Sefer Miẓvot Gadol* of R. Moses ben Jacob of Coucy. However, although it follows the enumeration and details of commandments in that work, it does not adhere to the *Semag*'s organization nor does it contain its detailed, involved *halakhic* discussions. There is no necessity or basis, from either the Torah or the Talmud, in the structure followed by the *Semak*. Intending it to be a popular work, Isaac included aggadic and ethical material.[7] As a result, *Amudei Golah* proved to be a popular work, combining contemporary *halakhah* for a large audience, with parables and similar matter of interest. It also found favor with other codifiers who often quote from *Amudei Golah*. The index of the commandments, found at the beginning of this edition, was included in a number of prayer books to be recited daily in lieu of *teḥinnot* (supplications) and psalms. Isaac of Corbeil had multiple copies made and distributed at his own expense. He requested that additional copies be made and be available to the public.[8]

Sefer ha-Terumah, by the *tosafist* R. Barukh ben Isaac (late 12th–early 13th century), is a popular *halakhic* code, well distributed in manuscript, and frequently quoted by later *rishonim* (early sages). R. Barukh ben Isaac was known as Barukh of Worms, after his birthplace, and, perhaps, although this latter identification has been seriously challenged, was known as Barukh of Regensberg, after his place of residence. Barukh spent considerable time in France—he was the foremost student of R. Isaac ben Samuel the Elder of Dampierre and later of R. Judah of Paris, and a colleague of R. Sampson of Sens—so that when he speaks of Germany he does not do so as a resident of that land. Barukh later immigrated to Eretz Israel, where he died.

First printed by Daniel Bomberg (Venice, 1523, 2^0: 139 ff.), this edition has a spare title page with a brief text that states that "All who look into it 'will find rest' (cf. Jeremiah 6:16) 'and will go out with a high hand'" (cf. Exodus 14:8) and the date 5283 (1523). The colophon dates completion of the work to Friday, 26 Nissan 5283 (April 21, 1523).[9] The title page is followed by a detailed digest of its

---

7 Meyer Waxman, *A History of Jewish Literature* (1933, reprint Cranbury, 1960), II pp. 127–29.

8 Ephraim Urbach, *Ba'alei ha-Tosafot* (Jerusalem, 1980), II pp. 571–75 [Hebrew].

9 26 Nissan 5283 (April 21, 1523) was not a Friday but a Saturday. Perhaps the non-Jewish compositors altered the date in consideration of the sensitivity of the book's Jewish readers (purchasers). More likely, this being the colophon and there being no necessity, in any case, to spell out the date, the 26 is simply a typesetting error.

contents, in effect a synopsis and the essence of the halakhot covered in the book's twelve subject areas, in 254 chapters (paragraphs) of varying length. The purpose of this comprehensive listing is to enable the reader to study concepts prior to learning them in greater detail and to review them afterwards. Barukh places great emphasis on this preliminary abstract, referring to it in the colophon.

Sefer ha-Terumah is an important Ashkenazic code, also from the time of the Ba'alei Tosafot. It varies from contemporary *halakhic* codes in that the material is arranged not according to the order of tractates of the Talmud but rather by subject matter, which, within the *halakhah*, is then presented by tractate order. The contents are: *Hilkhot sheḥitah* (1–8); *treifus* (9–25); *issur ve-heter* (26–79); *ḥallah* (80–85); *niddah* (86–109); *gittin* (110–132); *ḥaliẓah* (133); *avodah zarah* (134–160); *yayin nesekh* (161–188); *Sefer Torah* (189–202); *tefillin* (203–213); and *Shabbat* (214–254), the last divided into nine subheadings. These contents encompass religious and family law, but do not include civil law or communal customs. Barukh based *Sefer ha-Terumah* not on his own understanding of the *halakhah*, but rather on the rulings of his teachers, particularly R. Isaac ben Samuel. He quotes his sources, mostly naming French sages, particularly R. Samuel ben Meir (Rashbam), R. Jacob ben Meir (Rabbenu Tam), and R. Isaac ben Meir (Ribam). No Sefardic sages are mentioned. In the concluding paragraph Barukh states that he entitled this work *Sefer ha-Terumah* because it represents the best teachings of his time.

Sefer ha-Terumah was also a well distributed manuscript work, frequently quoted by later *rishonim*. Its popularity was due not to novellae or profundity, but rather due to its direct and concise summary of the *halakhah* and its being written in a clear and lucid style. Entire sections were copied by R. Simhah ben Samuel of Vitry in the *Maḥzor Vitry*. Barukh also wrote *tosafot* to tractate *Zevaḥim*, normally printed with the Talmud, and on a number of tractates that are not extant.[10]

Our next work, ***Sefer ha-Agur,*** is a concise *halakhic* compendium by R. Jacob Barukh ben Judah Landau (15th cent.). A member of a

---

10 Urbach, I pp. 345–56.

prominent rabbinic family in Germany, Landau relocated to Italy as did many other Jews in the fifteenth century. After about ten years in Italy he settled in Pavia (1480) and afterwards in Naples (1487), where he worked for a time as a proofreader at the press of Joseph Gunzenhausen. Among the works printed at that press in 1490, by Azriel ben Joseph Gunzenhausen, is Landau's *ha-Agur*.

This, the second printing (Rimini, Italy, 1526, 4^0: 102 ff.; reprinted, Venice, 1549), was published by Gershom Soncino, the preeminent pioneer of Hebrew printing. The title page, with an architectural frame, is dated from "the third year of our lord Pope Clement VII (Giulio de' Medici, 1478–1534, pope from 1523 to 1534)," that is, 1526. The text of the title page describes ha-Agur's subject matter as:

> *Hilkhot tefilah*, *ẓiẓit*, and *tefillin*, blessings, the laws of Shabbat and festivals, the laws of [ritual] slaughter, *issur ve-heter*, the scouring of utensils, the laws of *niddah*, *tevillah*, *mikva'ot*, Sefer Torah, *mezuzot*, and *eruvin*.

The text is followed by a table of contents and the book is completed with *Sefer Ḥazon*, also by Landau. *Ḥazon* is a small book of Talmudic conundrums. It does not, in this edition, have a separate title page, but its presence is noted on the title page of the *Agur*. In the introduction we are informed of the source of the title and Landau's purposes in writing the *Agur*. It begins,

> "The words of Agur the son of Jakeh" (Proverbs 30:1), to his distinguished pupil, R. Ezra ben David Ovadiah ha-Rofeh of the house of Leon. . . . "His soul longs" (Genesis 34:8) with a great desire to cleave to the sages all the day to plow יחרוש, to seek ידרוש "to spread יפרוש his wings" (Deuteronomy 32:11) to "frequent the shade of wisdom" (Ecclesiastes 7:12) ... And when I saw that his intentions were good and he was prepared to accept the wisdom of the Torah, with his good nature and clear intelligence, striving greatly to find the correct path. He cleared the path יסקל מסילות סלולות for him to go to "a city of habitation" (Psalms 107: 4, 7, 36) ... "He sought me daily to know" (cf. Isaiah 58:2) "the entrance to the city" (cf. II Samuel 17:17) the city of his intention "to enlighten his eyes" (cf. Ezra 9:8) to arrive at his "desired haven" (Psalms 107:30)...

> This was the primary reason that I aroused myself when I saw my distinguished student putting forth his hands for the fruit "of the tree of the knowledge of good and evil" (cf. Genesis 2:17), which are the commandments explained in the Talmud.

His student's time for Talmud was limited, however, by his studies of physics and metaphysics, necessitating this more concise work to instruct him in his Jewish studies. *Ha-Agur* is a distillation of *halakhah*, primarily in *Oraḥ Ḥayyim* and to a lesser extent from the other parts of the *Arba'ah Turim*. Although Landau makes use of a large number of sources, he relies primarily on the *Tur* of R. Jacob ben Asher, also following the arrangement of that work. Mention is made of the opinions of later decisors and their rulings subsequent to the *Tur*, among them R. Israel Isserlein, R. Jacob Weil, R. Joseph Colon and Jacob Landau's father, R. Judah Landau. *Ha-Agur* reflects the Ashkenaz tradition in *halakhah* and *minhag*. Landau also integrates kabbalistic content into the text, quoting from the *Zohar*, one, if not the first, to do so in a *halakhic* work, and provides a summary of the *halakhah*, all in a concise manner. An example of the conundrums in *Ḥazon* is:

> If a person does one *miẓvah* more than the required measure he forfeits the reward [for performing the *miẓvah*] and is not considered to have performed the *miẓvah*.
> Explanation: Terumah requires a first offering in which the remainder is recognizable. If one makes the entire heap terumah he has not fulfilled the *miẓvah* ...
>
> There is water in which it is permissible to *tovel* (immerse) one's entire body and which is unfit for *netilat yada'im*, and specifically in a utensil.
> Explanation: The thermal springs of Tiberias. If they are in their place it is permissible to *tovel* one's hands in them, but it is prohibited to do so in a utensil (*O. Ḥ.* 160; *Ḥullin* 106a).

The incunabula edition of the *Agur* was the second Hebrew book published in the lifetime of its author, the first being R. Judah ben Jeḥiel's (Messer Leon) *Nofet Ẓufim* (Mantua, before 1480) and the first book to contain rabbinic *haskamot* (approbations), from R. Judah Messer Leon, R. Jacob ben David Provenzalo, R. Ben Zion ben Raphael, R. Isaac ben Samuel Ḥayyim, R. Solomon Ḥayyim ben

Jeḥiel Raphael ha-Kohen, and R. Nethaniel ben Levi of Jerusalem, reprinted with this edition.[11] Messer Leon writes that he has examined *ha-Agur*, and that "it is a work that gives forth pleasant words ... and therefore I have set my signature unto these nectars of the honeycomb, these words of beauty." No other works by Landau are known.[12]

Piskei Halakhot is a *halakhic* work from the Italian kabbalist R. Menahem ben Benjamin Recanati (late 13th–early 14th centuries). Published by the Company of Silk Weavers, *Piskei Halakhot* (Bologna, 1538, 4^{0}: [12] 62 ff.) is the sole *halakhic* work known to have been written by Recanati. Little is known about him, although it is reported that Recanati was originally an ignorant person who became, miraculously, wise and understanding. Recanati is better known for his kabbalistic works, *Perush al ha-Torah* (Venice, 1523), *Ta'amei ha-Miẓvot* and *Perush ha-Tefillot* (Constantinople, 1544).

The title page, with a brief text and no ornamentation, notes the kabbalistic background of the author, stating "*Piskei Halakhot* from the kabbalist, Rabbenu Menahem of Recanati ... " The volume begins with a twelve-page table of contents, followed by 601 concise *halakhic* decisions, without discussion. For example,

> Those days that people are accustomed to fast, for example, between the ten days of repentance [between Rosh Ha-Shanah and Yom Kippur] even though they did not accept the fast upon themselves the day before, they may fast, for in such an instance prior acceptance is not necessary. 177.
>
> The *Halakhah* is like Rav Sheshet who says that even to wash before *Tishah be-Av* and to put aside is forbidden. 186.

This is not an original work, but rather is based on a large number of earlier authorities, primarily German and French

---

[11] Concerning this edition of Messer Leon's *Nofet Ẓufim* see Joshua Bloch, "First Hebrew Book Printed During the Lifetime of its Author" *Bulletin of the New York Public Library* 39:2 (1935), pp. 95-96 reprinted in *Hebrew Printing and Bibliography* (New York: New York Public Library and KTAV Pub. House, 1976), pp. 143-44.

[12] Moses Herschler, *Ha-Agur ha-Shalem* (Jerusalem, 1960), pp. 5B14 [Hebrew].

decisors, most importantly R. Eliezer ben Samuel of Metz (c.1115–c.1198), author of *Sefer Yere'im*. Recanati also relies on many other Ba'alei Tosafot, such as R. Eliezer ben Joel ha-Levi of Bonn (Ravyah, 1140–1225) and Rabbenu Tam (c.1100–1171), the latest being R. Meir ben Barukh of Rothenburg (Maharam, c. 1215–1293). Sephardic authorities are quoted, including Alfasi and Maimonides, but to a lesser extent. A number of Recanati's sources would be unknown if not for their being referenced in *Piskei Halakhot*. With one exception, references to Rashba are not to R. Solomon ben Abraham Adret (c. 1235–c. 1310), but to R. Simeon ben Abraham. Recanati, who frequently quotes the Ramban (R. Moses ben Nahman, Nahmanides, 1194–1270) in his Torah commentary, makes no mention of him here.

References within a *halakhah* are made without consideration to their chronological order and much of the material lacks apparent order, suggesting that the work was prepared by Recanati for his personal use, as an outline for a later expanded work, or that this brief work was sufficient for someone who did not wish to devote considerable time to *halakhah*, but preferred to turn to other studies such as Kabbalah.

Later editions of *Piskei Halakhot* are censored, missing entire entries, primarily those with material pertaining to non-Jews. Among the objectionable material are the sections *yayin nesekh* (gentile wine) and the laws of *avodah zara* (idol worship). An example of the former is:

> 251: There are those who say that a gentile who pours out wine of a Jew, even intentionally knowing that it is wine, it is not considered as *yayin nesekh* for it (the wine) gets lost and that is not the way of a libation, as it says in the chapter *Ein Ma'amidim*, "it is like pouring water into clay" [*Avodah Zarah* 33a], and since it is not a libation, what is in the utensil is permissible. However, from utensil to utensil everyone forbids it . . . and there are those who forbid it in any case.

The title page of the 1820 edition of *Piskei Halakhot*, printed in Poland/Russia, gives the date as 1538 and the place of publication as

Bologna. Most likely this unexpurgated edition was backdated to avoid problems with the censor.[13]

Shibbolei ha-Leket is a *halakhic* compendium by the Italian sage R. Ẓedekiah (ha-Rofei) ben Abraham (c. 1230–c. 1300) of the Anav family.[14] Although it is known that Ẓedekiah was a student of R. Judah ben Benjamin, R. Meir ben Moses, R. Avigdor Katz, R. Jacob of Wuerzburg, and, perhaps, R. Meir ben Barukh of Rothenburg, little else is known of his life. Nevertheless, it is clear from *Shibbolei ha-Leket* that, at least when he wrote this work, he was a resident of Rome and was alive when the Talmud was burned in Paris in 1242. Also, from the appellation *ha-rofei* it is clear that he was a physician. His brothers, Benjamin (*Massa Gei Ḥizzayon*, Riva di Trento, 1560) and Moses, were both liturgical poets, the former also a physician.

Shibbolei ha-Leket (Venice, 1546, 2^0: 55 ff.), printed by Daniel Bomberg, is a detailed compilation from earlier *halakhic* works and responsa covering prayers, holidays and the Jewish year. Ẓedekiah, without offering his own opinion, references a large number of early sources; quotes often from the Jerusalem as well as the Babylonian Talmud; notes divergent positions; and discusses various customs and laws. The title page, which does not mention Ẓedekiah, states,

---

13 Concerning further examples of backdating of books see my "Who can discern his errors? Misdates, Errors, and Deceptions, in and about Hebrew Books, Intentional and Otherwise" *Ḥakirah: The Flatbush Journal of Jewish Law and Thought* 12 (2011), pp. 284–87, and reprinted in *Further Studies in the Making of the Early Hebrew Book*, Brill (Leiden/Boston, 2013) pp. 410-414.

14 Anav (Anau) is an ancient Italian family, mostly resident in Rome. According to family tradition, the Anavs are descended from one of four aristocratic families of Jerusalem brought by Titus to Rome from Jerusalem after the destruction of the Temple. In addition to the members of the family noted here, other prominent members include R. Nathan ben Jeḥiel (Ba'al he-Arukh, 1035–c. 1110), author of the lexicon known as the *Arukh;* and several liturgical poets (Milano, Attilio. "Anau." *Encyclopaedia Judaica*. Ed. Michael Berenbaum and Fred Skolnik. 2nd ed. Vol. 2. Detroit: Macmillan Reference USA, 2007. 136. *Gale Virtual Reference Library*).

"Who is the man who desires life [and loves many days, that he may see good?]" (Psalms 35:13), for a sign, for the appointed times of the days and years, ... "I beg you, let (me) glean and gather after the reapers among the sheaves" (Ruth 2:7) in this book, full of the interpretations of the geonim and decisors ...

In the introduction, Ẓedekiah relates that he has named it *Shibbolei ha-Leket* (Gleaned Ears) for he has selected from "a field of the understanding of the geonim, here and there הנה והנה as he found them and arranged the halakhot one to another אחת אל אחת "like a bed of spices, like fragrant flowers" (Song of Songs 5:13). I did not come to fill my sack and bag with grain with a lengthy commentary for the "hand is not shortened" Isaiah 59:1.

This edition is much abridged, the now more familiar *Shibbolei ha-Leket ha-Shalem*, based on a manuscript, not having been printed until 1886. Unlike the complete version, divided into 13 *arugot* (rows, sections) and 372 *shibbolim* (ears), this edition is divided into 12 sections and 121 subsections. Among the omitted material is the recounting of the burning of the Talmud, with the accompanying *she'elot ḥolim* (request for a response via a dream), as to the appropriate time to fast; the commentary on the *Haggadah*; and numerous references to his brothers. In 1988 a second part of *Shibbolei ha-Leket*, previously unpublished, covering dietary laws, interest, and vows, was published from a manuscript. In the description of the burning of the Talmud, Ẓedekiah writes:

> Since we are occupied with the laws of fasts and the burning of the Torah we will write as a remembrance that what befell us in our own days due to our many iniquities, for the Torah of our God was burned in 5004 [1244, *sic.*] of the creation on the sixth day of *Parashat Ḥukkat* [Numbers 29]. Twenty-four wagons full of volumes of the Talmud, halakhot, and aggadot were burned in France, as we have heard. We have heard from rabbis who were there that they asked a *she'elot ḥolim* to know if this was a decree from the Creator, and He responded to them that it was a decree of the Torah ... and from that day on the leading individuals [of the community] accepted upon themselves to fast each and every year on the sixth day of *Parashat Ḥukkat*, not setting [the fast] by the day of the month, so that the ashes should be an atonement for us, as a burnt offering on

the pyre and may it be as pleasant for the sons of Judah as a meal offering brought according to *halakhah*. May our remembrance take place, and may God fulfill for us what is written, "Then shall the offering of Judah [and Jerusalem] be pleasant to the Lord, as in the days of old, and as in former years" (Malachi 3:4).[15]

The volume is completed by a brief colophon, a table of contents; and the tale describing the encounter of the *amora*, R. Joshua ben Levi and the angel of death, in which R. Joshua is assured of his place in the Garden of Eden, given a tour of the Garden, which is described, and gets the angel of death's sword (*Ketubbot* 77b). It concludes with a single brief responsum from R. Solomon ben Abraham Adret (Rashba, 1235–c. 1310) concerning an individual who wished to be relieved from a vow to cease gambling, so that he would not violate both his vow and the prohibition against gambling. The response was negative.

Shibbolei ha-Leket was sufficiently popular that it was abridged as, or was a major source for our next work, ***Sefer Tanya Rabbati,*** also a comprehensive *halakhic* digest. It is ascribed to R. Jeḥiel ben Jekuthiel ben Benjamin ha-Rofei Anav (late thirteenth century), perhaps a grandson of Ẓedekiah's brother. R. Jeḥiel was a scribe,[16] *paytan,* and author of *Ma'alot ha-Middot* (Constantinople, c. 1511 as *Beit Middot*, and Cremona, 1556). Little personal information is

---

15 Ẓedekiah ben Abraham ha-Rofei, *Shibbolei ha-Leket ha-Shalem*, ed. Solomon Buber (Israel, 1977) p. 252 no. 263 [Hebrew]; Tchernowitz, II pp. 186–91. The discrepancy between the date normally given for burning the Talmud, 1242, and the date in *Shibbolei ha-Leket*, 1244, has been addressed by S. H. Kuk and D. Tamar (*Kiryat Sefer* XXIX (1953-54). It is suggested that the discrepancy may have resulted from misreading a daled ד (4) for a *bet* ב (2) in the manuscript of the *Shibbolei ha-Leket,* a not uncommon occurrence when reading manuscripts. Parenthetically, this fast day is noted in modern *halakhic* works. For example, the *Magen Avraham*, *Mishnah Berurah*, and the *Kaf ha-Ḥayyim* on *Shulḥan Arukh O.Ḥ.* 580:3 and the *Arukh ha-Shulḥan* 580:4 all mention the burning of the Talmud and comment on the associated fast day.

16 His Leiden Manuscript (1289) is the only complete manuscript of the *Yerushalmi* in existence today.

available about Jeḥiel, except that he too was a scion of the Anav family.

Shibbolei ha-Leket was first printed in Mantua (1514, 4^{0}: [99] ff.) and reprinted in Cremona (1565). The Mantua edition was printed by Samuel Latif without a title-page. The date of printing is known from the colophon, given the completion date as "the month of Sivan, 5074 (*sic.*) from the creation, 'Then the Lord your God will turn your captivity, and have compassion upon you ורחמך ([5]274 = May 26-June 23, 1514), and will return and gather you from all the nations, where the Lord your God has scattered you' (Deuteronomy 30:3)."

The title page of the Cremona edition notes that it is "'The rear guard of all the camps' (Numbers 10:25), assembling all the laws and customs appropriate for every Jewish man in a clear and easy language." A preface from R. Simon ha-Levi, who brought the book to press, follows, then a page of verse, table of contents, and the text. *Sefer Tanya* is so entitled because it begins with the word *tanya* (we learn in a *baraita*). It later became known as *Tanya Rabbati*, to distinguish it from the much-reprinted *Tanya* of R. Schneur Zalman of Liadi.

The above attribution notwithstanding, the authorship of *Tanya Rabbati* is uncertain. R. Simon ha-Levi states that the author, "being most humble, not wanting to take the crown of greatness appropriate to him, did not mention his name," but there are those who say he was R. Jeḥiel, brother of R. Jacob, Ba'al ha-Turim, "which seems correct, for he mentions himself in this work as 'I, the scribe Jeḥiel.'" This attribution, often repeated, is no longer accepted. It is now believed that the author was R. Jeḥiel ben Jekuthiel, perhaps a great-nephew of Ẓedekiah (ha-Rofei) ben Abraham, author of *Shibbolei ha-Leket* to which *Tanya* has been compared.

Tanya differs from *Shibbolei ha-Leket* in a number of particulars. There are additions, omissions, rearrangement of entries, and abbreviations of supportive material brought by Ẓedekiah ha-Rofei. Nevertheless, the similarities, including identical language, leave little doubt as to the close relationship of the two works, *Tanya* being a concise edition of *Shibbolei ha-Leket*. The latter work, and Ẓedekiah ha-Rofei, are frequently referenced in *Tanya*, suggesting to some that Jeḥiel's intent, if it was he, was to conceal that his book was an abridgment of *Shibbolei ha-Leket* and not an original work. In response, it has been asked why, if Jeḥiel wished to plagiarize Ẓedekiah's work, did he omit his name and frequently reference *Shibbolei ha-Leket*?

Several additional possibilities have been suggested. Ẓedekiah wrote both versions, omitting his name from the earlier concise work; Jeḥiel, a copyist, discovered the manuscripts, and, intending to write a popular *halakhic* digest, rewrote the first, adding material from the second, not realizing they came from the same author. Possibly Jeḥiel, in fact Ẓedekiah's grandfather, wrote *Tanya* as a *halakhic* digest for the family, a work later greatly augmented by Ẓedekiah in *Shibbolei ha-Leket*. Finally, perhaps the two works are indeed independent, their likeness resulting from the fact that both authors were students of Jeḥiel's uncle, Judah ben Benjamin Anav.[17]

We began by referring to ***Ẓeidah la-Derekh***, R. Menahem ben Aaron ibn Zeraḥ's (c. 1310–1385) *halakhic* code. This concise code of law (Ferrara, 1554, 4^0: 297 ff.) is unusual in that it is directed towards the wealthier strata of Jewish society. In the introduction, Ibn Zeraḥ informs us about his background and difficult early years, relating,

> In the year 5088 (1328) "the anger of the Lord was kindled against his people" (Isaiah 5:25) "and the king [of France who ruled over Navarre] died" (I Kings 22:37) and the people rose up and took counsel together "to destroy, slay and annihilate" (Esther 7:4) "all the Jews who were" (*ibid.* 3:6) in their kingdom and they slew in Estella and other places in the land about 6,000 Jews, including my lord, my father, my mother, and my four brothers, younger than I, dying in sanctification of the Lord's name. I alone survived from my father's house "stricken, struck by God, and afflicted" (Isaiah 53:4), for twenty-five of the wicked "struck me and wounded me" (Song of Songs 5:7) and I was cast naked among the dead...

---

17 Solomon Buber, ed., *Tanya Rabbati* (Warsaw, reprint, Jerusalem, 1963), pp. 24–31 [Hebrew]; Saul Kook, *Iyyunim u-Meḥkarim* II (Jerusalem, 1963), pp. 270–72 [Hebrew]; S. K. Mirsky, ed., *Shibbolei ha-Leket ha-Shalem* (New York, 1966), pp. 40–49 [Hebrew].

A knight, a friend of his father, found Ibn Zeraḥ, removed him from among the dead, brought him home and nursed him back to health. After he recovered, Menahem went to Toledo, where he studied under R. Joshua ben Shuaib and R. Judah ben Asher, grandson of the Rosh (R. Asher ben Jeḥiel). Ibn Zeraḥ subsequently went to Alcala de Henarez (in the vicinity of Toledo), where he studied under R. Joseph ben al-Aysh, whom he succeeded as rabbi in 1361. Eight years later a civil war between two aspirants to the throne left Menahem impoverished. The courtier, Don Samuel Abrabanel, interceded on his behalf and Ibn Zeraḥ was appointed rabbi of Toledo and head of the rabbinical academy.

Ibn Zeraḥ composed *Ẓeidah la-Derekh* for the honor and benefit of Don Samuel, whom he praises in the introduction. The book is directed towards the wealthy who, because of their responsibilities and lifestyle, including social intercourse with non-Jews, are not always rigorous in the performance of *miẓvot*, nor do they have sufficient time to master a detailed code, as he informs in his introduction

> I saw that they [Spanish-Jewish nobles] who are in the courtyard of our lord the king, may his majesty be exalted, are a shield and shelter for the rest of their people, each according to his position and status. However, due to the tumultuous times and their desire for attention and matters that are unnecessary "going continually" (Joshua 6:13 II Kings 2:11), lacking in obligatory *miẓvot*, ... prayers, benedictions, *issur ve-heter*, Shabbat, festivals, *Seder Nashim*, and "they also reel through wine" (Isaiah 28:7). I loved the above [Don Samuel Abravanel], may God preserve him . . . and set myself the goal ... and entered within my limits and wrote this book and entitled it *Ẓeidah la-Derekh* ...
>
> I arranged his table for soul and body ... and entitled it *Ẓeidah la-Derekh* and said for my soul to clear the way ...

His code, therefore, is directed towards the practical. It provides, as its name implies, *Ẓeidah la-Derekh* "provision for the way" (Genesis 42:25, 45:21) implies, the traveler's necessities, not too burdensome to bear. In addition to its *halakhic* content, *Ẓeidah la-Derekh* provides reasons for the commandments, based on the

Rambam, as well as philosophical and moral precepts, and medical advice.

The title page of the first edition, printed in Ferrara at the press of Abraham ibn Usque, has that printer's device, the astrolabe and anchor, and gives a completion date of 8 Adar, "in the shadow of the Almighty שד"י ([5]354 = February 20, 1554) I will take refuge," (cf. Psalms 57:2). *Ẓeidah la-Derekh* is divided into five *ma'amarim* (articles) and further divided into *kelalim* (rules), which are subdivided into 372 *perakim* (chapters). The *ma'amarim* are 1) prayers, blessings, *tefillin* and *ẓiẓit*; 2) *issur ve-heter*; 3) laws of matrimony and divorce; 4) laws pertaining to the Sabbath and festivals; and 5) fast days, and the laws of mourning. This last part ends with a discussion of the coming of the messiah and the resurrection of the dead.

The second edition (Sabbioneta, 1567) varies from the previous Ferrara edition, reflecting the censor's expurgations and changes. Most notable is the section on the *Amidah,* which initially included a discussion of the twelfth benediction, *malshinim* (slanderers, informers). This paragraph, comprising almost an entire leaf, is omitted, and the enumeration of the prayers comprising the *Amidah* was correspondingly adjusted in the Sabbioneta and subsequent editions of *Ẓeidah la-Derekh* up to the present. In some instances, in the first unexpurgated edition, rather than ink out so many lines, the entire quire was removed.[18]

Among the most influential compilations of customs and laws is R. Jacob ben Moses's (Maharil, c. 1360–1447) ***Sefer Maharil***, composed by his pupil R. Eleazar ben Jacob (Zalman of St. Goar), from the discourses that he heard from Maharil. Maharil (Morenu ha-Rav Ya'akov Levi), the leading *halakhic* authority of his time, was also known as Mahari Segal and Mahari Moellin, these various appellations resulting in some confusion as to whether they referred to one or more individuals. Maharil was a student of R. Shalom ben Isaac of Neustadt (Sar Shalom) and the teacher of R. Jacob Weil

18 Shlomo Eidelberg, "Menachem Ben Aaron Ibn Zeraḥ," in *Medieval Jewish Ashkenazic History. Studies in European Jewry* II. Hebrew Essays (Brooklyn, 2000), pp. 204–26 [Hebrew].

(Mahariv, d. c. 1455). He was among the first, together with R. Shalom of Neustadt, to be given the title *Morenu*, done to prevent abuses in the performance of marriages and divorces by unauthorized individuals. The slaughter of Jews in Austria in 1420 was followed by the Hussite wars, a time of great suffering for the Jews of central Europe. They beseeched Maharil to pray for them. He, in turn, requested that they fast for three days and pray, which they did (September, 1421). At the end of that period the Imperial army dispersed and the very soldiers who had harassed the Jews came to beg food from them.

However, *Sefer Maharil* is not only a *halakhic* digest, but also a compendium of the customs of German Jewry. It begins with the laws pertinent to Nissan, for it "is the month concerning which the Torah writes, 'This month shall be to you the beginning of months; it shall be the first month of the year to you' (Exodus 12:2), therefore I am beginning the explanation of the customs relevant to each of the months of the year with [Nissan]." The text begins with Rosh Ḥodesh, thirty days before Pesaḥ, the laws of Pesaḥ, Shavuot, Yom Tov, Shabbat, fast days, continuing through Sukkot, and concluding with the laws of Purim. The halakhot of festivals are followed by laws pertaining throughout the year, such as prayer, marriage, *milah*, divorce, dietary laws, ritual slaughter, *ẓiẓit, tefillin*, *mezuzah*, *niddah*, and mourning. Interspersed with these halakhot are various customs and laws that do not fit into any of the above categories.

Sefer Maharil, much copied and often reprinted, is one of the most basic sources of Ashkenaz custom and practice, frequently referenced by R. Moses Isserles (Rema) in his glosses to the *Shulḥan Arukh*. Maharil wrote numerous responsa, collected by another student, and first published in Venice in 1549. He is also remembered for his cantorial abilities, composition of synagogal hymns, and advocacy for retaining traditional tunes. *Niggunei Maharil,* attributed to him, were sung until modern times by the Jewish community of Mainz. The volume, which measures 19 cm., is completed with an index, followed by the device of the printer, Tobias Foa. The Cremona edition, printed two years later, was an identical copy of this edition, including the text of the title page, and was printed at the expense of the apostate Vittorio Eliano.

Toledot Adam ve-Ḥavvah—Sefer Mesharim are two paired *halakhic* works, both by R. Jeroham ben Meshullam of Provence (Rabbenu Jeroham, c. 1290–1350). Jeroham was born in Provence, but with the expulsion of the Jews from France in 1306 wandered until settling in Toledo. He learned briefly by R. Asher ben Jeḥiel (Rosh) and for a longer period by R. Abraham ben Moses Ismail, a student of R. Solomon ben Abraham Adret (Rashba). Jeroham wrote two works, *Sefer Mesharim* in 1334, and *Toledot Adam ve-Ḥavvah* in 1340 (Venice., 1557, 2^{0}: 16, 13–238, 2–104 ff., printed previously in Constantinople (1516). The former work deals with civil law, primarily monetary issues, divided into thirty two paths (*netivot*).

Sefer Mesharim (uprightness) is not an original work, but rather a compendium of the decisions of earlier authorities. It is organized so that anyone, even if not a scholar, can benefit from the work. *Sefer Mesharim* begins with a long table of contents, unusual for that period. In the introduction he praises Alfasi and Rambam, but, with "the weakening of the heart" and the additions of later sages, it is not easy to find or master the law, which is not compiled in one location, as with the laws of property, where acquisition is dealt with in one place and laws of possession in another. Therefore Jeroham properly arranges each subject, reordering the organization of the Rambam, which is intended for scholars, following the Rosh. He is the first to include the laws of *shemittah* (Sabbatical year) and *prosbul* (formula for releasing debt in a Sabbatical year) as monetary matters, in contradistinction to Rambam who classifies them as agricultural laws. In this edition it follows *Toledot Adam ve-Ḥavvah*.

In the introduction to *Toledot Adam ve-Ḥavvah* Jeroham writes that friends, seeing the benefits of *Sefer Mesharim,* pressed and urged him to prepare a similar work on *issur ve-heter* (dietary laws). He accommodated them, writing *Toledot Adam ve-Ḥavvah*, remarking that God and Israel know that he did not do this for honor nor to be considered a scholar, for he merely transcribed the words of the sages that preceded him. *Toledot Adam ve-Ḥavvah* comprises twenty-eight paths, in two parts, according to the periods of a person's life, from birth to death. *Adam*, the first part, treats the precepts from a person's birth until marriage, encompassing birth, *milah*, benedictions, prayer, learning Torah, holidays, vows, *kashrut*, and contemporary customs, all matters a person should know prior to marriage. *Ḥavvah*, the second part, deals with the period from marriage until death, covering marital laws, such as betrothal, weddings, divorces, levirate marriage, *niddah*, and mitzvot applicable to women. Here too Jeroham brings the opinions of earlier decisors, particularly *Piskei ha-Rosh*, and records the customs of Jewry in France, Spain, and Provence.

Toledot Adam ve-Ḥavvah and *Sefer Mesharim* are the only works known from Jeroham ben Meshullam. Although well received when written, they were quickly superseded by the *Arba'ah Turim* of R. Jacob ben Asher. This edition and subsequent printings are based on the 1516 Constantinople edition, which was based on a corrupt manuscript. Nevertheless, *Toledot Adam ve-Ḥavvah* and *Sefer Mesharim* are highly regarded and referenced by decisors such as R. Joseph Caro and R. Samuel de Medina. It was more than two hundred and fifty years until the next printing of *Toledot Adam ve-Ḥavvah* (Kopyst, 1808).

Minhagim, by Abraham Klausner (d. 1407/8) is the earliest printed book of Jewish customs. The author was a student of R. Moses of Znaim, and, from 1380, rabbi of Vienna, together with R. Meir ben Barukh ha-Levi (d. 1404). R. Aaron of Neustadt (Blumlein) was his brother-in-law.

Minhagim (Riva di Trento, 1558, 16^{0}: 43 [1]) records the customs of the Jews of France and Germany for the entire year, encompassing benedictions, prayers and ritual practice. Although it is based on a number of writers over a period of time, including the geonim, a primary source is the *Siddur* of Rashi, which details the customs of medieval French Jewry. R. Ḥayyim Paltiel (d. 1307), a student of Eliezer of Touques, and, perhaps, the Maharam of Rothenburg (Meir ben Barukh), and rabbi of Magdeburg, Germany, added the customs of German Jewry, composing a *Sefer ha-Minhagim*. This work was the basis of Klausner's *Minhagim*. Klausner did not, however, simply rework Paltiel's book, but rather added considerable explanatory marginalia of his own.

The title page is simple, without any decoration. On the verso is a brief preface from R. Jacob Marcaria. Within the book the text is surrounded by glosses, which often exceed the text in length. Customs are given in a straightforward manner, beginning with *Seliḥot* (penitential prayers) recited from the conclusion of the Shabbat prior to Rosh Ha-Shanah through the festivals and fast days to *Tishah be-Av* (9th of Av). Emphasis is placed on those customs dealing with prayer, Torah readings, and the synagogue. It is a basic work on prayers for Shabbat, festivals, including *piyyutim* (liturgical poems) included in *maḥzorim*. Among the interesting features is that here, for the first time, the prayer *Av ha-Raḥamim* for martyrs is mandated.

Minhagim concludes, on the last page, with a paragraph (from Klausner) relating that he had "vowed to fast on Mondays, Thursdays, and Mondays for a complete year. It happened, however, that *Tishah be-Av* occurred that year on a Tuesday. R. Yom Tov Lipmann [Muelhausen] from Neustadt and R. Mendel Klausner permitted me to eat after *Minḥah* (afternoon prayers), but only one cooked item, from lentils, without any fat and without anything else." The colophon notes that it was completed on 2 Kislev [5]319 (November 22, 1558).

Minhagim is an important and influential work, and, because of it Klausner is known as the father of Minhag Ashkenaz. The book's recognized value was enhanced by the fact that Klausner's students included such luminaries as R. Israel Isserlein (*Terumat ha-Deshen*, Venice, 1519), Jacob Moellin (*Sefer Maharil*, Sabbioneta, 1556), and Isaac Tyrnau (*Minhagim*, Venice, 1566), all of whom drew upon *Minhagim* for their books, and through them influenced R. Moses Isserles (Rema) in preparing his glosses on the *Shulḥan Arukh*. Klausner also wrote responsa, noted in the responsa of Israel Bruna (c. 1400–80).[19]

A somewhat different *halakhic* compendium is ***Sefer ha-Aguddah*** (Cracow, 1571, 2^0: 4, 250 ff.) by R. Alexander Suslin ha-Kohen of Frankfort. One of the leading Talmudists of Germany in the first

---

[19] J. Freimann, ed., *Leket Yosher* (1904, reprint Jerusalem, 1964), pp. xviii-xix [Hebrew]; Jonah Joseph Disin, ed., *Sefer ha-Minhagim le-Rabbenu Abraham Klausner* (Jerusalem, 1978), pp. 9–15 [Hebrew]; David Wachtel, A Memorialization Through Ritual and Liturgy in Medieval Ashkenaz, Master's Thesis, Columbia University (1995).

half of the fourteenth century, Suslin was a student of R. Isaac of Dueren (*Sha'arei Dura*, late 13th century), and served as rabbi in Cologne, Worms, and Frankfort. Towards the end of his life he is reported to have settled in Erfurt, his birthplace, where, in the massacres following the Black Death, he reputedly suffered a martyr's death on March 21, 1349, one of more than one hundred Jews who perished that day.

Sefer ha-Aguddah is a *halakhic* digest organized by Talmudic tractates. It is dissimilar from similarly organized works, as here the tractates do not follow the order of the Talmud. Rather Suslin begins with *Nezikin* and *Niddah*, followed by *Nashim*. The subject matter also encompasses *Zera'im*, *Kodashim*, and *Taharot*, matters generally not applicable today and normally omitted from codes.

The purpose of the book, as suggested by its name, is to collect and present halakhot. Most, but not all, entries are brief, the *halakhah* being extracted from the Talmud without detailed explanations or elaboration. The Talmudic discourse on issues is absent, again in contrast to similar works, such as that of Alfasi, based on the order of the Talmud. Suslin brings the decisions of a large number of early decisors, including Alfasi, Maharam, Mordekhai, Rashbam, Rosh, Rabbenu Tam, Semak, and Tashbetz. He does not hesitate, however, to express disagreement when he differs with their conclusions.

Ha-Aguddah was prepared for publication by R. Joseph ben Mordecai Katz (*She'erit Yosef*, 1510–1591), brother-in-law of R. Moses Isserles (Rema). The manuscript he used was imperfect, however, and his attempts to correct the text were not completely successful. Katz's introduction is followed by a list of the halakhot in the book, and the text is followed by a more detailed listing, concluding with verses of thanksgiving by the printer, Isaac Prostitz. The work is accompanied by Katz's annotations, written, as he explains in the introduction, because the concise style of *ha-Aguddah* frequently made it difficult to comprehend. The text, ordered by tractate, is further divided and numbered, permitting, with the indexes, easy reference. Katz notes that the author, in his humility, did not call the book by his name, but rather Katz found it attributed to Suslin in an old manuscript. The title page has the decorative frame topped by a vignette of the *Akedah*, used previously in Cremona, Venice, and Padua and reused by Prostitz in Cracow over several decades.

Ha-Aguddah is highly regarded and considered authoritative, being quoted and praised by R. Jacob Weil, R. Jacob ben Moses Moellin (Maharil), R. Israel Isserlein (*Terumat ha-Deshen*), and Rema. Nevertheless, *ha-Aguddah* was not reprinted, and then in part only, until the late nineteenth century, when J. H. Sonnenfeld published, with notes, tractate *Bava Kamma* (Jerusalem, 1874) and Order *Nezikin* (Jerusalem, 1899). However, a much-abridged version, *Ḥiddushei Aguddah*, prepared by Weil, was published as an appendix to Weil's responsa (Venice, 1549), and republished in that form several times.

Minhagim is yet another popular compilation of customs written in the mid-fifteenth century by R. Isaac Tyrnau (b. 1380/85–1439/52) recording the religious conventions and practices of central European Jewry for the entire year. First printed in Venice (1566) and reprinted in Lublin (1571, 1581), Venice (1591), Cracow (1591, 1592, and 1598), it was also published in what proved to be a popular Yiddish translation by R. Simon Levi ben Judah Guenzburg (Venice, 1589, 1593). The latter Yiddish edition (8^{0}: 80, [10] ff.), printed by Giovanni di Gara, is noteworthy for being the first printing of *Minhagim* in which the text is accompanied by illustrations which were included in subsequent printings of *Minhagim*.

Tyrnau, born either in the Hungarian city of Tirnau (now in Slovakia) or in Vienna, resided in Tyrnau, Austria. He was a student of R. Abraham Klausner, R. Shalom ben Isaac of Neustadt (Sar Shalom), and R. Aaron of Neustadt (Blumlein) and later served as rabbi in Pressburg. It is reported that Tyrnau had a beautiful daughter with whom the Hungarian crown prince fell in love, renouncing the throne and converting to Judaism, studying under Sephardi rabbis and becoming a Talmudic scholar. Returning to Hungary he entered into a clandestine marriage with her and continued to study under his father-in-law. Discovered by Catholic priests who demanded his return to Catholicism, he refused and was burned at the stake; the Jews were expelled from Tyrnau.[20]

Although a Talmudic scholar of considerable accomplishment, Tyrnau wrote not scholarly works, but rather a popular and, given the times, a necessary book of customs for the average person. Guenzburg was involved previously in other Hebrew printing endeavors, most notably the Basle Talmud (1578–81), and later in an unsuccessful attempt to print a *Maḥzor* and *Ẓultot*, together with a R. Isaac Mazia, in Thannhausen in 1594.[21]

In the introduction Tyrnau informs as to his purpose in writing *Minhagim*, to arrange the customs for the entire year in a manner that will make it easy for everyone to find [what they need] in clear language for people who are not Talmudic scholars. Therefore he is concise in both his proofs and reasons, but elaborates somewhat and even repeates laws as necessary, for "due to our many iniquities, the number of students and scholars has decreased." After men of Torah and good deeds perished in the Black Death (1348–50) and the persecution of the Jews occurred in Vienna in 1421, Tyrnau "saw that there were communities in which not even two or three men could be found who are truly knowledgeable in the customs of their community, and all the more so of another city." He therefore "ordered, picked and gleaned after the gleaners (*Ta'anit* 6b, *Bava Meẓia* 21b) the conclusions only of the customs, for many times something is written in the [*Tur*] Oraḥ Ḥayyim, or the *Mordekhai, Or Zaru'a*, and *Maimoni* that is not our practice at all, for example, ... *Avinu Malkenu* on Shabbat Yom Kippur."

The text follows the order of the year, beginning with the start of the week, that is, the conclusion of Shabbat, then weekday practice, *Rosh Ḥodesh*, festivals, starting with the month of Nissan, and

---

20 Ashkenazi, Shmuel. "Tyrnau, Isaac." *Encyclopaedia Judaica*. Ed. Michael Berenbaum and Fred Skolnik. 2nd ed. Vol. 20. Detroit: Macmillan Reference USA, 2007. 219-220. *Gale Virtual Reference Library*. Web. 20 Aug. 2012; Mordekhai Margalioth, ed., *Encyclopedia of Great Men in Israel* I (Tel Aviv, 1986), cols. 129-30 [Hebrew].

21 Concerning the expurgated Basle Talmud (1578–81) see Marvin J. Heller, *Printing the Talmud: A History of the Earliest Printed Editions of the Talmud* (Brooklyn, 1992), pp. 241–65.

concluding with *berit milah*, weddings, various other customs, and finally matters dealing with orphans and Kaddish. This volume ends with ethical matter from *Orḥot Ḥayyim*. *Minhagim* is primary based on the work of Tyrnau's teacher, Abraham Klausner, also author of *Sefer ha-Minhagim* (Riva di Trento, 1558). *Minhagim* is highly regarded and frequently quoted by R. Moses Isserles (Rema) in his annotations to the *Shulḥan Arukh*. Its popularity is evidenced by its frequent reprintings, and by Guenzburg's Yiddish translation.

This Yiddish edition has a title page with, in the center, a depiction of a winged figure holding a shield with a pitcher in the middle. To the left and right, respectively, is the name Simon Levi/Guenzburg. At the sides of the depiction is the verse "[That this is] God, our God for ever and ever; he will be our guide [till death]" (Psalms 48:15). On the verso of the title page is an introduction, in Hebrew, from R. Solomon ben Isaac Selim, who praises Guenzburg for bringing this valuable book to press again, three years after the previous edition. Guenzburg has "removed the stones from the path for all whose souls desire to know the righteous customs followed throughout the dispersion of Judah and Israel, particularly according to the Ashkenaz custom ... " The book has, due to its great value, disappeared from the market, and Guenzburg has spared no expense in publishing this edition. It is Guenzburg's name, but not that of Tyrnau, that appears in several places, even though, the translation and Guenzburg's additions notwithstanding, it is clearly Tyrnau's *Minhagim*. As noted above, the text is accompanied by numerous woodcuts, making it the first *minhag* book to be published with illustrations. These woodcuts depict events in the Jewish life cycle and the celebration of Jewish holidays. Twelve woodcuts are of the Zodiac and twenty-six pertain to Jewish customs. Five of the latter illustrations appear several times in the book. Among the woodcuts are depictions of the search for leaven, baking matzah, building a Sukkah, and lighting Sabbath lights.[22]

---

[22] The third edition (Venice, 1601) has different and finer illustrations. Nevertheless, it is the illustrations in this edition of *Minhagim* that have been much reprinted, independently and in *siddurim* and other books. According to some sources, also in Mantua in that year, but that printing is likely a misdating of the Venice edition.

We conclude with the ***Shulḥan Arukh***, the single most influential and authoritative *halakhic* digest, of R. Joseph ben Ephraim Caro (1488–1575). The first edition of this seminal work was printed at the press of Meir ben Jacob Parenzo and Alvise Bragadin (Venice, 1564-65). The title page has the three crowns of the Bragadin press and dates the beginning of the work on the first volume, *Oraḥ Ḥayyim*, to 18 Kislev [5]325 (Wednesday, November 22, 1564) and the last volume, *Ḥoshen Mishpat*, to 6 Ḥeshvan [5]326 (Monday, October 1, 1565). It is, as stated on the title page, an abridgement of Caro's magnum opus, the *Beit Yosef.*

> *Shulḥan Arukh* from the *Tur Oraḥ Ḥayyim* entitled *Beit Yosef* ... an abridgement of his great work on the *Arba'ah Turim* entitled *Beit Yosef* which "He has declared to his people the power of His works" (Psalms 111:6) "and His eye sees every precious thing" (Job 28:10) in order "that everyone who sought the Lord" (Exodus 33:7) will find that which he seeks with ease ...

The *Shulḥan Arukh* follows the structure of the *Arba'ah Turim.* Unlike that work, and also differing from Maimonides' *Mishneh Torah*, it contains neither involved *halakhic*, theological or philosophical discussions, nor aggadic or kabbalistic material. Caro's intention in writing this *halakhic* summary is expressed in the introduction. He begins by referencing the *Beit Yosef*, noting that it includes "the laws found in all the *posekim* (*halakhic* adjudicators), new as well as old," and their sources, enumerates a variety of works, and notes that each law is explained in detail. Caro continues,

> I saw in my heart that it was good to collect the lilies and sapphires in a brief format, clear and succinct, in order that the Torah of the Lord will be complete, fluent in the mouth of every man of Israel, so that whenever a question in *halakhah* is posed to a [Talmudic scholar] he will not stammer, but will "say to wisdom, you are my sister (var. tractates)." Just as it is clear to him that his sister is forbidden to him, so shall every practical *halakhah* be fluent in his mouth. This book "built with turrets" (Song of Songs 4:4), a hill, divided into thirty parts, one part to be learned daily, so that he repeats his learning monthly, as it says, "Fortunate is he who comes here and his learning is in his hand" (var. tractates). Furthermore, young students may constantly reflect on it, learning the text by

heart, that which they learned as youths will be retained and have practical application and even when elderly will not be forgotten. Wise men (*maskilim*) will shine as the brightness of heaven when they have respite from their travail and the exertions of their hands ... I have called this work *Shulḥan Arukh* (prepared table), for in it can be found all manner of delicacies ...

Caro initially had a negative view of the concise *halakhic* works described in this article. His critical appraisal of them, according to Isadore Twersky, is expressed in his undertaking of the *Beit Yosef*, for the

> Need was great for a comprehensive guide, which would stem the undesirable and almost unconscious proliferation of texts and provide a measure of religious uniformity in this period of great turmoil and dislocation. This would be accomplished, however, not by producing another compact, sinewy model—a small volume such as the *Agur*, which R. Karo treats pejoratively—but by reviewing the practical Halakhah in its totality. The oracular type of code, containing curt, staccato directives and pronouncements, was neither adequate nor reliable. It did not provide for intellectual stimulus and expansion of the mind, nor did it offer correct guidance in religious practice.[23]

Nevertheless, as Twersky also observes:

> Ten years later, in the course of which the *Bet Yosef* spread far and wide and his authority was increasingly respected, R. Joseph Karo came full cycle in his own attitude towards the oracular-type code. Having previously and persuasively argued against the utility and wisdom of the apodictic compendium, he now conceded its need and efficacy. He himself abridged the voluminous *Bet Yosef* ... [24]

---

23 Isadore Twersky "*The Shulḥan 'Aruk: enduring code of Jewish law*," *Judaism* 16 (1967) pp. 142-43. In an accompanying footnote, Twersky suggests that the *Agur* was singled out either because it "was simply one of the most recent representatives of the genre" or because Landau stated that the Agur satisfied the reader's minimal *halakhic* needs.

24 Twersky, p. 148.

Bare of all commentaries, the *Shulḥan Arukh* is a small work. The text, divided into sections and subsections, is followed by a ten-page listing of the contents. The *Shulḥan Arukh* was printed nine times in the sixteenth century without R. Moses Isserles's (Rema, c. 1530–72) glosses and four times with them. The *Shulḥan Arukh*'s success may be attributed to a number of factors, not least the reputation and authority of its author. Nevertheless, the work was initially criticized by many leading rabbinic figures. Among their complaints were the *Shulḥan Arukh's* excessive brevity and that the *Shulḥan Arukh* reflected Sephardic and neglected Ashkenaz tradition in *halakhah*. However, in the end it is the glosses of the Rema and other commentators addressing those complaints, that make the *Shulḥan Arukh* the primary *halakhic* work that it is to the present day.[25]

The widespread acceptance of the *Shulḥan Arukh* resulted not only in numerous reprints with glosses and commentaries, but also in translations. ***Shulḥan ha-Panim*** (*Misa de El Almah*) by R. Meir Jacob ibn Me'iri is a Ladino (Judeo-Spanish) translation and abridgment of the *Shulḥan Arukh*. It was first printed in Salonika (1568, 152 ff.) at the press of Joseph Jabez, the title page having the florets typical of Jabez imprints. It dates the beginning of the work to 15 Av 5368 (Monday, August 19, 1568). The text of the title page is, excepting the header and footer, in Ladino in vocalized Hebrew letters. There are both Hebrew and Ladino introductions, the former in a small rabbinic type.

Shulḥan ha-Panim (*Misa de El Almah*) is primarily the laws in the first two parts of the *Shulḥan Arukh*, that is, *Oraḥ Ḥayyim* (5a–113b) and *Yoreh De'ah* (114a–166b), with selections from *Even ha-Ezer* (177a–180b) and *Ḥoshen Mishpat* (181a–187a). The text, in Ladino, is

---

25 Meir Benayahu, *Yosef Beḥiri, Maran Rabbi Joseph Caro* (Jerusalem, 1991), pp. 407-523 [Hebrew]; Reuben Margaliot, "The First Editions of the *Shulḥan Arukh*," *Sinai* XXXVII (Jerusalem, 1956), pp. 25-29 [Hebrew]; Heller, II pp. 554-55; Naphtali Ben-Menaḥem, "The First Editions of the *Shulhan Arukh*," in *Rabbi Yosef Karo: Iyunim u-Mehkarim be-Mishnat Maran Ba'al ha-Shulḥan Arukh*, ed. Yitzhak Raphael (Jerusalem, 1969), pp. 101-03 n. 1 [Hebrew].

set in a single column, in square vocalized Hebrew letters. In his introduction, ibn Me'iri defends translating the *Shulḥan Arukh*, noting that Maimonides wrote in Arabic, that many do not know Hebrew, and that perhaps this will encourage them to learn the Holy language. Ibn Me'iri forbids with an oath the reprinting of this book in Latin letters, even if the act is well meant, out of concern that it will then be reproduced by someone unfamiliar with Hebrew writing, as has been done with the prayer book, and he requires that one swear by His holy name not to do so, so that non-Jews will not read it. Ibn Me'iri further includes in this oath a prohibition on printing the book anywhere in Italy because the censors alter the text, and unsuspecting readers will be unaware that this has been done.

Shulḥan ha-Panim was, however, reprinted in Venice (1602) at the press of Giovanni di Gara. In his introduction, R. Joseph ben David Franco, who brought the book to press, omits any mention that *Shulḥan ha-Panim* was printed previously. However, as ibn Me'iri's introduction is of value, Franco includes it, but not wishing to show that he has transgressed the translator's oath prohibiting printing the book in Italy, he has modified the prohibition to a restriction on printing anywhere in Italy but Venice, since there the censors remove only that which is explicitly against their religion, so that nothing has to be removed. The reference to non-Jews has been modified to read Ishma'elim.[26]

The *halakhic* works described here are timeless but, despite being republished over the centuries, are now only occasionally reprinted. Moreover, they are little studied today by most individuals interested in contemporary *halakhah*. Although available, albeit with some effort, they have largely become antiquarian works. Part of the

26 Meir Benayahu, *Copyright, Authorization, and Imprimatur for Hebrew Books Printed in Venice* (Jerusalem, 1971), pp. 218–22 [Hebrew]; A. M. Habermann, *Giovanni di Gara: Printer, Venice 1564–1610*. ed. Y. Yudlov (Jerusalem, 1982), pp. 106-07 no. 216 [Hebrew]; Isaac Yudlov, *Ginzei Yisrael, The Israel Mehlman Collection in the Jewish National and University Library* (Jerusalem, 1984), pp. 231-32 no. 1494 [Hebrew with English Appendix].

chain of *halakhic* development, they are, today, infrequently a component of contemporary *halakhic* discourse except by learned decisors. This is due to the overwhelming acceptance of the *Shulḥan Arukh*, which, together with its numerous commentaries and supercommentaries, is now the touchstone of *halakhic* discourse. Nevertheless, for centuries these works provided provision for the way (*ẓeidah la-derekh*), upon which the *Shulḥan Arukh* drew and which still remain, for interested contemporary readers, *ẓeidah la-derekh*. ☙

The Emergence and Development of Tosafot on the Talmud

By: ARYEH LEIBOWITZ

Introduction

It is generally known that the *Tosafot* commentary on the Talmud is a compendium of Talmudic scholarship produced in France and Germany over a period of a century and a half. Less known are the stages of its development and the different elements of its production. By charting the development of the Tosafist academies in Northern France through their final editing stages in France and Germany, this article suggests three distinct elements in the production of the *Tosafot* commentary and provides the reader with a general perspective of the printed editions of *Tosafot* that adorn modern-day editions of the Talmud.

The Tosafist Enterprise

Dialectic study, the *sine qua non* of rabbinic Judaism in the period of the Amoraim, seemingly fell into disuse in the centuries following the final redaction of the Talmud. The talmudic commentaries that emerged from the Geonic era primarily focused on straightforward explanations of difficult talmudic lexicons or on the elucidation of specific complicated passages. Additionally, Geonic attention was turned toward the issuance of legal rulings for the many communities that looked toward the Babylonian academies for legal decisions. If dialectic study of the Talmud was engaged in by the Geonim, very little was recorded and available for the emerging

---

Aryeh Leibowitz is a *musmakh* of REITS and earned his Ph.D. from Yeshiva University. He is the Assistant Dean of the Moty Hornstein Institute for Overseas Students at Yeshivat Sha'alvim.

Tosafist schools in Germany and France.[1]

The re-emergence of dialectic study was seemingly initiated by the Tosafist scholars of Northern France and Germany in the twelfth and thirteenth centuries.[2] The focus of the Amoraim had

---

1 Avraham Grossman addresses the lack of Talmud commentaries in the Geonic period in his "Social Structure and Intellectual Creativity in Medieval Jewish Communities (Eighth to the Twelfth Centuries)," *Studies in Medieval Jewish History and Literature*, ed. I. Twersky and J. M. Harris (Cambridge, 2000), 3:1–19. In addition, see his *Ḥakhmei Ẓarefat ha-Rishonim* (Jerusalem, 1995), 429–436. For examples of Geonic commentaries on the Talmud, see *Seridim mi-Toratan Shel Geonim ve-Rishonim mi-Genizat Kahir*, ed. E. Hurvitz (New York, 1986).

2 Various approaches have been suggested to explain the re-emergence of the dialectical movement as an internal Tosafist movement. Haym Soloveitchik writes that the "multiple panzer thrusts of R. Tam's intellect" led to a "rediscovery" of the methods utilized by the Amoraim to analyze the mishnaic corpus and that R. Tam applied those methods to the talmudic corpus. See Haym Soloveitchik, "Three Themes in the Sefer Ḥasidim," *AJS Review* 1 (1976): 339, idem., "Can Halakhic Texts Talk History?," *AJS Review* (1978): 179, and idem, "Rabad of Posquières: A Programmatic Essay," *Studies in the History of Jewish Society in the Middle Ages and in the Modern Period*, ed. E. Etkes and Y. Salomon (Jerusalem, 1980), 19. However, Avraham Grossman has argued that the dialectic method popularized by the Tosafists emerged before R. Tam in the eleventh-century talmudic academy in Worms, Germany; see his *Ḥakhmei Ashkenaz ha-Rishonim* (Jerusalem, 1981), 343 and 419, idem., *Ḥakhmei Ẓarefat ha-Rishonim*, Chapter Seven and specifically 447–449, and idem., "Social Structure and Intellectual Creativity," 1–19. The relationship between the Tosafists and the early German academies was first suggested by Jacob Naḥum Epstein, "Perushei ha-Rivan u-Perushei Vermaiza," *Tarbiẓ* 4 (1933): 167–192, especially 177-178. [We also find remnants of such study in R. Nissim b. Jacob's 11th century work, *Sefer ha-Mafteaḥ le-Man'ulei ha-Talmud*. See for example tractate *Shabbat* 80a.] Ḥayyim Hillel Ben-Sasson, "Hanhagatah shel Torah," *Beḥinot be-Bikkoret ha-Sifrut* 9 (1956): 39–53, suggested that the Tosafists' writings merely represent an intensification of classic talmudic methodologies encouraged by the success of Rashi's Talmud commentary.

Other scholars have looked to explain this re-emergence by noting similarities between the Tosafist dialectics and the methods of other intellectual movements of the time, suggesting a possible cross-cultural influence. See José Faur, "The Legal Thinking of the Tosafot: A Historical Ap-

been dialectic analysis of the *Mishnah* in light of the entire Tannaitic corpus. Every *Mishnah* had to be understood in the context of all other relevant Tannaitic sources. This required cross-referencing from the *Baraita* and *Tosefta* collections, as well as collation of the many explanations and traditions of the various Tannaitic sages.

The Tosafists approached the talmudic text with a similar perspective: talmudic passages could be understood only in light of the greater Amoraic corpus.[3] The Tosafist schools set out to analyze the entire Talmud using all relevant talmudic passages as a context and backdrop for the text under scrutiny. For two centuries the Tosafist academies searched the Talmud noting contradictions and relevant passages. Their dialectic analysis and hairsplitting distinctions procured for the Tosafists a sacred position within the intellectual history of talmudic study, described by one historian as the "immortal accomplishments" of the Tosafists.[4] The product of the meticulous work undertaken during these two centuries is well represented by the *Tosafot* commentary that graces the page of the printed Talmud.

---

proach," *Dine Yisrael* 6 (1975): 43–72, Ephraim Urbach, *Ba'alei ha-Tosafot*, 17–31, 87, fn. 9, and 744–757. Note that these remarks of Urbach appear in the 1980 edition and are a revision from what he originally wrote in the 1955 edition, 27-28. Ephraim Kanarfogel, *Jewish Education and Society in the High Middle Ages* (Detroit, 1992), 168 fn. 27, writes that these revisions were made in response to Isadore Twersky's critical comments in his 1957 review article of Urbach's work that appeared in *Tarbiẓ* 26 (1957): 218–220. See also A. Grossman's remarks in *Ḥakhmei Ashkenaz*, 423, especially fn. 58. For other cross-cultural similarities, see Ephraim Kanarfogel, *Jewish Education*, 70–73, and Israel Ta-Shma, "Halakhah and Reality—The Tosafist Experience," *Rashi et la Culture Juive en France du Nord au Moyen Âge*, ed. G. Dahan, et al. (Paris, 1997), 313–329. In general, see also Salo Baron, *Social and Religious History of the Jews* (New York, 1958), 6:27–56 and 6:340-341.

3 Urbach, *Ba'alei ha-Tosafot*, 679 – 680 and 744.

4 Haym Soloveitchik, "Three Themes," 339. In another essay, "Catastrophe and Halakhic Creativity: Ashkenaz – 1096, 1242, 1306, and 1298," *Jewish History* 12:1 (1998): 72, Soloveitchik remarks, "If, as Whitehead once aphoristically said, all philosophy is a series of footnotes to Plato, we can say, with far less exaggeration, that all subsequent halakhic thought has been a series of footnotes to the Tosafists."

Elements of the Tosafist Enterprise

It is possible to identify at least three distinct elements in the development of the Tosafist Talmud commentaries. These elements are also manifest as distinct stages in the Tosafist period—for different generations showed propensities toward one element or another.[5] Similarly, when speaking of a particular generation, we can identify three different roles that individual Tosafists assumed in their own work. We will address these elements as stages and speak in terms of generations, but it should be stressed that most Tosafists engaged, to varying degrees, in each of these roles.

Element One: Independent Dialectics

Rashi's line-by-line explanations of the entire talmudic corpus opened the book of the Talmud in a way that was previously unparalleled.[6] However his commentary was a local commentary, and he did not seek to analyze each line of the Talmud in context of the entire talmudic corpus. Rashi's Talmud commentary focused on the local discussion, and he chose explanations that presented the local passage with the most clarity, even if this required ignoring a relevant discussion in another tractate.

This was not the case with the Tosafists. Working with an assumption that the entire talmudic corpus was one unified text—an assumption that Rashi likely agreed with but did not focus on when

---

5 Compare to Israel Ta-Shma, *Ha-Sifrut ha-Parshanit la-Talmud* (Jerusalem, 1999), 1: 94.

6 Unlike the commentaries of R. Ḥananel, R. Gershom, or the other various commentaries that preceded his commentary, Rashi's method highlighted key phrases in the talmudic discussion (*dibur ha-matḥil*) instead of the paraphrasing commentary style of the aforementioned scholars. His commentary quickly spread throughout France and Germany, replacing the previously utilized commentaries. Now that the Talmud had found its authoritative commentary, a path was laid for the Tosafist enterprise. For more on this relationship between the commentary of Rashi and the Tosafist enterprise, see Urbach, *Ba'alei ha-Tosafot,* 21-22, and Grossman, "Social Structure and Intellectual Creativity," 11, and idem, *Ḥakhmei Ẓarefat ha-Rishonim,* 439-440.

composing his commentary—the early Tosafists focused their work on more global, corpus-wide analysis.[7]

Yet their broader focus did not preclude their attention to local issues. Before engaging in any dialectic analysis, the Tosafists engaged in a close reading of the local passage, providing further elucidation of the talmudic discussion.[8] Indeed, the early Tosafists were likely seeking to complement, and not replace, the commentary of their ancestor Rashi, and it could be that for this intention they received the name *Tosafot*, meaning additions.[9]

With a more corpus-wide perspective, the early Tosafists pored over the Talmud, seeking to identify difficulties in talmudic passages or Rashi's explanations based on parallel, or at least relevant, discussion in other locations in the talmudic corpus. These difficulties were often seeming contradictions that demanded resolution. Sometimes the contradictions between passages related to issues of a technical nature,[10] but more often the contradictions related to fundamental talmudic principles and placed key passages at loggerheads with one another. While earlier schools of talmudic analysis had surely noticed contradictions, their approach was often to discern which passage was the primary talmudic approach and which was to be presumed the non-authoritative passage.[11] But the Tosafists

---

7 Israel Ta-Shma, *Ha-Sifrut ha-Parshanit la-Talmud*, 1:71–75.

8 Urbach, *Ba'alei ha-Tosafot*, 689–699 and 715. E. Kanarfogel, "Religious Leadership During the Tosafist Period: Between the Academy and the Religious Court," *Jewish Religious Leadership: Image and Reality*, ed. J. Wertheimer (New York, 2004), 265, describes the Tosafists as "rabbinic scholars" who "revolutionized and forever changed the study of the Talmud and the formulation of *halakhah* through the methods of close reading and dialectic."

9 Urbach, *Ba'alei ha-Tosafot*, 21-22, Haym Soloveitchik, "The Printed Page of the Talmud: The Commentaries and their Authors," *Printing the Talmud: From Bomberg to Schottenstein*, ed. S. L. Mintz and G. M. Goldstein (New York, 2005), 38, and Israel Ta-Shma, *Ha-Sifrut ha-Parshanit la-Talmud*, 1:65-66.

10 Such as contradictions relating to biographical or historical facts; see for example *Tosafot Gittin* 84b s.v. רבי, *Tosafot Eruvin* 63a *s.v.* רב, and *Tosafot Kiddushin* 8a s.v. רב כהנא.

11 This approach of identifying the "*sugyah de-shematsa*" and disregarding the other was the approach of the Geonim and, to a degree, Maimonides. See

operated with a different principle, and they sought out contradictions not in order to identify which passages were primary and which non-authoritative, but to resolve and unify the entire corpus. The resolution of contradictions often yielded a broadening of initial perceptions and led to a deeper understanding of the issues. Similarly, other relevant passages, not only contradictory ones, were noted by the Tosafists to broaden the talmudic discussion.

Tosafist dialectics consisted of cross-referencing, resolving contradictions, and suggesting innovative readings of talmudic passages.[12] They represent the most creative element of Tosafist scholarship and were the primary focus of the early Tosafists. The growth of this approach to Talmud study in the early Tosafist period was encouraged by a strong intellectual independence of the early Tosafists.[13]

The systematic study of the Talmud from a dialectic perspective comprised the first stage, chronologically, of the Tosafist enterprise. In addition, it laid the structural foundation for future Tosafist works.

Identifying contradictions and relevant passages was not always an easy task. The first challenge was the need to memorize, or utilize some other technique to keep at the fore of one's consciousness the entire talmudic corpus. Only by having all relevant discussions in mind could a Tosafist properly analyze every line of the Talmud and determine if a particular passage needed to be reinvestigated in light of a discussion elsewhere. For this daunting task the Tosafists were likely aided by their academies. One early description of a Tosafist academy relates that the lectures were attended by dozens

---

Haym Soloveitchik, "The Printed Page of the Talmud," 38, Israel Ta-Shma, *Ha-Sifrut ha-Parshanit la-Talmud*, 1:71–75 and for specific examples, Shlomo Toledano, "Darko shel Rambam le-Tapel be-Sugyot Sotrot le-Umat Darkam shel Ba'alei ha-Tosafot." *Mayim mi-Dolyo* 17 (2006): 165–178.

12 Haym Soloveitchik's terms to describe the focus of Tosafist dialectics are: collation, contradiction, and distinction. See Haym Soloveitchik, "Three Themes," 339.

13 It is in this context that Ephraim Kanarfogel, "Progress and Tradition in Medieval Ashkenaz," *Jewish History* 14 (2000), 287–315, applies Marie-Dominique Chenu's "Partisans of Progress" to the early Tosafists.

of other scholars, each an expert in a specific tractate. As talmudic passages were analyzed, each scholar contributed to the discussion based on his knowledge of the tractate he had mastered.[14]

An additional challenge was that of proper analysis of the talmudic discussion. Sometime contradictions are blatant, but often a contradiction is apparent only when correct implications are inferred from the text. Hence, beyond the mere mental necessity of remembering the vast corpus, prudence and clear thinking were needed to determine the applicability of the outside source to the passage under discussion.

After identifying contradictions and relevant discussions, the early Tosafists turned to resolution of the contradictions and application to the relevant discussions. Not every contradiction was resolved, and occasionally the Tosafists themselves resorted to choosing one text over another.[15] But this was a rarity, and in nearly all instances the Tosafists were able, occasionally by greatly sacrificing the plain meaning of the text, to provide resolutions. In this pursuit the genius and creativity of the Tosafist masters is the most detectable, and it was in this realm that the dialectic battles were waged.

---

14 R. Menaḥem b. Zeraḥ, *Ẓedah la-Derekh* (Lemberg, 1859), Introduction. R. Menaḥem goes on to suggest that this accounts for the wide range of sources found in the *Tosafot* commentary of Ri. This suggestion is questioned by J. Katz, "E. E. Urbakh, Ba'alei ha-Tosafot," *Kiryat Sefer* 31 (1956): 15. Additionally, E. Kanarfogel, *Jewish Education and Society in the High Medieval Ages* (Detroit, 1992), 66, argues that these numbers may be exaggerated, as data indicate that certainly some of the Tosafist academies were quite small. See also M. Breuer, "Le-Ḥeker ha-Tipologia Shel Yeshivot ha-Ma'arav" *Perakim be-Toldot ha-Ḥevrah ha-Yehudit Bimei ha-Beynayim u-be'ait ha-Ḥadash* (Jerusalem, 1980), 49–52, who also argues that the size of the Tosafist academies was small, the discussions often conducted in the house of the teacher.

15 See for example *Tosafot Gittin* 77a *s.v.* וכדרב, where *Tosafot* finally conclude "הש"ס דהכא לא סברי הכי." See also *Tosafot Bava Batra* 39b *s.v.* וצריך for another example. In *Tosafot Menaḥot* 58b *s.v.* ואיכא an apparent list of thirteen contradictory talmudic discussions appears. However, S. Toledano, "Darko shel ha-Rambam," 168, notes that the list in *Menaḥot* does not contain contradictions between anonymous passages, but rather is a list of either individual scholars who changed their mind or cases where there are different traditions about what an individual scholar taught.

Hairsplitting distinctions and ingenious use of *okimta*—the reduction of a principle, or limiting of a ruling, to specific parameters—were the methods that the Tosafist masters relied upon in their disputes over resolving and explaining contradictory Talmud passages. The more inventive or original a Tosafist's approach was, the more he was challenged by his colleagues to defend his position and bring proofs for his proposition.

In addition to noting contradictions and relevant discussions and then suggesting resolutions or applications, the early Tosafist commentaries also functioned in more traditional senses. They offered alternative translations of talmudic terms, questioned or explained a passage's initial position (*hava amina*), or ruled in favor of a particular view. These functions, while not unique to the Tosafist enterprise, also reflected the creativity and originality that were the hallmarks of the early Tosafists. The early Tosafists also confronted the rulings of Geonic masters, such as R. Simon Kayyara and R. Yehudai Gaon, and commented on the commentaries of pre-Tosafist Talmudists, such as R. Ḥananel.

The efforts of the early Tosafists yielded independent commentaries that contained the teachings of individual Tosafist masters. An early Tosafist's commentary primarily contained *his* questions, *his* resolutions, and *his* insights. Notwithstanding that the early Tosafists occasionally confronted the views of earlier scholars, their commentaries were nonetheless unique in that they generally read as independent works. The dominant tone of these commentaries was that they reflected one man's confrontation with the talmudic text, and certainly did not bear the imprint of an entire culture, as is the case with later Tosafist works.

It appears that over time the value of the early commentaries, which represented only single authors' teachings, decreased considerably. In an age when manuscripts were copied by hand and priority was likely granted based on utility, few of the early texts survived. Indeed, there are few extant fragments of these commentaries, many preserved only in later commentaries.

One early Tosafist who exemplified the initial stage of independent dialectics was R. Isaac b. Asher (Riba, d. 1133). Riba directed the talmudic academy in Speyer, Germany, conversed in study with Rashi, and authored a commentary on many tractates.[16] His commentary was the first German composition to be referred to as *Tosafot*,[17] and his central role in the emerging movement was noted by many later Tosafists.[18] Riba's creativity as an independent dialectician is strongly sensed in most tractates, as many passages in the printed *Tosafot* texts contain his dialectic contributions, such as questions he posed or contradictions he noted.

Riba's own original commentary has generally been lost, although a few remnants remain. For example, a lengthy passage from *Tosafot ha-Riba* is quoted in a later Tosafist commentary on Tractate *Bava Kamma*, and clearly demonstrates the nature of Riba's commentary as an early independent dialectic work.[19] The passages contain the teachings of Riba, and Riba alone. The reader immediately senses that he is reading the opinion of only one scholar.[20]

---

16 See *Tosafot Niddah* 39b s.v. אלמא for a record of Riba's interaction with Rashi. For more on Riba and his intellectual activity in a number of other German cities, see M. Ben-Ghedalia, "Ḥakhmei Shpira Bimei Gezeirot Tatnu ule-Aḥareihem: Koroteihem, Darkam be-Hanhagat ha-Zibur, ve-Yezeiratam ha-Ruḥanit," (Ph.D. Diss., Bar Ilan University, 2007), 85-107.

17 In France, R. Tam refers to his father's works as *Tosafot*, see *Sefer ha-Yashar*, #252.

18 There is debate regarding the stature of Riba. Urbach, *Ba'alei ha-Tosafot*, 165, positions Riba in the center of the emerging Tosafist movement and refers to him as "the head and first of the Tosafists in Germany." However, H. Soloveitchik, *Yaynam: Sahar be-Yaynam Shel Goyim – Al Gilgulah Shel Halakhah be-Olam ha-Ma'aseh* (Tel Aviv, 2003), 24, questions the position of Riba's centrality and argues that he was of lesser stature than the major Tosafist figures of France. Soloveitchik's denigration of Riba's stature was criticized by I. Ta-Shma in his review of *Yaynam*, *Zion* 69 (2004) 501–509, 507-508, which in turn was responded to by Soloveitchik, "Yaynam – Divrei Teguvot," *Zion* 70 (2005), 529–535. For more on this debate see M. Ben-Ghedalia, "Ḥakhmei Shpira," 87–89.

19 Oxford – Bodleian Opp. 388, printed by M. Blau, *Shitat ha-Kadmonim al Massekhet Bava Kamma* (New York, 1977); see Urbach, *Ba'alei ha-Tosafot*, 643–645. The passage under discussion is quoted on *Bava Kamma* 24b.

20 The same is true regarding another fragment of *Tosafot ha-Riba* on Tractate *Shabbat*. The fragment exists in manuscript form, Olomouc – Statni Vedecka Knihovna 138, and covers *Shabbat* 48a–51a, and was printed by

Although Riba's commentary is the earliest extant representative of the initial stage of the Tosafist enterprise, the true image of independent Tosafist dialectics was embodied in R. Jacob b. Meir (R. Tam, d. 1171). R. Tam, scholar and communal leader, was the towering figure of the emerging Tosafist dialectic movement. Few written remnants remain from R. Tam's own compositions, yet his influence is strongly felt on every page of the Talmud. His teachings became primary foci of later generations, and his opinions were always necessarily considered in all later Tosafist commentaries.[21]

Relying on his only known work, the *Sefer ha-Yashar*, we can surmise the nature of R. Tam's compositions.[22] *Sefer ha-Yashar* contains a commentary that boasts complete and utter independence. His strong personality and bold creativity are sensed in his detachment from earlier sources.[23] R. Tam forged his own path through the vast Talmud, and his personality stands at the fore of independent Tosafist dialectics.

As stated earlier, original dialectics are not exclusively found in the earliest stages of the Tosafist movement. Many later compositions contain original dialectic contributions of single independent Tosafists; however, the degree of independence in these later works was less than those of the earliest Tosafists.

Y. Shoshana, "Tosafot Riba al Massekhet Shabbat," *Yeshurun* 13 (2003): 21–36. The actual material in this fragment was not written by Riba himself but it quotes and paraphrases consistently from *Tosafot ha-Riba*. In this text as well, the *Tosafot Riba* reflect the independence of the early Tosafists.

21 For a brief description of R. Tam's influence on the Tosafist movement see H. Soloveitchik, "Catastrophe and Halakhic Creativity," 72, and "The Printed Page of the Talmud," 39. For a more expanded treatment see Urbach, *Ba'alei ha-Tosafot*, 60–113, and A. Reiner, "Rabbenu Tam u-Benai Doro: Kesharim, Hashpa'ot, ve-Darkei Limudo be-Talmud" (Ph.D. Diss., Hebrew University, 2002).

22 R. Tam's own *Tosafot* are not extant, yet they are referenced occasionally. See for example, "Tosafot Talmid Rabbenu Tam ve-Rabbenu Eliezer," ed. M. Blau, *Shitat ha-Kadmonim al Massekhet Bava Kamma* (New York, 1977), 272.

23 For more on R. Tam and his *Sefer ha-Yashar* see Urbach, *Ba'alei ha-Tosafot*, 92–106, and Reiner, ibid., 23–68.

Element Two: Integration

The independence of early Tosafist works notwithstanding, it is important to realize that talmudic scholars never operated in a complete intellectual vacuum.[24] Indeed, most Tosafists approached the talmudic text with the analysis of the earlier generations as a backdrop for their own analysis. In addition to engaging in the independent dialectics that typified the earliest Tosafist period, subsequent Tosafists also had the challenge of relating to the Tosafists that preceded them.

For the independent early Tosafists the Talmud text itself was the focal point of study, as they focused on identifying contradictions, suggesting resolutions, analyzing relevant passages, and other forms of commentary. However, in the following generations attention was also directed toward the works of the early Tosafists. Contradictions had been identified by the early Tosafist masters, and oftentimes multiple resolutions had been suggested by the different early masters. A later Tosafist had to collect the relevant discussions and weigh the strengths of the suggested solutions. In turn this would lead the later Tosafist to ultimately choose which questions, comments, comparisons, and resolutions he wished to teach to his students and integrate into his own commentary.

Collation of earlier material followed by selective integration constituted the second element of the Tosafist enterprise. The best questions, most cogent answers, and sharpest insights were spliced together to produce rich commentaries that reflected the choicest creativity of the early Tosafists. Integration was utilized by the generations following the earliest Tosafists, and was the hallmark of a second stage in the Tosafist enterprise.

---

24 In fact, we find instances, such as in *Tosafot Gittin* 82a *s.v.* אצ, where R. Tam is not only attentive to a dialectic assertion suggested by another Tosafist, in this case R. Meshulam of Melun, but he even openly embraces the opinion and augments it with a proof text. This example is additionally significant considering the stormy relationship between R. Tam and R. Meshulam. For more on this relationship, see Urbach, *Ba'alei ha-Tosafot*, 71–82, and for a new perspective see A. Reiner, "Parshanut ve-Halakhah – Iyun me-Ḥudash be-Pulmus Rabbenu Tam ve-Rabbenu Meshulam," *Shenaton ha-Mishpat ha-Ivri* 21 (2000): 207–239.

The transition from independent dialectic study to this second stage was gradual. The initial practitioners of integration also included in their works a large amount of their own independent dialectics. Their commentaries were independent texts, reflecting the initial stage of independent dialectics, yet also bore signs of integration, quoting and discussing the opinions of their colleagues.[25]

The first two elements of the Tosafist enterprise—i.e., (1) independent analysis and (2) integration of earlier teachings—were the focus of Talmud study for both French and German Tosafists in the late twelfth and early thirteenth centuries.[26] However, it was specifically the French works that ultimately formed the backbone of extant Tosafist commentaries, especially those that are printed today in the margins of the Talmud.

---

25 R. Tam's colleagues and students are representative of this cross between the independence of the early Tosafists and the dependence of later Tosafists who were part of an established tradition. His colleagues and students, including Tosafist scholars such as R. Jacob and R. Joseph of Orleans, R. Joseph Porat, and R. Hayyim ha-Kohen, contributed original dialectics to the Tosafist corpus in the form of questions, contradictions, and insights, while also addressing the many questions and contradictions raised by R. Tam and their other predecessors.

26 While it is the French Tosafists who are traditionally known as the authors of *Tosafot*, it is clear that German Tosafists also produced *Tosafot*-style commentaries on the Talmud. See E. Kanarfogel, "Tekstim ve-Yoẓeraihem: Hithakut Aḥarei Ḥiddusheihem shel Ba'alei Tosafot," *Ḥinnukh ve-Da'at: Samkhut ve-Autonomiyyah*, ed. I. Etkes, et al. (Jerusalem, 2011), 97. On some of the differences between the French *Tosafot* and the German *Tosafot*, such as the milder dialectics found in the German works, see E. Kanarfogel, "Rabbinic Leadership," 303. It is important to note that most extant *Tosafot* commentaries are associated with the French tradition, whereas many of the German *Tosafot* have been lost; see S. Emanuel, *Shivrei Luḥot: Sefarim Avudim shel Ba'alei ha-Tosafot* (Jerusalem, 2007), Introduction, 11, and Emanuel's specific discussions of the *Tosafot* of various German Tosafists, such as R. Samuel b. Natronai, 60-61, R. Joel ha-Levi, 81–86, R. Barukh of Magence, 122-123, R. Eliezer of Metz, 293–297, R. Simḥah of Speyer, 157, and R. Moshe Taku, 315 fn. 34. For a more general discussion on the difference between the literary activity of the French Tosafists and German Tosafists, see Ya'akov Sussman, "Mifalo ha-Madda'ei Shel Profesor Efrayim Elimelekh Urbakh," *Musaf Madda'ei ha-Yahadut* 1 (1993): 48–54.

The dominance of the French works is largely due to the emergence of R. Isaac of Dampierre (Ri, d. 1189) and the establishment of his Tosafist academy in Dampierre. Ri was a nephew of R. Tam and his greatest rival for prominence in Tosafist history. Ri's prolific lectures educated scores of Tosafists, and his students spread the Tosafist approach to all corners of Europe, including France, Germany, Italy, Provence, and the Slavic lands. Ri was a towering innovator and blessed with a creativity that allowed him to formulate many original contributions as an independent Tosafist. However, Ri was also the driving force and epitome of the second element in the Tosafist enterprise: integration.[27]

Ri is known to have lectured on the entire talmudic corpus and his academy reportedly boasted scores of students.[28] The lectures, culled from the erudite teachings of his uncle, R. Tam, and R. Tam's many colleagues, integrated the earlier sources with his own sharp insights. These sources included both French Tosafist teachings—such as those of R. Tam, R. Samuel b. Meir (Rashbam), R. Isaac b. Meir, R. Elijah of Paris, R. Ḥayyim ha-Kohen of Paris, R. Joseph of Orleans (Bekhor Shor), and R. Meshulam of Melun—and German Tosafists—such as Riva, R. Eliezer b. Nathan (Raban), R. Isaac ben Mordekhai (Rivam) and R. Ephraim of Regensburg. Ri also added countless new dialectic discussions that identified previously unnoticed contradictions and raised new questions. Hence, Ri's greatness was not only his ability to present his uncle's teach-

---

27 Ri's own writings contain both original material and integration. Hence some passages authored by Ri—such as those preserved in a commentary on tractate *Avodah Zarah*—are completely independent, lacking any references to Ri's predecessors and featuring only his own original insights. These passages appear in "Tosafot R. Yehudah of Paris," ed. M. Blau, *Shitat ha-Kadmonim al Massekhet Avodah Zarah* to *Avodah Zarah*, 41a - 41b, and on 51a. However, in other passages—such as those preserved in a commentary on tractate *Bava Kamma*—we find strong elements of integration, as Ri makes many references to Riba, Rashbam, and R. Tam. These passages appear in Blau's *Shitat ha-Kadmonim al Massekhet Bava Kamma* in what Blau titles "Tosafot Talmid Rabbenu Tam ve-Rabbenu Eliezer." The passages referred to here are on *Bava Kamma* 11b and 23b.

28 As alluded earlier, there is a significant debate regarding the size of the Tosafist academies. See Kanarfogel, *Jewish Education*, 66-67.

ings clearly and integrate them with the work of others, but Ri himself was also a creative innovator and independent dialectician par-excellence. His energies drew from both elements of the Tosafist enterprise discussed thus far, and his lectures were filled with both faithful transmission and originality. For this reason, Ri's academy became the center of the Tosafist tradition and bore the burden of transmitting the nascent enterprise.

Ri had many eminent students who dedicated themselves to recording his brilliance. Foremost of his students was his own son, R. Elḥanan (d. 1184), whose intellectual activity and life ended prematurely by marauding Christian crusaders, the brothers R. Isaac b. Abraham of Dampierre (Rizba, d. 1210) and R. Samson b. Abraham of Sens (d. 1214), R. Barukh b. Isaac (d. 1211), and R. Judah Sirleon of Paris (d. 1224). Other students of Ri also penned commentaries, of which some are extant, most notably R. Moses and R. Shneur of Evreux, as well as other lesser-known students, such as R. Isaac of Brienne and R. Ezra of Moncontour. In fact, nearly all extant *Tosafot* commentaries can ultimately be traced to Ri's academy.

Ri's students utilized the *reportatio* method of note-taking.[29] This method entailed Ri's dictation of his lecture to specific students who would capture his verbal formulations. After Ri confirmed the accuracy of the *reportationes* the authors would sign the

[29] The *reportatio* method of note-taking was widely utilized in the Middle Ages. An extant example from the non-rabbinic world is the *Sententie Abaelardi*, a *reportatio* of Peter Abelard's lectures; see John Marenbon, *The Philosophy of Peter Abelard* (Cambridge, 1999), 63. For more on *reportatio* in rabbinic works see, B. Smalley, *The Study of the Bible in the Middle Ages* (Notre Dame, 1964), 230, 200–204 (also quoted in H. Soloveitchik, "The Printed Page of the Talmud," 40, fn. 5), and M. Blau, Introduction, *Shitat Kadmonim al Massekhet Avodah Zarah*, 18. For a discussion about a very similar phenomenon in the broader medieval world of scholarship see M. B. Parkes, "The Influence of the Concepts of *Ordinatio* and *Compilatio* on the Development of the Book," *Medieval Learning and Literature: Essays Presented to R. W. Hunt*, ed. J. J. G. Alexander and M. T. Gibson (Oxford, 1976), 115–141, A. J. Minnis, "Late Medieval Discussions of Compilatio and the Role of the Compiler," *Beitrage zur Geschichte der Deutschen Sprache und Literatur* 101 (1979): 385–421, and N. Hathaway, "Compilation: From Plagiarism to Compiling," *Viator* 20 (1989): 19–44.

passage with a מ"ר, indicating that this formulation was "from the mouth" of Ri (מפי רבי).[30] The appearance of such signatures at the end of passages is found in manuscripts of many of Ri's students, most notably in the *Tosafot* of R. Elḥanan, R. Samson of Sens, and R. Judah Sirleon. The dominant characteristic in these commentaries is the high level of integration they contain, although the presence of independent dialectics is not lost completely. These records of Ri's lectures are the clearest extant examples of integrated commentaries, and demonstrate that much of this integration was undertaken by Ri himself. Ri's lectures and the intellectual activity of his academy were, in large measure, responsible for the integration of material from the early Tosafists that appears in the commentaries of subsequent generations.

The commentaries of Ri's students paint for us a general sketch of the nature of Ri's lecture. When studying a tractate in the academy, Ri would seemingly introduce the questions, contradictions, and insights of the earlier masters. He would then comment on the material, weigh the strengths of the questions and insights, and provide his own resolutions and comments. In addition, Ri would add his own independent dialectics that both raised new issues and augmented older discussions. This yielded, in the form of his students' *Tosafot*, sophisticated integrated texts that bore the teachings of Ri's predecessors through the unique prism of Ri's own teaching.

Ultimately, the success of Ri's teachings was a result of both his dependence on the earlier generations and his own confidence to operate, in the greater context of his academy, as an independent dialectician. This duality accounts for the unparalleled breadth of material found in the commentaries that emerged from Ri's academy. Scholars have noted the plethora of sources confronted in the commentaries that emerged from Ri's academy, and have tried to explain why these commentaries specifically boast a richness of sources not found in other rabbinic works.

In this context, the above-referenced tradition was recorded by R. Menaḥem b. Zerah regarding Ri: "My French teachers testified

---

30 They also used various other signatures when quoting Ri, such as לשון רבי when copying verbatim from Ri's own writings. See M. Blau, *Shitat Kadmonim al Massekhet Avodah Zarah*, 18.

to me in the name of their teachers that it is well known that sixty Rabbis would study in his presence."[31] R. Menaḥem continues with a description of how each of the sixty Rabbis was an expert in a specific tractate. As Ri analyzed a talmudic passage, each Rabbi was on hand ready to note if any discussions in the tractate he had mastered were at odds with the current passage or could be utilized for a deeper understanding.[32]

It appears that Ri wrote very little in terms of *Tosafot*.[33] But even if he himself wrote little, Ri's students wrote in abundance. Whereas many of Ri's students composed faithful transcripts of Ri's lectures, others followed Ri's example and added their own questions, resolutions, and insights, producing new Tosafist works that represented the earlier teachings as transmitted by Ri plus their own original insights.[34]

---

31 *Ẓedah la-Derekh*, Introduction. As we noted earlier, many scholars doubt the accuracy of this tradition; see E. Kanarfogel, *Jewish Education*, 66.

32 The late Prof. Jacob Katz questions the historicity of this account and is unhappy relying on this tradition to explain the wide range of sources found in the commentaries of Ri's academy. Instead, he ascribes this phenomenon to the rich tradition that preceded Ri, i.e., the teachings of the early Tosafists, R. Tam and his colleagues. For Katz, it was Ri's exposure to the teachings of the earlier generations and his willing reliance on his predecessors that accounts for the breadth of sources confronted in Ri's academy. See Jacob Katz, "E. E. Urbach, Ba'alei ha-Tosafot," *Kiryat Sefer* 31 (1956): 15, reprinted as "Al 'Ba'alei ha-Tosafot' le-Efraim E. Urbach," *Halakhah ve-Kabbalah* (Jerusalem, 1994), 348. In light of our presentation of the dual nature of Ri's lectures, that is, his mastery of independent dialectics as well as his heavy utilization of the Tosafist tradition that preceded him, R. Menaḥem's tradition and Katz's analysis are not mutually exclusive. The strength of Ri's lectures was exactly the fact that he not only conscientiously worked off of a rich tradition, but also infused the material, with the aid of his academy, with his own original dialectics. Both of these elements contributed to his success, as Ri's independent dialectics were augmented by his masterful integration.

33 See Blau, *Shitat Kadmonim al Massekhet Avodah Zarah*, 18, where he argues that Ri did not write much. This conclusion is seemingly shared by Haym Soloveitchik in "Catastrophe and Halakhic Creativity," 73 and "The Printed Page of the Talmud," 40.

34 It appears that not all of Ri's students followed his lead. The *Tosafot Evreux*, a product of the French Evreux academy led by R. Moses and R.

The most notable example of this is R. Samson b. Abraham of Sens. Ri's most prolific student, R. Samson authored his own *Tosafot* commentary, which gained wide popularity. While his commentary contained many passages that directly reported teachings that he heard from Ri, R. Samson also included significant amounts of original material. What Ri did to the integrated commentaries before him, R. Samson did to Ri's lectures. To wit, R. Samson produced an even further integrated commentary that contained much of the Ri's integrated material, but oftentimes through the prism of R. Samson's own teachings.

Element Three: Editing

The third element of the Tosafist enterprise, and the final stage chronologically, was the process of editing. In this stage, Tosafist attention turned from elucidation of the Talmud, original dialectics, and integration of early sources, and instead focused on the specific needs of presentation and clarification. Previously identified contradictions in the Talmud needed to be presented in a clear format, resolutions demanded skillful formulations, and creative insights of earlier masters required proper expression.

Historically, periods of literary creativity are often followed by periods of collation and organization.[35] It was the realization of these later goals that was sought out by the Tosafists who flourished in the generations following Ri's students. Indeed, two general

Shnuer of Evreux, is a Tosafist work whose nature and structure are considerably different from the other works that emerged from Ri's students. Most significantly, *Tosafot Evreux* do not contain the breadth of sources nor the highly sophisticated dialectic arguments that are typical of Ri's students' works. These characteristics are but some of the evidence presented by I. Ta-Shma and E. Kanarfogel that the Evreux academy was influenced by German Pietistic teachings, and that this influence affected the academy's curriculum and compositions. See I. Ta-Shma, "Ḥasidut Ashkenaz bi-Sefarad: Rabbenu Yonah Gerondi – Ha-Ish u-Fo'alo," *Galut Aḥar Golah*, ed. A. Mirsky, et al. (Jerusalem, 1988), 165–73, 181–88, and E. Kanarfogel, *"Peering through the Lattices," Mystical, Magical, and Pietistic Dimensions in the Tosafist Period* (Detroit, 2000), 26-27, 62–68.

35 I. Twersky, Introduction to the Code of Maimonides (Mishneh Torah) (New Haven, 1980), 72.

periods of Tosafist activity can be delineated, one categorized as an era of creativity, the second of collation and organization. The first extended until the death of Ri's primary students, at which point "the creative period of the Tosafists comes to an end." The second consisted of the remainder of the thirteenth century, when the Tosafists edited, "arranged and packaged the intellectual revolution of the twelfth [century]."[36]

A great challenge facing those who sought to edit the integrated commentaries was the need to responsibly condense and abridge the sometimes verbose dialectical arguments. Many of the Tosafists wrote voluminously, strengthening their arguments with multiple points, and supporting conclusions with many proofs. Shortening these passages was of supreme importance and required literary vision and editorial prudence. Only the most crucial proofs and arguments needed to be retained; the less crucial positions and arguments could be omitted.

At times, the editors of Tosafot also engaged in their own forms of integration. As part of the abridgment process, the Tosafist editors occasionally spliced together material from the already integrated commentaries that emerged from the second stage of the Tosafist enterprise. Further integration of the already integrated works produced new passages that contained spliced-together sections from earlier works. However, when operating as an editor a Tosafist seldom introduced new material into the text. His concern was not with including his own original contributions, nor integrating material from earlier commentaries. His primary focus was responsible presentation of the inherited material before him.

The aforementioned responsibilities of editing and transmitting the rich Tosafist heritage were the primary foci of the later

---

[36] H. Soloveitchik, "Catastrophe and Halakhic Creativity," 74-75. Similarly, the description of the Tosafists as "partisans of progress" in E. Kanarfogel, "Progress and Tradition in Medieval Ashkenaz," *Jewish History* 14 (2000): 287–315, is most befitting of the early generations of R. Tam and his colleagues, and is less applicable to the later generations of the Tosafists who were more occupied with presentation and transmission.

Tosafists.[37] Although earlier Tosafists also edited material they received from their predecessors, this sphere of activity was dominated by later Tosafist figures such as R. Perez (d. 1298) of Corbeil who operated in France, R. Meir (d. 1293) of Rothenberg in Western Germany, and R. Eliezer (d. late 13th century) of Tukh in Eastern Germany.

The undertaking of these editors signaled the closing of the creativity-dominated period, and ushered in the beginning of a new era, one where the focus turned to reformulating the received commentaries and transmitting them to future generations.[38] Expressing concisely and precisely the positions of the earlier masters, such as R. Tam and Ri, was the unstated goal of many Tosafists who flourished in this editing role.[39]

---

37 This article focuses on the *Tosafot* commentary on the Talmud and is not an exhaustive survey of all Tosafist activity; therefore, it has omitted some of the accomplishments of the Tosafists who flourished in the period between the students of Ri and those who engaged in this third and final stage of editing the *Tosafot*. For instance, no mention of the codificatory work of R. Moses of Coucy or R. Isaac of Corbeil is made, even though their works made significant contributions to halakhic literature.

38 Multiple factors likely contributed to this transition in roles. We have seen above the common pattern in intellectual history that periods of intense creativity are often followed by a period of collation and internalization. Additionally, in the case of medieval France and Germany there were political issues that also undoubtedly contributed to a decline in creativity. The Talmud disputations of the mid thirteenth century and Paris burnings of the Talmud changed the landscape of the intellectual centers in France, and ushered in the demise of the Paris center; see E. Urbach, *Ba'alei ha-Tosafot*, 460 and 521. In Germany, a new spate of anti-Semitic violence and the specter of further crusades contributed to a stunting of intellectual growth.

39 A statement by R. Asher b. Jehiel (Rosh) in his responsa, 20:27, illustrates this attitude. In response to a query based on a supposed Tosafist text representing the view of Ri, Rosh retorts that the commentary under discussion is not precise, as is typical of many of the commentaries in that region. He argues that such commentaries, including those elucidated in the presence of R. Perez, should not be relied upon. Rosh continues that he has the *Tosafot* commentaries of R. Samson and they are much more authoritative and precise in capturing the correct intent of Ri. One sees

The Printed Tosafot

The Tosafist redactions that emerged in the late thirteenth century were edited commentaries that contained the integrated teachings of the Tosafist masters of the past century and a half. Certainly, the redactions were not identical. Each editor produced his redaction by drawing from his own unique sources. Although most of these sources were rooted in the Dampierre academy of Ri and his students, there were nonetheless discrepancies in language, nuance in presentation, and even differences in content. Even within a single tractate, an editor may have drawn from multiple sources and hence varied opinions can appear even within a single tractate. This is certainly true between tractates, where an editor may have drawn from completely different sources.

The earliest printers made concerted attempts to procure one single redaction of *Tosafot* on the entire Talmud.[40] This would at least provide a modicum of consistency on the final level of editing and redaction. Yet their efforts were unsuccessful, and the printed *Tosafot* in modern-day editions of the Talmud are from varied editors and are attributable to numerous sources. Some tractates contain relatively early Tosafist works, such as *Tosafot Evreux*, or even *Tosafot Shanz*. Others contain later redactions, such as *Tosafot R. Perez* or *Tosafot Maharam*. Nonetheless, most of the major tractates contain the *Tosafot Tukh* of R. Eliezer of Tukh.[41]

This is not the venue for outlining in detail the many differences between the redactions. But it should be noted that the editors operated in different vicinities, and therefore had access to different primary sources. Also, each editor operated with his own

---

from this responsum that at least part of Rosh's judgment of texts was based on their accuracy in capturing Ri's teachings.

40 Gerson Soncino writes in the introduction to his edition of R. David Kimḥi's (Radak) *Sefer Mikhlol* that part of his preparation for issuing the first printed edition of the Talmud was an arduous search for the "*Tosafot Tukh* of R. Isaac and R. Tam" for inclusion on the page of the Talmud. For the text of Soncino's statement, see Raphael Nathan Nata Rabbinovicz, *Dikdukei Sofrim* (Munich: Huber, 1884), 48, fn. 16.

41 For more on the *Tosafot Tukh*, see A. Leibowitz, "Maḥutan Shel Tosafot Tukh," *Yeshurun* 27 (2012): 896–906.

unique methods of editing. Some editors contributed original content, while others did not. Some relied upon their students to partake in the editing process, while others operated independently. For certain, the many different redactions of *Tosafot* that emerged in the middle and end of the thirteenth century reflected unique records of the Tosafist tradition.

However, almost all of the redactions that have survived today share a common source: the prolific work of Ri's academy in Dampierre, France. Even those *Tosafot* collections edited in Germany, such as R. Eliezer's *Tosafot Tukh*, feature the *Tosafot* teachings of France at their core. For this reason, the use of parallel *Tosafot* works can greatly aid modern-day students of *Tosafot* in their study. Editing methods notwithstanding, the overall commonality between the works warrants their consultation during Talmud study.

ೋ

The Propriety of a Civil Will

By: A. YEHUDA WARBURG

During the last twenty-five years, approximately a dozen different formulations of halakhic *wills* have been disseminated in our community; nonetheless, to this very day, many segments of our community continue to utilize a civil *will* as the vehicle for their estate planning.

As we know, in accordance with secular law and the wishes of a testator, an attorney will draft a last will and testament that will distribute assets to a surviving spouse, son(s) and daughter(s) upon demise of the testator. Given the continued use of a secular *will* in our community, the purpose of this essay is to examine how halakhic authorities dealt with a secular *will*.

1. The Torah's Order of Hereditary Succession, the *issur* of "*avurei aḥsanta*" and "there is no *kinyan* after death"

A Jew's disposition of his property transpires during his lifetime. Upon his demise, human ownership ceases and halakhic succession law determines who will inherit his estate. Inheritance occurs by itself. As Rabbeinu Gershon notes,[1] no one benefits man but rather he automatically receives his ancestor's inheritance.

There is no transfer of assets between the testator and his heirs via the implementation of a *kinyan*, i.e., a symbolic act of transfer such as an exchange of money or writing a *shtar* (a halakhic-legal document). As the Talmud states,[2] and as it is restated in the Shulḥan Arukh,[3] there is no *shtar* after death.

---

1 *Bava Batra* 141b.

2 *Ketubbot* 55b; Bava Batra 152a.

3 *Ḥoshen Mishpat* (hereafter: *ḤM*) 250:9.

---

 rabbinic ordination, Hebrew University Faculty of Law, Dr. Jurisprudence, Dayan serving the *ḥassidic*, modern orthodox and yeshiva communities of NJ and NY.

The signing of a *shtar* is an example of a *kinyan* that may serve as a vehicle to transfer assets provided that the person is alive. Upon death, the person is incapable of transferring assets, or as the *posekim* state, "there is no *kinyan* after death."

In the words of the late Dayan Grunfeld of London, England,[4]

> ... In Jewish law we have the rules ... There is no gift after death and ... There is no effective document after death ... The logical consequence of this is that any money in the hands of a beneficiary of a will under the law of the land, which as far as Jewish religious law is concerned belongs to a different person, namely, the proper heir in accordance with the Jewish law of inheritance, has to be returned to that heir.

Unlike secular law which permits a transfer of assets upon death, for halakha the moment of death preempts this possibility. It is the halakhic system rather than the effectuation of a *kinyan* by a Jew that allows man to benefit his heirs. Pursuant to the Mishnah,[5] upon demise of the decedent, i.e., the father, the order of succession is as follows: (1) the sons, (2) their descendants, (3) the daughters, (4) their descendants, (5) the father, (6) the brothers, (7) their descendants, (8) the sisters, (9) their descendants, (10) the grandfather, (11) the brothers of the father, (12) their descendants, (13) the sisters of the father, (14) their descendants, etc.

After presenting the halakhot of succession, the Torah concludes by stating that the order of hereditary succession is "*ḥukat mishpat*" (a statute of judgment). The description of *hilkhot yerusha* as a "*ḥok*" implies, among other things, that these halakhot, despite dealing with monetary matters, are immutable.[6] Generally speaking, halakha allows individuals to determine their own monetary relationships, provided that the arrangement complies with a proper form, i.e., *kinyan,* and is not violative of any prohibitions such as

---

4 Dayan I. Grunfeld, *The Jewish Law of Inheritance*, New York: Feldheim, 1987, 53–55.

5 *Bava Batra* 88b.

6 *Mishneh Torah, Hilkhot Ishut* 12:9; *Hilkhot Naḥalot* 6:1; Ḥazan, *Naḥala le-Yisrael*, 49.

theft or the interdict against taking *ribbit*.[7] One of the exceptions to this rule is *hilkhot yerusha*. As Rambam states,[8]

> A man cannot cause his estate to descend to someone who is not potentially his heir; nor can he deprive the heir of the inheritance even though this is a money matter. For it says... 'And it shall be for the children of Israel a statute of judgment' ... that means, this statute cannot be altered and no stipulation can affect it.

In other words, stipulating that assets are to be distributed to a non-halakhic heir falls in the category of "*matneh al ma shekatuv ba-Torah, tnai batel*,"[9] and therefore for a testator to state "Reuven shall

---

7 *Kiddushin* 19b; *Shulḥan Arukh, Even ha-Ezer* 38:5; *Shulḥan Arukh, ḤM* 291:17; *Beit Yosef, ḤM* 305:4; *Shulḥan Arukh, ḤM* 305:4; *Rema, ḤM* 344:1.

8 *Mishneh Torah, Hilkhot Naḥalot* 6:1. See *Teshuvot Maharit, ḤM* 6; *Teshuvot R. Akiva Eiger, Mahadurah Tinyanah*, 83.

9 *Kiddushin*, supra n. 7. Whereas Rambam argues that an estate distribution at variance with halakha is a violation of "*ḥukat mishpat*," others contend that the execution of such planning presumes that the assets of the testator during his lifetime can be designated as his *yerusha*. But, in fact, during the testator's lifetime these are his assets. It is only upon the testator's demise that halakha determines that these assets are now designated as "*yerusha*," are no longer in the testator's possession, and automatically the Torah heirs receive their rightful distribution. See *Ḥiddushei ha-Rashba, Bava Batra* 113b. Alternatively, since the *yerusha* belongs to the heir only upon the testator's demise, during his lifetime he cannot execute an arrangement at variance with the Torah order of *yerusha*. See Ran on Rif, *Ketubbot* 41a.
Though *Shulḥan Arukh, ḤM* 282:1 states that diverting a share of the estate to a non-Torah heir is characterized as a transaction that merely does "not find pleasure" in the eyes of scholars, decisors construe such conduct as a formal issur. See *Teshuvot Maharam me-Padua* 60; *Teshuvot Maharashdam, ḤM* 336; *Teshuvot Ranah* 1:118.
Clearly, the *issur* of disinheritance devolves upon the testator.
Should a *beit din* affirm such a distribution, the *beit din* is not engaging in any *issur*. See *Teshuvot ha-Rema* 78; File no. 592010/1, Tel Aviv Regional Rabbinical Court, Ploni v. Almoni, June 14, 2010. Cf. infra text accompanying n. 171.

inherit me" regarding a non-Torah heir is null and void[10] and one is prohibited to execute such an arrangement.[11] Moreover, pursuant to many *posekim*, the Torah heirs are entitled to the entire estate and there is an *issur* to transfer any portion from the Torah heirs to non-Torah heirs.[12] Moreover, should a non-Torah heir retain the assets, such conduct is viewed as stealing from a rightful heir.[13] Consequently, a civil *will* that provides an estate distribution to a non-Torah heir ought to be null and void.

Barring any halakhically sanctioned arrangement that allows an estate to be distributed to non-Torah heirs,[14] it should be no surprise to find that many *posekim*, both past and present, have invalidated a civil *will* due to the rule that 'there is no gift after death' and

---

10 *Teshuvot ha-Radvaz* 1:543; *Teshuvot Mishpetei Shmuel* 103; *Teshuvot Maharashdam Even ha-Ezer (EH)* 110, *ḤM* 304; File No. 8820-41-1, Supreme Rabbinical Court, Ploni v. Attorney General, November 23, 2009.

11 Talmud Yerushalmi *Bava Batra* 8:6; Rashbam, *Bava Batra* 133b, s.v. *ma*; *Piskei ha-Rosh* 8:37; *Teshuvot ha-Rosh* 85:3; *Teshuvot Maharam me-Padua*, supra n. 9; *Maharashdam*, supra n. 9; *Teshuvot ha-Rema* 78; *Ranah*, supra n. 9; *Teshuvot Ḥatam Sofer, ḤM* 151; *Teshuvot Maharasham*, 7: 12; *Teshuvot Maharit* 1:29; *Teshuvot Zera Emet*, 2:110; *Mishpat ha-Yerusha*, Livorno, 1878, 25a. Cf. others who argue that it is improper rather than a prohibition to engage in disinheritance. See *Teshuvot Tashbetz* 2:177; *Shulḥan Arukh ḤM* 282:1; *Sema*, ad. locum. 2; *Teshuvot Divrei Malkiel* 1:103; *Agudat Eizov ḤM* 16.

For further discussion, see infra text accompanying note 80.

12 Rosh, supra n. 11; *Teshuvot Maharashdam*, supra n. 11; *Teshuvot Maharit* 1:29, 2, ḤM 5; *Teshuvot Mahari Ibn Lev* 3:31; Teshuvot *Ḥatam Sofer,* supra n. 11; *Teshuvot Yashiv Moshe* 2:236.

13 *Teshuvot ha-Rivash* 160; *Teshuvot Ḥatam Sofer, ḤM* 142; *Teshuvot Mahari ha-Levi* (Ettinger) 2:86; *Teshuvot Sha'ar Asher* 2, *ḤM* 29; *Teshuvot Maharsham* 2:15; *Dinei Mamanot* 3:208.

14 For a discussion of various halakha-sanctioned techniques that allow one to transfer one's possessions to non-Torah heirs, see Judah Dick, "Halacha and the Conventional Last Will & Testament," 3 *Journal of Halacha & Contemporary Society* 5 (1982); Feivel Cohen, *Kuntres me-Dor le-Dor*; Mattisyahu Schwartz, *Mishpat Hatzava'ah*, vols. 1-2; this writer's "Drafting a Halakhic Will," *Ḥakirah,* vol. 10, p. 73 (2010), which can be accessed at www.Hakirah.org.

For the validity of a revocable living trust, see this writer's *Rabbinic Authority: The Vision & the Reality*, volume 1 (*Urim*: 2013).

because compliance with a secular *will* would lead to "*avurei aḥsanta*" (disinheriting a Torah heir).[15]

2. The Propriety of a Civil *Will*

A. Rabbi Schwadron's and Rabbi Feinstein's Views

In reply to the contention that transfer of an estate based upon a secular *will* flies in the face of the recognized rule "there is no *kinyan* after death," Rabbi Moshe Feinstein states the following:[16]

> Although we are dealing here with a gift to be made after the death of the donor, and there is no such thing as a *kinyan* after death, as the object no longer belongs to the donor and such a gift is therefore not valid in Jewish law, nevertheless according to the law of the land a person can legally transfer with effect after death money or any other object that at that time no longer belongs to him or her ... but in essence it is clear, according to my humble opinion, that a testament of this kind, the disposition of which will certainly be put into effect by the authorities of the country, does not need a *kinyan* as one could not imagine a more effective *gemirat da'at* than this. Hence, since a *kinyan* is not necessary, the legal heirs can uphold their right also against those persons who are the proper heirs by Torah law, although there is no such thing in Jewish law as a gift after the death of the donor.

There are two ingredients required in transferring ownership to another individual: effectuating a *kinyan* and *gemirat da'at* (i.e., a concrete articulation of the parties' firm resolve to undertake this obligation). In other words, one requires a physical act such as the

15 Rosh, supra n. 11; *Maharashdam*, supra notes 10-11; *Teshuvot Maharit* 1:29, 2, *ḤM* 5; *Mahari ibn Lev*, supra n. 12; *Teshuvot Maharam Galante* 13; *Teshuvot Maharshach* 146; *Teshuvot Leḥem Rav* 219; *Teshuvot Ḥatam Sofer, ḤM* 151; *Teshuvot Lev Aryeh* 2:57; *Teshuvot Heishiv Moshe, ḤM* 90, 164; *Teshuvot Minḥat Yitzḥak* 2:95, 6:164-165; Cohen supra n. 14 at 3–7; Zalman N. Goldberg, 5 *ha-Yashar ve-ha-Tov* 3, 7 (5768).

16 *Iggerot Moshe, EH* 104. The translation is culled (with certain modifications) from Grunfeld, supra n. 4, at 72.

execution of a *shtar* that memorializes the assets that will be transferred and the intention of the parties to transfer the assets.[17]

In the absence of a *kinyan*, can one argue that the intention of the parties suffices to transfer an asset? In reply to this question, Rabbi Shlomo Kluger states:[18]

> The essence of the *kinyan* of the Torah is to resolve in one's heart to transfer (an asset), as we learnt that, in consideration of the pleasure of our children marrying each other, each father undertakes certain prenuptial obligations. Therefore this proves that in an instance where we can discern that there is was a firm resolution, one does not require an act of *kinyan*. And in cases where we require a *kinyan* it is because we do not know what he resolved in his heart and possibly he did not resolve to transfer (an asset) ... And every act of *kinyan* is only in order to ascertain what he resolved in his heart. However, if we know what he resolved and it is being transferred with a full heart (clear intention) we do not mandate an act.

Implicitly, following in R. Shlomo Kluger's footsteps, Rabbi Feinstein argues[19] "that a testament of this kind, the disposition of which will certainly be put into effect by the authorities of the country, does not need a *kinyan* as one could not imagine a more effective *gemirat da'at* than this."

To put it differently, the execution by a testator of a civil *will* that will be recognized by the civil court corroborates for us that he understood that his instructions will be followed and therefore he firmly resolved in his heart to transfer his estate and consequently a *kinyan* is not required.

---

17 Whether the *kinyan* is a vehicle for ascertaining that *gemirat da'at* exists or whether the performance of a *kinyan* is separate from the requirement of *gemirat da'at* is subject to debate.

18 *Teshuvot Tuv Ta'am ve-Da'at, Mahadura Kamma*, 269. For others who subscribe to this view, see *Ḥiddushei R. Shimon Yehuda ha-Cohen Shkop, Kinyanim* 11; Yeḥezkel Abramsky, *Monetary Laws (A Definition of Types)* (Hebrew), 9–13.
The citation of these authorities should in no manner be construed as an endorsement of a civil *will*.

19 See supra text accompanying n. 16.

Addressing a *will* prepared by Rabbi Me'sag that divided up his estate amongst his sons, daughters and grandchildren, relying upon Rabbi Doniel Tirnai,[20] Rabbi Shalom Schwadron states,[21]

> The requirement of a *kinyan* is to attest to his will and thought that he resolved in his heart to give with his soul. And wherever there is a presumptive *umdana* (sound inference / common sense) that demonstrates that he gave with his heart, a *kinyan* is superfluous.

To claim, in accordance with Rabbis Schwadron and Feinstein, that one can transfer an asset based on *gemirat da'at* without a *kinyan* is an argumentation based upon a well-trodden *mesorah* that is discussed in various places in the Talmud[22] and applied *halakhah le-ma'aseh* (practical halakha) in varying contexts by many authori-

---

20 *Ikrei ha-Da'at*, infra, n. 31.

21 *Teshuvot Maharsham* 2:224(2). See also *Maharsham* supra n. 11. In effect, his view is identical to R. Feinstein's position. See Yosef Goldberg, 1 *Shurat HaDin* 319, 323 (5754). See also, *Piskei Din Yerushalayim* 10:346, 350.
According to Rabbi Aharon Lichtenstein, Rav Joseph Soloveitchik prepared a civil *will*. It is Rabbi Dr. Dov Frimer's understanding, who was the drafter of Rav Soloveitchik's testamentary disposition, that Rav Soloveitchik endorsed Rabbi Feinstein's view that *gemirat da'at* could be obtained based upon the testator's awareness that the provisions of a secular *will* would be enforced by civil law and therefore no *kinyan* was necessary.
Cf. *Teshuvot Maharsham* 7:12.

22 1) *Ketubbot* 102a-b: "These are the matters that can be acquired via the medium of speech." See *Tosafot Ketubbot* 102b, s.v. *a'libai*. (2) *Bava Batra* 142b, acquiring for the benefit of an embryo: see *SA*, *ḤM* 210:1. (3) *Beḥorot* 18b, transfer ownership of a firstborn animal to a kohen. See *Teshuvot R. Akiver Eiger, Mahadura Kamma* 37 in the name of *Tosafot Beḥorot* 18b, s.v. *ak'neuyei*. (4) *Bava Batra* 123b, The transfer of priestly gifts to *makire kehunah* (acquaintances of the kohanim). See Rashash, ad. locum. (5) *Bava Kamma* 102b, someone dedicates his assets to the *beit hamikdash*. See *Sefer ha-Terumoth, Sha'ar* 1, 1:5 in the name of Ra'avad. (6) *Bava Metzi'a* 74a, *situmta*. Rashash, ibid.; *Mishpat Shalom* 194:2. See Ron Kleinman, "The Foundations of Transference: Intent & the Act of Acquisition" (Hebrew) 3 *Mishpetei Eretz* 91, 98–102 (5770).

ties, including the validation of a civil *will* by Israeli *dayanim* R. Shlomo Sha'anan, R. Domb and R. Ben Shimon.[23]

Nevertheless, many *posekim* demur and argue that a *ma'aseh kinyan*, act of transfer, is mandated. For example, Beit Yosef and Rema, who allow parties to execute an agreement without the prescribed *kinyan*, stipulate that only a recognized *kinyan* may be utilized. For example, both Beit Yosef and Rema will permit *metaltilin* (chattel) to be transferred with *kinyan kesef* (an exchange of money) though generally *metaltilin* cannot be transferred with *kesef*. [24] In other words, minimally, parties must implement a recognized *kinyan* even if it is not the one prescribed for the particular object. And other *posekim*, among them Drisha and Shakh, take issue with this position and argue that transfer of ownership requires the prescribed *kinyan* for the particular matter whether it is real estate or chattel.[25] The consensus is that a recognized *kinyan* must be used.

Secondly, should a non-Jew adopt halakha for a particular transaction and purchase with a bona fide *kinyan* from a Jew, such

---

23 *Aliyot de-Rabbeinu Yonah, BB* 84b; *Rashbam, BB* 123b s.v. *hokhi garsinan* [as understood by Rashash ad. locum; R. Engel, *Tziyunim la-Torah, Kelal* 39]; *Tosafot, BB* ad. locum, s.v. *hokha* [as understood by *Kovetz Shiurim BB* 374]; *Teshuvot Maharashdam ḤM* 380; *Teshuvot Maharshach* 1:46, 2: 46, 113; *Teshuvot Maharshal* 36, 135; R. Shlomo Kluger, *Teshuvot Tuv Ta'am Veda'ath, Mahadurah Kamma*, 265, 269, *Mahadurah* 3, 2:146; *Teshuvot Ḥatam Sofer Yoreh De'ah (YD)* 314 (as understood by *Teshuvot Shem Aryeh YD* 48 and *Teshuvot Dvar Yehoshua* 4: 48:1 Cf. *Teshuvot Dvar Avraham* 1:1's understanding of *Ḥatam Sofer* and *Teshuvot Ḥatam Sofer YD* 314 and *ḤM* 12; *Rashash, Bekhorot* 18b; *Teshuvot Pnei Mavin* 161; *Teshuvot R. Akiva Eiger Pesakim* 37; *Teshuvot Divrei Ḥakhamim*, vol. 1, *ḤM* 32; *Pnei Yehoshua Gittin* 77b; *Teshuvot Ḥemdat Shlomo YD* 33; *Avnei Miluim* 30:3 [in the name of Ran]; *Teshuvot Ohel Moshe* 2:138.
See Ron Kleinman, *Kinyan Situmta* (Hebrew) 24 *Meḥkarei Mishpat* 243, 257–259 (5768).
For validating a civil *will*, see *Piskei Din Rabbanayim* (PDR) 20: 297, 306-307, 21:28, 37-38; 22:133, 167, 179.

24 *Beit Yosef, Tur ḤM* 195; *Rema, ḤM* 195:5. See also, *Baḥ Tur ḤM* 198; *Ketzot ha-Ḥoshen* 198:3.

25 *Derisha, ḤM* 201:3; *Shakh, ḤM* 198:10.

an agreement would be valid.[26] Again it is a valid agreement because a *ma'aseh kinyan* was employed.

Moreover, let's assume that our ḥakhamim (sages) nullified the recognized *ma'asei kinyan* (acts of asset transfer). Can parties then stipulate between themselves that the *kinyanim* such as an exchange of money or executing a *shtar* are to be effective? The reply is that such private stipulation will be invalid.[27] Finally, for many *posekim*, *kinyan situmta* (a commercial practice of transferring ownership) is based on either *minhag* (custom)[28] or *kinyan ḥalifin* (barter),[29] or grounded in *kinyan meshikha/ḥazaka* (the act of pulling or possession of real estate for three years).[30] To put it differently, there is a requirement of some 'objective' act or minimally a collective understanding (*minhag*) that creates the *gemirat da'at* of the parties.

In short, a civil *will* is invalid since a *ma'aseh kinyan* is required to transfer an asset and there is no *kinyan* after death. As such, the view of Rabbis Schwadron and Feinstein is problematic.

B. Maharam of Rothenburg's View: A Gift in Contemplation of Death

Alternatively, some authorities[31] have recognized a secular *will* by invoking the position of Rabbi Meir of Rothenberg who states,[32]

---

26 *Ketzot ha-Ḥoshen* 198:3.

27 *Rema, ḤM* 198:5; *Shakh*, ad. locum, 10.

28 *Teshuvot haRashba* 2:268, 3:17, 4:125; *Teshuvot Ḥatam Sofer, YD* 314.

29 *Teshuvot Dvar Avraham* 1:1, *Anaf* 1.

30 *Piskei Halakhoth im Be'ur Yad Dovid, Ishut* 1, 228-229.

31 See decisors cited in *Ikrei ha-Da'at, Oraḥ Ḥayyim* (*OḤ*) 21; *Teshuvot Kapei Aharon*, 12; R. Shlomo Warmash, Rabbi in Fulda, Germany in 5639 cited in 58 *Moriah* 17 (5741).

32 *Mordekhai, Bava Metzia* 254, 602 and *Mordekhai Bava Batra* 591. For our understanding of *Maharam*, see *Teshuvot ha-Rema* 95; *Teshuvot Maharsham* 2:224 (1) in the name of Rabbi Meaglunza.
To avoid a challenge to his verbal instructions, the testator would have to memorialize his wishes into writing. See *Ikrei ha-Da'at*, supra n. 31, at p. 71a.
For the antecedents of this testamentary disposition, see *Gittin* 66a; *Bava Batra* 151b.

Even a healthy person who says "give to this person that and that if I will die" and this is to be designated a mitzva due to death and he (the heir) has acquired it.

In effect, despite the absence of a *kinyan* similar to a civil *will*, the assets have been transferred with the verbal instructions of the testator provided that he mentions the day of death. To put it differently, whereas a *matnas shekhiv mera* is a bequest communicated by a person on his deathbed, here this is a gift of a healthy person prepared in contemplation of death (*mitzva maḥmas mita*). In effect, by the testator's instructions there is an *umdana demukach* (sound inference/common sense) that he is resolute in giving this gift and therefore no *kinyan* is required.[33] Hence, a non-Torah heir may be a beneficiary of an estate, without the gifting being a violation of halakhic order of *yerusha*. Though many decisors reject his approach, it may be considered within the context of the doctrine of *muḥzak* and the *kim li* argument, as we shall demonstrate.

When a dispute is submitted to a beit din, the court has to determine which claimant retains certain assets. In halakha, there is a concept whereby one of the claimants is considered as the one who is in possession of the disputed item [the *muḥzak*], while the other claimant wants to "extract" this item and transfer it to himself. In case of a disputed inheritance, the beit din has to ascertain, first of all, who the *muḥzak* is. Which of the two parties—the Torah heirs or the non-Torah heirs, should be considered as "owning" the inheritance that the other is trying to take away? Seemingly, one could argue that, inasmuch as the Torah grants the inheritance to certain people, ipso facto they are considered as *muḥzakim*. But, as we explained, in accordance with Maharam's view, the gifting pro-

---

33 *Ikrei ha-Da'at*, supra n. 31. And many have adopted his approach. See *Kapei Aharon*, infra n. 42; Mahara Sasson in the name of Rif, Rambam, Ran, Rabbeinu Tam. See *Teshuvot Mahara Sasson* 151.
In fact some have rejected his approach. See *Teshuvot Maharam me-Padua* 53; *Darkhei Moshe, Tur ḤM* 257:4; *Rema ḤM* 257:7; *Teshuvot Har Hamor* 40; *Teshuvot Maharashdam YD* 203; *Mishpat ha-Yerusha*, supra n. 11, at 4–6. However, others have endorsed it. See sources cited by *Ikrei ha-Da'at*, supra n. 31. Cf. *Mishpat ha-Yerusha*, supra n. 11, at 13a who claims it is a minority view.

cess is not in violation of the Torah order of succession. So therefore, the two heirs are on the same footing and the Torah heir has no title, by dint of the Torah order of *yerusha* which preempts a non-Torah heir's right to the estate. Consequently, since there is a *safek* (doubt) whether we follow Maharam's posture or not, if the non-Torah heir is *muḥzak*, he will prevail.[34]

The *safek* whether we follow the Maharam's posture or not is equally significant with regard to invoking the *kim li* argument. Pursuant to halakhic court procedure, a party in a dispute can argue as follows: I want the court to rule in my favor, which is based on the position of Rabbi ______, who affirms my claim. Under certain prescribed conditions, we will accept his position even if Rabbi ______'s view is in the minority and the majority rule differently.[35] Such an argument can be invoked either by a *muḥzak* or by beit din. Thus, if the non-Torah heir is considered the *muḥzak*, he can request the court to uphold the secular *will* on the basis of a *kim li* argument that "I want the court to rule in accordance with Maharam," who validates a secular *will*.[36]

Since Maharam may have issued contradictory rulings regarding the effectiveness of this testator's directive and may have changed his mind regarding its effectiveness as a vehicle to transfer an estate, Maharam's view may possibly not serve as grounds to recognize a civil *will* either on the basis of rule of *muḥzak* or by advancing the *kim li* argument.[37]

---

34 *Teshuvot Maharsham* 2:224; PDR 19:1, 4 (Rabbis Elyashiv, Zolti and Hadas).

35 Ḥanina Ben Menaḥem, "Towards a Jurisprudential Analysis of the Kim-li Argument" (Hebrew) 6-7 *Shenaton ha-Mishpat ha-Ivri* 45 (1979-1980).

36 For those who contend that one can advance such a plea when the non-Torah heir is *muḥzak*, see *Netivot ha-Mishpat ḤM* 25, *Dinei Tefisah* 23 and other *aḥaronim* cited in *Teshuvot Yabia Omer*, 7, *ḤM* 2:6.
Others argue that even if the non-Torah heir seizes the assets, one may advance a claim of "*kim li*" on his behalf. See *Pitḥei Teshuva, ḤM* 25 (end); *Yabia Omer*, ibid. (end).

37 For the self-contradictory rulings that limit the Maharam's *psak* to instances of the testator dying, see *Mordekhai, BB* 592; *Teshuvot Maharam of Rothenburg*, Berlin ed., 46.

C. The Validity of *Minhag* in Estate Planning

Another approach focuses upon whether the existence of a *minhag*, to prepare and execute *wills* in accordance with secular law, ought to be recognized or not. To have binding force, a *minhag*, which is unaccompanied by rabbinic or communal sanction in the form of a legislative enactment,[38] must be clear and widespread amongst the majority of the members of the community, and have been practiced at least three times.[39] There are some eighteenth- and nineteenth-century authorities (and some of them despite various reservations) who have recognized the use of a civil *will* that employs the language of "giving" rather than "bequeathing" or "inheriting,"[40] if this is common practice (even among gentiles[41]) in the community wherein the testator and heirs reside.[42]And even if the Torah

For attempts to reconcile these rulings, see *Maharam me-Padua* supra n. 33; *Teshuvot Maharik* 94; *Teshuvot Maharil* 75; *Teshuvot ha-Rema* 95; *Teshuvot Mahara Sasson* 151.

38 For the independent status of a custom involving a monetary matter, see *Shulḥan Arukh, ḤM* 176:10, 218:19, 229:2, 230:10, 232:6; 330:5, 331:12; *Rema, ḤM* 72:5; *Teshuvot ha-Rema* 19-20; *Teshuvot Mahara Ashkenazi* 33.

39 *Teshuvot ha-Rosh* 79:4; *Teshuvot ha-Rivash* 475; *Teshuvot Terumat ha-Deshen* 342; *Rema, ḤM* 331:1.

40 *Ikrei haDa'at*, supra n. 31, at 76b. Cf. *Teshuvot Radakh* 26:3 who argues that *minhag hamakom* is determinative. Though Radakh's ruling addresses the case of *shekhiv mera*, R. Shlomo Sha'anan applies it to a testator who prepares a civil *will*. See Sha'anan, *Shurat ha-Din*, infra n. 55, at 319, 329.

41 *Ra'avad, Mishneh Torah, Malveh ve-Loveh* 25:10; *Tur ḤM* 132; *Teshuvot Maharashdam YD* 221; *Teshuvot Mahari ibn Lev* 2:23; *Teshuvot Bnei Avraham, ḤM* 13; *Teshuvot Makor Barukh* 55; *Teshuvot Ḥikekei Lev*, vol. 2, 30, vol. 3, *ḤM* 2:30; *Teshuvot Mahara Ashkenazi*, supra n. 38; *Teshuvot Kapei Aharon* 13; *Mishpat ha-Tzava'ah*, supra n. 14 at 423.

42 See *Ikrei ha-Da'at*, supra n. 31, at 72a-b, 73b, 76b, 77a and citations cited in *Teshuvot Kapei Aharon ḤM* 12-13; *Teshuvot ha-Ramah* (Abulafia) in *Ohr Tzadikim* (Salonika, 1799), 299; *Teshuvot Ḥedvat Ya'akov; Teshuvot Torat Ḥayyim* 2:13; *Teshuvot Ta'alumot Lev* 1:7; *Radakh,* supra n. 40; *Teshuvot Maharash* 2:13; *Teshuvot Mishpetei Tzedek* 2:52; *Tevuot Shemesh, ḤM* 33-34; *Mishpat ha-Yerusha*, supra n. 11, at 24; *Teshuvot ve-Zot le-Yehuda* (Mesalton) ḤM 9; *Teshuvot Betzeil ha-Ḥochma*, vol. 2, *ḤM* 6; *Teshuvot Mahara Ashkenazi*, supra n. 38.

heirs seize the assets from the non-Torah heirs, the assets would have to be returned to the designated heir(s).[43] As R. Yeḥiel Epstein rules, in places where the government is insistent that all legal documents be drafted in accordance with civil law, we must comply with their laws. *A fortiori*, he concludes if the local custom has validated these documents a civil *will* is equally to be recognized.[44]

Alternatively, others conclude that to impart credence to such a *minhag* it must have been approved by Torah scholars (i.e., *minhag vatikin*) in order for the civil *will* to be validated.[45] Adopting this approach (given as we will show in our presentation that there are some *posekim* who validate a civil *will*), the existence of a *minhag* to distribute assets in accordance with a civil *will* would be halakhically justified.

Even though there are *posekim* who reject the validity of a civil *will* based upon *minhag*,[46] nevertheless neither a *kim li* plea[47] by the

---

Clearly, there were instances where authorities sanctioned the use of a civil *will* based upon *minhag* or *dina demalkhuta dina* because the civil government would recognize only *wills* that were prepared in accordance with civil law. See *Teshuvot ha-Radvaz* 1:67; *Teshuvot Mahari* (R. Ya'akov) *ha-Levi* 75; *Teshuvot Rabach, ḤM* 8; *Teshuvot Aderet Eliyahu Riki* 23. As such these *teshuvot* fail to serve as grounds to validate a secular *will* today where the civil law allows individuals to execute estate-planning arrangements based upon halakha provided that the *will* is drafted in a legally acceptable fashion.

43 *Kapei Aharon*, 13 (159a).

44 *Arukh ha-Shulḥan, ḤM* 68:6. And R. Tzvi Yehuda ben Ya'akov concludes that therefore a secular *will* is valid. See *Teshuvot Mishpatekha Leya'akov* 4:7. In light of R. Epstein's ruling in *Arukh ha-Shulḥan ḤM* 369:17 this conclusion seems problematic.

45 *Teshuvot Mishpat Tzedek* 2:52 (end); *Mishpat ha-Yerusha*, supra n. 11, at 25a; *Teshuvot Torat Ḥayyim* 2:19; *Ikrei Hadat*, supra n. 31, at 75a; *Teshuvot Ramatz* 1:92; *Teshuvot Divrei Rivot* 78. For the definition of *minhag vatikin* as a practice approved by *posekim*, see *Ohr Zarua, Bava Metzia* 280.

46 *Teshuvot ha-Rashba* 6:254 cited by *Beit Yosef ḤM* 26; *Teshuvot ha-Radvaz* 1:545; *Maharashdam*, supra n. 10; *Teshuvot Maharik, Shoresh* 8; *Teshuvot Mishpetei Shmuel* (*Kal'i*) 53; *Teshuvot Tzit Eliezer* 20:71.

47 See supra text accompanying note 35.
In fact, pursuant to Ḥida, in cases where there is a clear *minhag* that distributes estate assets to a daughter based on civil law, one can invoke the

Torah heirs, nor a beit din will trump the *minhag*.[48] Since we have a dispute whether *minhag* can justify affirming a *will*, we have a *safek* what the halakha is. In cases where there is doubt in a monetary matter we cannot extract money from the defendant. Consequently, a defendant [in this case the non-Torah heir] can argue that there are authorities who agree that the *minhag* ought to be determinative and therefore the *will* should be validated. Others would contend that the Torah heirs, by dint of the Torah law of *yerusha,* are the muḥzak(im) and therefore retain the estate. As the Talmud instructs us, a Torah heir by virtue of *hilkhot yerusha* does not need to plead his right.[49] Consequently, the halakhic doubt concerning whether *minhag* ought to be determinative is irrelevant. The bottom line is that the Torah heir has possession of the estate.

One suggested justification for legitimating secular *wills* based on *minhag* dates back to a *teshuva* penned by Rivash. The *teshuva* deals with a fourteenth-century Jewish community composed entirely of *mumarim* (apostates) residing on the island of Majorca who decided to replace halakha with the governing civil law. Rivash ruled that their decision was to be understood as the communal practice and therefore binding.[50] Lest one assume that this ruling is limited to Jewish apostates,[51] Rivash clearly states that his decision is applicable to any Jewish enclave that decides to have their matters resolved according to secular law. And, in fact, Rema and R. Aharon ben Azriel understood Rivash in such a fashion.[52] Whereas numerous authorities have imparted validity to individuals who decide to resolve their matters in front of a beit din in accordance with secular law,[53] Rivash extends the applicability of civil law to a

---

kim li argument of those who endorse the validity of this *minhag*, such as Rivash and Maharshach. See *Tuv Ayin* 17 and see infra text.

48 *Ikrei haDa'at*, supra n. 31 at 31a, 38b; *Kapei Aharon* 12; *Kuntres Yismach Moshe* 12; *Teshuvot Baei Hayei*, *ḤM* 1, 73; Goldberg, supra n. 21 at 322; *Teshuvot Yaskil Avdi* 6, *ḤM* 18.

49 *BB* 41a.

50 *Teshuvot ha-Rivash* 52.

51 *Ḥatam Sofer*, supra n. 11; *Mishpat ha-Yerusha*, supra n. 11.

52 *Rema, ḤM* 248:1; *Teshuvot Kapei Aharon* 14.

53 *Giddulei Terumah, Sefer ha-Terumoth, Sha'ar* 62, *Ḥelek* 1; *Sma ḤM* 26:11, 61:14; *Netivot ha-Mishpat* 26:11; *Teshuvot Divrei Ḥayyim, ḤM*, 2:30; *Divrei*

communal adoption of civil law. Subsequently, Rivash's position has been endorsed by Rema and in contemporary times has been invoked as one of the grounds for affirming a secular *will* in Israel.[54] In fact, the validity of secular *wills* executed by some Israeli battei din stems not only from the acceptance of the view of Rabbis Schwadron and Feinstein, that there is no need for a kinyan regarding a testamentary disposition, but equally from the authority of *minhag*, a practice of using a secular *will*, which exists both in Israel and in other parts of the world.[55]

That said, should a Jewish community adopt the practice to arrange their estate planning in pursuance of secular law, a position that has met with trenchant criticism,[56] such *shtarot* (documents) of gentiles would be binding.[57]

And as Ḥazon Ish notes,[58] *dina demalkhuta dina* is determinative of the expectations of the parties. Hence, if the parties' expectation

---

Gaonim 25:3, 111:3; *Bnei Shmuel, ḤM* 26; *Maharitz ha-Ḥadashot*, no. 22; *Teshuvot Yosef Ometz*, no. 4; *Birkei Yosef* 26:3,8; *Tzedakah u-Mishpat, OḤ*, no. 7; *Leket Shikḥa* found in *Karnei Re'em*, Section 4 *Dayanim*; File No. 1-24-053917464, Haifa Regional Rabbinical Court; R. Ezra Batsri *Dine Mamanot*, vol. 3, 197; Z.N. Goldberg, *Lev ha-Mishpat*, volume 1, 286; Asher Weiss, 6 *Darkhei Horo'ah* 111 (2007); PDR 18:314, 324; *Teshuvot Minḥat Yizḥak* 9:112.

54 *Rema, ḤM* 248:1; *Piskei Din Yerushalayim*, supra. n. 21, at 347. To resolve the seemingly self-contradictory ruling of Rema, ibid. with *Rema, ḤM* 369:11, see *Sma, ḤM* 369:20.

55 *Piskei Din Yerushalayim*, supra n. 21; H. Shlomo Sha'anan, "A Will in Halakha," (Hebrew) 13 *Teḥumin* 317, 324-325 (5751); A Will that was Drafted Improperly, (Hebrew) 1 *Shurat ha-Din* 319 (5754) and in his decisions PDR 20: 297, 308, 21:28, 37-38. Cf. *Piskei Din Yerushalayim* 12: 329, 331 and *Teshuvot Mishpat Shlomo* 3:24.

56 *Teshuvot Tashbetz* 1:61, *Maharit,* supra n. 8; *Teshuvot Mishpat Tzedek* 2:68; *Ḥatam Sofer*, supra n.11, *Teshuvot Maharsham, EH* 131; and *Dinei Mamonot* 3, page 197.
Others have contended that the Rivash's position was not issued as an actual *psak*. See *Ketzot ha-Ḥoshen* 248:3 in the name of *Tashbetz* and *Maharit, Yosef Ometz* supra n. 53.

57 *Mahara Ashkenazi* supra n. 38; *Teshuvot Tevuot Shemesh,* supra n. 42.

58 *HM Likkutim* 16:1, 5, 9. Our citation of *Ḥazon Ish* is not to be misconstrued as implying that he validated the execution of a civil *will*.

is to arrange for a testamentary disposition in accordance with civil law, namely the *minhag*, the provisions of the secular *will* would be binding. Consequently, if the testator commissioned an attorney to prepare and draft a *will* in accordance with civil law, the expectation is to have his estate distributed in accordance with such law.[59]

Implicit in the above approach is the notion advanced by Rabbi Doniel Tirani of nineteenth-century Italy and others that such documents will be effective as a *kinyan situmta* (a transfer recognized by commercial practice).[60] To put it differently, just as authorities recognize a modern-day contract as a *kinyan situmta*,[61] halakha equally imparts validity to a civil *will* as another example of a *kinyan situmta*.

At first glance, invoking *kinyan situmta* in our situation poses various problems. Firstly, Rabbi Zalman N. Goldberg argues that *minhag*, which is reflective of civil law, is not binding. Since obedience to the law entails an element of coercion and *minhag* is predicated upon voluntary compliance, a *minhag* grounded in law is a self-contradiction and therefore is unenforceable.[62] As such, since the text of a civil *will* is drafted and executed according to the norms of secular law, we would deny its validity. Secondly, accord-

---

59 See infra text accompanying note 132.

60 *Ikrei Hadat*, supra n.31, at 70a, 73b; *Teshuvot Maharsham* 2:224 (30); *Erekh Shai*, *ḤM* 235.

61 *Maharashdam*, supra n. 23; *Teshuvot Maharsham* 3:8; *Teshuvot Zemech Zedek* (Lubavitch) YD 233; *Kesef ha-Kodshin, ḤM* 201:1; *Teshuvot Maharshag* 3:113; *Teshuvot Maharsham* 5:45; PDR 3:363, 4:193, 275; 6:202, 14:43.
Implicit in this approach, according to certain *posekim*, is that secular law can nullify an individual's ownership of property while simultaneously the execution of the *kinyan* that is utilized in commercial practice serves to transfer this property to another individual. See *Pitḥei Ḥoshen, Kinyanim*, 219, note 9 (end).

62 PDR 14: 334 (R. Z.N. Goldberg's opinion); R. Goldberg, 2 h*a-Yashar ve-ha-Tov* 9 (2006). Subsequent to the issuance of his *psak din* and authoring the article, R. Goldberg has emphasized that his position regarding the halakhic ineffectiveness of *minhag* is limited to matters dealing with commercial modes of undertaking obligations and transferring of assets. See R. Kleinman, "Civil Law in the Nation: Minhag ha-Medina," (Hebrew), 32 *Teḥumin* 261, 269-271 (5773).

ing to some authorities, notably the Baḥ, one cannot transfer *karka* (real estate) via a *kinyan situmta*.[63] And pursuant to other opinions, one cannot transfer assets that are not yet in the testator's possession (*davar she-lo ba la-olam*) at the time the testamentary disposition was prepared and signed.[64] Should we subscribe to these positions, a testator would be unable to earmark real estate for inheritance purposes and/or authorize a future estate distribution of assets that were not in his possession at the time of the drafting of the will.

Yet, there are numerous authorities who will recognize a *kinyan situmta* that is reflective of a *minhag* that is based upon civil law,[65] which entails the transfer of real estate that is in existence[66] as well as assets that are not yet in existence.[67] Generally speaking, assets cannot be transferred if not yet in existence at the time the disposition is prepared.[68] Nevertheless, should the prevailing law allow a testator to transfer future assets at the time of drafting the testamentary disposition, by dint of commercial custom many decisors would recognize the power of *kinyan situmta* to effectuate a transfer not only of current assets but equally of future assets.[69] Hence, a civil *will* that provides for a future disbursement of real estate and/or the future acquisition of assets would be halakhically binding.

The more vexing issue, however, is that the transfer of assets in accordance with a secular *will* transpires after the testator's demise

---

63 *Baḥ, ḤM* 202:1.

64 *Shulḥan Arukh, ḤM* 60:6, 209:4; *Rema, ḤM* 257:7.

65 *Teshuvot Divrei Yosef* (Iggeret), 21; *Teshuvot Nediv Lev* (David Ḥazan) 12; *Teshuvot Mahari ha-Levi* 2:111; *Iggerot Moshe, ḤM* 1:72,75; *Teshuvot Beit Yisrael* 172; *Pitḥei Ḥoshen, Hilkhot Halva'ah* 2:29.

66 *Teshuvot ha-Rashba* 3:132; *Beit Yosef, ḤM* 201:1; *Shakh ḤM* 201:1; *Sma, ḤM* 201:6; *Ḥiddushei R. Akiva Eiger, ḤM* 201:2; PDR 6:216, 12:292.

67 *Teshuvot ha-Radvaz* 2:278; *Teshuvot Ḥatam Sofer, ḤM* 66; *Teshuvot Aḥiezer* 3:79.

68 *Shulḥan Arukh ḤM* 60:6, 209:4.

69 *Teshuvot ha-Rosh* 13:20; *Mordekhai, Shabbat* 472-473; *Teshuvot Maharshal* 36; *Netivot ha-Mishpat* 201:1; *Teshuvot Maharashdam ḤM* 380; *Divrei Ḥayyim* 2, *ḤM* 26; *Teshuvot Beit Yitzḥak ḤM* 60:1; *Teshuvot Shoeil u-Meishiv, Mahadura Kamma* 2:39; *Teshuvot Mahariz Enzel* 1:37; PDR 3:363, 368-369, 2:193, 198-199.

and a *kinyan situmta* is effective in transferring ownership only during the testator's lifetime. As we noted, there is no *kinyan* after death. And for this very reason, Rabbi Z. N. Goldberg and Rabbi Judah Dick, Esq. rejected the effectiveness of *kinyan situmta* for halakhic estate planning.[70]

Others such as Rabbis Eliyahu Ḥazan, Yehuda Mesalton, Messas and a *psak* attributed to Rabbi Yosef Elyashiv contend that if there is a *minhag* to execute a civil *will*, the distribution will be effective based on *kinyan situmta* without elucidating the grounds for such a conclusion.[71]

The grounds for the effectiveness of a civil *will*, a form of a *kinyan situmta*, can be extrapolated from the positions of Rabbeinu Yonah of Gerondi, Spain and R. Yeshayahu Blau.[72] According to this position, the transfer of the assets from the testator to the heirs is subdivided into two stages.[73] Invoking the view that the rule of *dina demalkhuta dina* (the law of the kingship is the law), secular law divests the testator of the ownership of the assets.[74] Subsequently, based upon *minhag hasoḥrim* (commercial practice), utilizing a *kinyan situmta*, the assets are transferred from the testator to the heir. The execution of a *kinyan situmta* is contingent upon the fact (i.e. a *tenai*, condition) that the testator will pass away and with his demise the beneficiary(ies) will acquire the assets of the estate. In actuality, the *kinyan situmta* which embodies *minhag hasoḥrim* is

---

70 Goldberg, supra n. 62; Dick, supra n.14.

71 *Ta'alumot Lev*, supra n. 42; ve-*Zot le-Yehuda*, supra n. 42; *Teshuvot Shemesh u-Magen* 1, *ḤM* 1; *Ma'ase Beit Din* 1: p. 401 (Rabbi Yissachar Hagar in the name of R. Elyashiv); Moshe Toledano, 5 *Kovetz Darkhei Horo'ah* 280, 291 (5768).

72 *Aliyot de-Rabbeinu Yonah*, *BB* 55a s.v. *vearisa de-parsai*, s.v. *oleh beyadeinu*; *Pitḥei Ḥoshen* 8:, p. 219.

73 For this explanation, see Shmuel Shilo, *Dina Demalkhuta Dina* (Hebrew) Jerusalem, 1975, 324–326 and Sinai Deutsch, "The Validity of a Will Drawn in a Foreign Court" (Hebrew) 12 *Dine Israel* 193, 223–229 (5754-5755).

74 The notion that *dina demalkhuta* is based upon "*hefker beit din hefker*," loosely translated as the right of *beit din* to expropriate a person's property, resonates with others such as *Mahariz Enzel* 4; *Dvar Avraham*, supra n. 23.

being executed during the testator's lifetime only to be implemented upon his death.

Alternatively, echoing Rabbis Schwadron's and Feinstein's rationale, Rabbi Toledano states[75] that the customary practice demonstrates the *gemirat da'at* of the donor and recipient in the transaction that it will be effective in any fashion that it will be (as the law requires-AYW), and therefore it is effective instead of a kinyan, since it is clear that they firmly resolved the matter. And this conclusion should equally apply, as Rabbi Toledano claims, to matters of inheritance.

Regardless of which rationale is offered for the effectiveness of *minhag* relating to a civil *will*, seemingly this approach undermines the limited scope of the authority of *minhag*. As we know, *minhag mevatel halakha*, i.e., custom overrides the law, is limited to monetary matters.[76] In other words, the power of custom is that it can override an existing halakha in monetary affairs.[77] On the other hand, in matters of *issura* (prohibitions), custom cannot override the halakha.[78] In our instance, though we are dealing with a monetary matter (inheritance), nevertheless as we explained, *hilkhot yerusha* are labeled "*ḥukat mishpat*" (immutable) and therefore the *minhag* manifested in the execution of a *kinyan situmta* should be ineffective in overriding the halakhic order of testamentary succession. And, in fact, for the aforesaid reason, some authorities explicitly ruled that a *minhag* cannot override the Torah law of succession.[79]

Nevertheless, many authorities argue that if a significant share [fifty percent or twenty percent] of the entire estate, or according to others, a nominal amount is distributed to Torah heirs, one may distribute assets to non-Torah heirs.[80]According to Rabbi Wosner

---

75 Toledano, supra n. 71, at 293, 295.

76 *Talmud Yerushalmi BM* 7:1; *Mishnah BM* 7:1; *BM* 83a-b.

77 See supra n. 76.

78 RH 15b.

79 See supra n. 46.

80 *Sefer ha-Ittur, Matnat Shekhiv Me-ra* 59b (p. 118); *Teshuvot Tashbetz*, 3: 147; *Teshuvot ha-Rivash* 168; *Teshuvot Maharshal* 49; *Taz, EH* 113:1; *Teshuvot Maharsham* 7:12 in the name of Rema; *Teshuvot Beit David ḤM* 137;

of Bnei Brak, the import of the passage in Talmud Yerushalmi, *Bava Batra* 8:6 and *rishonim* is that one engages in *issur* only if one transfers the entire estate to non-Torah heirs.[81] And Rabbi Dovid Feldman of London, England argues in his treatise on *yerusha* that the same conclusion may be drawn from the discussion in Talmud Bavli *Bava Batra* 133b.[82] In effect, there is no commission of the *issura* (prohibition) of "*avurei aḥsanta*" since a potential Torah heir receives a portion of the estate.

Since halakha recognizes the possibility of a redistribution of the estate among Torah heirs and non-Torah heirs, the matter of *issur* is no longer existent. To put it differently, if a *minhag* overrides a matter of *issur* such as divesting the Torah heirs from benefiting from any portion of the inheritance, then such a custom is null and void, resulting in the need to redistribute all the assets to the Torah heirs. However, should some of the estate be distributed to the Torah heirs and the balance amongst non-Torah heirs, then the *minhag* of implementing a civil *will* and distributing assets to

Ḥiddushei ha-Rashash BB 133; *Zerah Emet* supra n. 11; *Teshuvot Pnei Moshe* 1:70; *Teshuvot Avkat Rokhel*, 92; *Teshuvot ha-Rema*, 92 [as understood by *Taz, Even Haezer* 113:1 and *Teshuvot Shoeil u-Meishiv, Mahadurah Batra*, 1:1 [in the name of *Teshuvot ha-Rema* 92]; *Naḥalat Shiva* 21:4, 6; *Agudat Eizov*, ḤM 15; *Ketzot ha-Ḥoshen* 282:2; *Teshuvot R. Akiva Eiger*, *ḤM* 16; *Iggerot Moshe*, *EH* 1:110, *ḤM* 2:49-50; *Teshuvot Shevet ha-Levi* 4:216; Rabbi Z. N. Goldberg, 2 *Shurat ha-Din* 360, n. 11. Pursuant to one opinion, as long as some of the same property that is distributed to a non-Torah heir(s) is given to the Torah heir there is no violation of *hilkhot yerusha.* See *Teshuvot Pnei Moshe* 1:70.

One exception to the rule is that one cannot withhold a portion of the *bekhor's* double share. See *Teshuvot ha-Geonim*, Harkavi ed. 260; *Shulḥan Arukh and Rema, ḤM* 281:4. For an exception to this rule, see infra, text accompanying notes 83–85.

The fact that the distribution of a portion to a Torah heir and the balance to a non-Torah heir does not contravene an *issur* cannot be taken as proof that a distribution based upon a civil *will* would be recognized by the above authorities.

81 *Teshuvot Shevet ha-Levi* supra n. 80.

82 *Otzrot ha-Mishpat, Naḥalot* 228.

non-Torah heirs should not be tainted by any element of *issura*.[83] Consequently, if there is a prevailing custom that divests a *bekhor* (firstborn) entirely from his double portion of inheritance, such a *minhag* has no validity. However, if he has been disinherited from only a portion of that share, the *minhag* will be determinative.[84] Similarly, if an estate is entirely distributed to a daughter(s) without distribution to the son(s), such a secular *will* is not halakhically effective. Nonetheless, if a Torah heir such as a son receives at least a portion of the estate, such an arrangement is valid.[85]

Whether the need to distribute a portion of the estate to the Torah heirs exists only when enforcing a civil *will* based upon *minhag*, we leave as an open question. Should a *posek* rely upon the positions of Rabbis Meir of Rothenburg, Schwadron and Feinstein for recognizing a civil testamentary disposition, or if the estate has been structured based upon one of the halakhically sanctioned techniques, [86]according to various *posekim*, provisions may have to be made for a distribution to Torah heir(s).[87]

Others contend that validating a secular *will* based upon a secular legal system contravenes the prohibition for Jews to litigate matters in a secular court. In other words, the prohibition is not limited to litigating one's affairs in secular courts but extends to adopting

---

83 *Ketubbot* 52b (the matter of *takanat benin dikhrin*); *Talmud Yerushalmi, Ketubbot* 9:1; *Rema, EH* 52:4 (end).

84 *Yad Rama*, supra n. 42; *Maharik,* supra n. 46; *Rema, ḤM* 281:4 (in the name of Maharik); *Maharashdam*, supra n. 10; *Radvaz* supra n. 46. The same is applicable when daughters inherit the entire estate and the son(s) receives nothing. See *Teshuvot Torat Ḥayyim* 2:19; *Maharit,* supra n. 8.

85 See supra n. 80.

86 See supra n. 14.

87 *Sefer Hashtaroth le-Rav Hai Gaon, Shtar* 48; *Teshuvot ha-Rivash* 168. However, R. Hai Gaon contends that if one utilizes a technique such as a matnas bari or a matnas *shekhiv mera* (a deathbed gift), one need not distribute a portion to a Torah heir. See *Sefer ha-Shtarot*, op. cit, *Shtar* 8-9 and 12. Cf. *Teshuvot Ḥatam Sofer*, supra n. 11.
Whether a testator executing a *matnas bari* (a gift donated by a healthy person) must avoid transferring property to a non-Torah heir is subject to debate. See R. Hai Gaon, ibid; *Teshuvot ha-Rosh* 25:3; *Rema EH* 113:1; *Ḥatam Sofer*, ibid.; *Teshuvot Maḥaneh Yehuda, ḤM* 282; *Mishpatekha le-Ya'akov* 3:28 (3).

practices that imbibe secular law.[88] Others contend that affirmation of such a *minhag* is a violation of "*avurei aḥsanta*."[89]

D. The Scope of *Dina de-Malkhuta Dina*

Under certain prescribed conditions, halakha is willing to recognize some secular laws based upon the rule "*dina de-malkhuta dina,*" lit., the law of the kingship is the law.[90] Though the rule addresses a kingship governmental structure, nevertheless the rule is applicable to any order that has been established with the consent of its citizens, has a legislative body[91] and enacts legislation that does not discriminate against its citizenry.[92]

Seemingly, a civil *will* drafted in accordance with the governing laws of a democratic order such as the United States ought to be recognized based upon the following *psak* of the Rema.[93]

> There are some authorities who state that the law of the kingship is the law in regard to taxes and tariffs dealing with immovables ... but other matters not. And there are others who disagree and argue that the law of the kingship is law regarding any matter that will be beneficial to the citizens of the state.

In accordance with Rema's commentary on the Tur, something beneficial for a state's citizenry is any matter that relates to interaction between individuals.[94]

---

88 See infra n. 54. For the *issur* of litigating one's matters in civil court, see Simcha Krauss, "Litigation in Secular Courts," 3 *Journal of Halacha and Contemporary Society* 35 (Spring 1982).

89 *Naḥalah le-Yisrael*, 38, 53; *Teshuvot Mishpatei Tishmaru* 25.

90 *Nedarim* 28a; *Gittin* 10b; *Bava Kamma* 113a-b; *Bava Batra* 44b-45a. Many of the sources dealing with *dina demalkhuta dina* have been culled from *Shilo*, supra n. 73.

91 *Teshuvot ha-Rashba* 1:612, 637; *Teshuvot Yaskil Avdi* 6:28; Yosef Henkin, "Dina Demalkhuta Dina," (Hebrew) 31 *Hapardes* 3–5; *Yeḥaveh Da'at* 5:63.

92 *Mishneh Torah, Hilkhot Gezelah ve-Aveida* 5:14; *Shulḥan Arukh, ḤM* 369:8; *Teshuvot Tashbetz* 1:158; *Teshuvot ha-Ritva* 53; *Teshuvot ha-Radvaz* 3:968; *Teshuvot Ḥatam Sofer EH* 126; *Teshuvot Torat Emet* 153; *Teshuvot Ḥikkekei Lev ḤM* 6.

93 *ḤM* 369:8.

Though the Shakh vigorously opposes incorporating a rule of secular law when it is contrary to halakha,[95] nevertheless, historically dating back to the *rishonim*, the majority of *posekim* endorse the position of Rema.[96]

Although in the past most authorities subscribed to Rema's view, in contemporary times in Eretz Yisrael and elsewhere, normative halakha endorses the Shakh's position.[97] Moreover, though Rema invokes *dina de-malkhuta dina* regarding matters relating to the benefit of the citizenry of a particular country, nevertheless, following in the footsteps of the Shulḥan Arukh,[98] Rema opposes applying this rule as grounds for validating a civil *will*.[99] Similarly, though R. Moshe Feinstein subscribes to Rema's view regarding the scope of *dina de-malkhuta dina*, nevertheless, R. Feinstein explicitly rejects the notion that a civil *will* can be validated based upon that view.[100]

Furthermore, since American law does not mandate that inheritance matters be resolved in accordance with civil law, there is no reason to invoke *dina demalkhuta dina* as a basis for validating a secular *will*.[101]

---

94 *Tur ḤM, Darkhei Moshe* 369.

95 *Shakh, ḤM* 73:19

96 *Teshuvot Doveiv Mesharim* 1:76. For a list of other *posekim*, see Shilo, supra n. 73, at 156. In addition, see *Tumim, ḤM* 26:1: *Teshuvot Ḥakham Tzvi* 148; *Teshuvot Noda be-Yehuda, Kamma ḤM* 10; *Teshuvot Harei Besamim Tanina* 2:41; *Teshuvot Avnei Tzedek ḤM* 9; *Teshuvot Divrei Yoel* 2:147.

97 *Ma'adnei Aretz* 18:1; *Amud ha-Yemini* 1:8; PDR 5:269-270; 8:78, 81. In the most trenchant terms, Israeli *posekim* lambast those who argue that *dina demalkhuta dina* can serve as grounds for validating a civil *will*. See Ben Tzion Uziel, "Mishpat Yerushat ha-Banot," (Hebrew) 9 *Talpiyot* 27, 44 (5725); Avraham Tzvi Yehuda Kook, "Dina Demalkhuta Dina Regarding Inheritance" (Hebrew) 3 *Teḥumin* 231 (5742); Eliezar Waldenburg, "The Proposed Inheritance Law according to Halakha" (Hebrew), Jubilee Volume to Federbush, Jerusalem, 5721, 221; *Teshuvot Yeḥave Da'at* 4:65.

98 *Beit Yosef, Tur ḤM* 369; *Teshuvot Rav Pe'alim*, vol. 2, *ḤM* 15.

99 *Rema, ḤM* 369:11.

100 *Iggerot Moshe ḤM* 2:72.

101 See *Aliyot de-Rabbeinu Yonah,* supra n. 72; *Teshuvot ha-Rashba* 1:895; *Teshuvot ha-Rivash* 495 in the name of Rashba; *Teshuvot Ḥukot Ḥayyim* 1;

Moreover, in cases where there is an element of *issur*, as Tashbetz notes, one cannot invoke *dina de-malkhuta dina*.[102] In fact, numerous *posekim* will reject invoking *dina de-malkhuta dina* in order to validate a civil *will* that provides for an estate distribution to a non-Torah heir which entails the commission of an *issur*.[103] For example, in the seventeenth century, R. Moshe Benveniste mandated that a daughter return her share in the inheritance to her brother because it was lost property [*hashavat aveida*].[104]And he records that all scholars of the period rejected the validity of a secular *will* based upon *dina de-malkhuta dina*. In R. Benveniste's words, "And they struck that opinion with a hundred measures against one." As such, at first glance, one must reject the validity of a secular *will*. Subsequently, addressing a case of inheritance that occurred in 1851 in Ancona, Italy, Rabbi Yisrael Moshe Ḥazan rails against those who equate the halakhic recognition of *dina de-malkhuta dina* in estate distribution with the halakhic validity imparted to parties who arrange their monetary affairs in variance with halakhah. R. Ḥazan explains,[105]

> What has the maxim of *dina de-malkhuta dina* to do with the Jewish law of inheritance? For the laws of inheritance and the laws ruling commercial transactions such as purchase and sale of goods, or deals in real estate, which are resolved according to the law of the land, are as removed from one, as is East from West.

Teshuvot Shemesh Tzedaka, ḤM 33:15; *Teshuvot Mahari Assad* 2:114; *Teshuvot Mishpetei Uziel* 3:28; Ḥazon Ish, *Likkutim ḤM* 16.

And therefore, if the validity of a *will* is based upon *situmta* (see infra text accompanying notes 109–113) and the governing civil law does not mandate the implementation of a certain *kinyan* regarding estate disposition, *situmta* will not be effective. See PDR 18:207, 240.

102 *Teshuvot Tashbetz* 1:158.

103 *Teshuvot Maharam me-Padua* supra n. 9; *Teshuvot Be'er ha-Mayim* 120–122; *Teshuvot Edut be-Ya'akov* 71-72.

104 *Teshuvot Pnei Moshe* 2:15.

105 *Naḥalah le-Yisrael*, 9. Cf. *Teshuvot Maharitz ha-Ḥadashot* 32.

As R. Akiva Eiger notes, these civil matters are monetary in nature while the laws of a *yerusha* have the element of *issur*.[106] Consequently, it is unsurprising to find numerous *posekim* who invalidate a civil *will* based upon *dina de-malkhuta dina*.[107] Hence, any assets, including but not limited to *yerusha* awarded by a civil court, halakhically continue to belong to the Torah heir(s), and as such a non-Torah heir who has won in court cannot enforce the award lest he be labeled a thief.[108]

Notwithstanding what we have presented here, without impinging upon the element of *issur* of *hilkhot yerusha*, according to contemporary *posekim* such as Rabbis Mesas and Sha'anan, one can still invoke the rule of *dina de-malkhuta dina*.[109] A last will and testament is a document that entails gifting an estate to various individuals. Though its provisions and the terminology employed by the document may not be in conformity with the halakhot of a *shtar matana*, a bona fide document that grants a gift, nevertheless, it is a *shtar matana* that is valid in the eyes of secular law. The question is whether halakha recognizes a *shtar kinyan* (vehicle to transfer an asset) such as a *shtar matana* that was prepared and valid in accordance with civil law.

Pursuant to the majority of *rishonim*[110] and some *aḥaronim*,[111] a *shtar matana* drafted in accordance with secular law will be recog-

---

106 *Teshuvot R. Akiva Eiger, Mahadura Tinyana* 83.

107 Supra n. 103; *Ḥida, Tuv Ayin* 17:4; *Teshuvot Yosef Omeitz* supra n. 53; *Teshuvot Rav Pe'alim* supra n. 98; *Ḥatam Sofer*, supra n. 13; *Teshuvot Minḥat Yitzḥak* 2:95; *Teshuvot Tzitz Eliezer* 6: 42(8); *Teshuvot Mishneh Halakhot* 9:326.

108 *Teshuvot Maharashdam, ḤM* 145; *Teshuvot Maharik* 154; R. Z. N. Goldberg, 5 *ha-Yashar ve-Hatov* 3, 5 (5768).

109 *Tevuot Shemesh*, supra n. 57; *Sha'anan*, supra n. 55. See also, R. Yirmeyahu cited in *Pnei Moshe*, supra n. 104.

110 *Ittur*, Vol. 1, *Ma'amar Shemini, Kiyum Tofsim ve-ḥotmim; Mordekhai, Gittin* 325; *Ḥiddushei ha-Ramban, Gittin* 10b; *Ḥiddushei ha-Rashba, Gittin* 10b; *Beit ha-Beḥira, Gittin* 10b; *Piskei ha-Rosh, Gittin* 1:10; *Ḥiddushei ha-Ritva, Gittin* 10b; *Magid Mishneh, Malveh ve-Loveh* 27:1; *Teshuvot ha-Ran* 37; *Teshuvot ha-Rivash* 203; *Tashbetz* supra n. 102; *Ḥiddushei Nimmukei Yosef, Gittin* 10b.

111 *Teshuvot ha-Radvaz* 1: 545, 6:1183; *Teshuvot Mayim Amukim* 53.

nized. The majority view of *rishonim* notwithstanding, *Shulḥan Arukh* and many *aḥaronim* relied upon the minority view of *rishonim*[112] to invalidate a *shtar matana*.[113] Nevertheless, relying upon the majority of *rishonim* and some *aḥaronim* who validate a *shtar matana*, Rabbis Mesas and Sha'anan argue that a civil *will* ought to be recognized. Since a *shtar matana* is a *shtar kinyan* and there is no *kinyan* after death, on what grounds can one legitimate such an estate distribution in accordance with a secular *will*?

Here again, as we mentioned previously in our presentation, the grounds for the effectiveness of a civil *will* as a *shtar matana* is based upon the position of Rabbeinu Yonah and Rabbi Yeshayahu Blau as an example of a *kinyan situmta*. According to this position, the transfer of the assets from the testator to the heirs is subdivided into two stages: Invoking the view that the rule of *dina de-malkhuta dina*, secular law divests the testator of the ownership of the assets. Subsequently, executing a *shtar matana* of estate distribution that is a *kinyan situmta*, the assets are transferred from the testator to the heir. The execution of a *kinyan situmta* is contingent upon the fact (i.e., a *tenai*, condition) that the testator will pass away and with his demise the beneficiary(ies) will acquire the assets of the estate. In actuality, the *kinyan situmta* that has been drafted in accordance with civil law is being executed during the testator's lifetime only to be implemented upon his death.

In short, clearly, the need to distribute a portion of the estate to the Torah heirs is not limited to an instance of enforcing a civil *will* based upon *minhag* or *dina de-malkhuta dina*. Should a *posek* rely upon the positions of Rabbis Maharam of Rothenburg, Schwadron and Feinstein for recognizing a civil testamentary disposition or if the estate has been structured based upon one of the halakhically sanctioned techniques,[114] according to various *posekim*, provision

---

However, clearly Radvaz will reject a *will* as a *shtar matanah* that reflects the *minhag* of disinheriting Torah heirs.

112 *Rif, Gittin* 1:410; *Mishneh Torah, Hilkhot Malveh ve-Loveh* 27:1

113 *Shulḥan Arukh, ḤM* 68:1; *Teshuvot Binyamin Ze'ev* 2:415; *Teshuvot Mishpetei Shmuel* 103; *Teshuvot Oraḥ le-Tzadik ḤM* 1; *Sha'ar Mishpat ḤM* 68:1

114 See supra n. 14.

has to be made for a distribution to Torah heir(s).[115] These approaches of Rabbis Rothenburg, Schwadron and Feinstein are predicated upon the fact that a partial distribution to a Torah heir will suffice to nullify the issue of "*avurei aḥsanta*."

Accordingly, the basis for the father's preparation of a civil *will* can be grounded in the *pesakim* of Maharam of Rothenburg, R. Schwadron and R. Feinstein and those *posekim* who affirm the *minhag* and the validity of *dina de-malkhuta dina*.

Based upon the foregoing presented in section 2, subsections a-d, assuming various conditions are obtained as dictated by the adoption of a particular view, we presented the positions of Rabbis Rothenburg, Schwadron and Feinstein as well as those *posekim* who endorse the effectiveness of *minhag* or *dina de-malkhuta dina,* which would serve as grounds for preparing and drafting a civil law as a vehicle for distributing one's assets to one's heirs. In fact, Rabbi C. Shlomo Sha'anan, a dayan serving on a Tel Aviv Rabbinical Court, factored all four views in order to validate a civil *will.*[116] What is important to stress is that all of these approaches are grounded in a particular halakhic-legal technique that allows for an estate distribution to any individual, regardless of whether the person is a Torah heir or not. In effect, the estate has been effectively transformed from a potential source of inheritance for a Torah heir into an asset that can be acquired by anyone no different from any article for sale in the marketplace.

---

115 See supra n. 80; *Sefer ha-Shtaroth le-Rav Hai Gaon, Shtar* 48; *Teshuvot ha-Rivash* 168. However, R. Hai Gaon contends that if one utilizes a technique such as a *matnas bari* or a *matnas shekhiv mera* (a deathbed gift) one need not distribute a portion to a Torah heir. See *Sefer ha-Shtarot*, op. cit, *Shtar* 8-9 and 12; *Teshuvot ha-Geonim*, supra n. 80. Cf. *Halakhot Gedolot*, Hildesheimer ed., Vol. 2, 511; *Teshuvot Ḥatam Sofer*, supra n. 11.
Whether a testator executing a *matnas bari* (a gift donated by a healthy person) must avoid transferring property to a non-Torah heir is subject to debate. See R. Hai Gaon, ibid; *Teshuvot ha-Rosh* 25:3; *Rema EH* 113:1; *Ḥatam Sofer*, ibid; *Teshuvot Maḥaneh Yehuda, ḤM* 282; *Mishpatekha le-Ya'akov* 3:28 (3).

116 Sha'anan, "The Matter of a Will Improperly Written," (Hebrew) 1 *Shurat ha-Din* 319 (5754); *Iyunim be-Mishpat, ḤM* 34; and supra n. 55.

As we have discussed, however, others reject these techniques and therefore affirm the Talmudic and *Shulḥan Arukh* rule that "*yerusha ein lo hefsek*" (the succession of inheritance cannot be interrupted)[117] and reject all of these solutions.

E. The Parameters of "*Mitzva le-Kayeim Divrei ha-Met*"

As we explained, many would argue that the *will* is ineffective in transferring an estate either because "there is no *kinyan* after death"[118] or because one may not disinherit a Torah heir from his rightful share as dictated by the Torah view of succession. Distributing a partial share to a Torah heir will not obviate the halakhic fact that the Torah view of succession is "*ḥukat mishpat.*" Any distribution of a share to a non-Torah heir entails the contravention of an *issur.*[119] Hence, even *be-di-avad* (ex post facto) one may not rely upon a secular *will.*

However, according to some *posekim* one can validate a secular *will* based upon "*mitzva le-kayeim divrei ha-met,*" the halakhic duty to carry out the wishes of the deceased.[120]

Amongst *rishonim* there are two primary approaches in trying to understand under what conditions one has complied with this mitzva:

Should the testator state "give to Reuven," such a clear instruction without transference of the actual asset to a *shalish* (a third party) will suffice to comply with "*mitzva le-kayeim divrei ha-met.*"[121] Others require that the assets be deposited for purposes of eventual

[117] *Bava Batra* 125b, 129b; *Shulḥan Arukh, ḤM* 248:1. See supra n. 15 and infra n. 164.

[118] See text accompanying supra notes 3-4.

[119] *Teshuvot Maharashdam ḤM* 336; *Teshuvot Maharit* 1:29; *Teshuvot Maharshakh* 2:164; *Teshuvot Ḥatam Sofer*, supra n. 11.

[120] *Gittin* 14b, 15a; *BB* 149a.

[121] *Ḥiddushei ha-Ramban, Gittin* 13a, s.v. *ve'od*; *Rashi, Gittin, ad locum* s.v. *be-bari*; *Tosafot, BB* 149a, s.v. *deka*; *Beit Yosef, ḤM* 252 who cites Rosh, Ritva and Ra'ah; *Teshuvot Binyan Tzion ha-Ḥadashot* 2:24; *Shakh, ḤM* 252:4.

estate distribution (*hashlasha*) with the *shalish*.[122] Normative halakha mandates that the asset(s) be deposited with the *shalish* for the express purpose of carrying out the testator's wishes, and the language of the *will* should preferably employ *matanah* (gift) terminology (such as "I give") rather than *yerusha* terminology (such as "I bequeath").[123]

Based upon the foregoing, Maharit contends that a civil *will* does not conform to the dictates of "*mitzva le-kayeim divrei ha-met*":[124] The absence in a civil *will* of a clear directive to the heirs,[125] and the need that full disclosure of the provisions of the future distribution have been delivered in the presence of the future heirs,[126] coupled with the fact that an *issur* is committed by disinheriting a Torah heir,[127] renders impossible for a civil *will* to be affirmed. Finally, to argue that the depositing of a *will* with an attorney and its subsequent enforcement by a probate court as a form of *hashlashah* and therefore a fulfillment of "*mitzva le-kayeim divrei ha-met*" is predicated upon invoking Rabbi Ḥayyim Ozer Grodzenzky's ruling which will be discussed later. However, argues Maharit, one cannot find support for such a position since his *teshuva* addresses charity bequests[128] and his ruling may therefore not necessarily extend to private testamentary dispositions.

---

122 Rabbeinu Tam, *Tosafot Ketubbot* 70a, s.v. *veho*; *Teshuvot ha-Rosh* 15:1; *Piskei ha-Rosh, Gittin* 1:15; *Teshuvot Mahari Ibn Lev* 2:39; *Teshuvot Maharit* 2, *ḤM* 95. Others claim that the deposit with a third party must have been executed prior to the verbal directive. See *Teshuvot Mahari Ibn Lev,* op. cit.

123 *Shulḥan Arukh, ḤM* 250:23, 252:2; *Teshuvot ha-Rema* 48.
Whether one can fulfill the wishes of the deceased by employing *yerusha* terminology in a testamentary disposition rather than the language of gifting is subject to debate. See *Ketzot ha-Ḥoshen* 248:1; *Netivot ha-Mishpat* 248:6.

124 *Maharit,* supra n. 8.

125 Supra n. 121.

126 *Ḥiddushei ha-Rashba, Gittin* 13a, s.v. *be-mai*; *Teshuvot R. Akiva Eiger* 1:150.

127 *Teshuvot Mishpatim Yesharim* 44; *Teshuvot Avkat Roḥel* 93.

128 *Teshuvot Aḥiezer* 3:34, 4:66.

Admittedly, both of Rabbi Grodzensky's decisions deal with *tzedaka;* nevertheless, in one of his rulings he writes,[129]

I have always doubted the propriety of the *wills* executed in civil courts since there is no *shtar* after death, yet a Jewish court will affirm their provisions.

As such, though his decision addressed matters of charitable bequests, clearly his ruling regarding the invoking of "*mitzva le-kayeim divrei ha-met*" applies equally to the conventional last will and testament. And, in fact, contemporary decisors understood Rabbi Grodzensky's *psak* in a similar fashion.[130]

To buttress his position, Rabbi Grodzensky found precedent in a *teshuva* of Rabbi Ya'akov Ettlinger dealing with a secular *will*.[131] The facts are the following: a healthy individual prepared a testamentary disposition in accordance with civil law wherein upon his demise, his estate would be distributed among Torah and non-Torah heirs. Since the estate arrangement failed to comply with halakha, the non-Torah heirs inquired of R. Ettlinger whether this civil *will* would be halakhically valid. Since the assets were in the hands of the beneficiaries in accordance with secular law, these individuals are *muḥzakim* in these assets. Lest one argue that the assets must be deposited with a third party prior to invoking "*mitzva le-kayeim divrei ha-met*," R. Ettlinger argues that since the testator communicated explicit instructions to transfer these assets upon his demise,[132] this suffices to comply with the mitzva. The fact that executors were appointed to ensure that his wishes would be fulfilled and the *will* would be enforced by secular authorities suffices to comply with the dictates of "*mitzva le-kayeim divrei ha-met*."[133] Relying upon R. Ettlinger's argumentation, R. Grodzensky posits,[134]

---

129 *Teshuvot Aḥiezer* 4:66.

130 *Teshuvot Ḥeshev ha-Ephod* 2:106; *Teshuvot Netzaḥ Yisrael* 20; *Pithei Ḥoshen, Yerusha*, pp. 145-146; *Mishpatei Tishmaru*, supra n. 89; *Kuntres me-Dor le-Dor*, supra n. 14, at 2; *Mishpat Shlomo*, supra n. 55.

131 *Binyan Tzion* supra n. 121.

132 See text accompanying supra n. 130.

133 Ramban, supra n. 120; *Teshuvot ha-Ritva* 54 in the name of Ra'ah; Ran on *Rif, Gittin* 5b; *Teshuvot ha-Rema* 48 in the name of Rambam.

> For some time, I have inclined to the view that the beneficiary in a *will* executed in accordance with the law of the land is to be considered as a *muḥzak*, since the testamentary disposition will be carried out in accordance with the law of the land, and as such we do not need the halakhic requirement of a deposit for the purpose of estate distribution. However, I have not found a source ("*gilluyei*") for this halakha.

In effect, the preparation and execution of a civil *will* and its subsequent enforcement by civil authorities is tantamount to depositing the assets with a third party for the express purpose of future estate distribution, i.e., *hashlashah.*[135] His position has been endorsed by some *posekim.*[136]

A similar approach has been espoused by Rabbi Shmuel Shor, who recognizes that *hashlasha* applies only when one gives a gift to a stranger. However, when one gives a gift to a daughter and she is considered *muḥzaketh* according to civil law, a deposit is not required and such a testamentary disposition is therefore valid.[137]

Arguing somewhat differently from Rabbis Shor and Grodzensky, Rabbi Henoch Padwa writes that the initiation of the executor's action to probate the *will* is to be viewed as a type of *hashlashah* and therefore, "*mitzva le-kayeim divrei ha-met*" at this juncture has been fulfilled. In other words, the preparation of a testamentary disposition in accordance with secular law and its enforceability by the court are insufficient to establish *hashlashah.* One requires the probating of the *will* by the executor. [138]

The existence of an executor of a *will* creates *hashlashah* (deposit). See *Teshuvot Ḥeshev ha-Ephod* (in the name of *Ḥelkat Meḥokeik*), 3:25.

134 *Teshuvot Aḥiezer* 3:34. Here again, R. Grodzensky's argument demonstrates that his decision is not limited to cases of *tzedaka*. Though in this *teshuva* he does not definitively resolve that executing a civil *will* is valid, elsewhere he validates it. See *Kovetz Iggreot*, No. 25.

135 See text accompanying supra n. 133.

136 *Binyan Tzion*, supra n. 121; *Teshuvot ve-Hanhagot* 1:853; *Teshuvot Minḥat Shai* 75. And *Minḥat Shai* argues that both Ḥatam Sofer, supra n. 13 and Radvaz, supra n. 42 agree with his position.

137 *Minḥat Shai*, supra n. 136.

138 *Ḥeshev ha-Ephod*, supra n. 130. See also, PDR 17: 175, 278.

The ramifications of Rabbis Grodzensky's, Shor's and Padwa's view that the preparation of a civil *will* and/or probating it is a form of *hashlashah* and therefore serves to ascertain *gemirat da'at* would be applicable to all segments of our Orthodox Jewish community. Many Jews who identify and affiliate with religious institutions in our Orthodox Jewish community execute such testamentary dispositions. Although many different documents have been suggested as complying with halakhic estate planning, and there are attorneys with the expertise and experience to address the observant Jewish community's concerns in drafting a halakhic *will*, it is not unusual to find, amongst our families across the Orthodox spectrum, numerous testamentary instructions prepared in accordance with civil law. And, in fact, many contested *yerusha* matters addressed in beit din today deal with civil *wills* executed by members of all segments of our community.

Seemingly, R. Yosef Elyashiv will invalidate such testamentary dispositions. He argues in a written *teshuva* that R. Grodzensky's view that the preparation and enforcement of a civil *will* is a form of *hashlashah* is applicable only to secular Jews who do not exhibit "a deficiency in their *gemirat da'at*."[139] To put it differently, since secular Jews do not comply with halakha, should a civil *will* be prepared, they firmly intend to have the *will* probated in secular court. Hence their *will* is valid. On the other hand, the allegiance of observant Jews is to halakha, and should they prepare a civil *will*, there is no firm intention to have the document probated civilly. The *gemirat da'at* of an observant Jew is to follow halakha, and since in R. Elyashiv's view a civil *will* cannot be validated for observant Jews either *lekhatḥila* or *be-di-avad*, a testator's *gemirat da'at* is actualized only if halakhically compliant in one's estate planning. A similar view is espoused by *Meishiv be-Halakha*, a publication of Machon Lehoro'ah, a beit din in Monsey, New York.[140]

However, as noted by R. Schwartz, R. Elyashiv's line of reasoning should equally apply to any observant Jew who files a civil divorce, trusting that his testamentary disposition will be executed in

---

139 *Kovetz ha-Teshuvot* 3:225.

140 *Meishiv be-Halakha* 211, n. 288.

accordance with his wishes upon his demise.[141] In fact, in a *mesorah* attributed to Rabbi Elyashiv, in situations where people recognize one mode of estate planning, i.e. executing a civil *will* and preparing such a testamentary disposition, we assess (*umdana*) that their intentions were to transfer the estate as a gift, similar to *hashlashah* in accordance with secular law.[142] To state it differently, even observant Jews who have their estate wishes executed in accordance with civil law trust that their instructions will be complied with, and therefore a civil *will* ought to be recognized as a vehicle for *hashlashah*.

Nonetheless, Rabbi Elyashiv contends based upon "*mitzva le-kayeim divrei ha-met*" that a *peshara* (compromise) should be executed by the Jewishly observant who utilize secular estate arrangements.[143] And *Meishiv be-Halakha* contends that it is "*midat ḥassidut*" to comply with the provisions of a civil *will* and invokes the possibility that confirmation of such a testamentary disposition is a fulfillment of *kibbud av*, a matter we will discuss later in our presentation.[144]

Finally, regarding Maharit's opposition to invoking "*mitzva le-kayeim divrei ha-met*" when executing a civil *will* is in violation of the *issur* of "*avurei aḥsanta,*" [145] we may reply, if one adopts the view that "*mitzva le-kayeim divrei ha-met*" is a form of a *kinyan*[146] and that therefore one may invoke it as grounds for recognizing a non-Torah heir's entitlement to estate assets, seemingly we are involved in the contravention of an *issur*. And, in fact, in another *teshuva* penned by Maharit, he seems to endorse this understanding of "*mitzva le-kayeim divrei ha-met*,"[147] and therefore we can readily

141 *Mishpat ha-Tzava'ah*, vol. 2, 309.

142 Shlomo Zafrani, 20 *Moriah, gilyon*, 122 (Tevet 5756). Cf. R Turetsky who attributes a contradictory *psak* to R. Elyashiv. See *Teshuvot Yashiv Moshe*, 475.

143 See supra n. 139.

144 See infra text accompanying notes 153–161.

145 See supra n. 80.

146 *Rashi, Gittin* 15b, s.v. *de-amru*; *Maḥaneh Ephraim Hilkhot Zekhiyah u-Mattanah* 29; *Teshuvot Maharsham* 2:224(10).

147 *Teshuvot Maharit* 2:95.

understand his opposition to invoking this notion in cases of disinheritance of Torah heirs.

However, most *posekim* contend that "*mitzva le-kayeim divrei ha-met*" is not an act of *kinyan*.[148] Rather this concept, as the words denote, informs us that it is a halakhic duty, a mitzva, to fulfill the wishes of the deceased. As Rabbi Shaul Nathanson notes,[149]

> It is a matter of kindness of truth [*ḥessed shel emet*] that we do with the departed... and it is a duty to comply with the wishes of the deceased.

Yet, as we explained,[150] should the testamentary disposition provide that Torah heirs, alongside non-Torah heirs, will benefit from the estate distribution, the *issur* of "*avurei aḥsanta*" is nonexistent and the mitzva may be fulfilled.

In short, though not explicitly stated, we assume that despite the recognition of a civil *will* by Rabbi Grodzensky, Rabbi Shor and the others who recognize a civil *will be-di-avad*, they will all concur that Torah heirs must receive a distribution from the estate[151] lest the execution of the *will* entail a contravention of this *issur* of "*avurei aḥsanta*." Even if the language employed by the testator is "to bequeath" or "to inherit" rather than "to give" his assets, such language will not invalidate the civil *will* that reflects the deceased's wishes.[152]

F. The Parameters of *Kibbud Av*

Finally, in the absence of affirming a civil *will* as a means to per-

---

[148] Rabbeinu Tam, *Tosafot Gittin* 13a, s.v. *ve-ho*; *Shitot Kadmonim* and *Ḥiddushei ha-Ramah, Gittin* 13a; *Mordekhai, BB* 629; *Teshuvot Tashbetz* 2:53; *Rema ḤM* 252:2; *Ketzot ha-Ḥoshen* 248:5; *Divrei Ḥayyim* (Urbach) *YD* 48.

[149] *Teshuvot Shoeil u-Meishiv, Mahadura Tanina* 1.

[150] See text accompanying note 80.

[151] See text accompanying supra n. 80.

[152] *Netivot ha-Mishpat* 248:1. Though *Ketzot ha-Ḥoshen* 248:1 and *Teshuvot ve-Hanhagot* 1:872 disagree, nonetheless, since there is halakhic doubt as to who ought to possess the assets, we do not extract them from the *muḥzak*. See *Mishpat ha-Tzava'ah* 2:22 (225). However, it is questionable whether such terminology will validate such a disposition based upon the mitzva of *kibbud av*. See infra text accompanying notes 153–157.

form the "*mitzva le-kayeim divrei ha-met*," there are *posekim* who argue that compliance with a parent's wishes is a fulfillment of the mitzva of either *kibbud av*, honoring one's father, [153] or *morah*, filial reverence.[154] The implicit premise of this position is that a *beit din* can coerce a child to comply with his parent's wishes[155] and that a child is obligated in *kibbud av* after his father's demise.[156] Such a conclusion would equally apply to a secular *will*.[157]

---

153 *Teshuvot Tashbetz*, 2: 53; *Mahari ha-Levi*, supra n. 13; *Minḥat Shai*, supra n. 136; *Maharashdam*, supra n. 33; *Teshuvot Ḥavot Yair* 214; *Maharsham*, supra n. 21, at 15–18; *Kovetz ha-Teshuvot ḤM* 215; *Iyunim be-Mishpat, ḤM* 33.
Rabbi Ya'akov Reicher argues that in accordance with the dictates of *lifnim meshurat ha-din* (lit. beyond the limit of the law), one may invoke *kibbud av* regarding a testamentary disposition. See *Teshuvot Shevut Ya'akov* 1:168. Even though he contends that one cannot coerce the child to respect his parent's wishes, nevertheless, should such a matter be resolved by a beit din, the signing of an arbitration agreement would be grounds to effectuate his compliance. A beit din can mandate compliance with one's halakhic-moral obligations. See *Teshuvot Mahari Bruna* 241; Rabbi Zalman N. Goldberg, *Shivḥei ha-P'shara* section 5 (letter sent to Kollel Mishpetei Aretz, Ofrah, Israel).
Since one is saved from transgressing an *issur* by performing the mitzva of *kibbud av*, we may assume that these *posekim* hold that as long as the Torah heir(s) receives a portion of the *yerusha*, there is no nullification of the halakhot of Torah succession.

154 *Ḥazon Ish, YD* 148:8. R. Akiva Eiger is unsure whether to affirm a *will* based upon these grounds. See *Teshuvot Rabbi Akiva Eiger* 1:68.

155 *Teshuvot ha-Rashba ha-Meyuḥosot le-Ramban* 88; *Sefer ha-Ḥinukh*, no. 33; *Rema, ḤM* 97:16; *Shakh*, ad. locum 1. Alternatively, even if one contends that there is no basis for coercing an individual to honor his parent, by dint of signing on the arbitration agreement, the child is duty-bound to obey a beit din that mandates that the parent be accorded honor and respect. See supra n. 153.

156 *Teshuvot Shivat Tzion* 58; *Birkei Yosef, YD* 240:17.
For example, after his father's demise the heir is obligated by the mitzva of *kibbud av* to pay off his father's debts and restore an object the father stole or *ribbis* he took. See *Ketubbot* 91b; *Bava Kamma* 94b, 112a; *Bava Batra* 157a.

157 *Ḥeshev ha-Ephod*, supra n. 130.

Others disagree for one of three reasons. Firstly, one cannot coerce a child to comply with his parent's wishes.[158] Some argue that *kibbud av* is limited to personal service of a parent, whereas incurring a financial loss by being unable to benefit from a testamentary distribution does not fall within the ambit of the mitzva.[159] Consequently, since foregoing one's share in an estate entails an expense to the child without reimbursement by the parent; the mitzva of *kibbud av* is inapplicable.[160] Finally, some argue that since there is no obligation to honor and/or respect a parent after his demise,[161] the child is exempt from complying with the parent's testamentary wishes, which will be actualized after his death.

We should be mindful of the words of a well-respected halakhic arbiter. After stressing the importance of complying with the order of succession prescribed in the Torah, drafting a halakhic *will* using a *matnas bari* or *shtar ḥatzi zakhar* to transfer assets to a daughter(s) in order to avoid the *issur* of "*avurei aḥsanta*,"[162] Rav Tucashinsky concludes with the following:[163]

> And if he erred and wrote to his daughter or wife in a language that is ineffective for estate transfer, it is desirable that the sons

158 Rashi, *Ketubbot* 91b, s.v. *mitzva*; *Piskei ha-Rosh, Ketubbot* 9:13-14; *Maharsham*, supra n. 21.

159 *Shulḥan Arukh YD* 240:1.
Firstly, though many *posekim* argue that there is no mitzva of *kibbud av* when he does not benefit from the child's action, there are decisors who disagree. See *Teshuvot Ḥavot Yair* 214; *R. Akiva Eiger* supra n. 154; *Teshuvot Maharsham*, 2:224 (in the name of Rivash and Tashbetz). Secondly, as R. Schwadron aptly notes, benefit accruing to a parent is not limited to personal service but encompasses equally his monetary assets. See Maharsham, op. cit, subsection 14. Hence, there should be unanimous agreement that a parent derive benefit, albeit it may be of a psychological nature, from his children's receiving his assets in accordance with his instructions.

160 *Emes le-Ya'akov ḤM* 282. Cf. *Mahari ha-Levi*, supra n. 13 and others who argue that the son has not benefited from receiving a *yerusha* rather than incurring a loss by being deprived of it.

161 *Teshuvot Tashbetz* 2:53; *Shevut Ya'akov,* supra n. 153.

162 See supra n. 14.

163 *Gesher ha-Ḥayyim*, vol. 1, 41.

> agree to distribute the estate equally with their sister and mother, and it is a mitzva to fulfill the words of the father...and also to avoid friction and controversy.

The *pesika* of Rav Tucashinsky which was forged in the crucible of his learning experience and investigation of the halakhic sources led to him to conclude that various halakhic techniques for drafting a will were the order of the day. And in his writings he suggested various texts of halakhically sanctioned *tzvaot*. Nevertheless, he concludes his presentation with the point that our Torah has been described as "ways of pleasantness and all her paths are shalom."

Though Rav Tucashinsky was hard pressed to find grounds to validate a secular *will*, nonetheless, he experienced clear personal anguish regarding disrespecting a father and his personal wishes, the potential family strife and instability that is caused by a son who contests a civil *will*, and therefore directed the son(s) to agree and accept the estate distribution to the non-Torah heirs based upon *mitzva lekayeim divrei ha-met*, *kibbud av*, and fostering shalom.

A similar approach, albeit much more subtle in form, resonates in the writings of Rabbi Mattisyahu Schwartz. After his exhaustive, over-four-hundred-page treatment of advancing the paramount importance of drafting a halakhic *will*, examining the advantages and disadvantages of the various techniques proposed for drafting a *will*, rejecting the views of Rabbi Feinstein and *posekim* who endorse minhag as well as *dina demalkhuta dina* as grounds for recognizing a secular will and his fifty-five-page review in Volume 1 of *Mishpat ha-Tzava'ah* of all the differing views on whether *kibbud av* is applicable, in Volume two, R. Schwartz summarizes his conclusion by stating[164]

> In Volume 1 of *Mishpat ha-Tzava'ah* we had a lengthy presentation in explaining why the *posekim* argue that one must affirm a civil *will* due to honor of a father [and we discussed the views that rejected *kibbud av*].

In other words, his aforesaid summary indicates that R. Schwartz is subscribing to the view that ex post facto one should affirm the *will* based upon *kibbud av*. In other words, a halakhic

164 *Mishpat ha-Tzava'ah*, vol. 2, 85.

will is the prescribed method for estate planning, however he affirms a civil *will* based upon *kibbud av*. In fact, R. Schwartz argues that even those *posekim* who opine that children are exempt from *kibbud av* regarding complying with his estate-distribution directives concur that if the children fulfill his wishes, they do fulfill the mitzva.[165]

His posture reverberates when dealing with the following scenario: A father's *will* mandates that portions of his estate be distributed to non-Torah heirs, but upon his demise his wife demands that the estate be distributed to other non-Torah heirs. Applying rulings emerging from different case patterns, R. Schwartz concludes with three approaches to parental precedence and the role of filial responsibility. Dealing with the situation wherein the parents dispute over whether their daughter should marry a particular man and upon the father's demise, the question emerges whether the mother's wishes should be complied or not, R. Yehzekel Landau concludes that since the wife is alive, *kibbud em* trumps *kibbud av*.[166] On the other hand, addressing whether a son should incur a financial loss if engaging in *kibbud av* becomes the subject of the dispute between the child's parents, R. Akiva Eiger contends that we comply with the husband's wishes due to *kibbud av*.[167] Should a father oppose his son's recitation of *Kaddish* for his deceased mother, some *posekim* argue that *kavod av* and *kavod em* in such a situation are on equal standing and that the *avel* (mourner) can therefore choose whose instructions he wants to follow.[168] In other words, eliciting from fact patterns dealing with a prospective marital mate, a child incurring a financial loss through *kibbud av*, and the propriety of *kaddish* recitation for a parent despite the other parent's protestation, R. Schwartz draws three diametrically contrasting conclusions regarding how to confront a mother's desire to modify her husband's estate disposition relating to a distribution to other non-Torah heirs.[169] To state it differently, there is no discussion whatsoever

---

165 *Mishpat ha-Tzava'ah*, vol. 1, 501.

166 *Teshuvot Noda be-Yehudah, Mahadura Tanina, EH* 45.

167 *R. Akiva Eiger*, supra n. 154.

168 *Teshuvot Ḥayyim She'ol*, vol. 1, 5; *Teshuvot be-Tzel ha-Ḥokhma*, 5:15.

169 *Mishpat ha-Tzava'ah*, vol. 2, 82–88.

about tearing up the *will* and giving all the assets to the Torah heirs. The question is simply whose *kavod* will be the determining factor in the estate distribution. And therefore, there are no grounds to distribute the entire *yerusha* to the Torah heir.

In conclusion, numerous decisors invalidate a civil *will* either because there is no *kinyan* after death and/or because affirming the *will* entails the violation of "*avurei aḥsanta*."[170] And should the assets earmarked in a civil *will* be distributed to non-Torah heirs, many battei din will redistribute the lion's share of the estate to the Torah heir(s) in accordance with the order of Torah sion.[171]And other battei din will rely upon the views expressed in our presentation that would validate a civil *will*.[172]

Should a beit din choose to invalidate the estate distribution in the will, a nominal distribution will be given to the daughter(s). Since legally, a daughter(s) must sign off in order for the son(s) to inherit his (their) share of the estate, a daughter(s) can rely on the *posekim* who do not obligate a daughter to sign off the estate distribution,[173] and therefore she has a right to receive a portion of the estate.

---

170 In addition to the *posekim* cited supra n. 15, see *Teshuvot Ḥatam Sofer*, *ḤM* 172; *Rav Pe'alim,* supra n. 98; File No. 5528-42-1, January 20, 2005, Ploni v. Plonit, Petach Tikva Rabbinical Court; File no. 8820-41-1, November 23, 2009, Ploni v. Attorney General, Great Rabbinical Court; Asher Weiss, 6 *Darkhei Horo'ah* 130, 133–137 (2007).

171 *Teshuvot Teshurat Shai, Mahadura Kamma* 259; *Kovetz ha-Teshuvot* supra n. 139.

172 See supra notes 55 and 116.

173 Whether one can coerce a daughter to sign a waiver is a matter of controversy. See *Pnei Moshe* supra n. 104; *Teshuvot Shoeil u-Meishiv*, 2, *Mahadurah Tiltali*, 1:78; *Teshuvot Mahari ha-Levi* 1:4; *Ḥeshev ha-Ephod*, supra n.130; *Erekh Shai, ḤM* 60:9; *Beit Shlomo* (Sklai) *OḤ* 85:3, *YD* 2:79, *ḤM*, 108-109; *Teshuvot Mahariz Enzel* 28; *Naḥalat Tzvi ḤM* 276.
However, if this matter is being resolved by a beit din empowered by signed arbitration agreement to address this matter, then even those *posekim* who contend that generally one cannot coerce a daughter to sign a waiver document, the beit din does possess such authority.

In exchange for her signature, there is a *minhag* to give her at least ten percent of the value of the estate's assets[174] or an amount determined by a beit din panel.[175] In effect, offering assets to a daughter is a *peshara*, a compromise. Generally speaking, in an instance of *issur*, one cannot implement a *peshara*;[176] nevertheless, the *issur* may be inoperative. As we earlier noted, though the entire estate belongs to the Torah heirs and consequently, according to certain decisors a partial distribution to a daughter entails a violation of "*avurei aḥsanta*,"[177] some *posekim* permit the distribution to a non-Torah heir. Implicit in their allowance of distribution to a daughter is their endorsement of the position that distribution to a non-Torah heir is permissible if he shares in the estate distribution.[178] Alternatively, since secular law mandates a daughter's signature for the son to receive his estate distribution, halakha allows her to sign off. Consequently, in the absence of an extant *issur*, a *peshara* may be implemented.

Others such as Rabbis Maharam of Rothenberg, Schwadron and Feinstein will sanction the use of a civil *will* either based upon the *gemirat da'at* of the testator, "the mitzva due to death" or *minhag*. Regardless of the grounds for validating a secular *will*, it may be effective in transferring assets to a non-Torah heir only if there is a partial distribution to a Torah heir.[179]

On the other hand, some *posekim* will validate a secular *will* based upon "*mitzva le-kayeim divrei ha-met*" or *kibbud av*. Here again, to avoid the *issur* of "*avurei aḥsanta*" such recognition may require that the Torah heir receive a partial distribution of the estate. Others as we have shown oppose both approaches.

---

174 *Pnei Moshe*, supra n. 104 (in the name of Maharit); *Ḥukot Ḥayyim* 73; *Seder Eliyahu Rabba ve-Zuta* 15.

175 *Teshuvot Mahari ha-Levi* 1:4; *Teshuvot Divrei Ḥayyim, ḤM* 2:3; *Teshuvot Birkat Yosef* (Landa) *ḤM* 22; *Teshuvot Divrei Malkiel* 5:211; PDR 9, 115, 126–131.

For a text of a waiver document, see *Teshuvot Tzitz Eliezer* 15:60.

176 *Teshuvot Avnei Nezer ḤM* 23; *Teshuvot Yad Eliyahu* 48; *Teshuvot be-Tzel ha-Ḥokhma* 3:36.

177 See supra n. 12

178 See supra text accompanying n. 80.

179 See supra n. 80.

Deciding between competing arguments regarding the propriety of a civil *will* will be the sole prerogative of the *posek* and beit din. The relative strength of each argument and plausibility will continue to be scrutinized within the framework of future *pesakim* and *piskei din*.

Conclusion

Since the halakhic propriety of a civil testamentary disposition is subject to debate, it behooves our community to seriously consider that a Torah heir may decide [based upon either his own halakhic convictions, desire for material aggrandizement or hatred of his siblings who are non-Torah heirs, or at the behest of his spouse's inveighing] to challenge in beit din his father's civil *will* that distributes portions of the estate to his siblings who are non-Torah heirs. Such claims have in the past been advanced in beit din and continue to this very day to be submitted to battei din. Never assume that family infighting regarding a *yerusha* will happen only in somebody else's backyard. Since there is no halakhic consensus to affirm a civil *will*, the chance of the overwhelming majority of the assets to be redistributed and awarded to a Torah heir(s) by a beit din is a distinct possibility. Optimally, our community ought to seek halakhic and legal counsel regarding halakhic estate-planning techniques that will avoid the potential challenges to the halakhic efficacy of a civil *will*.[180] Should a civil *will* be contested and settlement negotiations fail, it is advisable that one approach a rabbinic authority who has expertise in *Even ha-Ezer* and *Ḥoshen Mishpat* and preferably experience in *dayanut* for counsel on how to handle this matter. ☙

---

180 See supra n. 14.

Should Visiting the Cemetery be Encouraged or Discouraged?

By: MOSHE ZURIEL

The Problem

During the past few hundred years, a new custom has developed for people to visit the cemetery and pray there for Divine help. Some visit on a regular basis to honor the deceased, usually on the seventh and/or thirtieth day (*shloshim*) following the death of a dear one, or on the annual anniversary (*yahrtzeit*) of the *petirah*. In this Torah article we shall attempt to clarify what would be the best way to comply with *Chazal*'s directives and teachings on this matter. So, too, we shall explore whether the deceased can "hear" visitors talking to them.

This essay is divided into three parts. The first addresses the advisability of praying or reciting *Tehillim* and/or *Mishnayos* at the graveside; the second explores whether the deceased hear our words; and the last discusses whether or not it is proper to visit the cemetery on specific days to honor the memory of the deceased.

Undoubtedly, there are many reputable rabbis who condone and encourage each of these practices and beliefs, while other reputable rabbis condemn and forbid them. In general, the former rely

---

Rabbi Moshe Zuriel attended Yeshiva Torah Vodaath in Brooklyn and Ner Israel Rabbinical College in Baltimore. In 1958 he made *aliyah* to Israel and was a student of Rabbi Seraya Deblitzky and a *chavrusa* of Rabbi Chaim Friedlander (Ponevez). He served eighteen years as *Mashgiach* in Yeshivat ha-Hesder Sha'alvim and currently teaches in Yeshivat Rishon L'Tzion and Torat HaChaim. He has produced over thirty Torah volumes and pamphlets, many of them related to *Mussar*; ten biographies of ancient Torah giants with anthologies of their works; a four-volume encyclopedic work on *Aggados* of the Talmud; and republished twelve ancient kabbalistic works adding forewords and indices, and hundreds of comments.

on kabbalistic sources (*Zohar*, Arizal, etc.), while the latter rely on Talmud Yerushalmi.

Talmud Bavli records both opinions, but, as we shall see, the general tendency even there is to discourage the above practices in line with the Talmud Yerushalmi. The goal of this article is to inform those who wish to practice true *Chassidus* (as taught by *Mesillas Yesharim*, chap. 18) to do so without getting entangled in a *machlokes ha'poskim*.

1. Whether or not to pray or read a Torah-section in the cemetery.

> One should not be in the cemetery while wearing *tefillin* or reading Torah. One who does so is *loeg l'rash*, mocks the poor [i.e., the deceased] and insults thereby the Creator (*Berachos* 18a).

Rambam (*Aveilus* 14:13) adds the prohibition to pray there, as do the Rif (11a), Rabbi Yosef Migash (*Sh"ut* 47), and other *Rishonim*, and that is how it is codified in *Shulchan Aruch* (*Yoreh De'ah* 367:3). The additional prohibition to pray is based on the version of the Talmud in their possession (see *Dikdukei Sofrim*).

Rambam adds that if one recites *Krias Shema* in a cemetery, it is disqualified and he must recite it again after leaving the cemetery (*Hilchos Krias Shema*, chap. 3:2). He repeats this injunction concerning *Shemoneh Esreh* (*Hilchos Tefillah* 4:8), disqualifying it if recited in the cemetery.

During the 18th century there was a custom to organize a *minyan* to pray at the tombstone of great Rabbis. Rabbi Chaim David Azulai, the famous Chida, in *Shem HaGedolim* (article 199, "Rabbeinu Eliezer bar Nassan") discusses this custom, citing the *Shulchan Aruch* in *Orach Chaim* 71:4 who follows Rambam and prohibits saying *Krias Shema* at a graveside. Chida suggests that great Rabbis at whose graveside people pray are considered alive, based on the *Gemara* in *Berachos* 18b that *tzaddikim* are alive even after death. As additional support he quotes *Sefer Chassidim* (Section 1129) that Rabbi Yehudah HaNasi, the editor of the *Mishnah*, after his own funeral came to his home every Friday night to recite *Kiddush* for his wife and family. This can only be if he was deemed to be alive and therefore obligated to do *mitzvos*, since the dead are released from that obligation and therefore cannot be a proxy for others. The problem with the Chida's suggestion is that there is absolutely no source either in the Talmud or in any *Midrash* that Rabbi Yehudah HaNasi, after being buried, recited *Kiddush* or did any other *mitzvah* (see *Kesuvos* 103a where the *Gemara* does not mention *Kiddush* at all). As to the account of *Sefer Chassidim*, it's true that it was originally composed by the great Rabbi Yehudah HeChassid, yet it is known that many disciples added additional sections.[1] This may be one of them, and therefore unreliable.

Another Talmudic source prohibiting Torah study in the cemetery is in *Bava Kamma* 16b. *Divrei HaYamim* 2 32:33 relates that at the death of King Chizkiyah, he was accorded great honor. The *Gemara* asks what the great honor was and answers that the rabbis of that period convened a Torah study session at his graveside. *Tosafos* (s.v. *she'hoshivu*) ask how that is permissible, since the *Gemara* above (*Berachot* 18a) prohibits this? *Tosafos* suggests that they distanced themselves from the grave at least four *amos* so as not to infringe upon the law. We must remember that the ancient custom was not to bury the dead in the earth, but rather to place them in caves, which had excavated shelves in the cave-walls upon which the coffins were placed.[2] Therefore, by placing their yeshivah outside the entrance to the cave, they were permitted to study Torah.

Rabbi Yosef Migash (*Sh"ut* chap. 47) has a different answer. He teaches that at the grave of a great Rabbi the above prohibition does not apply. Just as he taught Torah while alive, so we continue to honor him even after death. The problem (for us in our discussion) with this answer is that this allows learning only at the graveside of a teacher of Torah, and not all of the dead fit into this category. Another problem is the issue of "*loeg l'rash*" (insulting the dead).

---

1 See *Sefer Chassidim*, Parma, published and annotated by Yehuda Wistensky וויסטינעצקי שנת תרפ"ד *Mavo* p. 14 as reported in *Otzar HaChochmah*. See also *Sefer Recanati* (14th century), *Parashas Bo*.
ד"ה ולכל בני ישראל לא יחרץ כלב לשונו כותב "וראיתי שכתב אחד מתלמידי ר' יהודה החסיד כי פעם אחת וכו' " וזה נמצא בספר חסידים פסקא תתשמ"ו.

2 See *Bava Basra daf* 101.

While it may be true that this deceased Rabbi is willing to have people learning by his grave, and is not insulted, what about the many others who are buried within a few short steps surrounding him, as is prevalent in modern-day cemeteries? Nevertheless, the *Shulchan Aruch* (*Yoreh De'ah* 344:17) permits reciting *pesukim* from Scripture and even *Torah derashos* at the cemetery if they honor the deceased.[3] Here we have a clear demarcation between learning Torah to fulfill the obligation of learning Torah, independent of the dead, which is prohibited in a cemetery, and Torah study in honor of the deceased, which is permitted.[4]

The *Gemara* in *Taanis* 16a explains the custom of visiting graves during droughts:

> Why do they go to the cemetery? Rebbe Levi and Rebbe Chanina, one says that it is to express that if we have no rain we are as good as dead, and the other says that the reason is so that the dead should pray for us. What is the difference between the two answers? The difference is whether to visit the cemetery of the gentiles.

Rashi explains that in those settlements where we have no Jewish cemetery, if the reason to go there is to humble ourselves, to

---

3 The *Shulchan Aruch* uses the *Nimukei Yosef* as his source.

4 We should mention that here Rabbi Yosef Karo, the author of the *Shulchan Aruch*, forsook his undertaking in his Introduction to the *Beis Yosef* on the *Tur*, that he would base his legal rulings upon the decisions of the Great Three *Rishonim*—the Rif, the Rambam and the Rosh. Here he decided as per Ri Migash et al., without paying attention to the rulings of the above three, who prohibit all and any Torah study in the cemetery. Why did he do so? The answer, I feel, is that it was the current custom in his day. He didn't want to record a ruling which would not be accepted by common practice. [We have several instances to cite, such as *Orach Chaim* (582:9), permitting the recital of the *tefillah* in a loud voice, due to the teaching of *Tosafos* and not that of the three *Rishonim* above. So, too, Rabbi Karo rules that one must wait to recite the blessing on the New Moon until seven days have passed from its inception (*Orach Chaim* 426:4). This is counter to the ruling of Rambam and other *Rishonim* that the benediction should be recited immediately at the first sight of the new moon. There are other exceptions to this rule in the *Shulchan Aruch*.]

inculcate our consciousness with the knowledge of our difficult situation, then going to the Gentile cemetery is fine. But if the reason is to have the dead pray for us, there is no benefit from notifying the dead Gentiles, since they will not pray for us.

Rambam, in *Hilchos Taanis* 4:18, rules according to the first reason. He explains that the rationale for going to the cemetery is to impress that "you will be as good as dead if you don't repent your ways." Generally speaking, the Rambam gives legal rulings without elaborating on the moral lesson involved. Here he does so, since he wants to reject the other explanation of the *Gemara*, i.e., to visit the dead so that they pray for us. Since we see that his habitual critic, the Raavad, doesn't disagree, we can assume that the Raavad agrees with his decision.[5]

Rambam's ruling is based on the Talmud Yerushalmi (*Taanis* 2:1) on this *sugya* which gives only one explanation for visiting cemeteries—that of teaching humility. Although in Talmud Bavli there is a dispute between two Rabbis, Talmud Yerushalmi accepted only the reason of humility. It is accepted that when we have an undecided Bavli versus a decisive Yerushalmi, we must rule according to the Yerushalmi (*Yad Malachi*, pt. 2, *Klalei Shnei HaTalmudim*, item 9).

The *Shulchan Aruch* (*Orach Chaim*, 579:3) copied the words of the Rambam verbatim, i.e., that the reason to go to the cemetery is to inculcate our spirit with humility. Here, too, the Rema is silent, apparently agreeing with the *Mechaber*.[6] Neither gives the other reason for visiting graves.

To summarize, we have here four of the major *poskim* who reject the opinion that we go to the cemetery to ask the dead to pray for us.

We still have to address the three instances where Bavli seems to suggest that visiting the cemetery is for the purpose of asking the dead to pray for us. [1] Kalev went to Chevron to ask the Patriarchs

---

5 This interpretation of Raavad's silence is based on the *Knesses HaGedolah* (*Klalei HaPoskim*, item 35); *Sh"ut Radvaz* (pt. 1, chap. 34) and the *Pri To'ar* (chap. 52:12).

6 See *Sh"ut Yabi'a Omer*, vol. 8, *Even HaEzer Responsa* 17, par. 2, who understands the Rema this way.

to pray for him to protect him from the cabal of the *meraglim* (*Sotah* 34b). [2] Rabbi Manny went to his father's grave (*Taanis* 23b). [3] A certain Rabbi had weakened eyesight and went to Rebbe Chiya's grave to request his intervention (*Bava Metzia* 85b).

All three of the above sources are *Aggados*[7] which are meant to teach moral lessons and not halachic practice; therefore *Chazal* say: "We do not learn from *Aggados*" (Yerushalmi, *Pe'ah* 2, end of *halachah* 4). The *Sefer HaKuzari* (end of *maamar* 3) explains that the editors of the Talmud included the *Aggados* without always giving us the key to unravel the riddles:

> ויש שההגדות הן משלים שנשאו על סודות החכמות שאסור לגלותם, הואיל ולהמון אין בהם משום תועלת, ולא נמסרו כי אם ליחידים שיחקרו וידרשו בהם.

The Noda BiYehudah (*Sh"ut Tinyana, Yoreh De'ah* responsa 161) accepts this rule using the Kuzari explanation as the reason for it:

> ובוודאי האדם לעצמו כשיש לו פנאי ראוי לחקור בכל כחו גם בדברי אגדה. אבל אני אמרתי שאין דרכי להשיב בהם לשואל, <u>כי כל דברי רז"ל בדברי אגדה סגורים וחתומים וכולם קשים להבין</u>.

The *Geonim*[8] (700–1000 CE) also write "the rule is that we do not rely on *Aggadah*." Rambam also agrees in his introduction to *Peirush HaMishnah*.[9, 10]

I want to make it clear that *Aggados* teach inner truths that are, however, not always evident to Torah students as they are written in code usually difficult to decipher. They therefore cannot be used in halachic rulings. Ignoring the above mentioned *Aggados*, we are left only with the halachic *sugya* of *Taanis* 16b, and there we see

---

7 *Aggadah* includes even stories about *Amora'im*, so long as the *Gemara* is not ruling for us what to do, or what is forbidden to do. See *Maamar al HaAggadah* of Rebbe Avraham ben Rambam, republished in the 5-volume *Ein Yaakov* books. There, three paragraphs before the end, ד"ה החלק השני, he includes the telling of stories about *Amora'im* as *Aggadah*, and holds that some of them are indeed dreams.

8 *Otzar HaGeonim*, *Berachos*, p. 91, *Peirushim* par. 271, and so, too, *Otzar HaGeonim* on *Chagigah*, p. 60, par. 69.

9 Mossad Harav Kook edition, pp. 19–20.

10 The encyclopedic work *Sdeh Chemed* (*Klalim, alef*, item 95) enumerates many other important Rabbis who agree with this rule; see also *Encyclopedia Talmudis*, article *Aggadah*, footnotes 60–63.

that the most famous *poskim* relied on the Yerushalmi which disagrees with the explanation of visiting cemeteries to ask the dead for their intervention on our behalf.

So far in the discussion we have worked with the proposition that the reason for not learning Torah or praying while within the confines of the cemetery is so as to not "shame" the dead, not insult them because they cannot do these *mitzvos*. That is the meaning of the term used by the Bavli, "*loeg l'rash.*"

The Talmud Yerushalmi, however, does not use this explanation. The reason it gives is that cemeteries are places that are unclean. "A person who is occupied with interring the deceased in his grave and the appointed hour of *Krias Shema* has arrived, must move to another clean spot, put on his *tefillin*, read the *Shema* and pray [*Shemoneh Esrei*]" (Yerushalmi *Berachos* Chap. 2:3).

In the context, the Yerushalmi is talking about saying *Shema* in an unclean location. Under the ground are moldering flesh and blood and remnants of bones; it is thus considered a foul location. This point is aptly expressed by Rabbi Joseph Kapach in his article "*Krias Shema* and Prayer in an Area of *Tum'ah*,"[11] and is repeated in his commentary to the *Mishneh Torah* of Rambam, *Hilchos Aveilus* 14:14, p. 218. Rambam makes this clear in the *Moreh* where he writes:

> וכל אלה הם גם דברים נגעלים כלומר נדה וזב וזבה ומצורע **ומת** ונבלה ושרץ ושכבת זרע. והנה הושג בדינים אלו מטרות רבות, האחת הפרישה מן הגיעולים, והשנייה נצירת המקדש.[12]

We see no mention here of "insulting the dead." As Rav Kapach explains, possibly the Bavli rabbis used this picturesque choice of language—"not to insult the dead"—to make sure that even the common folk comply properly with the law. The Rabbis may at times use extreme language, just like when they said that *lashon hara* is equivalent to murder, incest and idolatry, as a figure of speech, so as to exact compliance.

---

11 *Sefer HaYovel L'Rav YD Soloveitchik* [Jubilee book in honor of Rabbi Yosef Dov Soloveitchik] (Mossad Harav Kook, pp. 585–594).

12 *Guide for the Perplexed*, bk. 3, chap. 43, p. 389 in the Rav Kapach translation.

This attitude of Rambam, his reliance on the Yerushalmi rationale rather than the Bavli rationale, is taken up in the same way by *Smag* (*mitzvos asei*, 18, 22). So, too, Rav Yaakov, author of *Turim* (chap. 45) prohibited praying or learning within four steps of the dead, without mentioning "insulting the dead." According to this understanding, this rule applies to all deceased, whether the great teacher or the simple Jew, since they are all ritually unclean once no longer alive. Consequently, there is no "exception to the rule" to allow the saying of Torah *derashos* in honor of the dead next to the body or grave. Arguing that they are not insulted under the circumstances, mitigating "*loeg l'rash*," is untenable since this reason is not accepted by Yerushalmi, Rambam, *et al.*

The *Shulchan Aruch,* which, as we saw earlier, seems to lean towards permitting certain Torah activities in a cemetery, is clearly ambivalent. We are all familiar with the contemporary practice to say *Kaddish* while standing next to the coffin during the *levayah*, and also after burial in the cemetery. But not many know that the *Shulchan Aruch* (*Yoreh Deah* 376:4) prohibits this!

ומרחיקין מעט מבית הקברות ואומרים קדיש.

This prohibition is reiterated by Shach (367:3) who quotes the Maharshal on this point. Clearly these *poskim* are ambivalent and at times inconsistent on the permissibility of saying *divrei Torah* in a cemetery.[13]

We conclude this section with the testimony of Rav Moshe Sternbuch (of the Edah Chareidis, Jerusalem) that when the Chazon Ish accompanied a coffin to its funeral spot, he was silent and didn't recite *Yoshev B'seiser*, or any other *pesukim*.[14,15]

---

13 The prevalent custom to pray in the cemetery is based on the *Zohar* (Book 1, p. 225) which advises that when there is a great trouble for the community, they should go to the cemetery to arouse the dead to pray for us. Due to their intervention, many a time the *Ribbono shel Olam* cancels the trouble and saves His people. Rabbi Karo's contemporaries constructed their way of life to accord with the *Zohar*'s words and therefore even gave it precedence over the Talmud Bavli.

14 As aforementioned, we do have many Rabbis who permit praying by the graveside. Let us examine the words of one or two. The *Mishnah Berurah* (chap. 559:41) wrote concerning the custom to go to the cemetery on

---

Tishah B'Av "to the graves of Jews so that they beseech for us (the living) mercy," etc. These words are a quote from the *Darkei Moshe*, the primary work of the Rema, from which he glossed his remarks on the *Shulchan Aruch*, based on each chapter of the *Shulchan Aruch*. The following is the Rema's language regarding going to the cemetery on *Erev Rosh Hashanah* (chap. 581): "The Maharil wrote that it is customary to go to the cemetery on *Erev Rosh Hashanah* and *Yom Kippur* so to humble our hearts on the Days of Awe. The *minhag* is to recite entreaties and requests while there, because when the hearts are contrite the prayers are effective, and the wishes of the dead help as we find by Kalev who went to pray by the graves of the Patriarchs."

Here the words of the Rema must be read carefully so as not to misunderstand the quote from the Maharil. We see two sections of his words. First he records the reasoning "so to humble our hearts." Secondarily he adds, "The *minhag* is to recite entreaties," etc. In other words, the second clause is definitely NOT the Torah attitude, not the halachic reason. The matter of reciting entreaties and requests is common-folk activity, but not necessarily Torah-true. It is only *minhag ha'am*. Therefore, if the *Mishnah Berurah* would have been precise he wouldn't have copied the words about praying there, which is only common-folk practice. It is not the real reason that the Maharil and the Rema wrote for going to the cemetery.

15 Another *posek* whose words teach that it is proper to go to the graves of great Rabbis to pray is Rabbi Yaakov Emden. The Talmud Bavli (*Bava Metzia* 85b) tells us that Reish Lakish was wont to pour white plaster (*sid*) before the caves of burial of the Rabbis. Rashi comments: "So that the *Kohanim* are not contaminated by ritual impurity by stepping there. Why only the graves of the Rabbis (and not signify all of the graves then known)?" Rashi answers: "So that no *mich'shol* (problem) arise due to the *tzaddikim*." Rav Emden, in his gloss to this *Gemara* (printed at the end of the volume, p. 56), disagrees with Rashi and explains, "So that the people know where to go to pray when the community is in trouble." Therefore, we see that Rav Emden agrees with the practice we are discussing here.

Yet one must question, isn't this counter to what *Chazal* (*Shekalim* 2:5) taught, that we are not to erect tombstones for the *tzaddikim*, since their memories are kept alive due to their words or many great good deeds? And the Rambam wrote this halachic decision (*Aveilus*, Chap. 4:4). If, as Rabbi Emden thought, it was a good matter to go pray by the tombstones of the great Rabbis, why did *Chazal* prohibit putting up tombstones there? True, this is a Yerushalmi dictum, but we find no place in Talmud Bavli to contradict that law!

2. Whether the deceased can hear what people tell them at graveside.

Is there is any sort of communication between the living and the dead?

We will start with a quote from *Koheles* 9: 5: "The dead don't know anything." *Chazal* debate the issue in *Berachos* 18 a–b. There is disagreement amongst the commentators about the conclusion of the *Gemara*. *Tosafos* (*Sotah* 34b s.v. *Avosai Bakshu Alai*) understand it as simply so: the dead don't know. The living cannot deliver information to the dead. However, if somebody dies today he can notify those who already passed away, informing them of what is going on here in our world of the living. Rabbi Yeshayahu Pick (in the marginal notation *Masores HaShas*, in *Sotah*) questioned whether <u>this</u> conclusion of the *Tosafos* is indeed the final upshot of the deliberation in *Berachos*. Therefore, we append here the chart of the debate in *Berachos* 18b.

Question	Answer
Kasheh rimah l'meis.	The corpse knows only of its own distress, not that of others
Maaseh b'Chassid, etc. He overheard a conversation between two spirits who knew that their conversation was being overheard by the living.	Maybe a third party died in the meantime and he told the spirits that their conversation is overheard.
Ze'iri deposited monies etc. A certain girl will die.	Maybe it was the angel Duma that notified in advance.
The deceased father of Shmuel, who knew in advance that his son would die.	Shmuel is unlike the others of the dead, since he was an important figure.
G-d commanded Moshe to tell the Forefathers of Israeli redemption.	This is ambiguous. If they know, why tell them? And if they don't know, how does telling help? Maharsha answers here, too: somebody else died in the interim and notified them.

Maligning the dead is like demeaning a stone.	Some explain that the dead don't know, and some that they don't care at all.
A person slandered the deceased Shmuel. A stone fell from the ceiling and cracked his skull.	It is not that the deceased one knew at all. It was G-d who zealously punished the slanderer.

From the protracted deliberations, and the consistent repeal of the proposition that the dead hear what the living tell them, we see that the summing-up conclusion of the *Gemara* is that the dead do not know. When the *sugya* ends with the explanation that Rebbe Yonasan retracted his opinion, it is no contradiction to our conclusion. The Maharsha explains that Rebbe Yonasan retracted only his earlier position that the dead know nothing at all. But he now agrees that they do know, but not because of being informed by the living, but by those who died after them.

Actually this is quite simple and easy to understand. In most instances, after the passage of a year or two, the flesh of the dead disintegrates and is non-existent. If the physical "ears" are no longer there, how can they hear what the living are saying? Furthermore, the dead person is buried deep in the earth—at least five feet of dirt cover him; how can he physically hear the speech of the people above the ground? As to the claim that we are conversing with his soul, how do we know that we "connected"? The soul is a spiritual concept, above and beyond space. Who says that it is just there in the cemetery? It is everywhere, in the city as well as in the wilderness, not confined to any one area; why go to the cemetery to "make contact"?

One may argue that just as we dismissed the simple understanding of the *Aggados* earlier, so, too, this *sugya* (*Berachos* 18) should be considered irrelevant to our discussion, since it has no halachic basis. The response is that it certainly is halachic. We know that the principal *hesped* (eulogy) is the one held at the funeral. This is attested to by Ramban in his *Toras HaAdam* (Mossad HaRav Kook, pp. 80–85). The eulogies delivered after the thirty-day and twelve-month mourning periods are additional honors which the deceased himself doesn't hear at all, but they are dedicated so that the relatives and disciples of the deceased should give him his due honor. "Honor" is not necessarily what the honoree is cognizant of. We know, for example, that Rava stepped backwards when leaving the presence of his great teacher Rav Yosef. Walking backwards barefoot (going barefoot was customary among the Babylonians of that period), his bare feet bumped against the raised stone threshold which served as a doorstop. Rava's feet were badly hurt to the point that the threshold was covered with blood. Rav Yosef was blind and was unaware of this. When his other disciples told him about it, he fervently blessed Rava that he should eventually be the head *Rosh Yeshivah* in the city (*Yoma* 53a).

What honor accrued to the blind Rav Yosef who was unaware of Rava's behavior? Clearly "honor" is judged based on the feelings of the one who honors—how it educates him and brings merit to him. Similarly, when a son mentions his dead father's name and adds "*zichrono l'-vrachah*," certainly the father who is not here—his remains are possibly buried in some faraway place—is unable to hear those words of blessing and yet it is the duty of the son to honor his father thus. Similarly, there is an obligation to honor the deceased by giving a *hesped* (eulogy) long after the burial, even if the dead cannot hear it.

Is there a time period after death that the deceased can hear the words of the living eulogizers? Taz (*Yoreh De'ah*, chap. 344:1) teaches that the dead hear what is said until the grave is closed. He bases this on Talmud Yerushalmi (*Avodah Zarah* chap. 3:1).

Talmud Bavli records in *Shabbos* 152b: "Rabbi Avahu says: All that is spoken close to the dead he can hear until the grave is closed. But Rav Chiya and Rav Shimon, the son of Rebbe, one says that the corpse can hear until the grave is closed and the other says he can hear until his flesh is decomposed."

We already mentioned that when there are disagreements in the Bavli, and the Yerushalmi has a unanimous opinion, we follow the Yerushalmi; that is the reason for the Taz ruling.

But actually, Talmud Bavli comes to a similar conclusion. Rav taught that if one wants to know whether the deceased is deserving of *olam ha-ba* we should listen to the conversation of people at his funeral (*Shabbos* 153a). The *Gemara* bases this on the *passuk* (*Yeshayah* 30: 21):

וְאָזְנֶיךָ תִּשְׁמַעְנָה דָבָר מֵאַחֲרֶיךָ לֵאמֹר: זֶה הַדֶּרֶךְ לְכוּ בוֹ כִּי תַאֲמִינוּ וְכִי תַשְׂמְאִילוּ:

Your ears will hear, what is spoken after you, as follows: The path that this [deceased followed] you too follow; don't swerve to the right or the left.

Rashi (s.v. *v'oznecha tishmanah*) explains:

While **lying in your hearse and you hear** the mourners at the funeral say, "The path that this deceased person followed, do as he did," you can be reassured that you are a *ben olam haba.*

Why does Rashi add the words "While lying in your hearse"? Aren't a *hesped* and the accompanying praises of the dead done even later on, on the seventh day of mourning? On the thirtieth? After the twelve months? Clearly Rashi understands that the deceased no longer hears even if the *hesped* is delivered close to his grave.

Another important comment of Rashi on that same page in the Talmud should be noted. Rav requested of his student Rav Shmuel Bar Sheilat to show excitement during his eulogy so as to arouse the mourners' emotions "Since **I will be present there**" [and I will know what you are doing].

Rashi, s.v. *achim b'hespedo*, comments: "When I die, arouse yourself with vigor so that the people [at the funeral] get warmed up, they should feel compassion and weep (at my death)." Why does Rashi add the seemingly superfluous words "*b'she'as misasi*—at the time of my death"? Again, Rashi seems to emphasize that the dead are only capable of hearing **before** the burial, not afterwards, based on the *sugya* in *Berachos* 18 which now has a practical halachic application. Furthermore, it is important until when the dead can hear since it is nowadays customary that people (especially women) who are desperate for the intervention of an illustrious ancestor, a close relative, or of a great Rabbi, pour "their hearts out" and inform the dead of their needs. I quote here the words of Rav Avraham Danziger, the author of *Chayei Adam*, in his work *Chochmas Adam* (chap. 89:7):

איסור דורש אל המתים זה שמרעיב עצמו ולן בבית הקברות כדי שתשרה עליו רוח הטומאה (שם סעיף י"ג) ואותן נשים וכן עמי הארצות שהולכין על קברי מתים וכאילו מדברים עם המתים ואומרים להם צרותיהם, קרוב הדבר שהם בכלל זה. ונמצא שיש מן הגאונים היו רוצים לאסור להשתטח על קברי מתים.

The Torah (*Devarim* 18:11) prohibits to pray to the dead. Technically this refers to a person who fasts and spends the night in the cemetery so that the unholy spirit should rest on him. The women and some *amei ha'aretz*, ignoramuses, who visit graves to tell the dead about their troubles, probably commit the prohibition of *doresh el ha'meisim*. Some of the ancient *Geonim* wanted to prohibit the custom of visiting graves to pray there.

As for the *Gemara* (*Yoma* 87a) that rules that if someone slandered a person who is now dead, he must go to the cemetery and request his forgiveness—the intent is to ask for G-d's forgiveness and not of the deceased victim. The following is the language of the Talmud:

ואם מת, מביא עשרה בני אדם ומעמידן על קברו ואומר חטאתי לה' אלהי ישראל ולפלוני שחבלתי בו.

If [the insulted person] has already died, one must gather ten people, stand them at his graveside and say: I have sinned to G-d the Lord of Israel, and to this [now deceased] individual to whom I have inflicted pain.

Why is this formulated as if speaking to a third party? Why not address the deceased directly? Clearly we are not talking to him but to *Hakadosh Baruch Hu*, as the dead cannot hear. Then why go to the cemetery at all? Why not ask forgiveness in the synagogue? One should also ask, why bring ten people? Isn't it enough to ask person-to-person, at most in the presence of three people as is required when the insulted is still alive? The intent of *Chazal* is to humiliate the offender, to encourage him to desist from this evil habit and not repeat it again. Collect ten people, take the trouble to bring them all to the cemetery, involve the *Ribbono Shel Olam* in the ritual because the sin is now to G-d, not to the deceased who is already in another world. As *Chazal* said (in *Berachos* 19a) the deceased no longer cares that he was slandered. He is now in a higher spiritual world where these matters are insignificant to him, just as we no longer care what happened to us as young children in kindergarten or in elementary school.[16]

---

16 In the *Aggadah* of *Taanis* 23b, where Rebbe Manny went to his father's grave and exhorted him to help out, it is important to mention that in the Munchen manuscript of the Talmud (cited by *Dikdukei Sofrim*, item 5),

3. Is it proper to visit the cemetery on the thirtieth day or on the *yahrtzeit*, or just to honor the dead, like those who visit the Maharal's grave in Prague, the Vilna Gaon in Vilnius, etc.?

We find on this subject that the most prominent *poskim* frown on this matter. The *Mishnah Berurah* (chap. 559:41) writes: "All the above, i.e., to visit graves, is only if one stands four steps away from the grave, even from Jewish graves, since we fear the Evil Spirits."

The source for this is the Magen Avraham (end of chap. 559), who wrote: "We find in the writings of the Arizal that one should only go to the cemetery for the burial ceremony [not at other times] especially if one has not repented from the sin of nocturnal emissions, for then the Evil Spirit attaches itself to him." *Be'er Hetev* (chap. 559) quotes the Magen Avraham.

The *Aruch HaShulchan* (chap. 559:7) writes: "The Arizal was against visiting graves, other than at the time of burial. We already noted that nowadays people go there in groups and engage in idle chatter; it is better not to go."

The source of the Arizal's ruling is in *Shaar Ruach HaKodesh* (the block letter edition, p. 49) where it is recounted that Rav Chaim Vital asked advice from the Arizal regarding the obligation to go to the cemetery and ask forgiveness from a deceased Jew whom he had insulted. The Arizal advised him to walk around the entire cemetery on all four sides and to be careful not to enter with-

---

the words "Abba Abba" are deleted, so to say he didn't speak directly to the dead but was praying to G-d. This proves our contention that the dead hear no communications directed to them by living human beings. The reason he went to the graveyard to pray was to arouse contrition and humility in his heart. About the *Aggadah* that Kalev went to Chevron to implore the Patriarchs to help out, we already mentioned that the *Tosafos* claim that he spoke to G-d, not to the dead. Beyond that, in the ancient version of the Talmud, the book called *Aggados HaTalmud* (first printed in 1511, way before the printed version of the Talmud as we have it today), in the expression "*amar lahem*," the word "*lahem*" is lacking. So, too, in *Sefer HaMe'orot* of Rav Meir Hame'ily, *Berachos* 182, the word "*lahem*" is missing.

in four steps of any grave so that the Evil Spirits do not grasp hold of him, those spirits caused by the contaminated emissions.

So, too, the Vilna Gaon was against the *minhag* to visit graves. In the famous farewell letter that he wrote to his family when he traveled to the Holy Land, he writes to his wife and children: "Be very careful not to go to the cemetery at all, for there the Evil Spirits attach themselves unto you, especially women. All the troubles and the sins stem from this."[17]

If a person is not praying there, but is only going there to honor the dead, is this a kosher *minhag*?

The Chasam Sofer (*Sh"ut Yoreh De'ah*, response 338, paragraph "*U'bezeh Yuvenu divrei HaRambam*) was against it, and even called it "*darkei Emori*," a superstitious, idolatrous rite. He even based upon this the *Chazal* source of the Rambam's words not to visit the graves (*Aveilus*, chap. 4, par. 4) as follows:

> In *Maseches Semachos* (chap. 8, item 1), *Chazal* taught: "One may go to the cemetery to check the dead, up to three days without any fear of this being *darkei Emori*. It once happened

[17] It is important to clarify a mistaken understanding widespread amongst *bnei Torah*. The famous Kabbalist Rav Shlomo Elyashiv (the grandfather of our contemporary Rav Elyashiv, *zt"l*) wrote in his book *Gilyonos HaLeshem* (p. 313), in his remarks to the commentary of the Vilna Gaon to *Tikkunei Zohar* p. 22b, that "in a period when there are no *tzaddikim* in the generation, the *Shechinah* rests upon the graves of the *tzaddikim*." On the basis of these words, many *talmidei chachamim* in our day go to the graves of the *tzaddikim* to pray there, since the *Shechinah* is there.
But alas, in my opinion the Leshem had an incorrect understanding of the Vilna Gaon's words. The text involved (*Tikkunei Zohar*) has a Drashah of *gezeirah shavah* "*Ba'derech*." "*Ba'derech*" is the word used by the Torah for the tribes who died in the desert ("*meitu ba'midbar ba'derech*") and at the death of Rachel Imeinu ("*meitah alai ba'derech*"). The Vilna Gaon comments that *Sefiras Malchus* is called *Derech* and when there are not *tzaddikim* in the generation, the *Shechinah* rests upon the buried *tzaddikim*. The reference is only to Kever Rachel and to *meitei midbar* (who, as is well known, are called *Dor De'ah*, all the disciples of Moshe Rabbeinu). Neither the *Tikkunei Zohar* nor the Gaon of Vilna implies that this applies to *tzaddikim* in every generation. Even more so, it is well known that the Vilna Gaon was against visiting graves and didn't even visit his mother's grave (Aliyot Eliyahu) who was certainly a *tzaddekes*.

that the live visited the grave and found one (supposedly dead) and he lived afterwards for twenty-five years."

The *Nachalas Yaakov* (a commentary printed on the page of *Maseches Semachos*) commented: "The visit is to verify whether the buried just passed out or is really dead. The *Prishah* (commentary on the *Tur*) *Yoreh De'ah* 394, item 3, writes that this law was applicable only in the days of *Chazal* since in that period the dead were placed in caves (and were not covered with earth) and the visit was only intended to move the stone blocking the cave and look in [and check to see if the interred had only fainted and was now awake.] But today that the dead are covered by earth, there is no use in going to visit and to check."

This passage is explained by the Chasam Sofer as follows: "According to the *Prishah* [that in our age there is no need to check, since even if the supposedly dead man was really alive and we mistakenly thought him to be dead, after his being covered by earth for more than ten minutes, there is no point in checking as the person would be dead anyway by then], visiting the grave is once again *darkei Emori* [apparently a point in *doresh el ha'meisim*]. And this is the source of the Rambam's words."[18,19]

To summarize: the greatest of the prominent *poskim*—the Arizal, Vilna Gaon, Magen Avraham, Mishnah Berurah, Aruch

---

18 We know for a fact that that the Rambam had a source from *Chazal*, because whatever he adds as his own opinion, he precedes with the words "*Nir'im li ha'devarim.*"

19 **Editor's Note:** I believe that it is highly unlikely that Rambam or Chasam Sofer considered visiting graves to be *darkei HaEmori*. The relevant Rambam is in *Hilchos Aveilus* 4:4 where Rambam writes ולא יפנה אדם לבקר הקברות. Many explanations are given for this phrase. It is evident from Chasam Sofer's *teshuvah* that he interpreted it to mean, as some *Rishonim* do (see Radvaz, ibid., and *Teshuvas Rivash* 421), that it refers to opening the grave to examine the body. It is this that he considered *darkei HaEmori*. Radvaz says this is Rambam's intent and states explicitly that the custom of Israel is to visit graves. According to *Kesef Mishneh* (ibid.) based on Rivash, Rambam indeed means to discourage attachment to the grave, but not necessarily visiting it—and in any event this prohibition is not *darkei HaEmori*. We suggest that the reader consult these sources and make his own judgment.

HaShulchan—all disapprove of visiting graves. The Chasam Sofer considers it an out-and-out *issur* as does Rambam in *Hilchos Aveilus*, chap. 4, paragraph 4. Therefore, although those who do visit graves have reliable Rabbis who taught them to do so, he who wishes to be 100 percent proper, and not to do anything which is possibly forbidden, should take into account our great Masters listed above.[20] ☙

[20] Concerning the matter of women visiting the cemetery, this is even forbidden by the *Shulchan Aruch* (*Yoreh De'ah*, chap. 359. See there the words of the Shach). It is surprising that the most Orthodox Jewish women, *machmiros* in nearly all other matters, ignore this open and clear prohibition.

Kiddush HaShem: Israel's Mission

By: ASHER BENZION BUCHMAN

The *Shem*

"The *mitzvah* of *Kiddush HaShem* is stated [in the Torah] in the words 'I will be sanctified in the midst of the Children of Israel' (*Vayikra* 22:32). It consists in that we are commanded to publicize the true faith in public, and that we not fear from the damage threatened by any aggressor, to the extent that even if an oppressor demands of us to deny the Almighty—we will not heed him, but give ourselves up to certain death rather than let him be led to believe that we have denied even though in fact our hearts are still true to Heaven. This is the *mitzvah* of *Kiddush HaShem* that all of Israel was commanded in, to give ourselves up to death in the hands of the oppressor for the sake of the love of the Almighty and our belief in His Unity as did Chananiah, Mishael, and Azariah in the days of Nevuchadnetzar the Evil when he forced [all people] to bow to an idol, and all people bowed to it and Israel was amongst them, and there was none to sanctify (*mekadesh*) the Name of Heaven. And this was a matter of great shame to Israel that the *mitzvah* was lost from them all, and none was willing to fulfill it—all feared. And this *mitzvah* is only fulfilled in such a situation, where the entire world is in a state of fear, and then the obligation exists to publicize G-d's unity and to announce it at that time. G-d had already promised via Yeshayah that Israel's shame would not be total when this plight would arise, and that young men would step forward in that difficult situation, and not tremble before death and they would offer up their blood and publicize the faith and sanctify G-d in public as the Almighty commanded us via Moshe as it says: "And now Yaakov will not be embarrassed nor his face turn pale, when he

---

Asher Benzion Buchman is the author of *Encountering the Creator: Divine Providence and Prayer in the Works of Rambam* (Targum, 2004), and *Rambam and Redemption* (Targum, 2005). He is the editor-in-chief of *Ḥakirah.*

> sees his children, the work of My hands in the midst of him, sanctifying My name; they will sanctify the Holy One of Yaakov and stand in awe of the G-d of Israel" (*Yeshayah* 29:22–23). The language of the Sifra is "on this condition I took you out of Egypt—on the condition that you will sanctify me in public."[1] (*Sefer Hamitzvos, Aseh* 9)

As Rambam presents the *mitzvah* of *Kiddush HaShem* (קדוש השם) here in the *Sefer HaMitzvos*, its central theme is that Israel is obligated to demonstrate its loyalty in public to the One true G-d, who was revealed to them at Sinai. The crucial element of this publicizing is that the individual Jew demonstrates his willingness to give up his life rather than give the oppressor the impression that he has abandoned his religion because of the threat to his life. Although not stated explicitly here, in the time of *shemad* even for the smallest of *mitzvos* one must not relent before his oppressor.[2] The *mikra* itself speaks of making this demonstration specifically before a Jewish public: "I will be sanctified in the midst of the Children of Israel," ונקדשתי בתוך בני ישראל, and consequently halachah[3] requires that should the oppressor demand the Jew transgress a lesser violation for his personal gain rather than for the purpose of having him abandon his faith, he must only forfeit his life in refusal if this

---

1 הציווי שנצטווינו על קדוש השם, והוא אמרו: "ונקדשתי בתוך בני ישראל" (ויקרא כב, לב). ועניין מצווה זו: שאנו מצווים לפרסם דת אמת זו ברבים, ושלא נירא בכך מהזק שום מזיק, עד שאפילו יבוא אלינו אנס עריץ ויקרא אותנו לכפור בו יתעלה - לא נשמע לו, אלא נמסור את עצמנו למות בהחלט; ו[אפילו] לא ניתן לו לחשוב שכפרנו, אף שלבנו מאמין בו יתעלה. וזו היא מצוות קדוש השם שנצטוו בה כל בני ישראל, כלומר: שנמסור את עצמנו למות בידי העריץ על אהבתו יתעלה והאמונה בייחודו, כמו שעשו חנניה מישאל ועזריה בימי נבוכדנצר הרשע כשהכריח להשתחוות לצלם, והשתחוו כל בני אדם וישראל בכללם, ולא היה שם מקדש שם שמים. והיה בכך חרפה גדולה לישראל שאבדה מכולם מצווה זו, ולא היה שם מי שמקיים אותה אלא הכל פחדו. ואין מצווה זו נוהגת אלא בכגון אותו המעמד העצום שבו פחדו כל באי העולם, והיה חובה לפרסם ייחודו ולהכריז עליו באותה העת. וכבר הבטיח ה' על ידי ישעיהו, שלא תהיה חרפת ישראל גמורה באותו המעמד, ושיופיעו בהם בחורים באותו המעמד הקשה, שלא ירתיעם המות, ויפקירו דמם ויפרסמו את האמונה ויקדשו את ה' ברבים, כמו שציוונו יתעלה על ידי משה רבנו, והוא אמרו:"לא עתה יבוש יעקב ולא עתה פניו יחורו. כי בראותו ילדיו מעשה ידי בקרבו יקדישו שמי והקדישו את קדוש יעקב ואת אלקי ישראל יעריצו" (ישעיה כט, כב-כג). ולשון ספרא:"על מנת כך הוצאתי אתכם מארץ מצרים - על מנת שתקדשו את שמי ברבים" (סה"מ עשה ט).

2 *Hilchos Yesodei HaTorah* 5:3.

3 *Hilchos Yesodei HaTorah* 5:2.

transgression is to be done before ten Jews.[4] Thus on the one hand the central element of the *mitzvah* is standing up against the gentile oppressors and demonstrating to them our steadfastness and on the other hand it takes on an added dimension in front of a Jewish public.[5]

Rambam further states that it is only because the Jewish people would one day produce Chananiah, Mishael and Azariah, who would stand up against idolatry when the whole world gave in to it, that we were taken out of Egypt. The sense that Rambam conveys is that the Jews who witnessed Chananiah, Mishael and Azariah saw an example of faith, courage and love of G-d that would forever sustain the nation and preserve the mission they were entrusted in by the Creator. Rambam in *Moreh Nevuchim* (1:64) explains that שם ה' (the name of G-d) has several meanings and one of them is "G-d's mission," as in שמי בקרבו "My name is within him (Israel)" which means that Israel is "a vessel for My (G-d's) will"[6] and it is this meaning that it has with regard to *Kiddush HaShem*.[7]

Refraining or Resisting?

Some Rishonim[8] say that the requirement to give up one's life for *Kiddush HaShem* only pertains to cases where one is called upon to actively transgress a *mitzvah* in the Torah.[9] One must refrain from

---

4 See also *Lav* 63 that it is חלול השם ברבים when done before ten Jews. The *lav* of *Chillul HaShem* is the counter to the *mitzvah* of *Kiddush HaShem* and in general a failure to perform *Kiddush HaShem* includes a violation of *Chillul HaShem*. In this essay we will use the terms *Kiddush HaShem* and *Chillul HaShem* without dealing with the nuances that differentiate one from the other.

5 The הרוגי מלכות who are on the highest plane of existence resisted *shemad* before all of Israel, but according to Rambam's definition, in *Yesodei HaTorah* 5:4, they may have attained that status even if it was not the time of *shemad*.

6 Kappach's translation reads כלי לחפצי ורצוני.

7 Later on in this essay we will explain the term קדוש and sharpen the definition of the *mitzvah*.

8 See *Nimukei Yosef* (*Sanhedrin* 82a) and Ran (*Shabbos* 49a) quoted in *Kesef Mishneh* (Y.H. 5:1–3).

9 Following Abaye in his dispute with Rava.

doing a "sinful act" a *maaseh issur* (מעשה אסור). Thus, if the oppressor assaults a woman, as long as her submission is passive and requires no positive action, there is no need for her to give up her life—this is the principle that the Amora Abaye refers to as *karka olam* (קרקע עולם).[10] This principle applies to murder and *avodah zarah* as well; thus, if one would stay still and allow himself to be used as a projectile to kill another, that would be permissible.[11] Applying this principle further, these Rishonim deduce that in the case of refraining from doing a *mitzvah, bitul aseh* (בטול עשה), where the gentiles "could prevent one from acting" anyhow, the law would not apply. These Rishonim seem to see *Kiddush HaShem* more as a halachic principle than as a unique *mitzvah.*[12] The maintenance of the performance of *mitzvos* is so important that one should rather die than abandon them[13]—but if one will not be able to perform a specific *mitzvah* anyhow, there is no reason to give up one's life only to show resistance.

According to Rambam, the resistance itself is the *mitzvah* of *Kiddush HaShem* and thus refraining from doing a *mitzvah* is not an option.[14] Rabbi Akiva, who gave his life to preserve the *mitzvah* of *talmud Torah*, epitomizes this *mitzvah*. He steeled himself and even ordained others during a period of *shemad.*[15] The obligation is to

---

10 אסתר קרקע עולם היתה Literally, "Esther was [like] the ground of the Earth."

11 Likewise, an act of *avodah zarah* that is done without any action would be allowed.

12 This *mitzvah* is not found in all counts of the *mitzvos*. It is not found, for example, in Ibn Gabirol's. As we shall see, Rambam packages several diverse requirements under this one concept and in this he is certainly unique.

13 The Chinuch (296) writes as follows: שורש מצוה זו ידוע, כי האדם לא נברא רק לעבוד בוראו, ומי שאינו מוסר גופו על עבודת אדוניו איננו עבד טוב. והרי בני אדם ימסרו נפשותם על אדוניהם, קל וחומר על מצות מלך מלכי המלכים הקדוש ברוך הוא.

14 See *Hil. Yesodei HaTorah* 5:2 and 5:4. In *Iggeres HaShemad* he calls the refraining from *talmud Torah* and *milah* a מעשה which we must not acquiesce to.

15 See *Kesef Mishneh* (*Yesodei HaTorah* 5:3) who brings this as proof against *Nimukei Yosef.*

sustain the Jewish religion and positive acts of resistance are necessary for this.[16]

Kedushah

The *Baalei Tosafos*[17] and *Chinuch* (296) explain Rabbi Akiva's actions and similar conduct recorded in the Talmud by claiming that those people went beyond their legal requirement, *lifnim mi'shuras hadin.*[18] These Rishonim who on the one hand limit the cases where one is obligated to give up his life, on the other hand balance this by saying that it is saintly conduct, *middas chassidus* (מדת חסידות), to sacrifice one's life when it is not required.[19] This position itself also clashes with Rambam who states: "To whomever it is said that he should transgress rather than being killed, should he choose to be killed, he is guilty of shedding his own blood."[20]

To understand why *Tosafos* and Rambam argue on whether one may give up his life when it is not warranted, we must understand their respective positions on the concept of *kedushah.*

The Torah verse that commands the *mitzvah* of *Kiddush HaShem,*[21] ונקדשתי, comes at the end of a section in the Torah that begins with the verse "You shall be holy"—*kedoshim tihiyu* (קדשים תהיו)[22]—and the two concepts are clearly linked.[23] The position

16 Thus the *mitzvah* only applies to Jews and not gentiles (*Hil. Melachim* 10:2, TB *Sanhedrin* 74b, TY 3:5) as it is the obligation to preserve the Jewish religion and the Yerushalmi learns it from the words בתוך בני ישראל. But see *Minchas Chinuch* 296 (beginning) discussing other opinions who believe it does apply to gentiles.

17 See *Tosafos* to *Pesachmi* 53b.

18 The Chinuch stipulates that only those on the highest level are able to do this.

19 In the literature describing Ashkenazic Jewish communities sacrificing themselves and even slaughtering their children to avoid forced conversion during the Crusades, it is important to realize how different their halachic stance is from that of Rambam.

20 כל מי שנאמר בו יעבור ואל ייהרג, ונהרג ולא עבר—הרי זה מתחייב בנפשו.

21 *Vayikra* 22:32.

22 *Vayikra* 19:2.

Tosafos takes with regard to *Kiddush HaShem* is consistent with the famous Ramban on *kedoshim tihiyu*,[24] that the concept of *kedushah* consists in going beyond what the Torah demands. Thus, while the basic halachos of *Kiddush HaShem* might demand only a limited type of resistance, the fuller fulfillment calls for a higher level of devotion. In contrast, Rambam[25] believes that *kedushah* resides in doing the will of G-d which lies in performing all the *mitzvos* of the Torah exactly as they are defined and not more.

Rambam actually begins his definition of *Kiddush HaShem*[26] in *Mishneh Torah* by stating (*Hilchos Yesodei HaTorah* 5:1): "How is it performed? Under duress, one must violate any *mitzvah* rather than be killed" following the Torah's principle that the *mitzvos* were given to "live by"—*v'chai bahem* (וחי בהם). The simple reading of his words implies that in normal cases, by transgressing rather than dying for *mitzvos*, one is also engaging in *Kiddush HaShem.* Rambam believes that it is just as much a profanation of the name of G-d—*chillul HaShem* (חלול השם)—to portray His will as demanding that human life be sacrificed when it is unwarranted as it is to refuse to give up one's life when such a sacrifice is demanded.[27] According to Rambam, *kedushah* is not an extremist quality, but a balanced one like all the qualities *(middos)* of G-d, as the obligation to be holy is a part of the *mitzvah* to emulate G-d.[28]

---

23 To be מקדש השם is to fulfill מה אני קדוש אף אתה קדוש and to demonstrate שמי בקרבו and hence strengthen Israel in their mission in the world. We will explain this idea later in the essay.

24 See his commentary on the Torah at the beginning of *Parashas Kedoshim.*

25 *Sefer HaMitzvos, Shoresh* 4.

26 Before explaining under which conditions one must forfeit his life.

27 See also *Hilchos Shabbos* 2.

28 See *Moreh Nevuchim* where Rambam quotes this verse for the concept of והלכת בדרכיו while in *Mishneh Torah* he explains מה אני קדוש אף אתה קדוש. *Kedoshim tihiyu* is fundamental to the obligation of a Jew and in fact in *Sefer HaMitzvos* the *mitzvah* of *Kiddush HaShem* is immediately after *V'Halachta B'drachav.* Just as *kadosh* as a *middah* is in balance, so too *Kiddush HaShem* is in balance. *Kedoshim tihiyu* incorporates the requirement to be healthy and to not deprive oneself (*Shemonah Perakim*). See *Hilchos Shabbos* 2:3 where Rambam berates those who would not understand this concept. When Rambam speaks of לפנים משורת הדין it is in מעשיו—his dealings with others in monetary matters.

In *Iggeres HaShemad*, in response to the claim by some that there are other religions where more is demanded of practitioners than Judaism demands, Rambam notes that we dare not learn from other cultures what constitutes *Kiddush HaShem*, for if so "it would obligate us to say that since some idolaters sacrifice their children to their idols we should do likewise."[29]

Kiddush HaShem and the Fundamental *Mitzvos*

The Talmud says that the reason one may not kill another so that an oppressor will spare his own life is because "Who says your blood is redder than another's?" (מי יימר דדמה דידך סומק טפי?). As we have noted, the *Baalei Tosafos*[30] contend that one can nevertheless allow himself to be used in a murder as long as he is passive, as one's own life is equally worthwhile as another's and the law therefore just demands passivity. Since both lives are equal, one's obligation is merely to refrain from an act of murder, *maaseh retzichah* (מעשה רציחה).[31]

However, Rav Chaim Brisker notes that Rambam could not agree with this since he states that the married woman who is assaulted must resist even at the risk of her[32] life[33] and the requirement to give up one's life is unrelated to whether one need do a *maaseh*.[34] He thus explains that the concept of "Who says your

---

29 והיה מתחיב מזה ההקש שנאמר שכשיהיה עובד ע"ז בנו ובתו באש לנעבד ק"ו שנשרף אנחנו עצמנו ובשרנו ובנינו בעבודת הקל.

30 See *Tos. Sanhedrin* 74b d.h *V'Ha; Pesachim* 25b d.h. *Af;* and *Hagahos Rambam, Hil. Yesodei HaTorah* 5:7.

31 See section above: "Refraining or Resisting."

32 במה דברים אמורים, בזמן שהגוי מתכוון להנאת עצמו, כגון שאנסו לבנות לו ביתו בשבת או לבשל לו תבשילו או אנס אישה לבועלה וכיוצא בזה.(הל' יסודה"ת ה:ג) See the *Kesef Mishneh* who notes that Rambam decided like Rava rather than Abaye and thus does not use the logic of *karka olam.*

33 *Kesuvos* 3b speaks of פרוצות וצנועות and implication is that there are cases where a woman would not need to resist. Perhaps according to Rambam resistance should be to the act, to demonstrate non-compliance but not to the point where a provocation for murder would be created when the act could not be stopped anyway.

34 Dying for the three major sins—murder, *arayos* and *avodah zarah*—are exact parallels and should be governed by the same rules.

blood is redder?" teaches a principle that saving one person's life—*pikuach nefesh* (פקוח נפש)—is not grounds for permitting murder of another. Whatever constitutes murder, whether an act is involved or not, is not permissible for *pikuach nefesh.*[35]

> דכיון דשקולים הן ממילא אינה נדחית בפני פקו"נ ואין חלוק בין שב ואל תעשה למעשה בידים דלעולם אין בה דין דחיה (הל' יסודי התורה ה:א)
>
> Since the two are equal, thus it (murder) is not pushed aside for the sake of *pikuach nefesh,* and it matters not whether one is passive or performs an act, there are no grounds for pushing aside [the prohibition].

Rav Chaim does not elaborate further on this point, but we can explain this principle with the understanding that even with regard to the three *mitzvos*[36] that must never be violated even at the forfeiture of one's life, the reason this is so is because of the *mitzvah* of *Kiddush HaShem.* That is why the halachah pertaining to the requirement to sacrifice one's life rather than violating these three *mitzvos* is brought at the very beginning of the chapter of *Kiddush HaShem* (chapter five of *Hilchos Yesodei HaTorah*).[37]

Those who disagree with Rambam follow the reasoning that violating *arayos* and *avodah zarah* is as bad as an act of murder,[38] and since doing the act is as bad as refraining from the act one must be passive.[39] In fact, Ramban[40] is explicit that the three *mitzvos* are not

---

35 Even though indirect murder is not punishable by the death penalty, it is still prohibited under the אסור of רציחה.

36 *Avodah zarah, giluy arayos, retzichah.*

37 ב. במה דברים אמורים, בשאר מצוות—חוץ מעבודה זרה, וגילוי עריות, ושפיכות דמים. אבל שלוש עבירות אלו, אם יאמר לו עבור על אחת מהן או תיהרג, ייהרג ואל יעבור.

38 For *arayos* the *Geonim* say it is כאלו הרגה and with *avodah zarah* one loses even their *olam haba.* Thus, one *shittas Tanna'im* is that one can kill a person to save him from an act of idol worship. Rambam himself expresses this basic idea with regard to curing oneself through these sins.

39 We should also take note of the fact that the approach of the *Baalei Tosafos* rests upon the concept that submitting to an act of *arayos* is as bad as death. However, according to Rambam, this does not follow. These *halachos* are all governed by the principle of *Kiddush HaShem.* Israel's commitment to *tznius* and abhorrence of *arayos* demands of them that they not submit even in the face of death but this does not mean the

related to *Kiddush HaShem*.[41] According to Ramban it is only *Kiddush HaShem* when one resists because of his fidelity to the laws of the Torah when being forced to transgress even a minor violation in public or in the time of *shemad*. But according to Rambam, this case as well is *Kiddush HaShem* as the concept is that one cannot engage in murder even to save his life[42] and then claim to represent G-d. Even when the oppressor acts for his own benefit (להנאת עצמו)[43] and even when no *maaseh* is called for, it is a *chillul HaShem* to conduct oneself so as to save one's own life at the expense of another.

On the other hand, there are some who contend that since (in agreement with Rambam) the three *mitzvos* are based on *Kiddush HaShem*, one must therefore only submit in public.[44] But according to Rambam himself, just as *kedoshim tihiyu* applies in private, so, too, *Kiddush HaShem* can apply in private as well. Preserving the *Shem* within the individual is central to this commandment.[45]

Preserving *Taharah*

The Mishnah (*Terumos* 8:11) discusses whether one woman can be handed over to save multiple women from defilement. The preceding Mishnah raises a similar issue with regard to saving *terumah* from being made impure, *tameh* (טמא). With regard to purity—*taharos* (טהרות)—the rule is to preserve as much *taharah* as possible even though it means committing the positive act of handing over

---

harm done to the person is a "fate worse than (or at least as bad as) death."

40 *Milchamos, Sanhedrin* 74a–b.

41 Also Ran 74a and the Ramban are quoted by *Nimukei Yosef.*

42 He explains that this is דבר שהדעת נוטה לו, natural law declares this concept.

43 With no specific intent or concern that the Jew violate Jewish law.

44 By contrast, the שלטי גבורים quotes a view (apparently one opinion in *Tosafos*) that even the three *aveiros* can be transgressed in private. Since some believe that עבודה זרה מאהבה ומיראה, a lesser form of idolatry, refers to fear of being murdered, this is a likely interpretation—only the application to murder is startling.

45 This explains why Yosef, who bonded with G-d and did it all in his self-sufficient existence, embodied this as well (*Hilchos Yesodei HaTorah* 5:10).

the bread to be made *tamei* by the gentile.[46] But with regard to the women, the Mishnah legislates differently, and a single woman cannot be handed over to save the group. Although it is a logical principle to preserve as much *taharah* as possible and the first part of the Mishnah reflects this, this concept is not extended to the case of women even if the woman to be sacrificed is not married[47] and even if not in the presence of ten Jews (*Hil. Yesodei HaTorah* 5:5). Based on our understanding, there is no contradiction between these two parts of the Mishnah since in the latter case the principle of *Kiddush HaShem* becomes operable. Indeed, the Mishnah's principle is that as much *kedushah* and *taharah* as is possible must be preserved and in the case of the women the preservation of the most *kedushah* comes about by refusing to cooperate with the oppressors and acting for *Kiddush HaShem*.

Chazal utilize this concept as well, in ruling that the fugitive Sheva ben Bichri could not be handed over by the community leaders to save the lives of the rest of the city, unless he was indeed guilty of a capital crime. *Ramach* (*Hil. Yesodei HaTorah* 5:5) asks how this law can be rationalized. Our principle of "Who says your blood is redder?" would certainly dictate that since the alternative to handing over Sheva ben Bichri for execution is for the entire city—including Sheva—to be killed, then certainly we should hand him over. Should we not minimize deaths? *Kesef Mishneh* answers that apparently, though the Gemara presents this logic of "redder blood," this is not the complete explanation. His words, like those of Rav Chaim Brisker, point to the same principle—murder, even the mere handing over of one to be murdered,[48] is not an option, because such an act is not permitted even for *pikuach nefesh*. *Kiddush HaShem* is not dependent on the preservation of the most life, but of the most *kedushah*. *Kiddush HaShem* is not defined as giving up

---

46 וכיכרות של תרומה בידו, ואמר לו הנוכרי, תן לי את אחת מהן ואטמאה, ואם לאו, הריני מטמא את כולן—רבי אליעזר אומר, יטמא את כולן, ואל ייתן לו את אחת מהן; רבי יהושוע אומר, יניח לפניו אחת על הסלע. See *Hilchos Terumos* 12:6 that the halachah is like Rabbi Yehoshua.

47 And thus it is not an issue of the three *mitzvos* and thus for הנאת עצמו there is no need to resist at the risk of death, if not in the presence of ten Jews.

48 Not an act of murder.

one's life because of one's commitment to his faith, *Yahadus,* but rather preserving the values of *Yahadus* at the expense of one's life.[49]

Elisha Baal Kenafayim and Rabbi Akiva

The Gemara says that there was a time when the observance of the *mitzvah* of *tefillin* was "weak in the hands of Israel" and in this context it presents the story of Elisha Baal Kenafayim (*Shabbos* 130a) who wore *tefillin* at the time of *shemad* but when spotted by a government enforcer fled and hid his *tefillin* in his fist. Upon being caught, he opened his hand and the *tefillin* had turned to the wings of a pigeon and he was saved. It is generally understood[50] that Elisha was a saint whom G-d saved with this miracle,[51] as there had been no need for him to have worn *tefillin* in the first place, since one need not endanger himself to perform a positive command. However, according to Rambam his removal of his *tefillin* in the face of danger[52] was sinful and in fact embodies this weakness that was present in Israel. *Tefillin* is the sign (אות) of our covenant with G-d that we display to the world and at the crucial moment Elisha shirked his responsibility to publicize this *bris.* Rabbeinu Channanel[53] explains that *Chazal* bring his story not to praise him but to condemn him.[54]

---

49 According to the *Baalei Tosafos*, the issue of דחיית נפשות is governed by the rule of the equality of every life that dictates that one react with passivity and let nature take its course. This presented them with some difficulty in explaining why it would not be proper to hand over one's life to save many, and thus their reliance on refraining from a מעשה is crucial to their *shittah.* But according to Rambam that the principle is one of *Kiddush HaShem*, the nobility of the refusal to give up one's life to a cruel enemy even to save the many is readily understood.

50 As the Rishonim we noted above contend, and thus his act was לפנים משורת הדין.

51 See *Kesef Mishneh*, *Yesodei HaTorah* 5:3.

52 According to some Rishonim he was model of גוף טהור while according to Rambam he was the opposite.

53 Brought by *Tosafos*, ibid.

54 The Gemara is contrasting Elisha's actions with regard to *tefillin* with Israel's conduct with regard to *avodah zarah* and *milah* whose importance they understood and for whose performance they were willing to die.

Rabbi Akiva was brought to execution for having taught Torah. In his last moments, the Talmud tells us, he recited *Krias Shema* "and accepted upon himself the yoke of Heaven" (*Berachos* 61b.) In this retelling *Chazal* wish to impart to us the relationship between *Yichud HaShem*[55] and *Kiddush HaShem*, as his willingness to die for *Kiddush HaShem* was evidence of what Rambam referred to in the *Sefer HaMitzvos*[56] as his "love of the Almighty and belief[57] in his unity"— אהבתו יתעלה והאמונה בייחודו. In *Hilchos Yesodei HaTorah* (chapter 5), Rambam treats *Kiddush HaShem* right after explaining *yichud* as it is the way in which one concretizes *yichud HaShem.*[58] Elisha's fear, and a lack of what the Gemara (*Shabbos*, ibid.) refers to as a "pure body" caused him to remove his *tefillin.* The holy Rabbi Akiva embraced his mission[59] and reached a plane of existence that Rambam describes (ibid., halachah 4) as: "There is none higher than it"— שאין מעלה על מעלתם.

Healing with Sin

The Talmud (*Pesachim* 25ab) forbids a person to heal himself from a fatal disease by committing any of the three major sins. Elsewhere the Talmud (*Sanhedrin* 75a) adds, surprisingly, that even if one can be cured by having an inappropriate conversation with an unmarried girl, it is still forbidden, even though this does not qualify as *arayos*. Rishonim[60] note that even the first halachah is difficult to

---

Though *tefillin* relates to the same *bris* as *milah*, they did not think it was important to advertise the *bris* in the face of their oppressors and at the expense of their lives. Perhaps the כנפי יונה represents an attitude in which he saw the *mitzvos* as his protection in contrast to the *midrash* of יהודי או צלוב.

55 Many questions are asked by the *mefarshim* on why Rabbi Akiva would be saying *Krias Shema* at that time. They all become irrelevant when we understand that it was not a standard *Krias Shema* but the goal of that *mitzvah* which is of ייחודו.

56 See the passage quoted in the opening paragraph of this essay.

57 Perhaps the correct word is "knowledge of" rather than "belief in."

58 In *Sefer HaMitzvos* the *mitzvah* of *Shema* follows that of *Kiddush HaShem.*

59 For a Jew there is no life without Torah. See the Gemara (ibid.) that he argues אם במקום חיינו.

60 See *Tos. Pesachim*, ibid.

understand as the example in the Talmud for *avodah zarah* healing is curing oneself with the wood from the *asheirah*, עצי אשרה, in which the violation is having benefit from *avodah zarah* which is only an auxiliary sin to *avodah zarah* and not punishable with the death penalty. Thus some Rishonim[61] deduce from these laws that even auxiliary sins, *abizraihu*, אבזרייהו, of the major sins cannot be violated to save one's life. So severe are these fundamental sins that anything related to them is also worthy of giving one's life for.

When Rambam (*Hilchos Yesodei HaTorah* 5:6) quotes these halachos, he gives no indication that these laws are indicative of a broader principle of *abizraihu*. In general, he explains that the punishment for any sin is commensurate with the severity of the prohibition[62] and thus auxiliary violations, carrying minor punishments, would not logically be comparable to the major sins themselves. Moreover, some Rishonim[63] understand that the healing that comes through the wood of the *asheirah* is a result of the *segulah*/supernatural qualities of the wood, and Rambam is of course in disagreement with the belief that there is any efficacy to *avodah zarah* or the superstitions related to it.[64] Clearly he must have had a different understanding of these laws and this understanding is found in *Shemos Rabbah*.

> We learned. With all one may be healed by *avodah zarah*, uncovering *arayos*, and murder. How so?That if one tells a person to kill a person and you will be cured, don't heed him for it says (*Bereishis* 9:6) "He who spills the blood of a person, by a person shall his own blood be spilled" so how can one be cured by spilling blood? "How so via uncovering *arayos*?" If one tells you to commit sexual violations and you will be cured, do not heed him ... for all who touch a woman who is not his brings death to the world for it says (*Mishlei* 7:26) "for many bodies

---

61 See *Baal HaMaor, Sanhedrin*, (ibid); Chinuch 296; *Ran* (on Rif) *Pesachim* 25a who explains this based on the Yerushalmi.

62 See *Peirush HaMishnah* to *Avos* 2:1.

63 See *Tosafos Pesachim* 25a. Even according to this view, the healing via *avodah zarah* is not itself an act of idol worship but is not permitted lest it lead to idol worship.

64 See for example *Hilchos Avodah Zarah* 11.

> she has felled" ... since she has these qualities, **how can she give life to the ill?** Thus one may not be cured with it. "How so with *avodah zarah?*" For if a Jewish man was sick and one tells him to go to a certain *avodah zarah* and be healed, it is prohibited to go ... **for there is no substance to them and they do not help at all** ... The Holy One Blessed Be He said "Since they are like an inanimate stone with no substance and others must watch it that it not be stolen how can it give life to the ill?" That is why it is prohibited to heal with anything from it.[65]

It is precisely because these sins cannot cure that they may not be engaged in to protect against fatal diseases. Of course, they appeared to have efficacy, otherwise people would not have used them. Faith healers are often effective, even if the faith is in an idol. Killing a hated enemy can cure actual physical symptoms created by psychological factors. A lovesick person can be cured from actual symptoms by sating his lust.[66] Sick minds can require sin to sustain their bodies. The Gemara (*Sanhedrin*, ibid.) explains that only after the destruction of the *Beis HaMikdash* did the situation arise that a

---

65 **שמו"ר יב:כא** תנינן, בכל מתרפאין חוץ, מעבודת כוכבים וגילוי עריות ושפיכות דמים. כיצד? שאם יאמרו לו לאדם: בא והרוג את הנפש, ואתה מתרפא אל ישמע להן, שכן כתיב (בראשית ט, ו): שופך דם האדם באדם דמו ישפך, הואיל, וכל מי שהוא שופך דם האדם, באדם, דמו ישפך, היאך יכול החולה להתרפאות בשפיכות דמים?! גלוי עריות כיצד? אם יאמרו לו לאדם: עסוק בגלוי עריות ואתה מתרפא, לא ישמע להן, שאסור לו לאדם לעסוק בגלוי עריות. ...,
וכל מי שנוגע באשה שאינה שלו, מביא מיתה על עצמו, שנאמר (שם ז, כו): כי רבים חללים הפילה.וכתיב (שם ה, ה): רגליה יורדות מות שאול צעדיה יתמוכו, הואיל ויש בה כל המדות הללו, היאך יכולה היא ליתן חיים לחולה?! לכך אין מתרפאין בה.
עבודת כוכבים כיצד? שאם היה אדם מישראל חולה ויאמרו לו: לך אצל עבודת כוכבים פלונית ואתה מתרפא, אסור לילך, שכן הוא אומר (שמות כב, יט): זובח לאלהים יחרם בלתי לה' לבדו, והואיל שכל מי שעובד עבודת כוכבים יחרם, מוטב לו למות בחולי, ואל יעשה חרם בעולם הזה, ולא זה בלבד אסור, אלא כל דבר שהוא של עבודת כוכבים אסור להתרפאות בו. שאם יאמרו לו לאדם: טול ממה שמקטירין לעבודת כוכבים, או טול מן האשרה ועשה מהן קמיע והתרפא, אל תטול, שכן כתיב (דברים יג, יח): ולא ידבק בידך מאומה מן החרם, זו עבודת כוכבים. ואומר (שם ז, כו): ולא תביא תועבה אל ביתך והיית חרם כמוהו. למה? שאין בהם ממש, ואין מועילין כלום, שנאמר (ירמיה י, ה): אל תיראו מהם כי לא ירעו וגם היטב אין אותם. אמר הקדוש ברוך הוא: הואיל והיא כאבן דומם ואין בה ממש, ואחרים שומרים אותה, שלא יגנבו אותה, היאך יכולה היא ליתן חיים לחולה?! לכך אסור להתרפאות מכל אשר לה.

66 Ramban in *Milchamos* to the eighth *perek* of *Sanhedrin* also brings this *midrash*.

man could die of lust. Rambam explains (*Yesodei HaTorah* 5:9): "Let him die rather than he be permitted to speak with her from behind a fence, so that the daughters of Israel not be *hefker*, lest this sort of conduct lead to *arayos*." It is for the preservation of the values of Judaism that a Jew must give up his life.

Halachic Ramifications

There are ramifications to Rambam's position on *Kiddush HaShem* that would cause the *psak halachah* to differ from that of other Rishonim, and I will list some.

In the case of conjoined twins where one life can be saved if the other non-viable one is taken, some *poskim* look to the case of Sheva ben Bichri for guidance, where it is prohibited to actively give up one life in order to save the group. According to Rambam, since in this case the choice is not foisted on us by oppressors and thus *Kiddush HaShem* is not here a factor,[67] it is logical that preservation of the most life possible would be the operable principle.[68]

By contrast, in the case of the Cantonists where a quota of Jewish youth were drafted into a situation where their life was placed in great danger and performance of *mitzvos* was almost impossible, the principle of *Kiddush HaShem* would play a role. Some have argued based on the principle of חייך קודמין, that one has the right to put his own interests before that of others, as well as other halachic sources related to monetary matters, that one should be permitted to use his influence to save himself or others close to him at the expense of others who will subsequently be taken in his place.[69] But should we

---

67 See Arnold Enker, *Fundamentals of Jewish Criminal Law* (2007), chapter 7. For a different approach: Avraham Zucker, *Hakirah* 5.

68 Nor is it comparable to where the murder is committed to cure via satisfying one's anger.

69 See Rabbi Yitzhak Grossman's post <http://seforim.blogspot.com/2008/05/hunted-bears-cantonists-and-nazi.html> where he concludes that in the age of the Cantonists, it was permissible for the wealthy to use their influence to save their sons while it meant that the children of the poor would uniformly be taken. As this is really an issue of נפשות and בטול דת it would seem to come under the category of קדוש השם and require that none try to gain advantage over another.

apply Rambam's principle of *Kiddush HaShem*, our perspective changes.

In the death camps of Europe, Rabbi Zvi Hersh Meisels was approached by a man who was able to save his own son, but it would have meant that another would be taken in his place, and he asked if he could do so. Rabbi Meisels was unable to give him a definitive answer.

> But the father who asked decided, that because of the refusal of Rav Meisels to give a definitive answer the thing was prohibited, and said if so he was prepared to sacrifice his only son according to the Torah and the law, and he accepted this with love and happiness.[70, 71]

In the face of the impending Holocaust, some Rabbis escaped and lived to build thriving communities.[72] But it is the story of those who stayed to serve and comfort those who could not leave and who themselves perished and left no progeny that sustains our people and our religion. The stories of heroism displayed before *asarah m'Yisrael* are transmitted to future generations and remain in the consciousness of Israel until this day. This is the added importance of *Kiddush HaShem b'rabbim*.

Building the *Beis HaMikdash* is a central *mitzvah* to Judaism and incumbent upon the community as a whole.[73] Its centrality to Judaism explains why Israel's enemies built their place of worship on its place and to this day insist that Jews do not pray there. According to Rambam, when the oppressor wishes to uproot our ability to

---

70 אולם האב השואל החליט מתוך סרבנותו של הרב מייזליש להשיב תשובה ברורה, שהדבר אסור, ואמר שאם כן הוא מוכן להקריב את בנו יחידו על פי התורה וההלכה, ושהוא מקבל את זה באהבה ובשמחה, וכך עשה וגם ככה קיים דבריו ולא פדה את בנו, והיה כל היום, יומא דראש השנה, הולך ומדבר לעצמו בשמחה שזוכה להקריב את בנו יחידו לה' כי אף שיש ביכולת בידו לפדותו עם כל זה אינו פודהו מחמת שרואה שהתורה לא התירה לו לעשות כזאת ויהיה חשוב לפני השי"ת כעקידת יצחק אבינו שהי' גם כן ביום ראש השנה (מקדשי השם, שער מחמדים ב).

71 However, if an individual should volunteer to save another it would seem to be an act of saintliness and should be permitted. This is apparently the story of the brothers in Lud (see Rashi to *Pesachim* 60a and *Taanis* 18b) who did so and are considered with the הרוגי מלכות.

72 See *Hakirah*, vol. 9, "To Flee or to Stay."

73 See *Sefer HaMitzvos, Aseh* 20.

perform a *mitzvah*, even an *Aseh*, it is incumbent on a Jew to resist, and the principle of *Kiddush HaShem* calls on him to act without fear.[74]

As we have seen, it is fundamental to the concept of *Kiddush HaShem* that one be willing to give up his life rather than kill another, as this is a demonstration of our moral values. Based on our understanding of Rambam, even without a *maaseh retzichah* one who is a cause for this murder engages in *chillul HaShem* that the Torah forbids. If indeed whether brain death is death is a case of doubt, ספק, it does not automatically follow that a Jew can place himself on a list for receiving an organ since for him it is *pikuach nefesh*, but rather it could be argued on the contrary that the complicity in taking another's life for one's own is *chillul HaShem* and it should follow that taking an organ while not being willing to give is a *chillul HaShem.*[75]

On the other hand, perhaps since the "redder blood" argument does not mean that all lives should be treated equally, but that merely one may not rely on *pikuach nefesh* to save his own life at the expense of others, it follows that one should be able to willingly sacrifice his life to save another. The willingness to give one's life to save another emulates the act of the Martyrs of Lud[76] (הרוגי לוד) who saved a group by sacrificing themselves. A similar calculation could be made that sacrificing one's minimal existence to grant another a full life, would be a *Kiddush HaShem.*[77]

---

74 The concept is most specifically stated for conflict with religions. That Jews discuss the future of the Temple Mount—that we do not claim it— is certainly a *chillul HaShem.* Certainly the building requires Moshiach, but preserving the place for the eventual building should be a pressing obligation on the community.

75 A very similar argument based on Rambam's *shittah* as understood by Rav Chaim and explained by Rav Soloveitchik, *zt"l*, is presented by Rav Hershel Schacter, *shlita*, in *Assia* 7, pp. 188–206.

76 See Rashi to *Pesachim* 50a and *Taanis* 18b. See *Divrei Yirmiyah*, *Hil. Yesodei HaTorah* 5:4.

77 Especially since the brain-dead person is a *treifah.* Rav Schachter, in his article, also makes a similar point—but when we add the argument of *Kiddush HaShem* the argument is strengthened.

This *mitzvah* is specifically to show our dedication to Jewish values, G-d's values—to stand up against the world and not to adopt gentile values and curry favor with them. *Kiddush HaShem* is based on standing up against secular values when they contradict the Torah. Those Jews who fear that Rabbis who take strong public positions against homosexual "marriage" are creating a *chillul HaShem* since they oppose the "moral" values that are currently in vogue, are in error.

Servant of *HaShem*

The colloquial usage of the term *Kiddush HaShem* is when an Orthodox Jew acts in such a way as to reflect well upon the Jewish people. This is based on the last halachah of the *perek* of *Kiddush HaShem*.

> And so too if a *chacham* is exacting upon himself, and he speaks pleasantly to people, and relates well with them, and greets them with a smile, and takes abuse from them and does not return it, shows respect even to the smallest of them, and is trustworthy in his business affairs, does not spend much time with the activities that the ignorant engage in, and is constantly seen engaged in Torah study wrapped in *tzitzis* and crowned with *tefillin*, and conducts all his actions [with others] beyond the strict requirements of the law—and yet is not considered aloof [from the common people], nor an ascetic—so that it is found that all praise him and love him and wish to be like him. This is a *Kiddush HaShem* and of him Scripture says "And He said, 'You are my servant Israel' in whom I take pride."[78]

78 וכן אם דיקדק החכם על עצמו, והיה דיבורו בנחת עם הברייות, ודעתו מעורבת עימהם, ומקבילן בסבר פנים יפות, ונעלב מהן ואינו עולבן, מכבד להן ואפילו למקילין לו, ונושא ונותן באמונה, ולא ירבה באריחות עמי הארץ וישיבתן, ולא ייראה תמיד אלא עוסק בתורה עטוף בציצית מוכתר בתפילין, ועושה בכל מעשיו לפנים משורת הדין—והוא שלא יתרחק הרבה, ולא ישתומם הרבה—עד שיימצאו הכול מקלסין אותו ואוהבין אותו, ומתאווין למעשיו: הרי זה קידש את השם, ועליו הכתוב אומר "ויאמר לי, עבדי אתה—ישראל, אשר בך אתפאר" (ישעיהו מט,ג).

When a *talmid chacham*[79] acts in such a way as to reflect Jewish values, then Judaism is strengthened and Jewish values are strengthened. Moshe Rabbeinu captures the idea best in the blessing at the end of the Torah:

> ט יְקִימְךָ יי לוֹ לְעַם קָדוֹשׁ, כַּאֲשֶׁר נִשְׁבַּע-לָךְ: כִּי תִשְׁמֹר, אֶת-מִצְוֹת יי אֱלֹהֶיךָ,
> וְהָלַכְתָּ, בִּדְרָכָיו. י וְרָאוּ כָּל-עַמֵּי הָאָרֶץ, כִּי שֵׁם יי נִקְרָא עָלֶיךָ; וְיָרְאוּ, מִמֶּךָּ

> The L-rd will sustain you as a Holy nation as He swore to you, if you will keep the commandments of the L-rd your G-d and walk in His path. And all the nations of the earth will see that the name of G-d is called upon you and they will fear you.

☙

79 All religious Jews have this halachah even in the most technical of ways.

The Gaon of Rogatchov: A Study in Abstraction

By: DOVBER SCHWARTZ

Introduction

Rabbi Yosef Rosen, known as the Rogatchover Gaon (the Genius of Rogatchov), and also often referred to by the title of his main work *Tzafnas Paane'ach* (*Decipherer of Secrets*), was one of the most prominent Talmudic scholars and rabbis of the 20th century.

He was born in Rogatchov, Belarus, in 1858. His father, Fishel Rosen, was a well-known and respected Lubavitcher Chassid. At the age of five he was taken by his father to see the third Lubavitcher Rebbe, the Tzemach Tzedek, who instructed him to learn *Maseches Nazir*.[1]

Upon reaching the age of bar mitzvah, his father sent him to Rabbi Yosef Dov Soloveitchik, the Rav of Brisk, where he became a study partner of Rabbi Chaim Soloveitchik for a year. He was known there by the nickname of the *iluy ha'chatzuf* (the impish genius) due to his sharp wit and biting humor.

After this he went to the city of Shklov, where he studied with the Maharil Diskin (Rabbi Yehoshua Leib Diskin). In 1889, when the Rogatchover was 31, the Kapuster Rebbe, Rabbi Shlomo Zalman Schneersohn, appointed him to be the Rav of the Lubavitch-Kapust community in Dvinsk. The Lithuanian Rav there

1 There are those who posit that he took this as a sort of *nezirus* and therefore never cut his hair. Other theories are that he did not want to uncover his head since he would not be able to learn Torah, or that it hurt him to cut his hair.

Dovber Schwartz lives in Brooklyn with his wife and son, and is a student at Cardozo Law School. After studying in various yeshivos, he undertook the project of unraveling and presenting the writings of the Rogatchover Gaon to the English-speaking public.

was Rabbi Meir Simchah HaCohen (the author of *Ohr Same'ach* and *Meshech Chochmah*), with whom he enjoyed good relations.[2]

The Rogatchover was a unique personality. He would answer those who came to him with questions very concisely and summarily. Many of his responses were extraordinarily biting and sharp or, at the very least, incredibly short, with *ayin*[3] after *ayin* and nothing more.

His *sefer, Tzafnas Paane'ach*[4] was, and generally remains, a closed book even for scholars. It is written with extreme conciseness and is riddled with ambiguous hints as to his intent. Adding to the difficulty is that often the sources cited in building his theory are so numerous and dense as to make understanding the text a near impossible feat.

Another obstacle is that his theory on a given subject is not usually easily compartmentalized, nor is it presented as incrementally increasing building blocks. If that would be the case, it would be easier to digest a piece of his writing, since one would be able to focus on breaking down and understanding one line and then advancing. The problem is that often what he is trying to convey can only be understood in conjunction with all the other parts of the theory. Standing on its own, one part may not be comprehensible. The reader is forced to jump into the nucleus of the idea without the aid of independent pieces of information that indicate where he is headed with a certain concept.

This was his "Written Torah." His "Oral Torah," however, was entirely different. He had a unique ability to communicate even

---

2 Much of the following brief description of the Rogatchover's character is translated from an article written in Hebrew ("*Turei Yeshurun*" Volume 44, Shvat-Adar 1975) by Noah Zevulini who lived with the Rogatchover from 1932 until 1933.

3 *Ayin* means to look up the source referenced. For example he would write "*ayin Makkot* page 17." Aside from being indirect and forcing the questioner to look up numerous sources, these responses were often extremely ambiguous as to what part or concept on the page he was referring to.

4 Literally "Decipherer of Secrets," meaning the book deciphers the secrets of the Torah. However, there are those who, in a play of words, interpret the title that one must decipher the secrets of the book itself.

dense and technical ideas in a clear and lucid manner. Most of the content of his books was taken from what he wrote in the tiny margins of his *sefarim*. When asked what he meant in a particular place of his writing, he often explained it at length and in an unambiguous manner.

In this he was the polar opposite of the Lithuanian Rav of the town, Rabbi Meir Simchah HaCohen, who reportedly was extremely brief in his verbal responses to people, yet very clear and explanatory in his writing.

In stark contrast to all the other leading rabbis of his day, he had a small bookshelf and very few *sefarim* that he would use on a consistent basis. The *sefarim* he did have included a set of the Babylonian and Jerusalem Talmud, a *Tur* and some Rishonim. The crown jewel of his small study was his *Mishneh Torah*; he considered Rambam to be his teacher. He would refer to the *Rambam* as "my master" and reportedly would talk to him, bidding him good morning or expressing his delight when unraveling a complex concept from his works.

He was very popular with the yeshivah students for his humor and sharp wit. He often was critical of Acharonim, and while being respectful of the Rishonim, he would neglect to study them at times. Instead he would, on occasion, draw conclusions straight from the Talmud itself.

Shmuel Yosef Agnon, a Nobel Prize laureate writer and one of the central figures of modern Hebrew fiction, visited the Rogatchover and wrote the following:[5]

> I went into his room and found him suffering immensely from his sickness. When he noticed me he started to pour out his heart to me. "I am afraid," he said, "that all my suffering is a result of my not being respectful enough of the Rishonim. All my days I immersed myself in the Rambam's *Mishneh Torah*; it was my central focus and toil and even when I learnt other Rishonim, I only studied them to gain more understanding and perspective of the Rambam's approach."

"He then started to cry," continued Agnon, "and yelled out,"

---

5 As told by Yair Buruchav in his biographical book *HaRogatchovi*, p. 158.

> "Where are the other masters of the Torah? Where are Rashi and *Tosafot*? Where are the Raavan and the Ri? What have I done? Why did I not put effort into understanding and expounding upon their words? It is because of this I am being punished."
> He was silent for a bit, and then a spirit of calm settled over him.
> "It is all worth it," he declared suddenly. "If I am suffering because of my connection and bond to the Rambam I accept the pain joyously!"

Noah Zevulini relates the following:

> Every day I would enter his house and study and talk to the Rogatchover. One day the Rogatchover told me that Nachman Bialik had come to him and they had discussed various matters. The Rogatchover then gave him a copy of his book the *Tzafnas Paane'ach*, at which point Bialik left.
> Bialik later wrote that from the mind of the Rogatchover could be carved out two Einsteins. Legend has it that when the Rogatchover heard this statement he dryly remarked, "And from the leftover specks one could create numerous Bialiks."

The Rogatchover Gaon passed away in 1936 at the age of 78 and was buried in Dvinsk.

His main work, a commentary on *Mishneh Torah*, was published during his lifetime, as were five volumes of halachic responsa. The remainder of his surviving writings appeared in the United States many years after his death. All are titled *Tzafnas Paane'ach*, a title given to the Biblical Joseph by Pharaoh (*Bereishis* 41:45).

His manuscripts were smuggled out of Latvia on microfilm during World War II by his successor, Rabbi Yisrael Alter Safrin-Fuchs (1911–1942), who remained in Latvia to complete this task, and his daughter, who had come to Dvinsk from Eretz Yisrael to help preserve her father's manuscripts. Both died at the hands of the Nazis as a result. A portion of these manuscripts were edited and published by Rabbi Menachem M. Kasher.

His works include the following:

- *Tzafnas Paane'ach*—his magnum opus, a two-volume set on the Rambam's *Mishneh Torah*

- *Chibur al Moreh Nevuchim*—found in the back of his Torah commentary
- *Tzafnas Paane'ach al HaTorah*—a five-volume set on the Torah
- *Tzafnas Paane'ach al HaShas*—four volumes covering the tractates of *Bava Kamma, Bava Metzia, Makkot, Horayos* and *Sanhedrin.*
- *Tzafnas Paane'ach Responsa*—the Dvinsk edition contains two volumes. The Warsaw edition contains three volumes.
- *Sh"ut Tzafnas Paane'ach HaChadashos*—Responsa on *Orach Chaim* and *Yoreh De'ah* and glosses on the *Tur.*
- *Michtevei Torah*—a book of correspondence between the Rogatchover and Rabbi Mordechai Kalina, containing 290 letters from the years 1922 to 1926. The entire correspondence started with one letter from Rabbi Mordechai Kalina and the ensuing 289 letters were all derivative concepts and debates from the first letter.

Books on the Rogatchover's writings are few. The most extensive is the *Mefaane'ach Tzefunos* by Rabbi Menachem M. Kasher. The first part of the book contains several essays on the methodology and conceptual framework of the Rogatchover. The second part is a compilation of sources from the Rogatchover on several key concepts. Unfortunately, this part of the book is still essentially unintelligible unless vast amounts of time are spent unraveling the sources, since no explanatory or supplementary material is provided.

Another book was written by Rabbi Moshe Grossburg called *Tzefunos HaRagatchovi.* It is more conceptual and analytical then the *Mefaane'ach Tzefunos.* In it, the author takes several core concepts that the Rogatchover revolutionized and provides some background and context. Rabbi Grossburg also annotated much of the responsa of the Rogatchover, adding background information on the sources cited in the letters.

Another source is an essay written by Rabbi Shlomo Yosef Zevin. In his book *Ishim VeShittos*, which is a methodological and conceptual analysis of several of the giants of Torah scholarship in the last century, he explains some of the central guiding principles behind the Rogatchover's system of Torah analysis.

Another source—and probably the most readily understandable and user-friendly one—is the *Pirkei Mavoi* written by Rabbi Moshe Shlomo Kasher, the son of Rabbi M. M. Kasher. They are printed in the beginning of each volume of the *Tzafnas Paane'ach al HaTorah*.

Rabbi M. S. Kasher also translated an article written by Rabbi Chayim Sapir titled "*Der Lebediker Shas*" or "The Living Talmud."

Another two scholars who added to this area are Rabbi Yehoshua Mundshein (*Paane'ach Raza*) and Rabbi M.M. Tenenbaum (*Shittas Limudo shel HaRagatchovi*).

Recently a biographical book was published by Yair Buruchav on the life of the Rogatchover.

Part One[6]

6 This article is an excerpt from a book I am writing in English on the Rogatchover's system of Torah thought, focusing on the conceptual innovations inherent within it. I do research independently and in conjunction with several professors and Torah scholars who are knowledgeable on the topics. I hope to publish the first volume within the coming year. It will contain several sections, most notable being an analysis of the Rogatchover's conception of a Torah-based political theory—that is to say, how collectives are formed and what the individual's relationship is to societal obligation and collectivist constructs. Concurrently I am translating and annotating the Rogatchover's glosses on *Bereishis* and will be publishing a *chumash* with his commentary. This essay is an explanation of the unique style and approach of the Rogatchover Gaon.
The sources used for this article can mostly be found in *Mefaane'ach Tzefunos*, *Perek* 1, *Siman* 3 and in the various *Pirkei Mavoi* scattered throughout the chapter. I have primarily relied on the sources that the *Mefaane'ach Tzefunos* brings, although I have taken liberty with restructuring the order and often the thrust and theme of various sources. I have also relied on word searches, consultation with the few people well versed in *Tzafnas Paane'ach* and cross-referencing from the *Klalei HaTorah V'Hamitzvos*. *Mefaane'ach Tzefunos* greatly reduces the workload for the researcher trying to unravel the works of the Rogatchover. However, I have not bound myself to Kasher's understanding of the text and at times, after careful study of the source material, have deviated from the theme that Kasher understood that piece to fall into. Kasher's understanding itself is only implied by his ordering of the various sources from the *Tzafnas Paane'ach* since his comments are sporadic and terse.

To begin to understand the innovations and impact of the Rogatchover Gaon, it is helpful to start by considering the nature of the Talmud.

In its some 6,000 pages one engages with thousands of facts and arguments on a vast number of topics. Written as a series of conversations, the Talmud is fluid and tangential, jumping from topic to topic, unconstrained by subject or order. A conversation in tractate *Shabbos* can be picked up in *Sanhedrin*, and an argument touched upon in *Pesachim* is fully explained in *Rosh Hashanah*, despite their being many volumes apart.

Besides the lack of a structured sequential progression of ideas, the Talmud's content is complex and often intimidating, lending itself to multiple interpretations. The Talmud's structure demands careful scholarship and much commentary. Yet, as centuries of Jewish scholars discussed and debated the Talmud, the complex and fractious nature of the Talmud only expanded.

In the world of the Rogatchover, however, a Talmudic dispute is never just what it seems to be on the surface. The dispute recorded is simply the result of a long stream of more primary and basic disputes ending in the argument recorded in the Talmud.

This type of approach has numerous, profound consequences for how one views the Torah. If one would simply read the Talmud from cover to cover, one would come away knowing thousands of facts and arguments, yet they would all seem to be independent and fragmented items of information and disputes.

The Rogatchover radically altered and reconstructed the way one can view the body of Torah knowledge. From his perspective, all the fractious and disparate items of knowledge and disputation in the Talmud are derivatives of more basic and inclusive concepts. In field after field of Torah, the Rogatchover took numerous debates on seemingly disconnected subjects and showed how they are all predicated upon one core concept. All the disagreements were seen as ramifications and extensions of underlying core concepts.

The Rogatchover is reported to have said that he could refine and abstract all of Torah knowledge into ten ideas! Thus, in the eyes of the Rogatchover, the Torah is a unified, interconnected and harmonious body of knowledge, with all the apparent disparateness being merely the outer, superficial layer of thought.

A Mishnah in *Uktzin* regarding apple stems, a Mishnah in *Shabbos* concerning perfume, and a Gemara in *Bava Kama* discussing property damages may all be expressions of the same idea. The coherency and cogency that he developed in Torah was so pervasive and prevalent in his learning that one is hard-pressed to find a single piece of his writings that doesn't show how apparently unrelated laws are, in fact, all one and the same.

Minute technical laws about animal hides and candles were his building blocks for grand sweeping theories on the nature of life, religion and reality.

A debate about grass fibers became a debate about the very existence of our world, and whether halachah views physicality as the primary determinant or spirituality as the primary determinant.

An argument about slaves and converts was transformed into an argument about the ability of an entity to change its intrinsic identity.

A prophecy about the wolf lying with the lamb became a conceptual construct within which to discuss the advantages of quality versus quantity.

The finesse and grace with which the Rogatchover abstracted seemingly innocuous and technical Gemaras was and is unparalleled. The Rogatchover did not just excel in Torah. He created an entirely new field, not dissimilar to what Einstein did in helping to create the field of quantum physics and relativity.

His style differed somewhat from the schools of *lomdus* which were prevalent in his day and which still enjoy widespread dominance in the yeshivos. Although an analysis of the differences between Reb Chaim (the father of modern *lomdus*) and the Rogatchover's style is beyond the scope of this work, I think it might be captured somewhat by the following parable. Reb Chaim was a microscopic scholar. He took laws and delved into their complex ambiguous depths to discover their inner core, their molecular structure, if you will. He split hairs and refined each element of a law until the difference between all the parts became clear.

The Rogatchover, on the other hand, was a telescopic scholar. In each minute law he saw the universe of Torah. In his mind each subject of Torah orbited around the others until they were all intertwined and fused together. He abstracted each law until it took on massive proportions and gained immense applicability to all other fields of Torah.

The following quote from Rabbi Hillel Tzeitlin is somewhat in line with this characterization:

> זכורני, שגדולי הלמדנים החב"דיים שבעיירתי, פעם – תוך כדי שיחתם בגדלותו העצומה של "העילוי מרוגצ'וב" – אמרו זה לזה בלחישה: אבל בלימוד "על אתר", בזה הוא לא כל-כך "איי-איי-איי"... כלומר, כל הגדלות שלו מתבטאת בבקיאות וביכולת להקים בנין מורכב ממאות אבנים מהבבלי, ירושלמי, תוספות, רי"ף, רא"ש ובעיקר – רמב"ם. אבל לימוד "על אתר" היה נקרא, אצל הלמדנים שלנו: להתעמק בסוגיא כלשהי, לדייק בכל מלה ומלה, לחדור יותר ויותר לתוכה ופנימיותה עד שמגיעים לשורשה, ואז להצמיח משורש זה אילן, ענפים, זלזלים, עלים ופירות.
> ולא פעם היתה ההעמקה בסוגיא גדולה כל-כך, עד שהיו מסתבכים ותועים בה כבשבילי יער עבות.

> I remember that the greatest Chabad scholars in my town once were describing the exceptional greatness of the genius of Rogatchov. All of a sudden, they whispered to each other: "But his localized knowledge of each *sugya* is not so exceptional." In other words, all his greatness was expressed in his breadth and scope and in his ability to construct a tower comprised of hundreds of pieces from Bavli, Yerushalmi, *Tosafos*, the Rif, the Rosh, and most importantly, the Rambam. But localized learning meant to delve into the depths of the *sugya* as is; to be precise with every single word, to drill deeper and deeper into the internal structure of the *sugya* until reaching its roots. And then to grow from the roots a beautiful tree with branches, twigs, foliage and fruits.
> And it was not uncommon to delve so deeply into a *sugya* that we would stroll and wander [in the *sugya*] as if we were on a path in a gigantic forest.[7]

The following is a demonstration of this style of abstraction and harmonization.

---

7 His article can be accessed at: <http://www.shturem.net/index.php?article_id=64§ion=blog_new>.

Part Two: *The Spiritual and the Tangible*

The schools of Shammai and Hillel were intellectual and scholarly rivals for hundreds of years and were major influencers of the development of Torah. Between Hillel and Shammai there were only three (possibly five) disputes. But 316[8] arguments between the schools they founded are recorded in the Talmud. Of these arguments, 221 revolve around various halachos, 66 are *gezeiros* (preventative laws), and 29 are discrepancies over Biblical and legislative interpretations.[8] Despite Shammai's tendency to be strict and Hillel to be lenient, in 55 of these disputes (fully one-sixth), the school of Shammai ruled on the side of leniency.

Many theories have been proposed as to the central (or at least one of the central) differences between the schools. The theories as to the core conceptual difference between the schools range from psychological and hermeneutical, to socio-economic and analytical preferences.

The Rogatchover Gaon's key insight into the core difference between Hillel and Shammai is related to their differing perspectives on the degree to which spiritual versus tangible elements of reality should be taken into account in determining halachah.

The Talmud (*Chagigah* 12a) states: "The school of Shammai says, 'The heavens were created first and then the earth.' The school of Hillel says, 'The earth was created first and then the heavens.'" What does this argument revolve around? Is there an underlying theme?

Indeed there is.[9],[10] Shammai says the heavens were created first. By heavens, Shammai means spirituality and the intangible. In Shammai's view, spirituality is the primary determinant in halachah and is the main barometer of reality. It was created first since it is the dominant reality.

---

8 *Jewish Encyclopedia*, "House of Hillel and House of Shammai."

9 In *Michtevei Torah* letter #289: וזה שיטת ב"ה בחגיגה דף יב דחומר נברא תחלה ואח"כ הצורה היולית, אך ב"ש ס"ל להיפך, דצורה היולית נבראת תחלה ואח"כ חומר, וזה באמת בכל התורה דעיקר צורת הדבר.

10 In *Mahadurah Tinyana* p. 180: וזה הגדר דפליגי בחגיגה דף יב, דשמים נבראו תחלה לדעת ב"ש, ור"ל דהצורה הוא העיקרית, ע"כ. ובשו"ת צ"פ (ווארשא) סי' נ במחלוקת ב"ש וב"ה בחגיגה יב, שמים נבראו כוי, ר"ל אם המציאות הוא הצורה או החומר.

[Spirituality in this context does not have any sor worldly implication. It simply means something that e universe yet is immaterial and lacks concrete substance.]

Hillel says, however, that in our physical world, material considerations are of primary importance, and one must use the physical spectrum as the dominant factor in deciding halachah. Therefore the earth, meaning physicality, was created first.

The Rogatchover[11] proceeds to pinpoint this dispute as the epicenter of two Gemaras that seemingly have no connection to this. The Talmud in *Shabbos* 62b states the following (I paraphrase):

> A woman may not go out on Shabbos carrying a spice bundle (an ornament worn around the neck in which women would place spices so as to create a fragrance) or a flask of balsam oil. If she did go out she has transgressed the Shabbos and is required to bring a *korban chatas* (an atoning sacrifice in the Temple). This is Rabbi Meir's opinion.
>
> Rabbi Eliezer disagrees and says she has not transgressed the Sabbath and is exempt from a *korban*. The reason she is exempt is because a pendant containing spice or a small flask containing oil are considered to be in the category of *tachshit* (ornaments). Items that are categorized as a *tachshit* are Biblically permitted to be worn on Shabbos since it is not considered carrying when going out with them. Just as wearing a shirt on one's back is not considered "carrying," so, too, items that, while not being essential, have aesthetic or secondary uses and benefits are allowed to be worn on one's person.
>
> Rabbi Eliezer then qualifies his ruling and states that she is only exempt when the spice bundle contained spices inside and the flask contained oil inside. But if they did not have spice or oil inside them then she is obligated to bring a *korban* (meaning she has transgressed the Sabbath). Since it is not the norm to wear a pendant or a flask when they are empty, they are not considered ornaments when worn empty. Therefore, since they are not able to be classified as ornaments, they revert to *masa* (carrying) status.

11 In *Tzafnas Paane'ach Sh"ut Dvinsk, Siman* 50: דזה רק צורה ולא חומר, עי' ברכות מג, נשמה נהנה כו' דאין בו ממש, ופליגי בזה שבת סב, אם יש עליו גדר פחות משיעור.

[To facilitate a fluid, smooth understanding of the next part of the Gemara, it is necessary to preface the following principle about carrying on Shabbos. In order to transgress the Shabbos it is not enough to simply carry something outside in the public domain. One must carry a certain minimum quantity in order to be Biblically culpable. Each item has its own minimum requirement or *shiur*. For example, one carrying food must take out (generally) enough food equal to the size of a dried fig.

The minimum amount for other objects may be less or more, depending upon the specific item in question. For example, one taking out a vessel such as a jar would be Biblically liable even for carrying out a tiny jar, since one has carried a whole, complete vessel. With food, however, it is not dependent on whether one has carried a complete item, but rather on the amount of food.]

The Talmud in *Shabbos* 93b discusses an intriguing case concerning one who takes out a jar containing food, where the food does not satisfy the minimum requirement yet the jar does satisfy the *shiur* (since it is a complete vessel). What is the *din* (law)?

Seemingly, there should be no question as to their culpability. For the jar (which satisfies the *shiur*) they are liable, and for the food (which does not) they should not be liable.

Yet it is more complex than that. Since the jar is being used as a receptacle for the food, it is viewed as not having its own independent existence and is merely an accessory of the food. Thus, one is not liable for carrying the jar, since it is not its own halachic entity. Rather, it is an extension of the food. Yet for the food one also cannot be liable since the amount of the food is less than the *shiur*. Thus, counter-intuitively, for carrying out more (the food as well as the jar) one ends up not being liable (as opposed to if one would have just carried out the jar without the food, in which case one would indeed have been liable).

The Gemara attempts to deduce something from Rabbi Eliezer's opinion. Rabbi Eliezer said that when the flask is empty one is liable since then it is not a *tachshit* (because it is not the normal custom to wear an empty flask).

But what about the scent of the balsam oil that still emanates from the flask? Isn't that comparable to the case brought before where one took out food less than the *shiur* in a vessel?

Here too one is taking out two things: the scent that is wafting from the flask (which is less than the *shiur*, since scent has no substance to which we could pin a minimum *shiur*) and the flask itself (which satisfies the *shiur* since it is a complete vessel). Yet still Rabbi Eliezer holds that one is liable in this case! Is he not arguing on the Mishnah on 93b and forming his own opinion? According to the Mishnah on 93b, one should not be culpable for the scent since it lacks a minimum *shiur*, and also not for the flask, since the flask is carrying the scent, and is therefore merely an accessory and extension to the smell.

The Talmud answers that these two cases are not conceptually parallel. Smell has no tangibility *(leis bei mamasha)* since it has no substance, and the flask is considered empty and cannot be said to be an accessory to the scent.

What essentially is the discussion here in the Gemara? The Rogatchover sees it as being predicated upon the tension between the tangible and the intangible realms.

Scent here is classified as belonging to the spiritual realm. It is not tangible or concrete at all, and halachically it is viewed as being the only sense that is a sensory tool of the soul, as opposed to being a sensory faculty of the body. (This is why on Saturday night, at the closing of Shabbos, we smell spices to comfort the soul as we head into the lesser holiness of the week.)

This, then, is the point. Is smell part of our reality? Are non-tangible items viewed as determinants in our decisions and perspectives? If they are, then the smell of the oil in the flask should be viewed as being "something," albeit less than the *shiur*. If that is so, then the two cases are conceptually parallel and we can build a corollary from one case to the other. That would dictate that just as when one carries out food in a jar one is *patur* (exempt), since the jar is considered to be an accessory to the food and the food itself lacks the minimum requirement, so too when one carries out a scented flask without actually having scented oil inside, one should be *patur*, since again, one cannot be liable for the jar being that it is an accessory of the scent.

If scent is not viewed as part of our considerations, and halachah only deals with tangible factors, then fragrance is not considered an entity and the flask is properly defined as being empty, thus ending any hopes of building a comparison between the two cases.

Peppery Potential

Another expression[12] of this battle of perspectives is in a Mishnah in *Uktzin* 3:6. The *Mishnah* records a dispute between Beis Shammai and Beis Hillel regarding black cumin (*katzach*). Shammai says it is *tahor* (ritually pure) and not susceptible to *tumah* (ritual impurity) since it is not considered a food, as it is too harsh and bitter to eat. Hillel says it is susceptible to *tumah* since it is able to be eaten. On the surface they seem to be arguing about the physical existence of cumin and disputing a factual truth, which is not considered to be an optimal way of understanding halachah and Talmud *(ein machlokes b'metziyus).*

However, our analysis will shed light on this strange, seemingly factual, dispute. In order to do so, we must first avail ourselves of another statement from the Talmud.

The Talmud in *Berachos* 40a states:

> What is *katzach*? Rabbi Chama the son of Chanina said, one who eats a lot of cumin (*katzach*) will not experience illness or heart pains. Rabi Shimon ben Gamliel then asked, but *katzach* is recorded as being one of 60 plants that hasten death?

The resolution in the Talmud is that one of the teachings (that *katzach* averts pain and illness) was stated regarding its taste, and the other (that *katzach* hastens death) was concerning its smell. The smell is harsh and hastens death, whereas the taste is healthy and wholesome.

That being the case, Beis Shammai holds that black cumin is not susceptible to *tumah* since its smell is harsh and unhealthy and not fit for consumption; whereas Beis Hillel holds that we only consider tangible factors, and since smell is intangible it is not a factor. Thus we only consider the taste, and the taste is healthy and fit for

12 In *Mahadurah Tinyana* page 180: ועי' במאי דפליגי בסוף עוקצין פ"ג מ"ו ב"ש וב"ה דלב"ש קצה פטור מן המעשרות והטעם דס"ל דהעיקר הוא הריח, וזה ריחו קשה (ברכות דף מ). ובשו"ת שם: דס"ל (לבייש) דהעיקר הוא הצורה והיינו הריח.

consumption. Therefore it is susceptible to *tumah* since it is halachically considered a food.

Alcoholic Abstraction

This essential argument between these two schools is also reflected[13] in the following Gemara in *Berachos* 43b:

If one has wine (which he intends to drink) and scented oil (which he intends to smell) in front of him, he should take the oil in his right hand and the wine in his left hand. He should then make a blessing on the oil, smell it and then make a blessing on the wine and drink it. This is the opinion of Beis Shammai.

Beis Hillel says the opposite: One should take the wine in his right hand and the oil in his left, make a blessing on the wine and then proceed to the oil.

The explanation given by the commentaries is that Beis Shammai holds that the blessing on the oil takes precedence (and thus is held in the right hand) since the pleasure gained from it is immediate and does not require an action on one's part, whereas the wine's pleasure is only once one drinks it and digests it.

Beis Hillel, however, reasons that wine, which is consumed by the body, is more significant than oil, which is merely smelled, therefore the blessing on the wine takes precedence.

This does not explain, however, why Hillel holds that tangible intake of pleasure (consumption of the wine) is more significant than intangible intake of pleasure (smelling)?

Additionally, what does Shammai say to Hillel's point about consumption of pleasure versus merely smelling pleasure?

According to our analysis it is clear. Hillel holds that tangible pleasure is more significant than intangible pleasure in accordance with his world view that tangible factors are the primary determinants, as opposed to intangible factors. Shammai retorts that quite the contrary, intangible and abstract factors are the primary determinants. Thus the oil (merely smelling) takes precedence.

13 See footnote 8 above.

The Solidity of the *Sotah* Water

There is a debate in the Talmud about how much of G-d's name needs to be erased before we force the *sotah*[14] to drink the *sotah* water. Beis Hillel says at least two letters (the first *yud* and the first *hei*) need to be erased. Beis Shammai says even one letter is enough to compel the drinking of the water (Yerushalmi *Sotah* 2:4).

Elsewhere in the Gemara there is an inquiry concerning how many letters a Sefer Torah must possess in order to retain its status of sanctity. We know from the oral tradition that it needs 85 letters, but the Rabbis weren't sure if the 85 letters needed to be together, or even if they are all from different parts of a Torah scroll (*Shabbos* 115b).

In addition, there is an argument about how many extra letters invalidate a *mezuzah*—whether even just one or at least two extra letters are required to make it *passul* (*Menachos* 32b).

What is the thread running through these questions? The commonality they all share is that[15],[16] they all revolve around the identity and character of a single letter. In the Hebrew language there are no one-letter words. A word can be composed of even two letters, but a single letter can never be a word. That being so, perhaps a letter does not have its own inherent identity? Maybe it can never be

---

14 The *sotah* was a woman suspected of adultery who was brought to the Temple and given a special concoction to drink, which had Divine powers to ascertain the veracity of her claims of innocence. She had the option of demanding a divorce instead of drinking the potion. But if the potion had already been prepared, she was forced to drink it, because part of creating the drink involved erasing the Divine name. The Sages debated how much of the Divine name needs to be erased before she would be compelled to drink.

15 In *Mahadurah Tinyana* p. 180: וכן ס״ל לב״ש בירושלמי סוטה פ״ב (ה״ד) דאף אם כתב אות א׳ מן שם יש בו קדושה, וב״ה לא סבירא להו. עי׳ במה דפליגי בזה בשבת קטו, אם גם להציל מן הדליקה אם גם אותיות מפוזרין הוי כן לצרף לפ״ה אותיות, ע״ש.

16 And in *Mahadurah Tinyana* p. 52: והנה מבואר במנחות דף לב, גבי כתבו אגרת, ע״ש בדברי דבינו דאם הוסיף אפילו אות א׳ בפנים במזוזה אפילו בפ״ע פסולה המזוזה, ובאמת זה תליא בהך מחלוקת דב״ש וב"ה דהירושלמי פוטר, פ״ב ופ״ג אם אות א׳ יש עליו גדר מציאות, או לא חל עליו שם גדר בפ״ע רק חלק, כיון דכל תיבה באות אי, ע״ש דמבואר דאם כתב בפרשה פוטר לבייש אות אחת יתירה בפני עצמה שלא בתיבה שוב נפסלה כל הפרשה סוטה, ואז אם מחקה חייב מלקות משום השמות שבה, וב״ה ס״ל דוקא עד שיכתוב שתי אותיות יתירות.

seen as its own idea, and is always a building block of a word, without ever embodying meaning and content on its own.

Or perhaps there is some intrinsic meaning to a letter on its own and it is considered to be its own halachic entity, notwithstanding its deep-seated need to pair with another letter in order to form a word.

Although seemingly disconnected, this is actually the same debate that we saw regarding the *sotah* waters. Shammai says that even if only one letter of G-d's name was erased, it is sufficient to activate the full status of *sotah*. Shammai says this because in his view a single letter is its own entity, and thus by erasing even one letter from G-d's name, one has fragmented the name of G-d and the sanctity of the document has been destroyed.

Hillel disagrees. One letter on its own is nothing,[17] and is merely a part of the whole. Therefore, by erasing only one letter from G-d's name you have not erased a significant entity and therefore the sanctity of G-d's name is still there. Consequently, the *sotah* waters were not activated and the woman is not forced to drink and may still recant.

Obviously, this is also the debate regarding a *mezuzah*. If one letter has intrinsic identity, then even one extra letter adds to the *mezuzah* scroll and invalidates it.

This also applies to the "85-letters argument." If a single letter stands on its own conceptually and halachically, then the 85-letter requirement can be satisfied from 85 single letters. If a letter is not its own entity, then the 85 must be comprised of paired letters.

What does all this have to do with the differing *Weltanschauungs* of Shammai and Hillel? Well, if tangibility is the primary determinant of halachah and reality, then a single letter would not stand on its own. This is because in concrete terms and from an empirical

---

17 In *Mefaane'ach Tzefunos*, p. 55, fn. 1, Rabbi Kasher adds the following: ומבואר דס"ל שאות אחת לבייש הו' עליה גדר צורה, וחייב ולב"ה פטור משום שאין עליה גדר מציאות של תיבה. ועי' צפנת פענח השלמה צד 39 . ויש להוסיף עפמ"ש בתניא להגרש"ז וחיצונית וכו. .באגרת הקדש סה : "אך האותיות הן בבחינה חומר וצורה, הנקרא פנימית עיי"ש, ולפ"ז ב"ש לשיטתם דעיקר הצורה גם אות אחת יש לה פנימיות, משא"כ לב"ה דהעיקר החומר ופחות מהשיעור שתי אותיות אין על זה שם מציאות של תיבה. וראה צ"פ תרומות סג ע"א.

viewpoint, a single letter can never contain content or meaning. Thus, a single letter on its own is not considered its own entity.

If, however, as Shammai asserts, intangibility and spiritual elements are factors to be reckoned with, then a single letter does stand on its own. This is because spiritually each letter of the Hebrew alphabet contains intrinsic and individualized holiness and metaphorical and symbolical meaning.

This whole subject is further amplified in light of how the Rogatchover understands[18] the infusion of holiness into G-d's name. The Yerushalmi in *Berachos* 5:1 states:

> If a scribe was writing a Sefer Torah and was in middle of writing the name of G-d, then even if the king himself asks him a question, he is not allowed to respond.

Rambam codifies this in *Hilchos Tefillin* 1:15:

> If one was writing a Torah and did not have full intent when writing G-d's name (*kasav shelo lishmah*), the entire Torah is invalid. Therefore, if a scribe is in middle of writing G-d's name, he should not even respond to the king.

Simply speaking, the reason is that by responding to the king the scribe is partially distracted and not able to have full concentration on writing G-d's name. Yet, why can't the scribe stop writing, respond and then continue writing G-d's name? This way he could have full concentration while writing G-d's name, with only a short intermission between starting to write and finishing the name.

The reason the Rogatchover offers is that G-dliness is not able to be compartmentalized. What this means is that the name of G-d in a Torah is expressing and constitutes an actual embodiment of G-dliness. G-dliness is not an existence given to fragmentation and disparate parts. Thus, since it is absolute and not able to be partitioned, the physical letters of the name of G-d (which is the vehicle

---

18 In *Mahadurah Tinyana* p. 140 באמת הטעם דהוה מציאות אחת ואי אפשר לחלק לפיכך הכל מודים בכותב את השם (בשבת אינו חייב) עד שעה שישלים אף־על־פי שענין שיעור הכתיבה בשבת (שתי אותיות משם גדול) יש חילוקי דיעות, מכל מקום ביחס לכתיבת שם השם הכל מודים, שאינו חייב עד שישלים עצם פשוט ואינו זה אינו דבר מצטרף ח"ו רק מתחלק.

in which this G-dliness will be revealed and communicated to the world) must also be one and absolute.

We can ask, however, why can't the tangible expression be dissimilar in its character from the idea and truth it carries and embodies? This is because from the perspective of Torah and halachah the physical must resonate and be a transparent conduit through which G-dliness will flow into the world. There can be no friction between the physical and the G-dly. Therefore the physical letters (that are the expressers of the Divine truth inherent in the name of G-d) must reflect in their physical character the G-dly characteristics of Divine truth. They therefore cannot be written in a fragmented manner.

Thus we find that the authentic way of writing G-d's name was by holding four quills in between the five fingers and writing all four letters of G-d's name at the same time. The knowledge of how to perform this maneuver was known by one man who refused to share it with others, bringing down the condemnation of the Sages upon him.[19]

This explains an intriguing halachic discrepancy. The halachah is that one is not allowed to write on Shabbos. How much does one need to write in order to have transgressed this Biblical prohibition? The halachah is that writing two letters violates the Biblical directive not to write. Yet Yerushalmi *Shabbos* 13:1 states that "all agree that regarding writing G-d's name, one has not transgressed until he writes the complete name of G-d (more than two letters)."

What is the reason for this legislative inconsistency concerning writing G-d's name? After writing a *yud* and *hei* (the first two letters of G-d's name) one should be liable to the full extent of the law!

Our analysis on the nature of the relationship between G-dliness and the letters of G-d's name, however, sheds light on this enigma. Since the letters of G-d's name are not given to fragmentation and disparateness, therefore, by only writing two letters of G-d's name one has not written anything. The letters existentially do not stand on their own and are viewed as an entity only in their complete state of all four letters of G-d's name together.

---

19 See *Yuma* 38a.

Domestic Dualities

This distinction remains valid[20] in another important controversy, regarding the relationship between two women who were both married to a man who died childless. Generally, the deceased's brother would have a mitzvah to marry one of his brother's widows. There are situations, however, where a brother may be exempt from *yibum* (marrying his brother's widow) or *chalitzah* (performing the ritual that releases his brother's widow). One such case is if the brother is related to the widow in a way such that *yibum* would constitute a Biblically forbidden relationship — an "*issur ervah*" (see *Yevamos* 3b). The first Mishnah in *Yevamos* lists those cases where the widow would be forbidden to the brother but was not forbidden to the deceased.

What about the other wives? If only one of the deceased's wives is forbidden to the brother, does that automatically exempt all the other wives? There is a disagreement. Shammai permits the non-related widows to marry the brother, and Beis Hillel forbids it (Mishnah *Yevamos* 1:4).

According to Beis Shammai, from a legal point of view there is no point in linking the fate of the widows together. The widow who is his wife's sister cannot enter into a Levirate marriage with him because it is a prohibited marriage, while the other widows are autonomous and can marry the brother of the deceased.

Beis Hillel holds the opposite: the two women are not autonomous; their status is conditional on their being the ex-wives of the same deceased man and their destinies continue to be interconnected.

What is the core matter being debated? Beis Shammai holds that even though one of the wives is forbidden to the brother, this does not affect the other wife. Why is this, though? The Talmud in *Yevamos* 3b states that the other widows are released from any obligation to the brother if any one of them is forbidden to the brother.

---

20 In *Mefaane'ach Tzefunos* p. 55: במהד"ת ע' 180 וכן זה הגרר ביבמות רף יג ע"ב גבי צרת ערוה, ערוה אבראי קיימא, ע"ש דף מד ע"א. ובסגנון אחר בס' השלמה דף ב ע"א: וכבר כתבתי בזה אם איסורים הם רק תואר בהדבר או עצם, ובזה פליגי ב"ש וב"ה, ביבמות רף יג גבי צרת ערוה, דב"ש ס"ל דאיסור הוא עצם. וכמו איילונית שם רף יב, וע"ש בתוס' דף ח ואבראי קיימא ע"ש רף מד ע"א.

Shammai, however, doesn't view the prohibited wife as even existent (*ervah abrai kayma*), that we would then be able to say that due to her unavailability she exempts the other wives. Since she is *assur* (forbidden) she is not even considered to be in front of the court. This is because the *issur* is not peripheral or secondary, but rather, an *issur* is laid onto the very essence of the forbidden item or person. This is, of course, a more abstract and intangible "take" on the nature of an *issur*.

Hillel, on the other hand, views the related and forbidden widow as being here and existent in the case, just that the *issur* prevents her from marrying the deceased's brother. This is in keeping with Hillel's tangible and grounded worldview.[21]

Categorical Colors[22]

The Gemara in *Chullin* 136b brings a *machlokes* (dispute) between Shammai and Hillel regarding different colored figs. The halachah is that one cannot take *terumah* (one of five different types of tithes a Jew had to take from his produce) from one species of produce for another. So, for example, one could not take a tithe of oranges to permit apples, etc. Each plant, vegetable or fruit had to have the tithe separated from it to make the rest of that species of produce permitted for consumption.

---

21 This touches upon another well-known debate concerning the definition of a Torah prohibition: Whether the *issur* affects the very essence of the item *(issur cheftza)* or is instead merely a rule forbidding a person (*issur gavra*) to engage in the *assur* item. While one might make the argument that Shammai, keeping in tune with his intangible dominant theme, would gravitate more towards an *issur cheftza* opinion, and Hillel would relate to an *issur gavra*, I have not seen this correlation made anywhere. While the Rogatchover makes a very similar correlation in the above case, it is clear (to me at any rate) that he means it in a way that is very localized and specific to Levirate marriage.

22 See *Michtevei Torah* #283: בגדר צורה בלא חומר מחלוקת בית שמאי ובית הלל חולין דף קלו ע"ב אם מראה הוה מציאות אף דזה גדר צורה בלא חומר, דאם יטחן החומר לדק נתבטל המראה כמ"ש בספר המורה בהקדמות של המדברים.
See also *Michtevei Torah* #55: ותליא אם מראה הוה עצם איכות, או רק מכמות.
And *Tzafnas Paane'ach, Sh"ut, Warsaw, Siman* 50: ועיין בחולין דף קלו ע"ב דב"ש וב"ה פליגי אם שינוי מראת הוי מין אחד או ב' מינים.

Here the Gemara asks, what about taking *terumah* from black figs in order to exempt and de-sanctify white figs? Is that permissible? Beis Shammai says no and Beis Hillel says yes.

This is a dispute revolving around the tangible versus intangible question. What is color? Is it merely an accessory part of an item, or is it an absolute existence? Rambam in *Moreh Nevuchim* 1:73 discusses the nature of color. He brings the opinions of the Mutakallemim that color is intrinsic to physical matter. They say that if one takes snow, for example, the white color is there in every piece of snow and is part of its very existence.

Rambam, however, rejects their opinion and says that one sees that when things are ground down into tiny flecks and turn into powder the color is gone. Therefore, color is only part of the whole and not existent in the individual parts.

At any rate, we see that there are differing perspectives on the nature of color. According to some it is merely a superficial layer of existence while others view it as being firmly part of the item that it is coloring.

This, then, is the debate about black and white figs. According to Hillel, we permit the taking of *terumah* from black to white, because the different colors are not important and significant enough to make us consider the black and white figs as different species of produce. This is because the colors are only skin deep and not reflective of the essence of the figs. This, in turn, is because Hillel is grounded in concrete reality, which allows Hillel to see that different colors are simply just that, and not existential divides.

Shammai, however, considers the differently colored figs to be different types of fruit. Therefore, one cannot take *terumah* from one to the other. This is the result of Shammai's abstract perspective that different colors actually create a different category.

Sinai and *Harim*/Quixotic Quality[23]

Another instance of the Talmud's preference can be seen in *Horayos* 14a:

---

[23] In *Mahadurah Tinyana* p. 180: עיי יבמות דף יד דלכך ס"ל דעשו ב"ש כדבריהם משום דמחדדי טפי אף דב"ה רובא, וא"כ חזינן דאזלינ בתר הצורה אף דבהעצם הוי מיעוטא.

> Rabbi Shimon ben Gamliel and the Rabbis debated. One said that *sinai* is a superior quality in learning, while the other side said *oker harim* is a finer trait.[24]
>
> Who is a man embodying *sinai* qualities? Rav Yosef. Who is a man embodying *oker harim* abilities? Rabbah. They sent the debate to the east (Eretz Yisrael) for a resolution and the answer sent back was, *sinai* (vast knowledge) is superior.

Sinai verus *oker harim* is essentially a debate on quality versus quantity. *Sinai,* which is broad global knowledge, is equivalent to quantity of knowledge. *Oker harim,* which is localized sharp thinking, is equivalent to quality of thought.

With this in mind, we can uncover a further layer of depth, which is that quantity versus quality is, at its core, a debate about tangibility versus intangibility.

Quantity is a tangible and quantifiable (the very word implies concrete objective data) factor. It is a physical reality of having more. For example, the concept that majority rules, since there are more people who hold a certain view, is a concept predicated upon tangible, readily observed phenomena.

Quality, on the other hand, is a whole different beast. It is nonconcrete and intangible. Although the majority wants a certain approach, if the minority is smarter and more experienced, follow them, says quality.

We now come back to *sinai* versus *harim*. This is yet another place where the Talmud makes clear its position that tangible factors must outweigh (for the time being; see later) intangible elements. Hence *sinai* is superior, hence quantity is superior (i.e., majority rules in halachic decision-making), and hence tangible and

---

24 *Sinai* generally refers to Mt. Sinai. Here the Talmud uses *sinai* as a metaphor for the quality of vast knowledge and scholarship. As if to say, one who has the entire Torah at his fingertips as it was given at Mount Sinai. *Oker harim* literally means the "uprooter of mountains." The Talmud uses it as a metaphor for one who has sharp and incisive analytical skills. Although this individual may not know all of Torah by heart, and is not as knowledgeable as the other, he is possessed of superior and deeper intellectual abilities. Thus the Rabbis and Rabbi Shimon are debating which is the more desirable and admirable trait in Torah study.

physical phenomena must be of primary consideration to us, while spiritual factors are of secondary importance.

What does this have to do with Shammai and Hillel? The Talmud in *Yevamos* 14a records that Beis Shammai held the high ground in terms of superior thinkers and scholars, while Beis Hillel had a larger number of scholars and Torah legislators.

Beis Hillel, however, followed its own opinions *l'halachah* (practically). This was an astonishing phenomenon, when one considers that Beis Hillel knew and acknowledged Beis Shammai's superior caliber of scholars and legislators!

Yet according to our analysis, it was a phenomenon that makes perfect sense. Since Hillel held the view that tangible factors must always trump intangible ones, they concluded that their quantity of scholars outweighed the quality of Shammai's.

The Sin of Following Shammai's Rulings

The Talmud in *Berachos* 58b relates the following:

> Rav Pappa and Rav Huna were walking along a road and they met Rabbi Chanina. Rabbi Chanina proceeded to make the blessing of *chacham harazim,*[25] telling them that they are as wise as and equal to 600,000 people in his eyes.
> They then rebuked him, saying, "Are you indeed this smart and knowledgeable [to make such a character judgment]?" A short time later, Rabbi Chanina died.

What is the deeper meaning of this enigmatic story? Rabbi Chanina was a follower of Shammai.[26] He subscribed to their worldview. He therefore felt that since they were as wise as 600,000 people, he could make a blessing. Even though the required number

---

25 The blessing of *chacham harazim* is a blessing made upon seeing 600,000 people gathered together acknowledging G-d's omnipotent ability to create infinite variations of wisdom within people.

26 In *Mahadurah Tinyana* p. 180: ובזה יש לבאר הך דברכות דף נח ע״ב גבי עוברא דר״פ ור״י ורב אחא בריה דדב איקא דבריך עלייהו ויהבו ביה עינא ומת, וע״ש ברמב״ן במלחמות (ולא מברכינן חכם הרזים אלא על אוכלסיא ואע״ג דחשיבי טובא), ור״ל כך, משום חד, רק בגדר תואר (אוכלסא) והנה וכוי, עכ״פ כאן נמי חזינן דר״א בריה דרב איקא דאחשבינהו כמו אוכלסא ובריך עלייהו ברוך חכם הרזים ס״ל ג״כ כך, א״כ ס״ל כב״ש (דצורה הוא העיקר) ולכך נענש כמבואר בברכות דף יא (כל העושה כדברי בייש חייב מיתה), ובמ״א אבאר בזה.

of people to make the blessing was not gathered together, qualitatively there was the requisite amount of wisdom.

He was punished so severely because the halachah is that anyone who follows the opinion of Beis Shammai is liable to the death penalty (*Berachos* 11a).

Tangible Torah

Whom does halachah follow? Who has the final say? It turns out that it's not so simple. Although intangible and spiritual factors are considered to be a stronger reality, as we will see in a discussion about the era of Moshiach, tangibility is closer to the human experience, and as such is the primary determinant in the decision-making processes of Torah.

Since Torah is a system for dealing with our physical world and since physicality is a stronger reality to us, therefore it is the main factor in halachah. In light of this, consider the following halachah (Yerushalmi *Yuma* 6:1):[27]

> If one has two animals he can use for a *korban*, but one is stronger and of superior stock while the other simply looks better aesthetically, which one is he to bring? The one that is stronger physically is the preferred animal and is used as the *korban*.

The requirement regarding *korbanos* is to bring the best animal. Here we are faced with a decision in which one animal is superior physically while the other is superior in matters that are not as concrete. Take the tangibly superior one, says the Torah, thus informing us that when we need to make a decision, we should use tangibility as our main measuring stick of reality.

Messianic Times

The Rogatchover's pinpointing of the fundamentally different approaches related to spirituality versus tangibility can be applied to the well-known and fascinating assertion that in the times of the

---

27 *Pirkei Mavoi, Bereishis*, p. 21.

Moshiach the halachah will switch to be in accordance with Beis Shammai (*Mikdash Melech* to *Zohar*, Vol. I, 17b).

In day-to-day life we grant supremacy to the tangible and material while intangible factors are only accorded secondary status. However, when Moshiach comes it will be a time of, as the Rambam says (*Mishneh Torah, Hilchos Melachim* 12:5): "The Jews will be great sages, and know the hidden matters;" (*Mishneh Torah*, loc. cit. 11:4): "Moshiach will perfect the entire world;" and (Isaiah 11:9): "They will neither harm nor destroy on all my holy mountain, for the earth will be full of the knowledge of the L-rd as the waters cover the sea [bed]."

When Moshiach comes, our spectrum of reality will be elevated to a more refined and subtler level. Spiritual and intangible truths will resonate even within our physical spectrum.

The halachic switch to Shammai will be an instinctive natural gravitation instead of a conscious legislative effort. The fragrance of the small vessel being carried on *Shabbos* will seem real and practical, the intrinsic independent identity of a single letter will be clear, and the validity of subscribing to a spiritual-based worldview will seem compelling and precise. ❧

Jewish GIs and Their Dog-Tags

By: AKIVA MALES

My Father's Dog-Tag[1]

In May of 2012, my wife and I visited my parents in Cleveland, Ohio to help celebrate my father's birthday. As we all drove to a nearby park, I glanced at his keys in the ignition and noticed an item I had not seen for a few years—the dog-tag on his key ring.

During the Korean War, my father served in the US Air Force for four years (1951–1955). I grew up enthralled by the stories of his two years spent in Texas followed by another two years just outside Anchorage, Alaska.

As a boy, I was particularly interested in one detail of my father's dog-tag, the letter "H" impressed on the tag's lower right-hand corner. That "H" stood for "Hebrew," the religious classification assigned to Jewish servicemen at that time.

---

[1] I am greatly indebted to The Army Historical Foundation, and the office of the US Army's Chief Chaplain for answering many of my queries re lating to the history of dog-tags and religious affiliation; Rabbi Dr. Jacob J. Schacter as well as *Ḥakirah*'s editorial staff for their important comments on an earlier version of this article; and last but not least, my father, Mr. U.H. Males, for his invaluable editing assistance.

Rabbi Akiva Males serves as the rabbi of Kesher Israel Congregation in Harrisburg, Pennsylvania.

As my interest in halakhah and US history increased, I learned that this simple "H" had been a source of great concern to many brave Jewish GIs during World War II.

History of the US Dog-Tag

"Dog-tags" are the nickname for the government-issued identification tags worn by all members of the US Armed Forces.[2] Although dog-tags have become somewhat fashionable in popular culture, their intended use is rather grim—to ensure that the needs of seriously wounded soldiers are met, and that the remains of fallen soldiers are properly identified.

Surprisingly, the US did not begin issuing official identification tags to its troops until 1906. Prior to that time, the matter of identifying and providing vital information was left up to each individual soldier.[3] In 1916, the US Army amended its previous regulations

---

2 Some maintain that the nickname stems from the identification tags commonly worn by people's pet dogs. Others credit this nickname to the publishing magnate William Randolph Hearst. See <http://www.ehow.com/about_5212441_army-tags-called-dog-tags_html> for the following theory:

> The informal name for the ID tags used by soldiers, "dog-tag," was coined by William Randolph Hearst in 1936. Hearst used the term in print as a reaction to the news that the Social Security Administration was contemplating the use of such ID tags as means of identification for employees. As a staunch opponent of President Roosevelt, Hearst intended to undermine the campaign by lambasting this idea. The tags were never actually issued, but the name stuck and has been used to refer to the military ID tags ever since.

3 There are numerous US Civil War (1861–1865) accounts of both Union and Confederate soldiers pinning hand-written identification notes to their clothing before marching into battle. Private entrepreneurs soon realized that soldiers wanted forms of identification, and various ID medallions and pins were made to order for those soldiers who could afford to do so. It is little wonder that it is estimated that close to 42% of Civil War casualties were never properly identified. See "A Short History of Identification Tags" by Captain Richard W. Wooley, originally printed

and required that each serviceman be issued two identification tags. This way, in the event of a GI being killed in action, one tag would stay with and identify the body, while the other would be removed and delivered to the office charged with keeping track of records and burials. These two identification tags were to be worn by US servicemen at all times.

The vital information stamped on dog-tags evolved over time.[4] For the purpose of this article, we focus on US dog-tags issued between the years 1941 and 1952. All those tags contained the following personal information:

1) name
2) serial/service number[5]
3) date of most recent tetanus shots[6]
4) blood type
5) single letter denoting the serviceman's religious affiliation

Until 1952, the following letters were used to describe the religious affiliation of a US serviceman:

P = Protestant
C = Catholic

---

in the *Quartermaster Professional Bulletin*, December 1988. The article is available online at: <http://www.qmfound.com/short_history_of_ identification_tags.htm>.

4 For example, in the early years of WWII the name and address of a serviceman's next-of-kin was also included.

5 In 1969, the US stopped using serial/service numbers for military record keeping and began using soldiers' Social Security numbers instead. With identity theft becoming quite common in recent years, the military's casual use of soldiers' Social Security numbers has become a cause of growing concern. See these two news stories about US servicemen/women and identity theft: <http://www.nytimes.com/2010/12/07/technology/07identity.html?_r=1&pagewanted=all> and <http://www.stripes.com/news/jag-attorney-wants-to-prevent-pow-identity-theft-1.4804>.

6 The military stopped including this piece of information in the early 1960s. I was unable to find an official reason for this change in military policy.

H = Hebrew (Jewish)[7]

The first four items of personal and medical information were obviously vital for a soldier who was no longer able to speak for himself. A serviceman's religious affiliation was included on his dog-tags so the US military could ensure that in the event of death, the wearer's religious needs might be properly met. If a soldier had no religious preference, no letter would have appeared at all.

Jewish GIs and World War II

During World War II, approximately 550,000 self-identified Jews served in the US Armed Forces.[8] As per US military regulations, each of those Jewish soldiers/sailors/marines/airmen would have been issued dog-tags with the letter "H" stamped on them. While being identified as Jews may not have been a concern for those fighting the Japanese in the Pacific Theater, that one simple letter could have meant the difference between life and death for Jewish GIs serving in the European Theater. After all, during WWII, the Nazis were on a maniacal campaign to murder all Jews. As such, Jewish American soldiers had good reason to fear being taken prisoner by Nazi forces and identified as being Jewish.[9]

---

7 After 1952, the letter "J" was used instead of "H" on the dog-tags of Jewish US servicemen. (A member of my synagogue recently showed me his grandfather's WWII-era dog-tag with a "J" stamped on it. I cannot explain how any dog-tags from that period ended up with a "J" on them, rather than the regulation "H".) Also in 1952, the Army introduced the letter "X" to designate other religious affiliations not covered under Protestant/Catholic/Jewish faith groups, and the letter "Y" for those who did not have a religious preference. In November of 1962, the Army stopped using religious codes, and decided that a soldier's religion was to be fully spelled out on dog-tags. Since then, the word "Jewish" appears on the dog-tags of all US soldiers/sailors/marines/ airmen choosing to identify themselves as Jews.

8 <http://www1.yadvashem.org/yv/en/holocaust/about/07/jewish_soldiers.asp.>

9 There are numerous reports of Jewish American prisoners of war who were singled out by the Nazis for execution or slave labor. See for exam-

Jewish GIs, fearful of being identified as such by their Nazi captors, were left with the following options:

1) Have no letter of religious preference stamped on their dog-tags.
2) Make the "H" stamped on their dog-tags illegible.
3) Discard their dog-tags completely prior to being taken captive.
4) Have a letter signifying a different religious preference stamped on their dog-tags.

In the course of researching this topic, I discovered that during WWII, all four of these options were, in fact, employed by Jewish GIs. Of the many veterans' testimonies I have come across, I have chosen to include the following four.

In a letter to the editor of *The New York Times*, dated June 22, 1994, Paul Lippman of Hoboken, New Jersey wrote:

> ... Many Jewish G.I.'s omitted from their dog-tags the indication that their religious identity was Jewish for the prudent reason that in the event of falling into German hands, their lives would be at greater risk if they were identifiable as Jewish ... As a combat veteran I know that my dog-tags and those of many of my Jewish companions were religiously anonymous.[10]

In a 1999 *San Diego Jewish Press–Heritage* article about WWII-era Jewish US prisoners of war, several soldiers' experiences are reported. Seymour Brenner was

---

ple "Soldiers and Slaves" by Roger Cohen (2005) about the awful experiences of hundreds of Jewish US POWs whom the Nazis sent to a slave labor camp named Berga in Eastern Germany.

10 <http://www.nytimes.com/1994/06/22/opinion/l-in-world-war-ii-many-jewish-gi-s-left-religion-off-dog-tags-470333.html>. In his letter, Mr. Lippman uses this fact to explain why there are fewer Stars of David for fallen Jewish GIs in US military cemeteries in Europe than there ought to be.

> ... a field medic when he was captured in France after being knocked unconscious by an artillery blast. A quick thinking non-Jewish member of his unit broke Brenner's dog-tag in half, burying in the snow the part which had the "H" for his religion engraved upon it. When their capturers asked why Brenner's dog-tags were broken, the buddy said it was because they had been engraved with the wrong blood type and were expected to be replaced.
> The lie may have saved Brenner's life. Unaware that he was a Jew, the Germans decided to use his training as a medic to treat fellow prisoners at Stalag 5-A, which they reached after a 14-day forced march 'without food or water'."[11]

Earlier in that same article, the author writes of Sam Kimbarow, who

> ... threw away his US Army dog-tags identifying him as a Jew before he was captured by German soldiers during World War II's famous Battle of the Bulge. Later, at a camp for prisoners of war, he was in the middle of a crowd when a German officer asked if there were any Jews among the prisoners. About five American soldiers stepped forward, but Kimbarow was not among them. He watched as they were led away to uncertain futures.

Kimbarow added,

> ... "What we did was to deny our mothers and fathers," he said. "It was a terrible mental thing." ... He recalled that "a guy wrote a letter in a Jewish newspaper that he still has nightmares because one of the other (Jewish) guys met him years later and told him "you walked away and let me take it." Those who were separated went through hell; most of them died in the camp. And those of us who survived had a tremendous guilt feeling . . ."

---

11 <http://www.jewishsightseeing.com/usa/california/san_diego/veterans_administration/19990423-world_war_ii_pows.htm>.

Lastly, in an online group for WWII veterans, I found the following comment from one aging soldier who was told of an incident that had occurred in his friend's unit:

> ... Early in 1943 the Army came up with a bright idea. They were sending troops to England and getting ready for the invasions of Sicily and Italy. They wanted to insure that if a Jewish soldier were captured, the Germans would not know he was Jewish by looking at his dog-tags. So they issued a bunch of dog-tags to Jewish soldiers where they had changed the letter H (for Hebrew) to an over-sized letter P [for Protestant] ... [12],[13]

As we have seen, Jewish American GIs had good reason to fear being recognized as Jews by their Nazi captors. Accordingly, many took various steps to conceal the Jewish identities which their US Army-regulation dog-tags would have given away.[14]

At this point we must ask: Did any of these methods of concealing their Jewish backgrounds pose halakhic concerns?

---

12 <http://www.6thcorpscombatengineers.com/engforum/index.php?s=069ff09d597af3393a43cb3e7fce4880&showtopic=6938&st=25>.

13 This last account is of an official effort to have Jewish GIs list a religion other than their own on their dog-tags. There is no way to know how many Jewish GIs may have chosen this course of action on their own. According to one account, during the build-up to the first Gulf War the US Defense Department may have tried something similar for Jewish troops stationed in Saudi Arabia. See the chapter entitled "Protestant B, Not" in Debra Darvick's *This Jewish Life* (David Crumm Media, Canton, MI, 2012, pages 135-8). I thank Rabbi Raphael Davidovich of Cleveland, OH for bringing this source to my attention.

14 A number of reports indicate that Jewish US servicemen currently serving in the Middle East are taking similar steps. In October of 2007, US Army Chaplain Shlomo Shulman wrote:

> How many Jewish soldiers are stationed in Iraq? It's difficult to get an accurate count because they often avoid designating their "faith group" in military databases, especially once they find out they'll be deployed to an Arab country. They may not want the word "Jewish" printed on their ID necklaces (dog-tags). If they're captured in Iraq or Afghanistan, what kind of treatment could they expect?

Full article is available at: <http://www.aish.com/jw/s/48923202.html>.

The Search for Halakhic Precedent

Unfortunately, any student of Jewish history is well aware that the matter of concealing one's Jewish identity in the face of persecution is part of our people's collective narrative. Halakhic literature deals extensively with the circumstances under which one must forfeit his/her life rather than renounce one's Jewish faith.

Based on Talmudic and early rabbinic rulings, the following guidelines are found in *Shulḥan Arukh / Rema*:[15]

> אסור לאדם לומר שהוא עובד כוכבים כדי שלא יהרגוהו. אבל אם כדי שלא יכירוהו שהוא יהודי משנה מלבושו בשעת הגזרה, מותר כיון שאינו אומר שהוא עובד כוכבים. הגה: ואפילו לובש כלאים. ואף על גב דאסור לומר שהוא עובד כוכבים, מ"מ יוכל לומר להם לשון דמשתמע לתרי אפין, והעובדי כוכבים יבינו שהוא אומר שהוא עובד כוכבים והוא יכוין לדבר אחר. וכן אם יוכל להטעותם, שהם סוברים שהוא עובד כוכבים, שרי . . .
>
> It is forbidden for a Jew to declare that he is an idolater, so that he will not be killed. However, in times of religious persecution, one is permitted to change his clothing so that he will not be recognized as a Jew, since he has not declared that he is an idolater. [Rema]: He is even permitted to wear clothing containing forbidden mixtures of wool and linen. Even though it is forbidden for a Jew to clearly state that he is an idolater, it is permitted for him to make an ambiguous statement that can be understood in more than one way, so that the idolaters will think that the Jew declared himself to be an idolater—when in fact, the Jew meant something else. Similarly, if he is able to deceive them, so that they believe he is an idolater, it is permitted.

What seems to emerge from the *Shulḥan Arukh* and *Rema* is that during times of religious persecution, a Jew cannot openly declare him/herself to be an idolater, even if such a declaration would be life-saving. To save his/her life, however, a Jew can make use of any

---

15 *Yoreh De'ah* 157:2.

number of subterfuges so that others will incorrectly believe that he/she is in fact an idolater.

How would this ruling of the *Shulḥan Arukh / Rema* affect a GI's ability to conceal the "H" on his dog-tags identifying him as a Jew? Above, we suggested four methods employed by WWII-era Jewish GIs to conceal their Jewish identity. It seems clear that options 1, 2 and 3 would pose absolutely no halakhic concerns. After all, a Jewish GI who employed any of those three options never openly declared himself to be a member of a different religious community. He would have only concealed his true Jewish identity—something expressly permitted by the *Shulḥan Arukh / Rema*—thereby leaving it up to the enemy to assume he was part of the overwhelming non-Jewish majority of American soldiers.

What about option number four? Would there have been any halakhic issues for a WWII-era Jewish GI who chose to have a "P" for Protestant or "C" for Catholic stamped on his dog-tags instead of the "H"? Would such action be tantamount to a Jew openly declaring that he is an idolater—which *Shulḥan Aruch / Rema* clearly forbade?[16]

Responsa from the Holocaust

To answer this question, we turn to a tragic repository of halakhic guidance that was compiled at the time WWII-era Jewish GIs faced their dog-tag dilemma.

While serving as a rabbinic leader to the Jews of the Kovno Ghetto (Kaunus, Lithuania), Rabbi Ephraim Oshry (1914–2003) was presented with numerous heartbreaking questions of Jewish law.[17] During the dark years of the Holocaust, he recorded and hid brief notes of the halakhic questions he received and the answers he

---

16 The matter of whether or not Christianity (in any/all of its many forms) is classified as idolatrous in the eyes of Halakhah is quite complex. For simplicity's sake, this article classifies all forms of Christianity as idolatrous, so far as **this** ruling of the *Shulḥan Arukh / Rema* is concerned.

17 It is a strong testament to the religious will of the Jewish people that such concern for Halakhah was shown under such terrible circumstances.

provided. Following the liberation of the ghetto in August of 1944, Rabbi Oshry recovered and expanded his notes, and soon began publishing his set of Holocaust-era responsa entitled *She'eilot u-Teshuvot mi-Ma'amakim*.[18] A condensed English-language version was later published as *Responsa from the Holocaust* (Judaica Press, Inc. (New York) 2001).

While no record exists of any Jewish GI turning to Rabbi Oshry for halakhic guidance on this matter, one of Rabbi Oshry's responsa seems to resolve the above-mentioned dog-tag question. Here is the question Rabbi Oshry received, and the answer he provided, as condensed, translated, and printed in *Responsa from the Holocaust*:[19]

> **#58: May a Jewish Man Write the Letters R.C. (Roman Catholic) in His Passport?**
>
> **Question**: Among the imprisoned Jews in the Kovno Ghetto were German Jews who had been exiled by the Hitler regime. Among them was a Jewish man who possessed a German passport issued before the outbreak of the war, and whose name was absolutely not Jewish.
>
> As life for the ghetto prisoners grew more difficult, with new decrees appearing daily, this Jewish man decided to escape, hoping that he would be able to hide among the gentiles, since his appearance and name concealed his Jewish identity. He asked the following question: In order to complete the deception, he would have to write in his passport the letters "R.C." to show that the bearer of the passport was a Roman Catholic. Thus anyone inspecting his passport would be convinced that it was the passport of someone gentile by birth. Since adding these two letters might appear to be admitting or confessing to

---

18 All volumes were published in New York. Volume I was published in 1959, Volume II in 1963, Volume III in 1968, Volume IV in 1975, and Volume V in 1979.

19 Rabbi Oshry's original Hebrew responsum can be found in *She'eilot u–Teshuvot mi-Ma'amakim* 5:3.

a deity other than the G-d of the Jews, he wanted to make sure it was permissible.

Response: I ruled that he might write the two letters R.C. for, even though non-Jews would think they mean that he is a Roman Catholic, he was free to have in mind the Hebrew meaning of the two letters. It was irrelevant how non-Jews would construe those letters.

Not surprisingly, this short translated answer does not do justice to the nearly thirteen pages of complex argumentation and reasoning Rabbi Oshry recorded before answering the question he was asked.

After going through Rabbi Oshry's original Hebrew response to this question,[20] I would summarize his final answer as follows:

In his *Sefer ha-Mitzvot*,[21] Rambam teaches:

והמצוה התשיעית היא שצונו לקדש השם והוא אמרו (ויקרא כב,לב) ונקדשתי בתוך בני ישראל ... ואע"פ שבא עלינו מכריח גובר יבקש ממנו לכפור בו יתעלה לא נשמע ממנו אבל נמסור עצמנו למיתה ולא נתעהו לחשוב שכפרנו ואע"פ שלבנו מאמין בו יתעלה.

The ninth *mitzvah* is that we are commanded to sanctify G-d's name. As He stated (Leviticus 22:32), "that I may be sanctified amidst the Jewish people" ... and even if a powerful oppressor were to come upon us and ask us to deny our exalted G-d, we may not listen to him. Instead, we must submit ourselves to death, and not deceive him to think that we have denied [the Exalted One]—even if we still believe in Him in our hearts.

Rabbi Oshry wonders how Rema could have issued a ruling which clearly contradicts that which Rambam had ruled before him. If Rambam ruled that a Jew must forfeit his/her life rather than make a statement that would fool his persecutors into thinking he had renounced Judaism and accepted idolatry, how could Rema

20 I thank Rabbi Barry Nussbaum of Harrisburg, Pennsylvania for studying this responsum with me during Hurricane Sandy on October 29–30, 2012.

21 Positive Commandment #9.

rule that making such a statement was permissible—so long as it was ambiguous?!

Rabbi Oshry answers that there are two types of deceptive statements one can make: A) a deceptive statement which has but one meaning, and B) a deceptive statement which can be understood in more than one way. Accordingly, Rambam and Rema are in perfect agreement. Under no circumstance could a Jew faced with the threat of death or apostasy save his/her life by making the first type of deceptive statement. However, both Rambam and Rema agree that one could save his/her life by making the second type of deceptive statement, that is, an ambiguous one.

That being the case, Rabbi Oshry wondered what Rema was adding with his next statement of:

> וכן אם יוכל להטעותם, שהם סוברים שהוא עובד כוכבים, שרי . . .
>
> Similarly, if he is able to deceive them, so that they believe he is an idolater, it is permitted ...

In his previous statement, Rema had already ruled that one could save his/her life using an ambiguous deceptive statement. That being the case, what was Rema adding in his subsequent ruling? This second statement of Rema prompted Rabbi Oshry to develop a novel idea regarding the permissibility of saving one's life via a statement which indicated apostasy.

According to Rabbi Oshry, until this last ruling of Rema, the discussion in the *Shulḥan Arukh / Rema* regarding which verbal statements a Jew could make in order to save his/her life, were limited to scenarios where the Jew's persecutor knew that he/she was, in fact, a Jew. One recognized as a Jew, and given the awful choice of death or apostasy, had extremely limited options. Renouncing his/her Jewish faith outright and accepting an idolatrous one—even while remaining a loyal Jew at heart—was clearly forbidden. The only halakhic option for a Jew in such a scenario was to offer an ambiguous statement—one that his/her persecutors would understand as apostasy, while carrying a very different meaning for the Jew who uttered it.

What if, however, a Jew was not recognized as a Jew by his/her oppressors? What if he/she was seized and asked to state which faith community he/she belonged to? Rabbi Oshry claimed this is precisely the case which Rema is addressing in his final statement. In such a scenario, according to Rabbi Oshry, Rema is teaching us that there is no need for ambiguity at all. If a Jew is not recognized as such, and merely asked to identify his/her religious affiliation, in order to save his/her life that Jew may overtly identify him/herself as an idolater.

In Rabbi Oshry's own words:[22]

> ... בכדי להציל את עצמו מסכנת נפש מותר לו להטעות את הגויים שלא יכירוהו שהוא יהודי, ואינו דומה כלל למה שכתב הרמב"ם בספר המצות, דהרמב"ם איירי שיודעים בו ומכירים אותו שהוא יהודי אלא שבכדי להנצל הוא רוצה לומר שהוא עובד כוכבים היינו שהוא מתכחש לדת אבותיו, בזה אית ליה לרמב"ם שאסור, אבל היכא שהגויים אינם מכירים בו ואינם יודעים שהוא יהודי מותר לו להטעות אותם בכל טצדקי ואמצעים אפילו באמירה שהוא כאחד מהם מאז ומעולם ...

> ... To save himself from the threat of death it is permissible to deceive the gentiles so they will not recognize that he is a Jew. This [case] is not at all similar to [the case which] Rambam wrote of in *Sefer ha-Mitzvot*. For Rambam was dealing with a scenario in which the gentiles know him and recognize him as a Jew, and to save himself, he wants to declare that he is an idolater, i.e., that he renounces his ancestral faith. In such a case, Rambam rules that it is forbidden. However, if the gentiles do not recognize him, and are not aware that he is a Jew, he may deceive them using any trick and means, even declaring that he is no different from them [i.e., the idolaters][23] then or ever ...

Rabbi Oshry backs up his novel approach with the opinions of several major halakhic authorities,[24] and concludes that there was no halakhic problem with his questioner writing the letters "R.C."

---

22 *She'eilot u-Teshuvot mi-Ma'amakim* 5:3, p. 49.

23 A bit earlier in the responsum, Rabbi Oshry states explicitly that in this scenario, a Jew can claim that he is an idolater: אבל היכא שאינם יודעים ומכירים בו שהוא יהודי בזה אין איסור כלל להטעות אותם ולומר שהוא עובד כוכבים.

24 *Terumat ha-Deshen* 196, Shakh to *Shulḥan Arukh, Yoreh De'ah* 157 note 17, and *Nimukei Yosef* to *Bava Kamma* (p. 40a in *Ran*).

in his passport. Since this questioner's "appearance and name concealed his Jewish identity," his would-be persecutors would have had no idea that he was Jewish. As such, he could even have come straight out and verbally declared himself to be a Roman Catholic.[25] Therefore, merely writing the letters "R.C." in his passport was certainly permitted.

Before ending his responsum, Rabbi Oshry offers one additional reason why writing "R.C." in his questioner's passport posed no halakhic problem. Even without his above-mentioned novel approach, Rabbi Oshry had shown that Rema and Rambam agreed that when faced with the threat of death, it was permissible for a Jew to make an ambiguous statement of apostasy. Rabbi Oshry argued that including the letters "R.C." was in fact an ambiguous declaration. To the would-be persecutor, those letters identified the passport's holder as a Roman Catholic. The passport bearer, however, could see the letters "R.C." as a transliteration of the Hebrew word רק or "*rak*"—as in *Devarim* 4:9 in speaking of the Divine Revelation, the Torah states:

רק ... ושמור נפשך מאד פן תשכח את הדברים. . .

---

25 In *Hidden in Thunder* (Mossad Harav Kook, Jerusalem, Israel, 2007, p. 260), Dr. Esther Farbstein explains why some Holocaust-era rabbis allowed Jews to falsely claim to be Christians. In doing so, she mentions another early halakhic authority who weighed in on the matter:

> The permission may also have been based on the opinion of the Rosh, who wrote that the prohibition stems from concern that this statement would be interpreted by the gentiles as conversion; when a Jew who is forced to convert says he is not Jewish, he is acknowledging their religion. After all, "he is definitely an apostate. Since they want to kill him unless he switches to their religion and becomes a gentile like them, when he says he is a gentile he is certainly acknowledging their religion and adopting their god." It may be concluded that if the gentiles do not know the person is Jewish, the statement is not a desecration of God's name and is permitted in a life-threatening emergency.

[See *Piskei ha-Rosh*, *Avodah Zarah*, chap. 2, section 4.]

Just ... and be greatly aware for your soul not to forget the matters ...

Since the letters "R.C." could mean "*rak*" to the owner of the passport, Rabbi Oshry felt this case met Rema's criteria for an ambiguous assertion of apostasy—which even Rambam would agree—that a Jew was permitted to make if threatened with death.

The Jewish GI and His Dog-Tags

It would seem that the case of a Jewish GI who wanted to stamp a letter designating a religion other than Judaism on his dog-tags is perfectly analogous to the fellow who wanted to include the letters "R.C." in his passport.

In both cases, the bearer of such a passport / dog-tag offers no indication that he is a Jew.[26] For all the enemy knows, the bearer of those items is part of the overwhelming number of people who were born into the faith designated by the letters appearing in their passports and on their dog-tags. Accordingly, in both cases a Jew who feared for his life—but was not recognized as a Jew by his persecutors—could verbally claim to be a Christian.[27] If so, he could certainly indicate this by means of including some identifying letters on his passport/dog-tags.

---

26 This is assuming the name on the Jewish GI's dog-tag was not Jewish-sounding. If his name did in fact indicate he was Jewish, the permissive ruling would not apply, and he could not openly declare himself to be a member of a different faith community.

27 This is an important point. After all, as per fn. 7 above, in November 1962, the US government stopped using a single letter on dog-tags to denote its wearer's religion. Since then, one's religious affiliation is fully spelled out. Thus, a Jewish GI no longer has the option of having an ambiguous letter stamped on his dog-tags. Should he choose to have a religion other than "Jewish" stamped on his dog-tags, the name of that religion would be fully written out in a clear manner. This would only be permitted according to Rabbi Oshry's novel understanding of *Rema* and *Rambam* on this matter.

Furthermore, the bearer of the passport / dog-tags could have in mind that those letters designate whatever he would like them to, while his enemy assumes they signify that their owner is a member of a non-Jewish faith. This would be tantamount to making an ambiguous statement to convince one's enemies that he is an idolater. As we have seen, this is a course of action expressly permitted by Rema and even Rambam before him—as Rabbi Oshry showed in his responsum.

Conclusion

From the sources cited above, it seems clear that a Jewish soldier serving in the US military during WWII[28] would have had no halakhic issues in concealing his Jewish identity. Moreover, it seems clear that, according to Rabbi Ephraim Oshry, it would have been halakhically permissible for Jewish GIs (with non-Jewish sounding names)[29] serving in the WWII European Theater to have a letter signifying a faith other than their own stamped on their dog-tags.

I conclude with the words of one of our people's most beloved prophets. In describing the Messianic Era for which all Jews so eagerly await, Isaiah declared:[30]

> ד ... וְכִתְּתוּ חַרְבוֹתָם לְאִתִּים, וַחֲנִיתוֹתֵיהֶם לְמַזְמֵרוֹת--לֹא-יִשָּׂא גוֹי אֶל-גּוֹי חֶרֶב, וְלֹא-יִלְמְדוּ עוֹד מִלְחָמָה.

> 4... and they shall beat their swords into plowshares, and their spears into pruning hooks; nation shall not lift up sword against nation, neither shall they learn war any more.

I am sure that in the Messianic Era, if we put our minds to it, we will be able to find an agricultural use for our soldiers' dog-tags

[28] This should also apply to the recent wars in Iraq and Afghanistan.

[29] See note 26.

[30] Isaiah 2:4.

as well. Until that day, however, may it be G-d's will that no member of our people ever again fear being identified as a Jew.[31] ☙

---

31 In the course of writing this article, I discovered that Rabbi Oshry's responsum discussed herein is at odds with some of his other related responsa. I hope to treat these apparent contradictions at greater length in a future article.

Pointing to the Torah and other Hagbaha Customs

By: ZVI RON

The idea of displaying the text of the Torah to the listening congregation is already found in Tanakh. Before Ezra read to the assembled Jews from the Torah scroll, we are told that "Ezra opened the scroll before the eyes of the people ... and when he opened it, all the people stood silent. Ezra blessed the Lord God, and all the people answered, 'Amen! Amen!' with their hands upraised, then they bowed and prostrated themselves before the Lord, faces to the ground" (Neh. 8:5-6). It is not clear if the showing of the Torah and the reaction of bowing was meant to be a onetime practice or something that would accompany every public Torah reading. Still, this source forms the basis of the idea of displaying the Torah scroll as codified in *Masekhet Soferim* 14:13.[1] Just as reported in Nehemiah, *Masekhet Soferim* instructs that the Torah is to be shown before the reading, at which time the congregation should bow: "It is a mitzvah for all the men and women to see the writing, bow and say, 'This is the Torah that Moses placed before the Children of Israel' (Deut. 4:44). 'The Torah of the Lord is perfect, restoring the soul' (Ps. 19:8)." This source is quoted by Ramban in his discussion of

---

1 See Morekhai Zer-Kavod, *Da'at Mikra: Ezra v–Nehemia* (Jerusalem: Mossad Harav Kook, 1994), p. 105, note 6. See there also an alternate interpretation that the word *vayiftaḥ* in this verse means "began reading" rather than "opened." According to that interpretation there was not necessarily a public display of the Torah at this event, and the people reacted to hearing the words of the Torah, rather than to seeing the scroll. See also Daniel Sperber, *Minhagei Yisrael*, vol. 1 (Jerusalem: Mossad Harav Kook, 1989), p. 78–81.

Zvi Ron received semikhah from the Israeli Rabbanut and his PhD in Jewish Theology from Spertus University. He is an educator living in Neve Daniel, Israel and the author of Sefer Katan ve-Gadol (Rossi Publications, 2006) about the big and small letters in Tanakh.

hagbaha[2] as well as by other *rishonim.*[3] *Masekhet Soferim* forms the basis for the law as formulated in the *Shulḥan Arukh* (*Oraḥ Ḥayyim* 134:2). In all of these sources the only actions incumbent on the congregation during *hagbaha* are bowing and reciting two verses.

There are a few differences between the way *Masekhet Soferim* describes *hagbaha* and current practice. In accordance with *Masekhet Soferim*, R. Yosef Karo in the *Shulḥan Arukh* has *hagbaha* taking place before the Torah reading, the universal custom in Talmudic times.[4] R. Moshe Isserles adds that the Ashkenazic custom is to do *hagbaha* after the Torah reading, even though the early Ashkenazic work *Kol Bo,* quoting *Masekhet Soferim,* indicates that *hagbaha* is done before the reading.[5] It seems that some textual variants of *Masekhet Soferim* state that *hagbaha* is done after the Torah reading, leading to the different customs.[6] R. Chaim Benvenisti (1603–1673), an important Turkish halakhist, explains in his book *Sha'ayarei Knesset ha-Gedolah* that the Ashkenazic custom originated because uneducated people thought that seeing the Torah at *hagbaha* was more important than hearing the Torah reading, so they would walk out of the synagogue right after *hagbaha.* By postponing *hagbaha*, people would leave only after the Torah reading.[7] Some Sephardic authorities approved of the Ashkenazic custom,[8] and in

2 Ramban, commentary to Deut. 27:26.

3 See *Beit Yosef*, *Oraḥ Ḥayyim* 134:2.

4 *Arukh ha-Shulḥan, Oraḥ Ḥayyim* 147:9.

5 *Kol Bo*, siman 20. *Darkei Moshe*, *Oraḥ Ḥayyim* 147:4.

6 See *Bayit Ḥadash*, *Oraḥ Ḥayyim* 147:3. See also *Talmudic Encyclopedia* (Jerusalem: Talmudic Encyclopedia Publishing, Ltd., 1957), vol. 8, p. 167, note 12.

7 *Shayarei Knesset ha-Gedolah*, *Beit Yosef*, *Oraḥ Ḥayyim* 134:2. This is similar to the contemporary practice in some synagogues to place *Anim Zemirot* in the middle of the service rather at the end so that people do not walk out of the synagogue while the Ark is open. For more on Benvenisti, see Bezalel Naor, *Post-Sabbatian Sabbatianism* (Spring Valley, New York: Orot, 1999), p. 167.

8 R. Ḥayyim Yosef David Azulai, *le-David Emet* (Jerusalem: 1847), 4:2. He notes also that in some communities it was customary not to do *hagbaha* at all for fear that the Torah may be dropped or touched with bare hands, 4:1. See also *Talmudic Encyclopedia*, vol. 8, p. 167, n. 5–7.

some Ashkenazic communities *hagbaha* is done before the Torah reading.[9]

Masekhet Soferim gives two verses (Deut. 4:44, Ps. 19:8) for the congregation to recite during *hagbaha*. These along with various additional verses are found today in Ashkenazic and Sephardic prayer books.[10] Some editions of *Masekhet Soferim* have the word "or" between the two verses, indicating that either verse can be said, and it is not necessary to recite both, so it is not surprising that many prayer books leave out Ps. 19:8.[11] Contemporary Ashkenazic prayer books generally add the words "According to the word of the Lord through Moses" to the verse from Deut. 4:44, and leave out the verse from Psalms.[12] This addition is found in the very influential prayer book composed by R. Isaiah Horowitz (the *Shenei Luḥot ha-Brit* (*Shelah*), 1565–1630),[13] but is considered unusual since it is only a fragment of a verse with seemingly no connection to Deut. 4:44 or to *hagbaha*. [14] It seems not to be a kabbalistic addition since it does not appear in kabbalistic prayer books before the

---

9 See *Kaf ha-Ḥayyim*, *Oraḥ Ḥayyim* 134:17, Simcha Rabinowitz, *Piskei Teshuvot* (Jerusalem: 2002) volume 2, 134:9, p. 107, note 42. The differences in the placement of *hagbaha* may also be related to the different customs found in Israel and Babylonia regarding standing when the Torah is taken out and returned to the Ark; see Daniel Sperber, *Minhagei Yisrael*, vol. 8 (Jerusalem: Mossad Harav Kook, 2007), pp. 142–145.

10 Daniel Sperber, *Minhagei Yisrael*, vol. 3 (Jerusalem: Mossad Harav Kook, 1994), p. 99, note 75.

11 The word "or" appears in parentheses in the standard Vilna edition of *Masekhet Soferim*; however, the Gra in his notes to *Masekhet Soferim* deletes that word. The version of *Mesekhet Soferim* found in *Maḥzor Vitry* indicates that both verses are said (p. 707). See also *Piskei Teshuvot* volume 2, 134:8, p. 107, n. 38.

12 Ps. 19:8 is included in many prayer books at the end of the formula for calling up the first aliya, *v-tigaleh*. This is already found in works of the Rishonim; see for example *Sefer Abudraham* (Jerusalem: Frank, 1995), p. 142, and *Perushei Siddur ha-tefilla l–Rokeaḥ* (Jerusalem: Machon Harav Hershler, 1992), p. 422.

13 *Siddur ha-Shelah, Sha'ar ha-Shamayim* (Amsterdam: 1717), p. 117b. The addition is not commented upon by the *Shelah*.

14 See for example *Arukh ha-Shulḥan*, *Oraḥ Ḥayyim* 134:3, and Eliyahu Munk, *Olam ha-Tefillot* (Jerusalem: Mossad Harav Kook, 1992), p.185.

Shelah.[15] Although this phrase appears multiple times in the Torah,[16] some prayer books note that these words are taken specifically from Num. 9:23, "According to the word of the Lord would they encamp, and according to the word of the Lord would they journey; the charge of the Lord would they safeguard, according to the word of the Lord through Moses."[17] This verse reference is based on the opinion of R. Ḥayyim of Volozhin that originally this entire verse was said, but it was mistakenly abbreviated.[18] This verse is considered fitting for when the Torah is in motion, during *hagbaha* and on the way to the Ark.[19] There is no evidence from any early prayer book that the whole verse was ever recited. It has been suggested that these additional words proclaiming that this is the complete divine Torah were added in Ashkenazic lands to negate the theology of their Christian neighbors.[20]

While *Masekhet Soferim* instructs the congregation to bow during *hagbaha*, it is more common today to see people pointing at the Torah during *hagbaha*. This despite the explicit statement by the *Shulḥan Arukh* (*Oraḥ Ḥayyim* 134:2) that one should bow. R. Moshe Isserles writes that this was the custom of Maharil as well.[21] This bow is performed the same way one bows during *Modim* in *Shemoneh Esreh*.[22] Many authorities have decried the fact that some

---

15 Daniel Reimer, *Sefer Tefillat Ḥayyim* (Ẓrur ha-Hayyim Publications, 2004), p. 107.

16 Num. 4:37, 4:45, 9:23, 10:13, and once in Jos. 22:9.

17 See *ArtScroll Siddur*, p. 146. *Rinat Yisrael*, which usually provides chapter references, does not do so for this passage.

18 R. Avraham Landa, *Siddur Ẓluta d–Avraham* (Tel-Aviv: Grafika, 1958), p. 373.

19 R. Isaac Landa, *Mikra Soferim* (Suwalki, Poland: 1862), 13:4; see also his commentary *Dover Shalom* in *Oẓar ha-Tefillot*, p. 422. Based on this, in *Ishei Yisrael*, a prayer book based on the teachings of the Vilna Gaon, the entire verse is brought, Isaac Moltzin, *Ishei Yisrael* (Tel Aviv: Yakov Landa, 1968), p. 164.

20 Daniel Sperber, *Minhagei Yisrael*, vol. 3 (Jerusalem: Mossad Harav Kook, 1994), pp. 95–102.

21 *Darkei Moshe*, *Oraḥ Ḥayyim* 147:4.

22 *Talmudic Encyclopedia*, vol. 8, p. 170, n. 44.

people today do not bow during *hagbaha*.[23] Various reasons have been offered to justify this. R. Isaiah di Trani (c. 1235–c. 1300), known as Riaz, is quoted in *Shiltei Gibborim* (*Kiddushin* 14b) as saying that one should stand for the Torah but not bow to the Torah. He explains that there is no source anywhere that indicates that people should bow to the Torah or the Ark.[24] Some authorities understood this to mean that it is in fact prohibited to bow to the Torah and only standing for the Torah is allowed.[25] This ruling is considered the main justification for those who do not bow during *hagbaha*.[26] The statement of Riaz seems to be in direct conflict with *Masekhet Soferim*, a source that clearly mandates bowing. Ḥida reconciles this blatant conflict by explaining that Riaz was not referring to an open Torah scroll, only to a closed one, and thus one should bow to the open Torah during *hagbaha*.[27] Others have justified not bowing during *hagbaha* because the Torah may not be kosher,[28] or because the person lifting the Torah is standing between the congregation and the Torah scroll,[29] or that *Masekhet Soferim* only meant that it is good to bow during *hagbaha*, but not obligatory.[30] Whatever the justification, today in many congregations pointing is much more prevalent than bowing.

Pointing during *hagbaha* is not mentioned in any early sources and is not found in the *Shulḥan Arukh*, or in the traditional commentaries to the *Shulḥan Arukh*. Some works claim that there is no real source for this custom and it should be avoided.[31] Certain rab-

---

23 See Yehuda Levi Ben-David, *Sefer Kara Ravatz* (Jerusalem: Birkei Yosef, 1996), p. 267.

24 ולא נמצא בכל התורה שמשתחוין אפילו לארון הקודש.

25 See R. Ḥayyim Yosef David Azulai, *Birkei Yosef*, 134:3, where he discusses this at length.

26 Simḥa Rabinowitz, *Piskei Teshuvot*, volume 2, 134:7, p. 105, n. 28.

27 R. Ḥayyim Yosef David Azulai, *Birkei Yosef*, 134:3.

28 Yekutiel Yehudah Halberstam, *Divrei Yaẓiv* (Jerusalem: Shefa Ḥayyim, 1997), *Oraḥ Ḥayyim* vol. 1, 76:6.

29 *Piskei Teshuvot*, volume 2, 134:7, p. 106, n. 29. This would explain why bowing during *hagbaha* is more prevalent in Sephardic congregations where the person doing *hagbaha* is not blocking any of the writing.

30 *Sefer Kara Ravatz*, p. 267.

31 Yehudah Chesner, *Siaḥ Tefilla* (Ofakim: 2003) p. 248.

binic leaders in modern times, such as Rav Shlomo Zalman Auerbach and Rav Eliyashiv, would not point to the Torah during *hagbaha*.[32] The earliest mention of pointing during *hagbaha* is found in *Divrei Mordekhai*, a book of responsa by R. Moredekhai Krispin, a rabbi in Rhodes in the 1800s. No source for the custom is given, only a justification for why it is not considered inappropriate. In *Bamidbar Rabbah* (2:3) R. Ḥanina explains that while it is generally considered insolent and punishable by death to point to the image of a king using a finger, because of His great love for the Jewish People, God allows young children to point to His Name in the house of study. R. Krispin writes that this is what people rely on when they point to the Torah.[33] This justification is quoted by R. Ḥayyim Palaggi (1788–1869), who served as the *Ḥakham Bashi*, the Chief Rabbi of the Ottoman Empire, in his book *Sefer Ḥayyim* when he discusses this custom.[34] This work is the most common source referenced for the custom.[35] R. Palaggi discusses this custom in other works as well. In his book *Ruaḥ Ḥayyim* he explains that pointing with a finger is not considered inappropriate in connection with God, bringing proofs from the Talmud and midrash. For example, the famous comment at the end of *Ta'anit* (31a), based on Isaiah 25:9, that in the Garden of Eden the righteous will form a circle around God and point to Him with their finger.[36] He references *Divrei Mordekhai* there as well.[37] In his book *Lev Ḥayyim*, R. Palaggi once again discusses the custom of pointing to the Torah. This time he explains that the most appropriate finger to point with is the index finger, since it is the second finger if we begin counting

---

32 Avraham Schigel, *Doleh u-Mashkeh* (Kiryat Sefer: 2007), p. 95, n. 272.

33 R. Mordekhai Krispin, *Divrei Mordekhai* (Salonika: 1836), siman 9.

34 R. Ḥaim Palaggi, *Sefer Ḥayyim* (Salonika: 1863), 3:6. This book is often mistakenly referred to as *Sefer ha-Ḥayyim*.

35 See for example *Doleh u-Mashkeh* (Kiryat Sefer: 2007), p. 95, and *Aliba d-Hilkheta* 31, Shevat-Adar 5769, p. 34, where R. Ḥayim Kanievsky references R. Palaggi as the source of the custom.

36 A similar exposition of Psalms 48:15 found in the Jerusalem Talmud *Mo'ed Katan* 3:7 is suggested by Jacob Neusner to be the source for pointing as showing respect and thus pointing to the Torah. See Noam Neusner, "The Pinkie Paradox," Jerusalem Post Magazine, June 13, 2003.

37 R. Chaim Palaggi, *Ruaḥ Ḥayyim* (Izmir: 1876), *Yoreh De'ah* 285: 4.

with the thumb, corresponding to the second word in the series of five-word statements describing the Torah in Psalms 19:8–10. In each of the six statements, the second word is the Name of God. For example, "The Torah of the Lord is perfect, restoring the soul; The testimony of the Lord is trustworthy, making the simple wise, "תורת ה' תמימה משיבת נפש, עדות ה' נאמנה מחכימת פתי" (Ps. 19:8). Pointing with the second finger is therefore ideal since the entire Torah is understood to be the Name of God.[38]

A popular explanation for the custom to point is based on the idea found in *Menaḥot* 29a that the word *zeh* in the Torah implies pointing with a finger. "A Tanna of the school of R. Ishmael stated, 'Three things presented difficulties to Moses, until the Holy One, blessed be He, showed Moses with His finger, and these are they: the menorah, the new moon, and the creeping things. The menorah, as it is written, 'And this was (*v-zeh*) the work of the candlestick' (Num. 8:4). The new moon, as it is written, 'This (*ha-zeh*) month shall be unto you the beginning of months' (Ex. 12:2). The creeping things, as it is written, 'And these are (*v-zeh*) they which are unclean' (Lev. 11:29). Others add, also the rules for slaughtering beasts, as it is written, 'Now this is (*v-zeh*) that which thou shall offer upon the altar' (Ex. 29:38)."[39] Thus, when reciting the verse 'This is (*zoht*) the Torah that Moses placed before the Children of Israel' (Deut. 4:44) during *hagbaha*, people point with their finger.[40] Other *derashot* connecting the word *zeh* to pointing with a finger are found in rabbinic literature,[41] but always only in connection

38 R. Chaim Palaggi, *Lev Ḥayyim* (Jerusalem: Siaḥ Yisrael, 1996), vol. 2, 167:6.

39 *Exodus Rabbah* (15:28) adds a fourth, the anointing oil, based on the verse "This (*zeh*) shall remain for Me oil of sacred anointment for your generations" (Ex. 30:31).

40 Yosef Lewy, *Minhag Yisrael Torah, volume 1* (Brooklyn, New York: Fink Graphics, 1990), p. 181. He introduces his discussion of the custom by stating that he searched through many books and could not find anywhere a reference to pointing during *hagbaha*.

41 See *Torah Temima*, Gen. 25, note 30 and Ex. 13, note 29 for examples from the Jerusalem Talmud and midrashic literature. There the custom to point to the matzah and *marror* at the *seder* is explained based on the verse "And you shall tell your son on that day, 'It is because of this (*zeh*)

with the word *zeh*, never *zoht*. This would make pointing irrelevant to *hagbaha* where the verse recited uses the word *zoht* and not *zeh*. Still, in his discussion of Lev. 11:2 'These are (*zoht*) the creatures that you may eat from among the animals that are upon the earth,' R. Eliyahu Mizraḥi indicates that the idea of pointing can be learned from both *zeh* and *zoht*, so this is considered by some a support for the custom.[42] However, in the discussion of this verse in the Talmud (*Ḥullin* 42a) it says only that God showed Moshe the kinds of *tereifot*, without specifically mentioning showing with a finger. Still, this explanation is very popular, and seems to resonate with many people. This reasoning, along with the opinion of Divrei Mordekhai as quoted by R. Palaggi, are the explanations given in the popular *Oẓar Ta'amei ha-Minhagim*.[43]

These sources are concerned with justifying a preexisting practice and bringing support to something commonly done,[44] but raise the question of why people started pointing to the Torah in the first place. It has been suggested that it arose from people attempting to kiss the Torah as it is taken from the Ark to the *bimah*. People who were far away and could not reach the Torah would stick out their hands in the direction of the Torah, sometimes holding *ẓiẓit*, and then kiss the *ẓiẓit* or their finger. In Sephardic congregations where *hagbaha* takes place right after the Torah arrives at the *bimah*, some people would still be sticking their hands out during *hagbaha*, leading to the impression that people should point to the Torah during *hagbaha*.[45] This would explain why all the early references to the custom of pointing appear in Sephardic sources. R.

---

that the Lord acted on my behalf when I left Egypt' " (Ex. 13:8). Similarly, *Tiferet Yisrael* on the Mishnah (*Sanhedrin* 8:4) explains that when the parents of a rebellious son (*ben sorer u-moreh*) declare "This (*zeh*) son of ours" (Deut. 21:20) they point to their child with their finger.

42 *Minhag Yisrael Torah* also references the commentary *Iyun Yaakov* to *Ein Yaakov, Ḥullin* 42a, where the word *zoht* in Lev. 11:2 is understood as indicating pointing with a finger. See also Efraim Greenblatt, *Rivivos Ephraim* (Brooklyn, NY: Mazel, 1993) *Oraḥ Ḥayyim*, vol. 6, no. 4.

43 Shmuel Gelbard, *Oẓar Ta'amei ha-Minhagim* (Petaḥ Tikva: Mifaal Rashi, 1996), p. 224.

44 Yehudah Chesner, *Siaḥ Tefilla* (Ofakim: 2003) p. 248, n. 65.

45 *Siaḥ Tefilla*, p. 249, n. 65.

Palaggi specifically notes that most people hold their *ẓiẓit* in their hand when pointing to the Torah (although he explains that it is not necessary to do so),[46] and the custom in many Sephardic congregations today is to lift the *ẓiẓit* towards the Torah during *hagbaha* with or without a finger extended,[47] further indicating that the custom may have arisen as a long-distance way of kissing the Torah with the *ẓiẓit* on its way to the *bimah*.

Another factor that may have contributed to the prevalence of pointing is the practice of looking at letters in the Torah during *hagbaha*. The kabbalistic work *Sha'ar ha-Kavanot* compiled by R. Shmuel Vital, son of R. Ḥaim Vital, relates that R. Isaac Luria, the Ari, would get close to the Torah during *hagbaha* so that he could see the actual letters, and that this practice draws down a great light.[48] This was quoted by R. Abraham Gombiner (c. 1633–c.1683) in his *Magen Avraham* (*Oraḥ Ḥayyim*, 134:3) and was later included in *Sha'arei Efraim* (10:13) and the *Mishnah Berurah* (134:11). Previous to kabbalistic influence, an indistinct view of text of the Torah during *hagbaha* was considered sufficient, but making out individual letters was not stressed.[49] By being included in the *Magen Avraham* and *Mishnah Berurah*, this kabbalistic custom became well known and widely practiced. R. Yosef Chaim of Baghdad (the Ben Ish Ḥai, 1832–1909) adds that he saw in a book that during *hagbaha* a person should look for a word in the Torah that begins with the first letter of his name.[50] This idea is included in R. Yaakov Ḥayyim Sofer's *Kaf ha-Ḥayyim* (*Oraḥ Ḥayyim* 134:13). While none of these sources instruct people to point at the Torah, pointing is a natural way for people to make sure they can make out an actual letter, and certainly to find a particular letter. Justifications for pointing to the Torah are found only after the time of the *Magen Avraham*, when the kab-

---

46 *Sefer Ḥayyim*, 3:6.

47 *Sefer Kara Ravatz*, p. 275.

48 Shmuel Vital, *Sha'ar ha-Kavanot* (Jerusalem: Yerid ha-Sefarim, 2005), *Inyan Kriyat ha-Torah, derush alef*, p. 48b.

49 Moshe Hallamish, *Kabbalah in Liturgy, Halakhah and Customs* (Ramat Gan: Bar-Ilan University, 2000), p. 311 (Hebrew).

50 R. Yosef Chaim of Baghdad, *Sefer Ben Ish Ḥai* (Jerusalem: 1932), year 2, *Toldot* 16, p. 19a.

balistic practice of looking at the letters during *hagbaha* became more widely known.

In contemporary synagogues when the Torah is opened and lifted up during *hagbaha*, many congregants can be seen pointing to the Torah with their little finger. The earliest reference to this custom is found in the encyclopedic work *me-Am Lo'ez*, a Ladino commentary to Tanach. This work was begun by R. Yaakov Culi in the 1700s to facilitate Torah study among Turkish Jews who were not fluent in Hebrew. Rabbi Culi died in 1732, having completed the commentary on Genesis and most of Exodus. The rest of *me-Am Lo'ez* on the Torah was written by different authors. The custom of pointing to the Torah using the little finger is mentioned as part of the commentary to *Ki Tavo* (27:26) in a discussion of customs related to *hagbaha*.[51] There it simply states, "It is customary to point to the writing with the little finger and to kiss it." No explanation is given for the custom. *me-Am Lo'ez* on Deuteronomy was begun by R. Isaac Behar Arguiti of Constantinople and completed in 1772. However, beyond the commentary to the first three portions of Deuteronomy, *Devarim*, *va-Etḥanan* and *Eikev*, only a few pages of his work were found. The rest of the *me-Am Lo'ez* commentary to Deuteronomy, including the discussion of *hagbaha*, was written by R. Shmuel Kroizer (1921–1997),[52] a fifth-generation Jerusalemite who lived most of his life in the Beit Hakerem neighborhood of Jerusalem.[53] Rabbi Kroizer was a well-known Jerusalem rabbi and *talmid ḥakham* who was on the staff of the *Talmudic Encyclopedia* at a very young age. He authored many books and was responsible for translating *me-Am Lo'ez* from Ladino to Hebrew. He wrote the *me-Am Lo'ez* commentary to the remainder of Deu-

---

51 *Yalkut me-Am Lo'ez, Devarim: volume 3* (Jerusalem: Wagshal, 1969), p. 1,037.

52 *Yalkut me-Am Lo'ez, Devarim: volume 1* (Jerusalem: Wagshal, 1969), introduction, pp. 5-6.

53 Kroizer's wife was the daughter of Yisrael Ber Odesser, famous for his discovery of the "Letter from Heaven," containing the now ubiquitous *na-nach* phrase. For an overview of the life and works of R. Shmuel Kroizer, see the article in Haaretz, May 5, 2010, <http://www.haaretz.co.il/hasite/pages/ShArt.jhtml?itemNo=1168741&contrassID=1&subContrassID=18&sbSubContrassID=0>.

teronomy, as well as most of the *me-Am Lo'ez* Tanakh commentary. Due to his great modesty he often used pseudonyms, and in the title page of *me-Am Lo'ez* he goes by Shmuel Yerushalmi. Thus, the earliest reference in writing to the custom of pointing to the Torah with the little finger is in fact in the book *me-Am Lo'ez*, but that particular section dates to 1969, making this a very recent source. Pointing with the little finger was popular enough by Kroizer's time that he called it "customary" (נהגו), however it was never considered significant enough to be mentioned as a legitimate custom in any halakhic work or book of Jewish customs before he wrote about it. The contemporary halakhic work *Piskei Teshuvot* claims that the custom of pointing to the Torah with the little finger has an ancient source, מקורו קדמון, apparently not realizing that R. Kroizer is the author of this part of *me-Am Lo'ez*.[54] However, Yehudah Chesner in his book *Siaḥ Tefillah* correctly points out that this part of *me-Am Lo'ez* was written recently, and the custom has no ancient sources at all, ואין בזה שום מקור קדמון.[55] Since *me-Am Lo'ez* is a Sephardic work, many people assume that using the little finger to point is a Sephardic custom; however R. Kroizer is Ashkenazic and the sections that he wrote draw upon both Sephardic and Ashkenazic customs. In the same section he notes the differences between Sephardic and Ashkenazic congregations regarding when to do *hagbaha*, and the custom of the Ari to get close and see the actual letters.

Pointing with the little finger can be seen in many congregations today, but there is no clear reason for it.[56] Generally people explain that they do it because they have seen others doing so, even though they were never specifically taught to point to the Torah with their little finger.[57] In recent years a few explanations have

---

54 *Piskei Teshuvot* (Jerusalem: 2002) volume 2, 134:3, p. 104.

55 *Siaḥ Tefilla*, p. 248, n. 65.

56 Correspondence with the son of R. Kroizer, friends and neighbors did not shed any light on the custom. It may be that R. Kroizer himself did not know of a reason for the custom, since contrary to other customs, he did not provide a reason for this one in *me-Am Lo'ez*.

57 See Noam Neusner, "The Pinkie Paradox," Jerusalem Post Magazine, June 13, 2003.

been offered for this custom. One popular explanation is that pointing to the Torah with the littlest finger demonstrates the classic teaching that only a humble person can acquire Torah greatness.[58] Other approaches are somewhat more obscure. The ten fingers can be seen as representing the Ten Commandments, and if we begin counting the fingers with our hands palms down, the little finger on the right hand corresponds to the First Commandment, making it an appropriate finger to point to the Torah.[59] However, this way of counting fingers is in opposition to the way people commonly count using fingers and to the method of R. Palaggi noted earlier, where counting begins with the thumb.[60] Rabbenu Baḥya in his commentary to the Torah (Lev. 8:23) mentions an idea current among scientists of his time that each finger assists one of the five senses. For example, the index finger is commonly used to clean out nostrils, so it serves the sense of smell; the ring finger is used to clean out the eyes, so it serves the sense of sight. The little finger is used for cleaning out the ear, thus serving the sense of hearing. Based on this, it has been suggested that pointing with the little finger recalls the Israelites saying *na'aseh v-nishma* at the giving of the Torah at Mount Sinai.[61] The connection between cleaning out ears and pointing to the Torah seems tenuous. In general these explana-

---

58 Nissim Dayan, *Na'eh Zivam* (Bnei Brak: 2002), p. 43. The exact same text also appears in Dayan's book *Shavatenu Kabel* (Bnei Brak: 2009), p. 184.

59 *Sefer Kara Ravaẓ*, p. 275.

60 On the various places to begin counting via fingers, see Oliver Lindemann, Ahmad Alipour and Martin H. Fischer, "Finger Counting Habits in Middle Eastern and Western Individuals," *Journal of Cross-Cultural Psychology*, May 2011, vol. 42:4, pp. 566–578.

61 *Sefer Kara Ravaẓ*, p. 275. The connection between the little finger and ear cleaning is found in many cultures. The Anglo-Saxons called the little finger the ear finger; it is also known as the auricular finger, *Brewer's Dictionary of Phrase and Fable* (New York: Harper Collins, 2005), p.509. It is interesting to note that in medieval times, a raised little finger indicated that an actor in a play was eavesdropping on another character; see Charles Reginald Dodwell, *Anglo-Saxon Gestures and the Roman Stage* (Cambridge: Cambridge University Press, 2000), p. 23.

tions do not seem particularly satisfying, but the prevalence of the custom demands some sort of explanation.[62]

There may be another reason for the choice of using the little finger to point to the Torah. Finger pointing sometimes has negative connotations in Tanakh. For example, "If you remove from your midst perversion, finger pointing and evil speech" (Is. 58:9), is explained by Radak as referring to the way of belligerent people to point one finger at each other. In Proverbs 6:13 finger pointing is listed as one of the actions of a lawless man. Among both ancient and modern peoples, in both Islamic and European cultures, many consider pointing at someone with the index finger offensive.[63] There are some positive references to finger pointing in rabbinic literature, such as Ta'anit (31a) noted above,[64] but negative connota-

---

62 Rabbi Yehuda Schwartz explains that actually people are making the *kemiẓa* sign with their hand, folding down the middle three fingers, as the priests did when preparing the meal offering: "And so, we can say that the pinky is not pointing at all. Rather it is the result of forming that *komeẓ* with our fingers as the Torah is being returned, in effect, as we seek to 'take with us' that little portion we can, a *komeẓ* so to speak, to carry us through until the next reading" (personal correspondence). See his letter in the Jerusalem Post Magazine, June 20, 2003. Other "cute" explanations are given for the custom, such as the idea that since all the other body parts have mitzvot to do but not the little finger, it was decided to leave this for the little finger to perform.

63 When I was serving in the IDF and was responsible for training a group of new *olim* from Ethiopia, we were specifically instructed not to point to them as it was considered a very offensive gesture in Ethiopia. Regarding the negative associations of pointing among ancient cultures in Biblical times, see Aron Magen, *Beit Aharon: Klalei ha-Shas, volume 10* (Brooklyn, NY: Deutsch Publishing, 1975), p. 712. Regarding the pointing taboo in the modern era, see Larry A. Samovar, *Communication Between Cultures* (Boston, MA: Wadsworth, 2007), p. 257; Mai Moua, *Culturally Intelligent Leadership: Leading Through Intercultural Interactions* (New York: Business Expert Press, 2010), p. 123; Lillian Glass, *Say it Right* (New York: Putnam's Sons, 1991), p. 164; J.K. Yates, *Global Engineering and Construction* (Hoboken, NJ: John Wiley and Sons, 2007) p.32; Craig Steven Cravens, *Culture and Customs of the Czech Republic and Slovakia* (Westport, CN: Greenwood, 2006), p. 63.

64 See also Chanoch Zundel Grossberg, *Zer ha-Torah* (Jerusalem: 1979), p. 12, n. 8.

tions are found as well, such as the midrash mentioned by *Divrei Mordekhai* that it was considered an unpardonable offense to point to the likeness of a king. The reason for this is that "pointing with the finger is often held to be of magical efficacy, the power streaming, as it were, from operator to victim ... hence it is indecorous to point with a finger towards, e.g., the heavenly bodies or other worshipful objects or at friends or superiors."[65] Even in modern times, in many cultures pointing with the finger to what were considered supernaturally powerful objects, such as the sun,[66] moon, stars,[67] rainbows[68] and tombstones,[69] is considered inappropriate and a source of misfortune. This is extended to pointing to anything considered of value, such as ships in fishing cultures.[70] The index finger was considered a particularly offensive finger to use for pointing.[71] Because of this some people bend their index finger down a bit so that they are not actually pointing at the Torah. It may be that once the custom of pointing to the Torah became prevalent, it was considered inappropriate to use the index finger for pointing because of negative cultural connotations, leading to the use of the little finger as an alternative with no offensive connotations.[72] The fact that the

---

65 James Hastings, ed., *Encyclopaedia of Religion and Ethics* (Edinburgh: T & T Clark, 1913), vol. 6, p. 496.

66 Frank A. Kmietowicz, *Slavic Mythical Beliefs*, (1982) p. 174.

67 J.G. Frazer, "Some Popular Superstitions of the Ancients," *Folklore* (1890) vol. 1, p. 151-152.

68 Francisco R. Demetrio, *Encyclopedia of Philippine Folk Beliefs and Customs, vol. 2* (Cagayan de Oro City, Philippines: Xavier University, 1991), p. 19.

69 Wayland Debs, *Popular Beliefs and Superstitions: A Compendium of American Folklore*, vol. 1 (G.K. Hall, 1981) p. 1,241.

70 Morag Cameron, "Highland Fisher-folk and Their Superstitions," *Folklore* (1903) vol. 14, p. 303, not to point to boats going out to sea. John Rhys, "Manx Folklore and Superstitions," *Folklore* (1892) vol. 3, p. 84, superstition of fishermen not to point to anything with a finger.

71 Charlotte S. Burne, "Presidential Address," *Folklore* (1911) vol. 22, p. 27, the index finger is considered poisonous.

72 See *Sefer Kara Ravaẓ*, p. 275, where he explains that it is not standard to point with the thumb. Dr. Roman Katsman of Bar-Ilan University confirmed that the gesture of pointing with the little finger is "positively a non-offensive one." There have been some reports of a German custom of

little finger, affectionately known as the pinky,[73] is considered cute is probably a factor in the popularity of this custom.

The original custom to bow to the Torah during *hagbaha*, codified in the *Shulḥan Arukh*, has in many congregations been usurped by finger pointing. Finger pointing during *hagbaha* first appears in sources from the 1800s, where the index finger was used to point. Today the little finger is used by many people, a custom attested to in writing for the first time less than fifty years ago. The reasons for using specifically the little finger remain unclear. ☙

using the little finger to point in general; see Geraldine Michael and Frank N. Wills, Jr., "The Development of Gestures in Three Subcultural Groups," *The Journal of Social Psychology* (1969) vol. 79, issue 1, p. 39. This is repeated in many books about gestures but in fact appears to be very uncommon and unrelated to the development of the custom to point to the Torah with the little finger.

73 The term "pinky" for little finger derives from the Scottish use of the word "pink" to mean "small"; this is also the derivation of "pink eye," meaning a small or contracted eye. See John Jamieson, *An Etymological Dictionary of the Scottish Language* (Edinburgh: Abernathy and Walker, 1818), under "pinkie."

חקירה

כרך ט"ו – שנת תשע"ג

חקירה

כרך ט"ו – שנת תשע"ג

תוכן עניינים

הלכה

תלמוד תורה

נאמנות כפולה להלכה ולמדינה ופתרונה: פסיקתו של הרב שלמה גורן כמקרה בוחן

מאת: אביעד יחיאל הולנדר

מאמר זה עוסק בהבנת תהליך פסיקת ההלכה בתחומים בעלי זיקה למדינה בכלל, ולמדינת ישראל בפרט. במוקד המאמר עומדת פסיקת ההלכה של הרב שלמה גורן, אך דומני שיש בו בניין אב להבנת דרכם של פוסקים ציוניים-דתיים אחרים.

רקע: מעט מקורות חייו של הרב שלמה גורן[א]

כשדוד בן-גוריון ביקש למנות רב לצבא ההגנה לישראל, הוא חיפש אחר אדם שיוכר על ידי הממסד הרבני, אך לא פחות חשוב מכך, יהווה דמות איתה יוכלו החיילים להזדהות ולהעריך. הרבנים הראשיים דאז, הרב יצחק אייזיק הלוי הרצוג והראשון לציון הרב בן ציון מאיר חי עוזיאל, בעצה אחת עם הרב יהודה לייב פישמן-מיימון, המליצו פה אחד על הרב שלמה גורן.[ב]

[א] רוב האמור כאן מבוסס על חומר שאספתי והצגתי בעבודתי, *דיוקנו ההלכתי של הרב שלמה גורן: עיונים בשיקולי הפסיקה ודרכי הביסוס במאמריו ההלכתיים*, עבודה לשם קבלת תואר דוקטור, אוניברסיטת בר אילן, תשע"א, עמ' 1-21, והמבקש את המקורות הראשוניים עליהם התבססתי יעיין שם. לאחרונה התפרסמו שני חיבורים חשובים אודות חייו של הרב גורן. הראשון הינו מעשה עריכה של קטעי זכרונות אותם הרב גורן תיעד בכתב ובהקלטה על גבי קלטות: אבי רט (עורך), *הרב שלמה גורן: בעוז ותעצומות – אוטוביוגרפיה*, תל אביב: ידיעות אחרונות, 2013 (להלן: בעוז ותעצומות). פרטים רבים שיובאו להלן מצויים שם. דיונים נוספים בקורות חייו מצוי בעבודתה של שפרה משלוב, *בעין הסערה: דמותו הציבורית ויצירתו התורנית של הרב שלמה גורן בשנים 1948-1994*, עבודה לשם קבלת תואר דוקטור, אוניברסיטת בר אילן, תש"ע.

[ב] במשך השנים התהדק הקשר בין הרב גורן לבין דוד בן-גוריון. לאחרונה סקרה שפרה מישלוב את יחסיהם של השניים במשך השנים, ראו: הנ"ל, "'ידידי וידי כל בית ישראל': הרב שלמה גורן ודוד בן-גוריון", *קתדרה* 145 (תשרי תשע"ג), עמ' 147-172. מבט נוסף על הקשר בין השניים מצוי במאמרו של צבי צמרת, "שלמה ודוד – שני חולמים, לוחמים ובונים:

אביעד הולנדר כתב את עבודת התואר השני בהנחייתו של פרופ' אהרן שמש על פרשנותם של חז"ל במדרשי ההלכה. את עבודת הדוקטורט אביעד כתב אודות פסיקת ההלכה של הרב שלמה גורן, בהנחייתם של פרופ' חיים מיליקובסקי וד"ר חיים בורגנסקי מן המחלקה לתלמוד באוניברסיטת בר-אילן. בשנים האחרונות אביעד לימד באוניברסיטת בר-אילן ובמכללת "אורות ישראל" ברחובות.

הרב גורן, שנולד בפולין בשלהי העשור השני במאה העשרים, הגיע כילד עם משפחתו לכפר חסידים. לאחר כמה שנים, בהם השתתף בייבוש ביצות ושאר פעילויות חקלאיות, העתיקה המשפחה את מגוריה לירושלים. הרב גורן למד תקופת מה בחדר "שיבת ציון" של העדה החרדית ולאחר נדודים שונים של המשפחה, עבר ללמוד בישיבת "עץ החיים". בישיבה המפורסמת, שבין בוגריה ניתן למנות את הרב צבי פסח פרנק, הרב שלמה זלמן אוירבך והרב אליעזר יהודה ולדנברג, הוא התקדם, עד אשר הוחלט כי הנער הצעיר יעבור לישיבה הנכבדה – ישיבת "חברון".

הרב גורן נודע בשנים אלו כלמדן ושקדן. בדברי הספד שכתב הרב יהודה עמיטל לאחר פטירת הרב גורן, הוא העיד שהתהלכו שמועות על כך שבלילות נהג להניח רגליו בקערה ובה מים קרים, למען לא ירדם.[ג] הרב גורן עצמו נהג לספר סיפור משעשע המלמד על מעמדו המיוחד בישיבה והמחיר ששילם: בהתמדתו הספיק ללמוד מידי יום כשבעה דפים בעיון. חבריו לספסל הלימודים, מהם היה צעיר בכמה שנים, לא האמינו שאכן הוא לומד, וחמדו לצון. בלכתו לשרותים הם סגרו את ספר הגמרא בו למד. הידע היכן לפתוח חזרה, כך הסתקרנו. בשובו של הרב גורן, ובראותו את ספרו סגור ומבטים שובביים בעיני חבריו, הבין מיד את שקרה. הוא פנה לחברים ואמר: אנא, התחילו כל "תוספות" עד הדף אליו הגעתי, ואדע להשלים את דברי התוספות בעל פה על בוריים. במבחן זה, כמובן, עמד בהצלחה.

לא רק בקרב הישיבה נודע כ"עילוי". בזיכרונותיו האריך הרב גורן לתאר את יחסיו עם הרב ארבהם יצחק הכהן קוק.[ד] פרופ' אריה אדרעי פרסם מסמכים מהם מתברר כי בצעירותו זכה במילגת לימודים מהמשורר הלאומי – חיים נחמן ביאליק.[ה] אביו לקחו לחצרות רבנים ותלמידי חכמים, למען יכירו בגדלותו של הנער הצעיר. אמנם, היו כאלה שראו זאת בשלילה. בשם הרב יעקב ישראל קנייבסקי, הסטייפלר, נאמר כי אביו התגאה בו כדרך שפיראט משוויץ בתוכי שעל כתפו, וכישרונו כתוכי המשנן על פה.[ו]

בגיל שבע עשרה כבר נסמך לרבנות, ובגיל שמונה עשרה פרסם ספר חידושים על הלכות "פסולי המוקדשים" במשנה תורה לרמב"ם. בגיל עשרים ושתיים ערך הרב גורן חיבור מיוחד אותו כינה "שערי טהרה", ובו כינס וערך מקורות ממרחבי ספרות חז"ל לכדי תלמוד למשניות מסכת מקוואות. לתלמוד שערך הוסיף פירוש פשט וביאורים

הרב הראשי לצה"ל שלמה גורן וראש הממשלה דוד בן-גוריון", בתוך רט, בעוז ותעצומות, עמ' 339-361.

ג הרב יהודה עמיטל, "וי לארעא דישראל דחסרה גברא רבה", *עלון שבות - בוגרים*, ו (תשנ"ה), עמ' 122.

ד רט, בעוז ותעצומות, עמ' 66-82.

ה אריה אדרעי, "מלחמה, הלכה וגאולה: צבא ומלחמה במחשבת ההלכה של הרב שלמה גורן", *קתדרה*, 125 (2007), עמ' 121, הע' 3.

ו הרב אברהם הורביץ, *ארחות רבנו*, בני ברק: הוצאת המחבר, תשס"ה, עמ' קעג (תודה לידידי רועי זק שהפנה את תשומת ליבי למקור זה).

עיוניים. בגיל עשרים וארבע השתתף הרב גורן בכנסת החכמים שכינס הרב הרצוג לשם דיון בשאלת מעמדו ההלכתי של "קו התאריך".

במהלך שנות הארבעים הרב גורן למד באוניברסיטה העברית לימודים קלאסיים, יוונית, פילוסופיה כללית ומתמטיקה, וזאת, לפי דבריו, כהכנה לכתיבת פירוש על התלמוד הירושלמי.[ז] הוא נשא לאשה את צפיה, בתו של הרב דוד כהן ("הנזיר"). בביתם הסתירו בני הזוג תחנת שידור של הלח"י, ולימים הצטרף הרב גורן לשורות "ההגנה". הוא השתתף בקרבות לכיבוש קטמון ומלחה, תוך שהחליף תפקידים בין צלף ומקלען.

כרב צבאי ראשי נאלץ הרב גורן להתמודד עם לחצים מבית ומחוץ. הרבנים הראשיים סברו שהרב גורן כפוף למרותם, ואילו הוא עצמו סבר שהוא ה"מרא דאתרא" בצבא. אף בין הפוליטיקאים הדתיים היו שקראו להדחתו, באשר אופיו הנוקשה נודע ברבים, והיו שחששו שיוציא שם רע לרבנות הצבאית. אף בצבא פנימה, מהלכיו של הרב גורן זכו להתנגדות. בעיניו של הרב גורן הרבנות הצבאית היתה אמורה למלא את התפקידים שעד כה נועדו ל"שירות לחייל הדתי" בראשותו של נתן גרדי. לפיכך, בין השתיים התגלעו מחלוקות, עד שהאחרון עזב את הצבא. אף מש"קי הדת שמינה הרב גורן לא היו אהודים, וקצין האספקה הראשי, האלוף שמעון מזא"ה, כינה אותם "מרגלים". עימות חשוב היה גם זה שבינו לבין הרמטכ"ל האגדי משה דיין. לרגל הקמת גדוד 890 על ידי אריאל (אריק) שרון, החליט דיין לחוג את ליל הסדר ברוב עם והדרת מלך. לשם כך הזמין דיפלומטים זרים ושאר אח"מים. הרב גורן הפעיל את קשריו עם בן-גוריון, והלה ביטל את המסיבה שהיתה כרוכה בחילולי יום טוב. דיין מצידו לא נכנע, והודיע שיגיע לחוג בחברת החיילים. בחג הגיע ברכב, ועימו זמרת ונגן. בין הרב גורן ודיין התעורר ויכוח באשר להופעה המתוכננת, והשניים התפשרו שההופעה תתקיים ללא ליווי כלי הנגינה.

שלא כמו המינוי לתפקיד הרב הצבאי הראשי, במהלך חייו היה הרב גורן מעורב בכמה וכמה מערכות בחירות לתפקידים רשמיים אותם מילא. בשנת 1946, כשהוא רק כבן עשרים ושמונה, הרב גורן התמודד על תפקיד הרב הראשי לתל אביב. המועמד השני היה הרב איסר יהודה אונטרמן שהכריע את הרב גורן. בראשית שנות הששים, כשהוא כבר מכהן כרב הצבאי הראשי, הרב גורן התמודד על תפקיד הרב הראשי לישראל, שוב, מול הרב אונטרמן. גם הפעם גבר הרב אונטרמן, ברוב של שלושה קולות בלבד. בחירות אלה לא היו נקיות מבעיות ציבוריות. עוד קודם לקיום הבחירות, הרב גורן הביע במסיבת עיתונאים חשש מפני אפשרות שזרח ורהפטיג, חבר כנסת מטעם המפד"ל, יפעל למען הרב אונטרמן. ורהפטיג, כמובן, התנער מההאשמות. אולם, גם לאחר הבחירות המים לא שקטו. ישראל ישעיהו, שכיהן כסגן יושב ראש הכנסת, טען לספירה מסולפת של הקולות,

[ז] רט, בעוז ותעצומות, עמ' 90-91.

ודרש ספירה שניה של הקולות. השופט משה זילברג, שכיהן כיושב ראש ועדת הבחירות, הורה על ספירה מחודשת שאישררה את התוצאות הראשונות.

כשלוש שנים מאוחר יותר הגיע אחד מרגעי השיא של הרב גורן בקריירה הצבאית שלו. הימים ימי מלחמת ששת הימים, והרב גורן, ששהה עם הכוחות בגיזרה הדרומית, הבין שכוחות צה"ל נערכים לכניסה לירושלים. הוא חש לירושלים והצטרף לכוחות הלוחמים בתקיעה בשופר כשספר תורה בידו. עם כיבוש הר הבית הרב גורן נכנס לכיפת הסלע, ועודד את החיילים לשירת "בשנה הזאת בירושלים הבנויה". בנאום לחיילים הוא העניק משמעות משיחית להצלחת הלחימה: "חזון כל הדורות נתגשם לעינינו. עיר האלוהים, מקום המקדש, הר-הבית והכותל-המערבי – סמל הגאולה המשיחית של העם נגאלו היום על ידכם גיבורי צבא הגנה לישראל".

בשנת 1969 הרב גורן מונה לרב ראשי לתל-אביב, ובפועל החל במילוי תפקיד זה רק שנתיים מאוחר יותר. אחת הבעיות הקשות מבחינת יחסי "דת ומדינה" באותם הימים נגעה לשאלת פסולי חיתון. מקרה שפרץ לתודעה הציבורית היה זה בו הוכרזו אח ואחות, חנוך ומרים לנגר, כממזרים, ובשל כך נאסרה חתונתם עם בחירי לבם. ניסיונותיו של הרב גורן לעזור על ידי מתן עצות הלכתיות עלו בתוהו. משכך, ומשגבר הלחץ הפוליטי, הרב גורן ביקש מהרב יצחק נסים להקים בית דין מיוחד שידון בעניין על בסיס פסק דין מקל שכתב הרב גורן עצמו. הרב נסים ניאות לבקשה, אך בסופו של דבר לא הקים את בית הדין הנדרש. בשלב זה התברר לכל הגורמים שהמוצא היחידי הינו מתן סמכויות לרב גורן להקמת בית דין כזה, ובמילים אחרות – יש למנות את הרב גורן לרב ראשי.

מינויו של הרב גורן לרב ראשי היה כרוך בעשיה פוליטית מרובה שתוארה על ידי אשר כהן ואהרן קמפינסקי.[ח] התברר שבוועדת הבחירה הוא לא יזכה לרוב, ולפיכך, זרח ורהפטיג פעל להרחבת הגוף הבוחר, עד היווצרות רוב לתמיכה ברב גורן. גם בין רבני הציונות הדתית היו שהתנגדו למינוי הרב גורן, שהיה כרוך בהדחת הרב אונטרמן שכבר עבר את גיל השמונים, והרב שאול ישראלי עזב את ועד הרבנים של "הפועל המזרחי" במחאה על התמיכה ברב גורן. היתה זו ההתמודדות השלישית בין הרב גורן והרב אונטרמן, והפעם ידו של הרב גורן היתה על העליונה.

משמונה הרב גורן, הוא מילא את הבטחתו, הקים בית דין מיוחד והתיר את האחים לנגר מכבלי הממזרות. בכך אמנם זכו השניים למזור, והמצוקה הפוליטית באה על

ח Asher Cohen and Aaron Kampinsky, "Religious Leadership in Israel's Religious Zionism: The Case of the Board of Rabbis", *Jewish Political Studies Review* 18:3-4 (Fall 2006), available online [2.6.2010]: <http://www.jcpa.org/JCPA/Templates/ShowPage.asp?DRIT=4&DBID=1&LNGID=1&TMID=111&FID=625&PID=1631&IID=1645&TTL=Religious_Leadership_in_Israel's_Religious_Zionism:_The_Case_of_the_Board_of_Rabbis>.

פתרונה, אולם צעדו החריג של הרב גורן, ממנו אף נדף ריח פוליטי, גרר תגובות חריפות. בעצרות ענק נערכה "קריעה" טקסית, על חילול כבוד התורה, והרב אלעזר מנחם מן שך הכתיר את התנהגותו של הרב גורן כשריפת התורה. ההתקפות על הרב גורן לא היו רק מילוליות. כאשר זכה הרב שלמה זוננפלד בפרס ירושלים לספרות תורנית, הוא הודיע שיחרים את הטקס אם הרב גורן ינכח בו. בלווייתו של הרב ישראל הלוי בארי, רבה של נס ציונה, ארבעה צעירים תקפו את הרב גורן במכות, ונהגו אף נפגע בהגינו עליו.

הרב גורן כיהן כרב ראשי לישראל לצידו של הרב עובדיה יוסף, ויחסיהם האישיים של השניים ידעו עליות ומורדות. לקראת סוף שנות השבעים נחקק חוק ולפיו כהונתם של רבנים ראשיים מוגבלת לעשר שנים. הרב גורן פנה אל ראש הממשלה מנחם בגין בבקשה שישנה את החקיקה. פעולה זו דרשה את הסכמתו של שר המשפטים משה נסים, בנו של הרב יצחק נסים, אשר הודח על ידי הרב עובדיה יוסף. נסים לא נתן את קולו, וכהונתם של הרב גורן והרב יוסף הסתיימה בקץ עשור.

בשנות השמונים הרב גורן ביקר את עמדת הרבנים הראשיים בכמה עניינים, ביניהם השתתפות במפקד האוכלוסין, יהדותם של העולים מאתיופיה, היתר המכירה והכניסה להר הבית. את עמדותיו פרסם הרב גורן בעיתונות, ובכך לא חסך מבוכות מהרבנות הראשית.

בשנות התשעים הסעיר הרב גורן את המדינה כשקרא לחיילים לסרב פקודה לפינוי ישובים. אמנם, בכך הוא המשיך את הוראתו הקדומה לסרב לפקודה לחילול שבת, ובכל זאת, הפרת הממלכתיות היתה ניכרת. בהמשך הפתיע שוב, כאשר הבהיר שמבחינה הלכתית הגולן אינו חלק מארץ ישראל, ולפיכך אין כל מניעה לחתום על הסכם שלום עם סוריה שיכלול נסיגה ישראלית מרמת הגולן תוך פינוי הישובים והמתיישבים.

ימי המאבקים של הרב גורן באו לקיצם עם פטירתו בליל שבת, כ"ד חשון תשנ"ה.

עיקרי תפיסת ההלכה של הרב גורן

במהלך כהונתו הרב גורן הבהיר פעמים רבות שהאתגר העומד בפני פוסקי דורו היא הוכחת התאמתה של ההלכה לקיום מדינה יהודית-דמוקרטית. כך לדוגמה, בסימפוזיון שנערך בתאריך 5.9.1966 בהיכל התרבות בתל אביב, בהשתתפותם של דוד בן-גוריון וד"ר נחום גולדמן, הוא אמר:

> בדור זה אנו זקוקים לגדולי תורה והלכה שתהיה להם גישה ממלכתית לבעיות, ויחס חיובי למפנה ההיסטורי בעם היהודי שחל עם הקמת המדינה.[ט]

[ט] הרב שלמה גורן, *דיון פומבי על היהדות בעולם המודרני - סיכונים וסיכויים*, תל-אביב: חמו"ל, תשכ"ז 1967, עמ' 23. בשער החוברת ובה דברי הסימפוזיון הוגדר נושא הסימפוזיון כך: "בכל דור ודור – וכן גם בדורנו – מאיימות על היהדות סכנות של התבוללות וטמיעה; של

כיצד הבין הרב גורן את קביעתו זו? מהם הצידוקים להטיית הדיון ההלכתי לכיוון מסויים? מדוע נחשב דיון שכזה לדיון הלכתי, ולא לדיון המשעבד את ההלכה לגורמים חיצוניים? בשורות הבאות אציג את האופן בו אני מבין את עמדותיו של הרב גורן בשאלות אלה, ואבקש לתאר בקצרה את הדרכים בהם נעשות ההטיות בדיון ההלכתי אל עבר המסקנה הרצויה.

דומני, שהבנה נכונה של גישתו של הרב גורן תלויה בהגדרתו את מושג "נצחיות ההלכה" אותה הוא ניסח בבהירות באותה הרצאה. בדבריו הבהיר הרב גורן כי לטעמו מושג זה כרוך בהיות ההלכה "גמישה":

> **נצחיותה של התורה היא במרחב התימרון והאפשרויות הפתוחות לפני שומריה, חוקריה ומקיימיה.**
>
> יש מאמר בתלמוד הירושלמי "אילו נתנה התורה חתוכה לא היתה לרגל עמידה, כדי שתהא התורה נדרשת מ"ט פנים טמא ומ"ט פנים טהור". כלומר, **אילו ניתנה התורה קבועה כמו קוד, כך תעשה וכך לא תעשה, לא היתה אפשרות לעמוד על הרגלים ולחיות על פיה, אלא ניתנה בצורה גמישה** מ"ט פנים טמא ומ"ט פנים טהור, מ"ט פנים חייב ומ"ט פנים זכאי. בכל דור ודור יש חידושים של הדור הזה בתורה, אבל כל זה אך ורק במסגרת התורה, במסגרת ההלכה.[י]

אליבא דהרב גורן, ההלכה מושתתת על ערכים מקודשים ונצחיים, אלא שהביטוי המעשי של ערכים אלה משתנה בהתאם לתנאי המציאות המשתנה. אשר על כן, פסיקת הלכה המתעלמת מתנאי החיים הינה מאובנת ולקויה, ואילו פסיקה ראויה היא זו אשר מודעת למלוא הפוטנציאל הגלום במערכת ההלכתית ובוחרת את הפתרון הראוי לנסיבות ההיסטוריות.

ניתן למנות דרכים שונות בהן עיצב הרב גורן את פסקיו:[יא]

א. הגדלת טווח המקורות. הרב גורן הביא בחשבון את מדרשי ההלכה והאגדה, התוספתא, המסכתות הקטנות, תרגומי המקרא, התלמוד הירושלמי, ספרות הגאונים ועוד. חשוב להדגיש שבבואו לפסוק הוא נמנע מלפסוק כנגד כללי פסיקה מקובלים, אך עם זאת השתדל להציג עושר מקורות אשר למעשה מעמעם את כוחם של כללים אלה. כך לדוגמה הוא בדרך כלל לא פסק כתלמוד הירושלמי נגד התלמוד הבבלי, אך צירף לתלמוד הירושלמי מקורות נוספים מספרות חז"ל או ראשונים אשר צידדו בהכרעה מקומית כדעת

דכוי רוחני, לאומי ודתי ושל השמדה. מקומם, חשיבותם והשפעתם של הגורמים היסודיים לקיום היהדות: עם ישראל – תורת ישראל – מדינת ישראל, והקשר ההדדי ביניהם".

[י] שם, ההדגשות שלי.

[יא] בכך הרחבתי את הדיבור, תוך מתן דוגמאות רבות בעבודתי הנזכרת לעיל, הע' א.

הירושלמי. בכך נפתחה הדרך לפסיקה כעמדת הירושלמי נגד הבבלי, מבלי לכפור בכלל הפסיקה המקובל.[יב]

ב. פרשנות תכליתית. פעמים שמקור הלכתי ניתן להתפרש באופנים שונים. כיצד יכריע הפוסק אם להרחיב או לצמצם, אם לרבות או למעט? בכמה מפסקיו של הרב גורן ניתן לראות שהוא מבקש לחשוף את תכלית ההלכה שבמוקד הדיון, ופרשנות המקורות נעשית באופן שיתאם את תכלית ההלכה.[יג]

ג. הכרעה ברברנית. יש והכרעתו של הרב גורן מצדדת בדעת מיעוט, וזאת בצירוף טענות כגון "שעת הדחק" או "הפסד מרובה". במקרים אלה ברור שאל מול הכלל "כדאי הוא פלוני לסמוך עליו" עומד הכלל "ויש לחוש לדעת אלמוני". כן ברור שמול הכלל "המיקל יש לו על מי שיסמוך" ניצב הכלל "המחמיר תבוא עליו ברכה". הבחירה כעמדה אחת כנגד השניה מהווה הכרעה אקטיבית לכיוון שנתפס כרצוי.[יד]

[יב] כך, לדוגמה, בפסקו אודות כיבוי שרפה במחנה צבאי (*משיב מלחמה: שאלות ותשובות בעניני צבא, מלחמה ובטחון, חלק א*, ירושלים: האידרא רבה ומסורה לעם, תשנ"ד[2] [להלן: ממ"א], עמ' רנט), הוא מסיק שלפי התלמוד הבבלי אסור לומר לגוי לכבות שריפה שפרצה בשבת, ואילו לפי הירושלמי אמירה שכזו מותרת (שבת פט"ז ה"ג). הרב גורן אימץ את עמדת הירושלמי, בכפוף לפרשנות שניתנה לה בדברי הבית יוסף (אורח חיים סימן שלד), וראו גם בהע' הבאה.

[יג] דוגמה לכך מצויה בדיונו אודות טלטול במחנה ללא עירוב טוען הרב גורן שלפי סוגיית הבבלי (עירובין יז ע"ב) הפטור ההלכתי למחנה מלחמה מדיני עירובין אינו תלוי בגודל המחנה, ואילו לפי סוגיית הירושלמי (עירובין פ"א ה"י) מגבלה שכזו קיימת. הרב גורן אמנם אימץ את ההגבלה הנזכרת בירושלמי (ממ"א, עמ' קנז), אך זאת לאחר שהביא תימוכין מדיוניהם של הריטב"א (על אתר), מגיד משנה (הל' עירובין פ"א ה"ג) והגר"א (אורח חיים סי' קנה ס"ק כא). הרב גורן ציין לדברי החזון איש (אורח חיים, הלכות עירובין, ליקוטים, סי' קיד, ו) שסובר שההקלה דווקא למחנה בו מקובצים עשרה חיילים, אולם "אם הלוחמים מרובים אבל הם מפוזרים – אינם מצטרפים". הרב גורן מסכים שמבחינה עקרונית ניתן להבין כך את המקורות ההלכתיים, אלא שלטעמו, הבנה שכזו נוגדת את תכלית ההקלה למחנה הלוחם: "והרי דוקא להם חשוב ההיתר הזה של הליכה מחוץ לתחום בשבת, כדי לאפשר להם להתארגן למנין של מתפללים בשבת ובמועד לכל דבר שבקדושה [...] אין צורך שבכל מוצב ומוצב יהא בו עשרה חיילים, אלא כלם מצטרפים לדין מחנה, גם כשהם מפוזרים" (ממ"א, עמ' קנח).

[יד] כך לדוגמה הוא הציע דרך הלכתית שתתיר לימודי רפואה לכהנים, על אף שהדבר כרוך בניתוח גופות (יהודים), תוך שהוא טוען "וכדאי הוא בעל היראים לסמוך עליו בשעת דחק גדול מעין זה, שאם לא נסמוך עליו יופקעו הכהנים ממקצוע חשוב זה של הרפואה" (*תורת הרפואה: מחקרים הלכתיים בנושאי רפואה* (בעריכת ישראל תמרי), ירושלים: האידרא רבה ומסורה לעם, תשס"א, עמ' 243), וממשיך ומסביר: "אין לטעון כנגד זה, שהרי יכול ללמוד אומנות אחרת, ולאו דווקא רפואה. התשובה היא – שאין אדם למד אלא מה שליבו חפץ, כמו שאמרו במס' ע"ז (יט, א) לענין לימוד תורה. הוא הדין בשאר חכמות שבעולם, כי יתכן שרק ברפואה שקרוב לליבו יראה ברכה ויצליח, וגם היא מקצוע המפרנסת ומכבדת את בעליה, ונפשו חשקה במקצוע זה" (תורת הרפואה, עמ' 255).

בשלב זה ראוי להדגיש שאין מדובר בגישה אנרכיסטית העושה בהלכה כבתוך שלה. המעיין במרחבי פסיקתו של הרב גורן יוכל לזהות בין בתרי דבריו כוחות סמויים, דוגמת "מהיות טוב אל תהי רע", המרסנים את החדשנות ושומרים על קירבה לפסיקה המקובלת והמסורתית.

הווה אומר, הרב גורן בקש לקשר את המפעל הציוני, הנתפס בעיניו כבעל פוטנציאל משיחי, ולו הוא נאמן בכל מאודו, אל מסורת ההלכה המקובלת מדורי דורות, לה הוא חש מחוייבות בעומק נשמתו.[טו] בעיניו של הרב גורן הוטלה עליו האחריות להוכחת התאמתה של ההלכה להוות תשתית לחוקי מדינת ישראל, ולשם כך הוא קרוא לנצל את מלוא הפוטנציאל הגלום בעולמה של ההלכה.

מקרי בוחן

הבה נפנה לבחינת שלוש פסיקות של הרב גורן המבטאות באופן יפה את העקרונות האמורים, ובהן יש כדי להביע את המורכבות שבעשייתו ההלכתית.

מקרה הלן זיידמן

בהיסטוריה של התנגשויות הלכה ומדינה במדינת ישראל ישנו מקום של כבוד לבעיות מתחום "המעמד האישי". כבר במסמך המוכר "מסמך הסטטוס קוו", אשר נכתב בשנת 1947 על ידי הנהלת הסוכנות היהודית ומוען להסתדרות אגודת ישראל העולמית, ישנה הבטחה להתייחס באופן מיוחד לסוגיות מתחום האישות למען לא יפרד העם לשני מחנות.[טז] היישום של הבטחה זו בא בצורת חוק הקובע שבישראל נישואין וגירושין יכולים להיעשות רק על פי ההלכה. בשנות החמישים סערה הארץ בשל שאלת "מיהו יהודי".[יז] העיסוק בשאלה זו ליווה את המדינה במשך שנים רבות, ודי להזכיר את פרשיית "האח דניאל", כומר ממוצא יהודי שבקש להרשם כיהודי, ו"פרשת שליט", בה תבע קצין צה"ל שהיה נשוי לגויה להכיר בילדיו כיהודים.

טו תיאור של מורכבות גישתו התיאולוגית של הרב גורן לציונות וזיקתה לדיוניו ההלכתיים מצוי במאמרי: "הלכה ציונית-משיחית – הגותו הציונית-משיחית של הרב שלמה גורן והשפעותיה על פסיקותיו ההלכתיות", בתוך: ידידיה צ' שטרן ויאיר שלג (עורכים), *הלכה ציונית*, ירושלים: המכון הישראלי לדמוקרטיה (טרם פורסם).

טז ניתוח המסמך והצעה מרתקת לסיבות כתיבתו מצויים אצל מנחם פרידמן, "ואלה תולדות הסטטוס-קוו: דת ומדינה בישראל", בתוך: ורדה פילובסקי (עורכת), *המעבר מיישוב למדינה 1949-1947: רציפות ותמורות*, חיפה: אוניברסיטת חיפה, 1990, עמ' 47-79.

יז בעניין זה ראו את מאמרו של אליעזר דון-יחיה, "דת, זהות לאומית ופוליטיקה: המשבר בשאלת 'מיהו יהודי' – 1958", בתוך: מרדכי בר-און וצבי צמרת (עורכים), *שני עברי הגשר: דת ומדינה בראשית דרכה של ישראל*, ירושלים: יד יצחק בן-צבי, תשס"ב, עמ' 88-143.

הלן שנון, ד"ר לביולוגיה מאוניברסיטת אילינוי, עלתה לישראל לאחר פרידה מבעלה, ולה בת.[יח] בתחילה התגוררה בקיבוץ מפלסים, ובהמשך עברה לקיבוץ נחל-עוז, שם הכירה את בנימין זיידמן, לו נישאה בנישואין אזרחיים במקסיקו.[יט] את בנם הראשון, יהודה, היא ילדה בהיותה גויה. אולם, אז ביקשה להתגייר, אולי מפני שהרתה בשנית. בפנותה לבית הדין באשדוד נענתה בסירוב, ככל הנראה משום שהתגוררה בקיבוץ, והסיכוי לכך שתהיה כשומרת מצוות היה נראה נמוך ביותר. יתר על כן, מאחר ובנימין, בעלה, היה כהן, נדרשה זיידמן מבחינה הלכתית להיפרד ממנו, ולא נראה היה שבכוונתה לעשות זאת.[כ] זיידמן המאוכזבת פנתה ועברה גיור רפורמי. עתה ביקשה להירשם כיהודיה, על מנת שבנה יחשב כיהודי גם כן. מאחר ונענתה שמדינת ישראל אינה מכירה בגיור רפורמי, פנתה בערעור לבית המשפט העליון, ובקשה מזור – על המדינה להכיר בגיור הרפורמי, ולהחשיב את בנה כיהודי.

במערכת הפוליטית היו שדרשו להפקיע מהרבנות את המונופול באשר לנישואין וגירושין, ולאפשר בישראל הסדרת זוגיות אזרחית שלא על פי ההלכה.

כמה ימים לפני הדיון בבג"צ חל מפנה דרמטי בפרשה. הרב גורן, שכיהן עדיין כרב ראשי לצה"ל, הודיע כי נפגש עם זיידמן והשתכנע כי רצונה להיות יהודיה כנה. לפיכך, הסביר הרב גורן, בתום פגישתו עמה אסף שני דיינים נוספים וגייר את הלן זיידמן, שמעתה קרויה גם רות, בגיור אורתודוכסי, שיכול להיות מוכר על ידי הרבנות הראשית ומשרדי המדינה.[כא]

מהלכו של הרב גורן שמט את הקרקע תחת הפרופגנדה שהתנגדה לחיוב נישואין וגירושין על פי ההלכה. במערכת הפוליטית היו מי שהביעו שביעות רצון ממהלך זה אשר מנע מבוכה מהממשלה. מאידך, הגיור המהיר עורר גם תמיהה וביקורת, באשר לא תאם את העמדה הרבנית המסורתית, לפיה הגיור הינו תהליך ארוך ומתמשך.[כב]

[יח] רבים מהפרטים אודות סיפורה האישי של הלן זיידמן הופיעו בכתבתו של דב גולדשטיין, '"תנו לי לחיות בשקט בנחל עוז"', *מעריב*, 19.6.1970, עמ' 11.

[יט] לפי החוק, מדינת ישראל הכירה בנישואין אזרחיים שנערכו מחוץ לגבולותיה. בשל כך נפוצו "נישואי קפריסין" ומאוחר יותר גם "נישואי מקסיקו".

[כ] כך לפי נתנאל פישר, *המרת דת ומדינה: מדיניות הגיור של ישראל מהקמת המדינה עד ראשית שנות האלפיים*, עבודה לשם קבלת תואר דוקטור לפילוסופיה, האוניברסיטה העברית בירושלים, תשע"א 2011, עמ' 167. ניתוחו של פישר, וקישור פרשיית זיידמן לפרשיות גיור אחרות בשנות השבעים מאירי עיניים, יעויין שם.

[כא] תיאור של התפתחות הקשר בין זיידמן והרב גורן והליך הדיון בבית הדין מצוי אצל דניאל דגן, '"זאת לתעודה: גב' הלן זיידמן התגיירה כדת וכדין ונקרא שמה בישראל - רבקה"', *מעריב* 16.6.1970, עמ' 3.

[כב] יש לציין שמאחר והרב גורן היה רב צבאי, היו שטענו שהוא חסר את הסמכות החוקית לגייר אזרחים. כנגד טענות אלה הכריז הרב עובדיה יוסף על גיורה של הלן זיידמן כהלכה. מאחר והרב יוסף היה אזרח לא היו על גיורו עוררין.

אחד המבקרים את מהלכו של הרב גורן היה הרב יחזקאל אברמסקי, אשר כיהן כנשיא ועד הישיבות בישראל. במכתב אישי פירט הרב גורן את מכלול שיקוליו. הוא הסביר שהאשה שומרת כשרות, אם כי מאידיאולוגיה צמחונית, והוסיף וטען שבגיור יש בכדי להציל את בן-זוגה הכהן מחטאים חמורים. עוד טען הרב גורן כי הרב חיים עוזר גרודז'ינסקי סבר גם כן שבמקום הפרץ יש להקל בהלכות גיור, ובכך למנוע התבוללות. לאחר פריסת שיקולים הלכתיים נוספים, שיתף הרב גורן את הרב אברמסקי בשיקול ריאל-פוליטי שלו:

> ובנידון דידן בודאי **שהיה בזה משום הצלת התורה והדת במדינה ובעם, כפי שידוע לי בבירור מה זממו חוגי הכנענים להפיק ממשפט זה**, שעמד להתקיים אילו לא הקדמנו רפואה למכה, שנתגיירה כדת וכדין. והגיורת בעצמה ליבה לא היה כלל שלם עמם מלכתחילה; היא חיפשה רק דרך להתייהד. אחרים **בקשו לעקור את כל חוקי התורה של הגירות, הנישואין והגירושין במדינה**, והרפורמים עמדו לתקוע יתד בלב ישראל, ואחריתה מי ישורנה. ראיתי בסכנה הזאת, וחשתי בה בהיותי זמן קצר לפני כן בתפוצות ישראל בעולם. שמעתי איך שמתנגדי התורה והדת התכוננו לכך, שהנה בא הזמן עבורם לתקוע יתד בארץ ולקבל לרשותם את הרבנות, ולהשיג הכרה בכל מה שיעשו בגירות, נישואין וגירושין, עד **שהיה חשש גדול להנהיג באופן רשמי חוקי נישואין וגירושין אזרחיים, ח"ו, מה שעלול היה להרוס את כל חיי המשפחה בעם.**
>
> והנה ברגע האחרון ממש **באה ישועת ה' כהרף עין להצלת המצב**, וזכות התורה והרבים עמדה לנו בזה, **שיכולנו לקדש שם שמים ושם ישראל, ולהציל את אחדות התורה והעם במדינה ובתפוצות.** כי כל הנעשה כאן יש לו מיד השלכה על העם היהודי בגולה. ויותר ממה שכתבתי כאן יש לי באמתחתי, מקורות רבים ללבן ולברר את ההלכה שהיתה כדת וכדין.[כג]

הנה כי כן, פיו של הרב גורן מלל דברים ברורים: השאיפה להשארת החוק המחייב נישואין וגירושין על פי ההלכה, והרצון לזיכוי הרבים בחיים התואמים את המסורת היהודית, הם אשר הכווינו את פסיקתו. בעיניו הוא לא פסק הלכה שלא על פי המקורות, אלא העצים מקורות המבססים את העמדה ההלכתית שנדרשה בעת הזאת.

[כג] המכתב מופיע בספר תשובות של הרב גורן שנערך לאחר פטירתו: *תרומת הגורן: תשובות בהלכה, חלק שני – יורה דעה*, ירושלים ותל אביב: האידרא רבה וידיעות אחרונות, תשע"ב, עמ' 124 (ההדגשות שלי, אי"ה).

"האח והאחות"

הפרשייה הבאה בה אעסוק כאן מערבת סיפור אישי כאוב המעורב בסיפור הלאומי של יחסי דת ומדינה במדינת ישראל. תחילתה של הפרשייה, בדומה למקרה זיידמן, בסוף שנות השישים, אם כי העניין הציבורי בה התעורר רק בשנות השבעים.

עת בקש חנוך לנגר להינשא בדק רשם הנישואין את תעודותיו והודיעו כי הוא פסול חיתון, ולא יוכל להינשא. לנגר הופתע, ורשם הנישואין הסביר שאמו נישאה לאביו בטרם קיבלה גט מבעלה הראשון. בעיית הממזרות לא נגעה רק לחנוך, אלא גם לאחותו, מרים, חיילת בשירות סדיר שרצתה גם כן להינשא לבחיר לבה. בצר לה פנתה לרב הצבאי הראשי, הרב גורן, לבקשת מזור.

מאחר והרב גורן היה בתפקיד רשמי בצבא, הוא עזר רק בעצה ותושיה לעורך הדין שניהל את תיקם בבתי הדין. דייני בית הדין בפתח תקווה טענו לממזרות, ובשל טענות הרב גורן ועורך דינם של האחים לנגר נידון העניין גם בבית הדין הרבני הגדול, המהווה ערכאת ערעור על בתי הדין האזוריים. מאחר ודייני בית הדין הגדול לא הגיעו לכלל החלטה, הם החזירו את התיק לבית הדין האזורי להמשך בירור העניין, וכך עבר התיק רצוא ושוב. בישיבה האחרונה בבית הדין הרבני הגדול אומצה עמדת בית הדין הרבני בפתח תקווה, ללא מתן הנמקות.

משמעות ההחלטה היתה שחנוך לנגר, קצין במילואים, ואחותו, חיילת בשירות סדיר, לא יוכלו להינשא במדינת ישראל. העניין עורר סערה. הטענה היתה שהרבנות וההלכה מתנכרות למדינה וגומלות רעה תחת טובה לצעירים שמעניקים את שנותיהם הטובות למען המדינה.

בפגישה שהתקיימה בביתו של הרב הראשי הספרדי, הרב יצחק נסים, השתתפו אישים חשובים במערכת המדינית הישראלית: שר המשפטים, איש מפא"י, יעקב שמשון שפירא, שר הדתות זרח ורהפטיג, איש המפד"ל, והיועץ המשפטי לממשלה – מאיר שמגר. ההנחה היתה שעל אף שהרב גורן הכיר היטב את התיק לפרטיו, ולטענתו במישור ההלכתי ניתן להתיר את האחים לנגר מממזרותם, הרי שהוא אינו מוסמך לעשות כן, שכן אין בסמכותו לחלוק על פסק דין של בית הדין הרבני הגדול. היחידים שיכולים לערער על פסק הדין האמור הם הרבנים הראשיים, באשר הם ממונים על מערכת בתי הדין בכללותה. הרב יצחק נסים, הרב הראשי הספרדי דאז, ניאות לסידור הבא: הרב גורן יכתוב פסק הלכה מנומק להתרת האח והאחות, והרב נסים יושיב הרכב מיוחד של דיינים שידון מחדש בתיק לאור הערותיו של הרב גורן.[כד]

[כד] תיאור מהלך העניינים מבוסס על סיכומו של הרב גורן את השתלשלות המאורעות, ראו: הרב שלמה גורן, *פסק הדין בענין האח והאחות*, ירושלים: דפוס ממשלת ישראל, תשל"ג, עמ' 191-185. הרכבי הדיינים בבתי הדין השונים הינם: 13.11.55 – הדיינים א' גולדשמידט, י'

הרב גורן אמנם חיבר פסק דין שכזה, אותו הפיץ בין מאה רבנים ובקש את הערותיהם.[כה] בפתיחת החוברת הוא הבהיר שאין לו כוונה להכריע בדין, אלא רק לעורר את הדיון המחודש:

> עלי למסור מודעה רבה שאין בכוונתי בהרצאת דברים בקונטרס זה, כדי להורות נגד חכמי ישראל שישבו על מדוכה זו, ולא מצאו פתח להיתר, כי אם לפענח מקורות חדשים ולפרוס יריעה הלכתית חדשה על מנת להביאה לפני גדולי התורה, כדי שיכריעו בדבר לאור העדויות והמסמכים החדשים שנתגלו על ידינו.[כו]

ברם, הרב נסים לא הקים את ההרכב המיוחל. האח והאחות נותרו אסורים, והמהומה בתקשורת הלכה וגברה.

ההכרה שהלכה והתחדדה היתה שאם הרב גורן יהיה הרב הראשי הוא יוכל לכנס הרכב דיינים המזדהה עם עמדתו, ובכך להביא להתרת האח והאחות. הלחצים הפוליטיים היו עצומים, ואף התקשורת תרמה את שלה.[כז] הרב מנחם מנדל שניאורסון, מנהיגה של חב"ד, הזהיר את הרב גורן:

> עוד נקודה עיקרית במצב המיוחד בבחירות אלו אשר מנצלים מועמדות כת"ר למלחמה נגד הדיוק בשמירת ההלכה [...] ועוד, אשר דוקא חוגים הידועים בעמדתם לכל עניני תורה ומצותי' הם התומכים ומרעישים וכו' למועמדות כת"ר [=כבוד תורתו].[כח]

הויכוחים סביב מינויו של הרב גורן לרב ראשי חצו גם את מחנה הרבנים הציוניים-דתיים, וכאשר ועד הרבנים של הפועל המזרחי בחר לתמוך במועמדותו של הרב גורן,

---

בבליקי וש' קרליץ (תל-אביב); 17.5.66 – הדיינים מ' שלזינגר, י' וילנסקי וי' סורוצקין (תל-אביב); 8.10.67 – הדיינים ש' קרליץ, מ' זולטי וש' ת' רובינשטיין (פתח-תקווה); 4.6.69 – הדיינים ש' קרליץ, מ' זולטי וקרייסמן (פתח-תקווה); 20.1.70 – הדיינים י' ש' אלישיב, ש' ישראלי וע' יוסף (בית הדין העליון בירושלים).

כה הרב שלמה גורן, *חות דעת הלכתית בנושא מעמד אישי*, ישראל: המטה הכללי-הרבנות הצבאית הראשית, תשל"א. כעבור שנתיים, אחרי שהרב גורן כבר התיר את הממזרים וערך להם חתונות, הוא שב ופרסם את פסק הדין: גורן, פסק הדין (לעיל, הע' כד). בין שתי המהדורות יש שינויים, שברובם הינם חסרי משמעות, ובמיעוט החשוב אדון אי"ה במקום אחר.

כו הרב גורן, חות דעת, עמ' 5.

כז ראו לדוגמה: טוביה מנדלסון, "מהצפוי ברבנות הראשית", *דבר*, ד' חשון תשל"ג, 12.10.1972, גליון 14501, עמ' 3; ש. פרידמן, "בדרך הקולות והעקלקלות", *המודיע*, ה' חשון תשל"ג 13.10.1972, גליון 8328, עמ' 3; הועד להצלת הרבנות הראשית, *המערכה על הצלת הרבנות בישראל והסכנה במועמדותו של הרב שלמה גורן*, ירושלים: דפוס עקיבא יוסף, תשל"ג, עמ' 3.

כח מכתב שהתאריך עליו הוא ימי הסליחות תשל"ב, מועתק ב*אגרות קודש*, כרך כז, אגרת י'תפו, עמ' תקיא-תקיב.

הודיע הרב שאול ישראלי על עזיבתו את הועד. השדה הפוליטי רחש גם כן. כשהתברר שלפי תנאי הבחירות הנתונים צפוי הרב גורן להפסיד בבחירות, שונו חוקי בחירת הרב הראשי, עד שיובטח שהרב גורן יבחר. ואכן, בחודש אוקטובר 1972 הרב גורן נבחר למשרת הרב הראשי האשכנזי לצדו של הרב עובדיה יוסף.

הרב גורן אכן עמד בדיבורו. בתאריך 19.11.1972, כחודש לאחר שנבחר, הוא הודיע כי הקים הרכב מיוחד של דיינים אשר טיהר את האחים מכתם הממזרות, ובו ביום נישאו הללו עם בחירי לבם.

מהלך זה זכה לתגובות שונות. היו שראו בפעולה זו צורך השעה, והמליכו את הרב גורן כגיבור. "אינני סבור, כי בארץ שלנו ובמציאות שבה אנו חיים נמצא עוד רב אחד בשיעור קומתו, שהיה נכון להשליך נפשו מנגד ולפתור את הבעיה ההילכתית והאנושית בדרך זו. כאן נתגלה הרב גורן כיחיד בדור הרבנים שלו", נכתב בשבועון מפלגת "העבודה".[כט] ראש הממשלה גולדה מאיר בירכה את הרב גורן,[ל] ומשה דיין קבע שאילו הרב גורן החליף את הרב אונטרמן במשרת הרב הראשי לישראל כמה שנים קודם לכן "היו חילוקי-הדעות בין הדתיים והלא-דתיים נדונים באווירה נאותה וחיובית יותר".[לא]

לעומת זאת, היו שביקרו את הרב גורן חריפות. בציניות אופיינית כתב אורי אבנרי בעיתונו:

> הפסוק האהוב ביותר על הרב שלמה גורן אינו לקוח מן התלמוד, אלא מהסלנג בצה"ל. כה אמר, מאות פעמים, כשהביאו בפניו בעייה: "יש לי פאטנט!".
>
> השבוע עלה הפאטנט של הרב על כל הפאטנטים הקודמים שלו. גם הוא נלקח ישר ממחסני צה"ל. הכל דמה לפשיטה של יחידה 101, בימים הטובים שבהם מלך רב-אלוף משה דיין על צה"ל, ולידו כיהן בקודש האלוף-הרב גורן.[לב]

גם בעולם הדתי עצמו לא היתה עמדה אחידה לגבי מהלכו של הרב גורן. בבני ברק כונסה עצרת ובה נערך מעמד קריעה, אבילות על השפלת קרנה של התורה, באשר מהלכו של הרב גורן נתפס ככניעה של ההלכה לדרישות הפוליטיקאים. מילים חריפות ביותר השמיע הרב אלעזר מנחם מן שך:

> להוי ידוע, כי בוערת אש, מתלקחת להבה, שורפים את התורה, ותולשים ממנה גוילים גוילים, ויש לזעוק לנוכח שריפת התורה שכזו געוואלד! [...]

[כט] "פריצת דרך חדשה", *אות - שבועון מפלגת העבודה*, 23.11.72.

[ל] ראו לדוגמה: *מעריב*, י"ד כסלו תשל"ג, 20.11.1972, גליון 8623, עמ' 1.

[לא] שם, עמ' 2.

[לב] אורי אבנרי, "זבנג וגמרנו!", *העולם הזה*, 22.11.72, עמ' 14-15.

יש הטוענים כי הרב הראשי למדן הוא, ברם מאי משמע למדן – אומרים בשם ר' יוסף דובער זצ"ל כי למדן אינו זה היודע ללמוד, כשם שגנב אינו זה היודע לגנוב, אלא הלומד תורה ביראת שמים צרופה הקודמת לחכמתו – לזה למדן יקרא.
וזה אשר הביאני לכאן, להודיע קבל עם ועדה, למען יהא הדבר מושרש בלב כל אחד מאתנו, כי הוא אינו רב ופסקיו אינם פסקים, אין לאכול ע"פ [=על פי] הכשריו, ומחוץ למחנה מושבו, ואם מותרים הממזרים לבוא בקהל, הרי שאסור הוא לבוא בקהל. ואין להתייחס כלל לדבריו, ואליו לא תשמעון, וגרוע הוא מהרפורמים, באשר ובדעתו מתחשבים רבים, כי הלא רב הראשי הוא כביכול.[לג]

מאוחר יותר אף התפרסמו כרוזים של ועדי רבנים מן התפוצות, ובהם הכרזות נוקבות נגד הרב גורן. כך, לדוגמה, נכתב בכרוז עליו חתום הרב משה פיינשטיין, כנשיא ועד הרבנים האורתודוקסיים:

בדבר ענין הנורא שנעשה בארץ ישראל, שהרב הראשי שנבחר זה לא כבר, כפי שמפורסם, אמר שיכול למצא דרכים בהוראה להקל בשאלות חמורות וגם עשה תיכף מעשה, שהכשיר אח ואחות לקהל אחרי שנאסרו בבית דין חשוב, ועשה עובדא זו רעש בין גדולי התורה שבארץ ישראל, וקבלנו דעת תורה מהגאון ר' יחזקאל אבראמסקי שליט"א, והסכימו לו כל גדולי וראשי הישיבה בארץ ישראל, איך שהם מכריזים שכל פסקיו והוראותיו בטלים [...] גם אנחנו מצטרפים [...] שכל פסקיו והוראותיו בטלים.[לד]

מאידך, היו שתמכו במהלכו של הרב גורן גם בתוך העולם הרבני. לפי עדותו של הרב יוסי הראל, הוא התלווה לרב גורן בביקור אצל הרב יחזקאל סרנה, ראש ישיבת 'חברון', בה למד הרב גורן בצעירותו. כשצעירים חרדים קראו לעברו קריאות גנאי נזף בהם הרב סרנה, ואמר: "אתם יודעים על מי אתם מדברים?! זה גאון בתורה!".[לה] בציונות הדתית אמנם היו שהסתייגו ממהלכו של הרב גורן, אולם דמויות מפתח צידדו בו. בחוברת שהופצה על ידי המפד"ל היו ראיונות עם הרב כתריאל פישל טכורש, רבה של תל אביב, והרב צבי יהודה קוק, ראש ישיבת מרכז הרב, ודמות דומיננטית בין רבני הציונות הדתית

[לג] הרב אלעזר מנחם מן שך, *מכתבים ומאמרים ממרן הגאון רבי אלעזר מנחם מן שך שליט"א*, א-ב, בני-ברק: חש"מ, תשמ"ח, עמ' עג.

[לד] ההודעה הובאה בצד הפנימי של עטיפת גליון *הפרדס* 47:4 (ינואר 1973). בתוך החוברת, עמ' 24-26 הובאו מודעות נוספות, מישראל ומן העולם, הקוראות שלא לראות ברב גורן רב. בין החתומים על המודעות ניתן למנות דמויות מפתח כמו הרב יחזקאל אברמסקי, ר' חיים שמואלביץ, הרב אלעזר מנחם מן שך, הרב יעקב ישראל קניבסקי, הרב יוסף שלום אלישיב, הרב שמואל הלוי ואזנר, הרב נתן געשטטנר, ר' משה שטרנבוך והרב שלמה זלמן אוירבך.

[לה] כך אצל יאיר שלג, *משוח מלחמה: סיפורו של הרב שלמה גורן*, פרק עשירי (טרם פורסם). אני מודה ליאיר שלג שנתן בי אמון והעמיד לרשותי את טיוטת ספרו.

של אותם הימים, אשר צידדו ברב גורן.[לו] הרב צבי יהודה קוק אף הביע דעתו שבהיבט ההלכתי יש צדדים לכאן ולכאן, וההכרעה נוטה אחר העמדה הבסיסית באשר ליחס לשיתוף פעולה עם הציבור החילוני בישראל:

> הרב הראשי הוכיח, שבמיקרה זה לא היתה גירות, ואילו המתנגדים אינם משיבים תשובה שיש בה משקל וטעם. הודעות כלליות, ללא הוכחות, אי-אפשר לקבל אותן. ידוע, ש"מועצת גדולי התורה" של אגודת-ישראל מתנגדת לרבנות הראשית. זו שיטתה והיא הקובעת.[לז]
>
> אחר הראש הולך הגוף. מקור התורה של המזרחי עיצב אותו בדמותו, והיפוכו ב"אגודה". כאן [בציונות הדתית, אי"ה] אחדות-ישראל כיסוד היסודות, ושם [באגודת ישראל, אי"ה] קרע בין יהודים ליהודים.[לח]

בהקשר זה מעניין גם לציין את טיב הסיקור לו זכה העניין בעיתון לונדוני:

> Rabbi Goren's coup, which by-passed normal Bet Din (rabbinical court) procedure and avoided involving Rabbi Ovadia Yosef, the Sephardi Chief Rabbi of Israel, caused a sensation all over the country (Israel, AY"H). His action pushed almost every other topic out of the head-lines for 24 hours... [p. 3.] The middle-of-the-road religious section of the population represented by the National Religious Party and most non-observant Israelis, who form the majority, now regard Rabbi Goren as a folk hero.[לט]

הנה כי כן, טענות הרב שך על כך שהרב גורן חסר יראת שמיים, טענותיו של הרב צבי יהודה קוק על כך שההתנגדות לרב גורן נובעת מחוסר באהבת ישראל, כמו גם הסיקור התקשורתי, מלמדים על ההבנה שהפסיקה ההלכתית במקרה זה אינה מנותקת מעמדות אידיאולוגיות הנוגעות לחברה הישראלית. מצד אחד עמדו אלה שראו בעין שלילית את מציאת הדרך ההלכתית לפתרון הבעיה והסערה הפוליטית, ומאידך עמדו אחרים, שראו בכך מעשה גבורה אמיץ מצדו של הרב גורן.[מ]

[לו] פנחס פרבר (עורך), *הרבנות הראשית – רבנות לעם כולו*, תל-אביב: המחלקה להסברה בכתב של המפלגה הדתית לאומית המזרחי-הפועל המזרחי, תשל"ג 1973.

[לז] פרבר, רבנות לעם כולו, עמ' 10.

[לח] פרבר, רבנות לעם כולו, עמ' 11.

[לט] "Goren's coup on mamzerim", *Jewish Chronicle*, 24.11.1972, 18 Kislev 5733, No. 5405, pp.1-3.

[מ] מעניין לציין שההתנגדות למהלכיו של הרב גורן לא פסקה עד זמננו. בעקבות פרשיית "האח והאחות" פרש הרב יוסף שלום אלישיב מחברותו בבית הדין הגדול של הרבנות הראשית

נראה שהרב גורן עצמו היה מופתע מעוצמת ההתנגדות לו. במסיבת עיתונאים שכינס לביתו הוא קרא לרבנים להפסיק את המחאות, ולהיפגש לשיחה עמו בה יוכל להבהיר את עמדתו:

אף פעם לא אמרתי שיקבלו את דברי, רק שיזמינו אותי לבוא ולשאול על סמך מה חתמתי[מא] [...] אני שואל ראשי-ישיבה וגדולי תורה אלה, שאינם משמשים כרבנים בפועל בשום מקום ואין להם שום מעמד של דיינות, איך הוציאו פסק-דין עלי בלי לשמוע אותי, בלי לראות את החומר, ובלי אפילו לנסות לבוא איתי בדברים?[מב]

במכתבים אישיים מאותם הימים הוא כתב בטון חריף ביותר. הוא הציג את ההתנגדות לו כרדיפה שאינה עניינית, ואת עצמו כמי שמבקש לייקר את מעמד התורה בחברה הישראלית. כך הוא כתב אל מכתב לרב אליעזר ברנשטיין, נשיא הסתדרות הרבנים בארה"ב, בתאריך כ"ח בטבת תשל"ג, 2.1.1973:

מערכת ההשמצה הזדונית ומסכת השקרים שרקמו אנשי האגודה ועושי דברם מסביב ל"היתר" סופה לנחול כשלון חרוץ, כי תורה לא בשמים הוא, כל אחד יוכל כעת להוכח, בדברי האמת לאמיתה של תורה עליהן מבוסס ההיתר... [עמ' 2] אני סמוך ובטוח בע"ה שאם נעמוד כחומה בצורה נגד בני חושך אשר פיהם דבר שוא וימינם ימין שקר המנסים להשתלט עלינו ולהכתיב לרבני ישראל ודייניו את פסק הדין וההוראות, נצליח בדרכנו דרך התורה האמת והשלום.
הבה נמשיך להתקדם בדרך התורה הרצופה, נסע ונלך לאורו הגדול של גאון ישראל אהבו ואהובו פארו והדרו, מרן הגראי"ה קוק זצ"ל, שהתווה את דרכי המחשבה ההוראה והעשיה, לא נרתע מפני איש ולא נחת בפני מהלכי אימים.[מג]

זאת ועוד, עם היבחרו הודיע הרב גורן שיפנה אל גדעון האוזנר בבקשה שיסיר מעל שלחן הממשלה את הצעת החוק להנהגת נישואין אזרחיים במדינת ישראל.[מד] פעולה זו

לישראל. לאחרונה נדפסה ביוגרפיה אודותיו ובה הוקדש מקום רחב לפרשיות הלן זיידמן והתרת הממזרים תחת הכותרת "מלחמתו נגד מפירי התורה בקרב הרבנים המזוייפים", ראו: י' סג"ל, *השקדן: פרקי מופת אודות יגיעה ופירות משקידתו בתורה של רבינו רשכבה"ג מרן הגרי"ש אלישיב שליט"א*, א, ירושלים: הוצאת המחבר, תש"ע, עמ' 178-203.

מא בהקשר זה מעניינת עדותו של הרב אברהם הורביץ, *ארחות רבנו*, עמ' קעד, לפיה הרב קנייבסקי התמודד עם טענה מעין זו שהעלה הרב גורן שהושמעה באזניו בשם האדמו"ר מגור: "אמר מו"ר כתגובה על מה שספר לו מרן הגאון הרב שך (שליט"א) זצ"ל ששמע לשה"ר [=לשון הרע] כאילו האדמו"ר מגור אמר, האם ראו את הקונטרס שלו שצועקים עליו, אולי יש בזה משהו, ע"ז ענה מו"ר, שיודע שאין בזה כלום, כי אילו הי' בזה איזו סברא אחת להתיר, כבר אונטרמן(!) הי' מתיר".

מב אברהם רותם, "הרב גורן: גם אם יקרעו קריעה – אני אמשיך ללכת בדרכי", *מעריב*, 24.11.1972, עמ' 5.

מג אוסף משפחת גורן, תיקייה: *מכתבים אישיים מאת הרב בעקבות פסה"ד*.

צלחה, ובתגובה לצעדיו של הרב גורן הכריז האוזנר שיפנה לוועדת מפלגתו (ליברלים עצמאיים) וכי הוא צופה שזו תסכים להסרת הצעת חוק הנישואין אזרחיים.[מה]

צעדיו של הרב גורן לא השפיעו רק בזירה הפוליטית. בראיון שערך מתי גולן עם חנוך ומרים לנגר הוא שאלם לגבי עמדתם באשר לחוק נישואין אזרחיים שהציע האוזנר. האחים הביעו התנגדות, וקבעו שיש להתמודד עם הבעיות ההלכתיות בדרכים הלכתיות. דני, בעלה הטרי של מרים קבע:

> הדת היא דבר חשוב למדינה. היא מחזיקה את היהדות ובגללה אנו ממשיכים להתקיים כעת. אין לי טינה כלפי אף אחד, אלא רק כלפי הסחבת שנמשכה שבע שנים. תמיד שאלתי את עצמי: מדוע אי-אפשר לגמור עם זה.

ומרים החרתה החזיקה אחריו:

> הדת היא שליכדה את העם היהודי. לא ייתכן לקיים שתי רשויות – חילונית ודתית. מי שדורש להפריד את הדת מהמדינה אינו חושב מספיק על ההשלכות לגבי שלמות העם ואופיה היהודי של המדינה. אם אתה יהודי אתה קשור לדת היהודית.

בסיכום הדברים, נראה אפוא שהמניע העיקרי של הרב גורן לא היה רק הדאגה לאושרם של חנוך ומרים לנגר,[מו] אלא שבעיניו על כפות המאזניים עמד חוק הנישואין וגירושין בישראל, ומעמדה של הדת במדינה היהודית. בדומה למקרה זיידמן, גם במקרה האח והאחות סבר הרב גורן שיש להימנע מפסיקה הלכתית שתרחיק את הקהל הישראלי מהתורה ויש להעדיף פסיקה חדשנית שתקרב את עם ישראל למסורת ישראל.

בשלב זה עלינו לנסות ולהבין מה היו השיקולים ההלכתיים שהציג הרב גורן. ובכן, הרב גורן הציג רצף של טענות הלכתיות. ראשית, אמם של חנוך ומרים, חווה, הכירה את בעלה הראשון, אברהם בורקובסקי, בהיותו גוי. שמו העברי, בו הוכר בישראל, אמנם היה אברהם, אך שמו המקורי היה בולק. היא היתה נערה כבת ארבע עשרה, והוא היה מבוגר ממנה בלמעלה מעשר שנים. החברות בין הנערה היהודיה לבן זוגה הגוי היתה למורת רוח

[מד] כך בכותרת עיתון *דבר*, ח' חשון תשל"ג 16.10.1972, גליון 14504, עמ' 1: "גורן ויוסף נבחרו רבנים ראשיים: הרב גורן מבקש מהאוזנר אשראי של שנה".

[מה] *מעריב*, י"ד כסלו תשל"ג 20.11.1972, גליון 8623, עמ' 1.

[מו] כך כתב בחוברת שפרסם: "תחילת התעניינותי בפרשה אנושית מזעזעת ורווית-צער זו, בשנת תשכ"ח [...] מצבם הנפשי של שני הצעירים התערער מאד, והם מצאו פורקן נפשי במשרדי במטכ"ל ופתח לתקוה ולנחומים. בכל עת אשר הרגישו שמר להם היו באים אלי להוזיל דמעות, ולבכות את מר-גורלם [...] התחלתי להתענין בגורלם המר. התקשרתי מיזמתי עם עורך הדין שלהם [...] נוכחתי לראות שמבחינה הלכתית ישנו זיק של תקוה" (עמ' 3 בעמ' ההקדמה).

להוריה. בשלב כלשהו פשטה בעיירה לוקוב, בה גרו השניים, השמועה כי בולק התגייר והשניים נישאו בחתונה ביתית.

הרב גורן תקף את עצם עובדת הגיור של בולק בורקובסקי. כשנשאל על דבר גיורו לא זכר את פרטי הגיור. הוא טען שהברית נעשתה בבית חולים, וכלל לא ידע שהיה אמור לבוא בפני שלושה דיינים. לדבריו הרב המקומי גייר אותו, ולא בית דין.

לטענת הרב גורן, אף אם היה גיור, הרי שהוא היה בכפיה. הרב גורן הביא עדים שגרו בלוקוב בתקופה האמורה, והללו סיפרו שאבי הנערה היה עשיר, והוא כפה על בולק את הגיור נגד רצונו.

נוסף לכך, לדעת הרב גורן, אף אם לגיור היה תוקף, הרי שיש להפקיע אותו. הרב גורן הביא מסמכים של עובדת סוציאלית של עיריית תל אביב, ולפיהם לבורקובסקי נולד בן אותו הוא הטביל לנצרות בתל אביב. יתר על כן, הוא המשיך לבקר בכנסיות בתל אביב, והובא גם עד שידע לספר שאכל עם בורקובסקי חזיר ביום הכפורים.

הרב גורן הציע צדדים נוספים להתרת האחים. גם אם הגיור היה תקף ואין להפקיעו, הרי שאין כל ראיה לכך שבני הזוג נישאו. לחווה לא היתה כתובה, ואין בנמצא עדים שהיו בחתונתם.

לבסוף, לפי ספר העיטור גיטו של מומר אינו תקף מדאורייתא, וכחו כהפקעת קידושין. על כן, טען הרב גורן, מאחר ובורקובסקי פקד את הכנסיה, יש לראות את גיטו כגט של מומר, והרי שבנותנו את הגט הפקיע את קידושיו מעיקרא. נמצא שאף אם הגט ניתן לאחר נישואיה לאביהם של חנוך ומרים, הרי שנישואיה הראשונים הופקעו.

מעתה, טען הרב גורן, אם בולק בורקובסקי אינו יהודי או שהוא יהודי שלא נישא לחווה, הרי שכשהתחתנה עם אביהם של חנוך ומרים היא היתה פנויה, והשניים אינם ממזרים. במילים אחרות, ההחמרה בדינו של בורקבוסקי היא המהווה את הפתח להקלה במעמדם של האחים לנגר.

הרב גורן היה מודע למורכבות הנושאים ההלכתיים עליהם התבסס. לפיכך, משרבתה המהומה הוא פרסם נוסח מורחב של פסק ההלכה בעניין.[מז] חוברת זו, המונה כמאה וחמישים עמודי דיון הלכתי, מלמדת על דרכו של הרב גורן בפסיקה. הוא מונה ומפרט דעות שונות ומחלוקות, ונראה שאין כוונתו לשכנע שפסיקתו היא הפסיקה האפשרית היחידה, אלא שהיא פסיקה מבוססת היטב במקורות ההלכתיים.

[מז] הרב גורן, פסק הדין (לעיל, הע' כד). העובדה שמוסדות המדינה הדפיסו את פסק הדין של רש"ג עוררה ביקורת בקרב מתנגדיו. כך לדוגמה כתב מנהיג הזרם הליטאי באותה תקופה, הרב אלעזר מנחם מן שך, *מכתבים ומאמרים ממרן הגאון רבי אלעזר מנחם מן שך שליט"א*, ג, בני ברק, תשמ"ח, עמ' צח: "הגידו נא רבותי, וכי יש צחוק גדול מזה. למה הדפיסו רק פסק זה, ולא פסקים אחרים מהרב הראשי שלהם? הדפיסו פסק זה מפני שזהו פסק נגד התורה, זהו פסק שעוקר לאו בתורה, זהו פסק שלהם, ולא פסק של איזה רב שכשר להורות ולפסוק, זהו פסק שהוציא אחרי שביזה [את] כל גדולי [ה]תורה מימות עולם, עד התנאים והאמוראים לחוות דעתו המורעלת מספרי המינים".

דומני שבפרשיה זו יש ביטוי להלך המחשבה של הרב גורן: מצד אחד הוא מכיר את המסורת ההלכתית על שלל הטענות וכיווני המחשבה שיש בה, ומאידך הוא מכיר את החברה הישראלית והנהגתה הפוליטית. האתגר העומד בפניו הוא כיצד לחבר בין שני צדדי המשוואה, וכיצד להביא את החברה הישראלית לראות בהלכה מערכת היקרה ללבה ושיכולה לתרום לה. בשל כך הוא בחן את כלל האפשרויות ההלכתיות, וביסס את העמדה ההלכתית התואמת את רחשי הלב של החברה הישראלית. באופן זה, כך תקוותו, יעלה בידו לקרב את ישראל לאביהם שבשמיים, ואת חוקי המדינה לדרכה של תורה.

הכניסה להר הבית

בשתי הסוגיות בהן דנתי לעיל, הרב גורן בקש להגן על מעמדה של ההלכה במסגרת חוקי מדינת ישראל. בסוגיה הבאה, שאלת היתר הכניסה להר הבית, המצב מורכב יותר: ברובד הגלוי הרב גורן מצהיר שפסק ההלכה שלו מבקש להשפיע על קובעי המדיניות לשמור על הריבונות הישראלית בהר הבית, גם במסגרת הסכמי השלום עם הפלסטינים. לדעתי, ברובד הנסתר הרב גורן בקש להציע עמדה רבנית אשר מחד תגן על הריבונות הישראלית בהר הבית , ומאידך תיזהר מלהביע תמיכה, אפילו במשתמע, בפעילות טרור נגד מבני הדת המוסלמיים שבהר.[מח]

כבר בשנת תשכ"ב, בכינוס הארצי החמישי לתורה שבעל-פה, נשא הרב גורן הרצאה שכותרתה "חידוש העבודה בתקופת בר-כוכבא",[מט] ובה טען כי במידה והר הבית יכבש ישנה חובה הלכתית להקים בו את המקדש.[נ] הדיון התיאורטי הפך בתוך מחצית העשור לדילמה מעשית.

[מח] דיון בבירור עמדתו של הרב גורן בעניין הכניסה להר הבית תוך השוואה לפוסקים ציוניים-דתיים אחרים מצויה במאמר שכתבתי במשותף עם ידידי ד"ר אליאב טאוב: "The Place of Religious Aspirations for Sovereignty over the Temple Mount in Religious-Zionistic Rulings", in: Marshall. J. Breger, Yitzhak Reiter and Leonard Hammer (eds.), *Sacred Space in Israel and Palestine: Religion and Politics*, London and New York: Routledge, 2012, pp. 139-167. הדיון כאן תמציתי יותר, ודברי תורה עניים במקום אחד ועשירים במקום אחר.

[מט] כך בסיכומו של י"ש, "הכינוס הארצי החמישי לתורה שבעל-פה", *תורה שבעל פה* ה (תשכ"ג), עמ' ו.

[נ] "הרב גורן בכינוס לתורה שבע"פ: אילו היינו כובשים היום את הר-הבית היינו מחוייבים לבנות עליו בית-המקדש", *דבר*, 15.8.1962, עמ' 4; דיווח זהה הופיע באותו היום, תחת אותה כותרת גם בעיתון *חירות*. יש לציין שבזמן הויכוח בשאלת הר-הבית לאחר מלחמת ששת הימים הרב גורן הבהיר שאינו מתכוון שעל מדינת ישראל לבנות מקדש מייד, אלא להקים בית תפילה ליהודים, ראו לדוגמה: רות בונדי, "הרב וריבו", *דבר השבוע – מוסף ערב שבת של "דבר"* 40 (13.10.1967), עמ' 3-5. פרופ' יעקב לוינגר הביע דעתו שנסיגה זו של הרב גורן הינה טקטית, ותכליתה קידום עניינו של הרב הבית עד לכדי השלמת החזון – בניין

בימי הלחימה של מלחמת ששת הימים, הרב גורן הצטרף לכוחות שלחמו בגיזרה הדרומית. במהלך הלחימה הוא התוודע לכך שכוחות צה"ל הגיעו לירושלים ועורכים שם קרבות. הרב גורן עזב את הגיזרה הדרומית ונסע במהירות לירושלים, שם פגש את עוזי נרקיס, אלוף פיקוד המרכז באותם הימים. נרקיס פנה לרב גורן והתעניין בנעשה בדרום, ואילו זה האחרון מחה: "מה חשוב הדרום, ירושלים והר-הבית, הם העיקר!". השניים סיכמו שנרקיס יצרף את הרב גורן לכוחות הפורצים לירושלים, ובלבד שהלה ידאג להביא עמו שופר.[נא]

במוזיאון רוקפלר, שם התרכזו כוחות צה"ל, הרב גורן הסביר את בואו כך: "באתי הנה להיכנס לכותל המערבי, לכבוש את [הר] הבית, ולכבוש את הכותל המערבי, ואת העיר העתיקה, ולערוך את התפילה הראשונה בציבור ליד הכותל המערבי, עם מוטה [גור] ועם כל יחידת הצנחנים".[נב]

הרב גורן אכן הצטרף לכוחות שכבשו את העיר העתיקה, בידיו ספר תורה והוא קורא קריאות עידוד. כשניסה קצין המבצעים של גדוד 28 לעצור את התקדמותו של הרב גורן, הוא מאן ודרש "*אל תתחצף*", ואף למפקד הגדוד הוא הבהיר: "*אותי לא יזיזו אחורה*".[נג] עם הצנחנים הגיע הרב גורן להר-הבית, ובמרחביו, וכיפת הסלע בכלל, הוא סייר תוך כדי תקיעה בשופר שהוכן מראש.[נד] רק לאחר מכן, הוא ניגש לכותל המערבי, שם אמר "קדיש" ו"אל מלא רחמים" לזכר הנופלים,[נה] והצטרף לשירת הלוחמים.[נו]

המקדש, ראו הנ"ל, *בין שיגרה לחידוש: קוים למחשבת היהדות בזמננו*, ירושלים: דעות, תשל"ג, עמ' 131.

נא לפי עדותו של עוזי נרקיס, *אחת ירושלים*, תל-אביב: עם עובד, 1975, עמ' 161-162 (להלן: אחת ירושלים).

נב כך בהקלטה אותה ניתן לשמוע בתכנית רדיו ששודרה ברשת 'מורשת', מצוי במרשתת בכתובת:
http://www.iba.org.il/moreshet/moreshet.aspx?classto=InnerKlali&entity=642784&type=1&topic=952 (נצפה בתאריך 9.3.2013). דבריו של הרב גורן מתחילים בדקה 15:25.

נג לפי עדותו של מפקד חטיבת מילואים של הצנחנים דאז, מרדכי (מוטה) גור, *הר הבית בידינו!: קרבות הצנחנים בירושלים במלחמת ששת הימים, כ"ו-כ"ח אייר תשכ"ז*, תל-אביב: מערכות, משרד הבטחון, תשל"ד, עמ' 321 (להלן: גור, הר הבית).

נד הרב מנחם הכהן מעיד על כך שבביתו ישנה תמונה של הרב גורן במבנה כיפת הסלע, ראו: שלום כהן, *שיח אחים – על "מלחמות היהודים"*, תל-אביב: זמורה-ביתן, תשמ"ז 1987, עמ' 125. תמונה כזו אכן התפרסמה אצל שבתי בן-דב, *סולם למלכות ישראל היעודה: כתבי שבתי בן-דב, חלק ג* (בעריכת יהודה עציון), ירושלים: סלמות, תשס"ז, עמ' 171. לאחרונה פורסם ברשת האינטרנט סרטון משידורי הטלויזיה הישראלית, ובו ניתן לראות את כניסת הרב גורן לכיפת הסלע (נצפה בתאריך 9.3.2013): <http://www.youtube.com/watch?v=SuLOLj-vUWI> (הכניסה נערכה משניה 37 ואילך).

נה גור, הר הבית בידינו, עמ' 333; נרקיס, אחת ירושלים, עמ' 250.

נו בהקלטת הרדיו מורשת, דקה 21:15 ואילך, ניתן לשמוע את הרב גורן שר ומעודד את החיילים לשיר עמו "לשעה הזאת בירושלים" (פרפראזה על השיר המוכר "לשנה הבאה

באותה שנה הרב גורן תיאר את המחשבות והרגשות שמילאוהו באותה השעה. הוא חש פעמי משיח, וסבר שמן הראוי היה לפוצץ את המסגדים, ולכל הפחות לשלם למוסלמים פיצוי בעבור עזיבתם את ההר.[נז] יתכן אף שדרש זאת ממשה דיין בישיבת מטכ"ל.[נח] כעבור שנים הרב גורן טען כי אמנם הרהר בכך, אך מחשבותיו לא היו רציניות, שכן ברור היה לו שהמדינה לא היתה מוכנה לצעד שכזה, ואף אילו נקטה בו, הרי שהיתה בונה מחדש את המסגדים.[נט]

לאחר כיבוש ההר, הרב גורן ארגן מדידות שנערכו על ידי חיילי חיל ההנדסה. מגמתו של הרב גורן היתה לקבוע היכן בשטח הר הבית עמד המקדש, באשר לדעתו, לשטחי ההר שעליהם לא עמד המקדש אין כל איסור הלכתי להיכנס. הרב גורן ייסד מניין שהתפלל בשטח המותר, מתוך מגמה שבעתיד אף יבנה בו בית כנסת. תפילות אלה לא עוררו עניין מיוחד, אך תפילה שהרב גורן ארגן בתשעה באב באותה שנה עוררה מחאה בעולם המוסלמי. כעבור כמה ימים, כשהרב גורן ביקש לקיים תפילה המונית בשבת "נחמו" בהר הבית, נחלץ דוד בן-גוריון ותבע למנוע את מימוש תוכנית זו. ועדת שרים שדנה בעניין כניסת יהודים להר הבית, קבעה שיש לאסור על יהודים את התפילה בהר. הרב גורן הזדעק כנגד קביעה זו, ובמכתב נרגש הוא התחנן שיחזרו בהם. לדידו, התפילה בכותל המערבי מסמלת את הגלות, ואילו הר הבית הוא גולת הכותרת של שיבת ישראל לארצו. אין כל כוונה, כך הוא הדגיש, לפגוע בהר. הבקשה היחידה היא שיהודים יכנסו להר, ויתפללו בו. אולם תחנוניו של הרב גורן לא נשאו פרי, והאיסור עמד בתוקפו.[ס] לענייננו חשוב לציין שאת המוטיבציה לארגון תפילות אלה הרב גורן הסביר בכך שיש להפגין את הזיקה בין עם ישראל להר הבית.[סא]

פעילותו של הרב גורן למען זכויות היהודים בהר הבית התחדשה לאחר מינויו לתפקיד הרב הראשי לישראל. לאחר שהסתיימה המלחמה, התפרסם כרוז עליו היו

בירושלים"). דיווח עיתונאי על שירה זו מצוי אצל יונה כהן, "ברוך שהחיינו וקימנו והגיענו לזמן הזה – תפילת מנחה ראשונה ליד הכותל", *הצפה*, 8.6.1967, עמ' 1.

נז נדב שרגאי, *הר המריבה: המאבק על הר-הבית – יהודים ומוסלמים, דת ופוליטיקה מאז 1967*, ירושלים: כתר, 1995, עמ' 29 (להלן: שרגאי, הר המריבה).

נח כך לפי חגי סגל, *"אחים יקרים": קורות "המחתרת היהודית"*, ירושלים: כתר, 1987, עמ' 47 (להלן: סגל, אחים).

נט שרגאי, הר המריבה, עמ' 29-30. יצויין שנרקיס עצמו סיפר שהרב גורן ביקש ממנו לפוצץ את המסגדים. עדותו זו מצוטטת במחקרים שונים העוסקים בהר הבית, אך מבלי להזכיר את הכחשותיו של הרב גורן עליהן דיווח שרגאי.

ס שרגאי, הר המריבה, עמ' 30-34.

סא כך בדיווח עיתונאי תחת הכותרת "הרב גורן לא יערוך תפילה בהר-הבית בשבת", *דבר*, 17.8.1967, עמ' 2: "הרב הסביר את צעדו זה באמרו, כי על העם היהודי להפגין זיקה למקום בו היה בית-המקדש".

חתומים מאות רבנים, ובו נאמר כי הכניסה להר הבית אסורה מבחינה הלכתית.[סב] עמדה שכזו נקטה גם הרבנות הראשית.[סג] לאחר מינויו לרב ראשי, הרב גורן פנה לחברי מועצת הרבנות הראשית בבקשה לדון מחדש באיסור הכניסה להר הבית. בחודש מרץ 1975 הוא הרצה את דבריו בפני חברי המועצה. הרב גורן הסביר שהוא אינו מבקש להתיר הסתובבות בהר כולו, אלא רק בשטחים בהם ניתן לקבוע בוודאות שהמקדש לא עמד עליהם. כמו כן, היתר הכניסה יותנה בכך שהנכנסים להר יעברו סדרי טהרה כהלכה. הצעתו של הרב גורן נתקלה בהתנגדות חריפה. החלטת המועצה היתה שעל הרב גורן להגיש את טענותיו בכתב, ואז עמדתו תידון מחדש.[סד] כחודש לאחר מכן כבר ידע גיסו של הרב גורן, הרב שאר-ישוב הכהן, לספר כי החיבור מוכן להדפסה.[סה] אולם, לאכזבתו של הרב גורן, גם בכך לא היה די, ומועצת הרבנות לא שבה לדון בטענותיו. הרב גורן מצדו לא פרסם את חיבורו והשעה את פעילותו למען הכניסה להר הבית למשך שנים. רק בסוף השליש השני של שנות השמונים הוא החל לקרוא שוב לכניסה להר הבית, ובשנת 1992 ראה ספרו אור.[סו]

שתי שאלות חשובות ינחו את דיוני בעמדתו של הרב גורן: האחת, מהן הטענות המצדיקות את הכניסה להר הבית, והשניה, מדוע התעכב בפרסום עמדתו בתורת פסק הלכה עד לראשית שנות התשעים.

ובכן, בספרו של הרב גורן מאות עמודים המהווים דיון הלכתי ובו הבחנה בין אזורים אליהם מותר להיכנס לבין שטחים שהכניסה אליהם אסור, וכן בירור מגבלות הלכתיות שונות על הכניסה. הטענה העיקרית המוליכה את קו המחשבה לאורך הספר היא ששטח ההר היום גדול מזה שבעבר, ולכן לא כולו מוקדש בקדושת המקדש. בירור מציאותי של השטח המקורי והצבעה על איזורי הקדושה, תוציא מן הכלל איזורים מסויימים, ואליהם הכניסה מותרת.

[סב] רשימה ביבליוגרפית לפסקים האוסרים או מתירים את הכניסה להר הבית או לחלקיו מצויה אצל שמואל ברקוביץ, *מה נורא המקום הזה!: קדושה, פוליטיקה ומשפט בירושלים ובמקומות הקדושים בישראל*, ירושלים: כרטא, תשס"ו 2006, עמ' 111, הע' 514.

[סג] על עמדותיה של מועצת הרבנות הראשית לדורותיה ראו אצל יואל כהן, "הרבנות הראשית ושאלת הר הבית", בתוך: איתמר ורהפטיג ושמואל כ"ץ (עורכים), *הרבנות הראשית לישראל: שבעים שנה לייסודה*, *ב*, ירושלים: היכל שלמה, תשס"ב, עמ' 763-786.

[סד] Yoel Cohen, “The Political Role of the Israeli Chief Rabbinate in the Temple Mount Question”, *Jewish Political Studies Review* 11:1-2 (Spring 1999), by ff. 35.

[סה] הרב שאר-ישוב כהן, "ושם נעלה ונראה", בתוך: י' גליס (עורך), *הר הבית – מקומו וגבולותיו: הרצאות שהושמעו בשני ימי עיון כ"ב-כ"ג בניסן תשל"ה* (3-4.4.75), ירושלים: עיריית ירושלים והמכון ללמודי היהדות ש"י המדרשה הגבוהה לתורה, תשל"ה, עמ' 11.

[סו] הרב שלמה גורן, ספר *הר הבית: משיב מלחמה חלק רביעי – מחקר הלכתי והיסטורי מקיף על הר המוריה ומקום המקדש בצירוף מפות מעודכנות*, ירושלים: האידרא רבה ומסורה לעם, תשס"ה[2] (להלן: ממ"ד).

לצד הטיעון הזה מופיע לאורך הספר אמירות שונות לפיהן החיבור נועד להתיר את הכניסה כנגד מגמת המדינאים, אשר מוכנים לוותר על הריבונות הישראלית בהר הבית כחלק משיחות השלום עם עמי האיזור. כאן, השאיפה לריבונות אינה מהווה שיקול להיתר הכניסה, וכל כוחה בכך שהיא מניעה את הרב גורן לדון את הדיון ההלכתי, ואולי אף לתור אחרי מקורות הלכתיים מקילים.

הלך מחשבה זה מובע בפיסקה בה הצהיר הרב גורן על מטרות חיבורו (ממ"ד, עמ' 42-43):

> לאור כל האמור, וכדי שלא יוכלו מסגירי הר הבית לגויים לתלות את הקולר [עמ' 43] ברבנים האוסרים לעלות לשם, החלטתי לחקור, ולמדוד ולברר, את ההלכות הקשורות עם הר הבית ומקום המקדש, לתחם תחומין המותרים והאסורים בכניסה, וכן לקבוע את סדרי הטהרה שיש לנהוג לפני העליה להר.[סז]

אולם, לאורך הספר ישנן כמה נקודות בהן מתברר שלרב גורן עמדה אחרת, ולפיה השאיפה לריבונות על הר הבית איננה רק גורם מניע לבירור הלכתי מיקל, אלא היא מהווה בעצמה שיקול בעל תוקף הלכתי. לדעת הרב גורן, ההלכה מחייבת את ניקוי המקדש, ובמקרה שאין אנשים טהורים שיעשו זאת, מותרת הכניסה להר הבית ולשטחי המקדש אף לטמאים. לדעתו, אם ניקוי המקדש מתיר כניסת טמאים, הרי שעל אחת כמה וכמה שהכשרת הר הבית לבניין המקדש תהיה מותרת, גם לטמאים.[סח] מטעם זה היתה הכניסה להר הבית מותרת בשעת כיבושו במלחמת ששת הימים, ומטעם זה תהיה הכניסה מותרת במידה שיש בה כדי לחזק את הריבונות הישראלית בהר הבית (ממ"ד, עמ' 41):

> אין ספק שבמקרה כזה, כאשר קיימת סכנה להשתלטות נכרים על הר המוריה, מותר אפילו להכנס לשטח העזרה, כדי לא לתת להם חניה בהר ה', כי העליה של היהודים על ההר במצב זה נחשבת ככיבוש וחזקה ומניעת השתלטות זרים עליו.[סט]

סז ראו גם בממ"ד, עמ' 403: *"יש עלינו חובה ומצוה להכנס ולהתפלל במקום שמותר בכניסה עפ"י דין, כדי שלא יוסגר הר הבית לגויים"*.

סח ממ"ד, עמ' 403-406.

סט ראו גם בממ"ד, עמ' 45: "ככל שהזמן חולף, הולך ונחלש מעמדנו בהר הבית, ביחוד מזמן פרוץ האינתיפאדה. אנו מאבדים שליטה על הר הבית [...] כעת שאנו נמצאים תחת איום על חיינו ועל חרותנו, ארצנו ומולדתינו, מצווים אנו ע"פ [=על פי] התורה וההלכה להפגין נוכחות בכל פינה ובכל אזור בארץ". יש לציין כי ביום הכיבוש נכנסו הרב צבי יהודה קוק והרב דוד כהן ("הנזיר") לשטח הר הבית בדרכם לכותל המערבי. הרב כהן מספר בזיכרונותיו שהרבנים התלבטו האם הכניסה מותרת, והכריעו, שהעובדה שהם נכנסים עם כוחות הצבא ביום הכיבוש מתירים את הכניסה, ראו יוסף טולידאנו (עורך), *קול צופיך: אגרות וקטעי יומן מכתבי נזיר אלהים מרן הרב רבי דוד כהן זצ"ל אל מורו ורבו רבן של ישראל מרן הרב רבי אברהם יצחק הכהן קוק זצ"ל*, ירושלים: מכון הרי-פישל, תשל"ג, עמ' קכז.

הרב גורן לא היה היחיד שהבין שכניסת יהודים להר הבית תחזק את הסכמת העמים לשמירת הריבונות על ההר בידיים ישראליות. בשנת 1986 יזמה קבוצת חברי כנסת כניסה הפגנתית לשטח ההר. בין חברי הכנסת נמנה גם דב שילנסקי, אז יו"ר הכנסת, שפנה לרב גורן בשאלה אודות עמדתו ההלכתית באשר לכניסה להר.[ע] בהזדמנות זו הביע הרב גורן את גישתו הלכה למעשה, בהתירו לו את הכניסה להר כמעט ללא סייג (ממ"ד, עמ' 405-406, ההדגשות שלי):

> על אף הסייגים ההלכתיים הקיימים בכל הנוגע לכניסה להר הבית בימים כתיקונם, במצב שהתהווה שקיים חשש לאבדן הרבונות היהודית על הר הבית, **והנוכחות של היהודים בהר הבית כיום תחזק את הרבונות שלנו שם**, וכל שכן בקורם המופגן של חברי הכנסת בהר הבית, בודאי שיוכיח קבל עם ועולם שהר הבית הוא ברבונות ישראל. **במצב זה ולמטרה זו, לא רק מותר, אלא מצוה קדושה מוטלת עלינו להכנס להר הבית כדי לחזק את זכותנו, אחיזתנו והרבונות שלנו על מקום המקדש** [...]
>
> [עמ' 406] ובנדון דידן שהמטרה היא שחרור הר הבית מהשתלטות נכרים, וככל שיכנסו יותר ויותר חברי כנסת ויהודים אחרים, תהיה התוצאה המדינית גדולה ומרשימה יותר, כלפי הערבים והעולם כולו, שידעו כי לא ויתרנו חס וחלילה על הריבונות שלנו על הר המוריה. **אין להטיל על הנכנסים להר הבית למטרה זו, של מניעת השתלטות מוסלמית על הר הבית, סייגים הלכתיים קשים.** אבל זאת העצה היעוצה, שכל הנכנסים להר הבית מבין חברי הכנסת, ויהודים אחרים, לא ינעלו נעלי עור כי אם נעלי גומי [...] וכל הירא את דבר ה' יטבול באותו יום במקוה טהרה.

כאן אין זכר לחלוקה בין אזורים מותרים ואסורים, ואף הטבילה בגדר רשות והידור מצווה גרידא, וכפי שהרב גורן עצמו מדגיש, הדברים נאמרים אמנם לשילנסקי ושאר חברי הכנסת, אך נכונים לא פחות לגבי כל יהודי. גישה זו, המתירה את הכניסה לכל מרחבי ההר ורואה בטבילה הידור מצווה בלבד, שונה מהגישה שהציג הרב גורן בפני מועצת הרבנות הראשית בשנות השבעים.

ברם, מה הביא לשינוי במעמדה של השאיפה לריבונות על ההר, ומדוע הבליט הרב גורן את בירורי התחומים כאשר היה בידיו פסק מיקל עוד יותר?

[ע] על ביקור חברי הכנסת, ובהם דב שילנסקי, בהר הבית, ראו: שמואל ברקוביץ, *מלחמות המקומות הקדושים: המאבק על ירושלים והמקומות הקדושים בישראל, יהודה, שומרון וחבל עזה*, ירושלים ואור יהודה: מכון ירושלים לחקר ישראל והד ארצי, 2000, עמ' 90-91. ברקוביץ (שם) אף מציין שהרב גורן אירגן עצומות רבנים ובהם קריאה לעליית יהודים להר הבית. למעשה, בשנה זו נערכו שני ביקורים בהם השתתף שילנסקי, ושניהם היו כרוכים בגילויי אלימות מצד המוסלמים, ראו שרגאי, הר המריבה, עמ' 307-315.

כיצד עלינו להבין את הפער בין היתר כניסה המותנה בקיומן של מיגבלות קבועות, לבין היתר גורף המוצא אף הוא את מקומו בפסיקתו של הרב גורן? התשובה לשאלות אלה נעוצה, להבנתי, בשיקוליו של הרב גורן לעיכוב פרסום עמדתו מחד, והחלטתו לפרסמה מאידך.

כשנשאל על ידי פעילי תנועות העליה להר הבית בראשית שנות השמונים לטעם גניזת חיבורו ולסיבת הימנעותו מלהורות את היתר הכניסה להר הבית הלכה למעשה, הכחיש הרב גורן מכל וכל את ההקשר הפוליטי, ונימק את עיכוב הפרסום בכך שטרם הגיע למסקנה באשר להיתר כניסת נשים למרחבי ההר.[עא] לפניה רשמית של עורך דין חיים שטנגר, ביוני 1981, ובה בקשה שיפרסם את עמדתו, נענה הרב גורן בשלילה. את סירובו הוא הסביר בבקשתו להימנע מריבוי מחלוקות בישראל.[עב] לפי עדות אחרת, הימנעותו של הרב גורן מפרסום חיבורו נבעה מפחד מפני ביקורת שתימתח עליו בעולם הרבני.[עג] אולם, כפי שראינו לעיל, הרב גורן טוען בחיבורו שלפרסום הספר יש מטרה פוליטית – השפעה על הפוליטיקאים בשיחות השלום.

אם כן, שתי סתירות לפנינו: מן ההיבט ההלכתי, הרב גורן שינה את כח השפעתה של השאיפה לריבונות משיקול המעניק מוטיבציה לשיקול בעל תוקף הלכתי ממש. בנוסף, הרב גורן טען שאי פרסום פסקו אינו נובע משיקולים פוליטיים, אך את פרסום הפסק הוא נימק ברצונו להשפיע על הפוליטיקאים. להבנתי, שני השינויים כרוכים זה בזה, ושניהם גם יחד תלויים בשינויים במצב הריאל-פוליטי של מדינת ישראל בכלל, ומעמד הר-הבית בפרט.

בעיני הרב גורן היתה כניסת הצנחנים להר הבית מותרת, וכך גם הכניסה לכיפת הסלע, אליה נכנס הוא עצמו, כשהצדקתו בכך שהוא חלק מן הכוחות המוודאים שהשטח נקי מסכנה.[עד] עם שכוך הקרבות, הרב גורן נעזר בחיל ההנדסה וביצע מדידות, שתכליתן קביעת השטחים המותרים בכניסה, ואלו האסורים. נראה אם כן, שכבר בשנת 1967 הרב גורן הבחין בין רמות שונות של איום על ריבונות ישראלית על הר הבית. ככל שהסכנה לריבונות גדולה יותר, כך יהיו ההיתרים מופלגים יותר.

לפיכך, לאחר השגת הריבונות שוב אין עילה להיכנס לאזורים ברמת קדושה גבוהה, וההיתר מתמצה לאזורים שלפי המדידות מותרים בכניסה, ובכך יהיה די כדי להפגין את הזיקה בין העם היהודי לבין הר הבית. אף המוטיבציה לפרסום מוגבלת, שכן התקבע המצב לפיו הריבונות היא יהודית והניהול בפועל בידי הוואקף. ברם, בחילופי השנים

[עא] שרגאי, הר המריבה, עמ' 63. כך גם כתב הרב גורן עצמו בממ"ד, עמ' 15.

[עב] שלג, משוח מלחמה, פרק עשירי.

[עג] סגל, אחים יקרים, עמ' 50 מצטט את הרב גורן כאומר: "אני חושש שיאכלו אותי חיים וימיתו אותי". לפי סגל "הוא לא התכוון לשלטונות וגם לא לציבור החילוני".

[עד] רט, בעוז ותעצומות, עמ' 277.

התברר לרב גורן שישנה כוונה לחתום על הסכמים שיוותרו על הריבונות הישראלית בהר לצמיתות. מעתה, באופן עקרוני שב המצב לזה שהיה בימי המלחמה, ואם כן, ניתן להתיר את הכניסה להר על כל מרחביו, ללא הגבלות ודרישות טהרה גבוהות. אכן, בלשון מכתבו של הרב גורן לשילנסקי ניכר שהדגש הוא על המצווה הגדולה שיקיימו הנכנסים להר, ואילו הוראת ההגבלות נכתבת בשפה רפה, כהמלצה, בבחינת "מהיות טוב אל תהי רע".[עה] מעתה גם מתעורר הצורך לפרסם את ההיתר בשער בת רבים, ולעודד יהודים להיכנס להר הבית, ולהביע את חשיבותו של ההר לעם היהודי.

אולם, פרט אחד עדיין חסר בתיאור זה של עמדת הרב גורן. כאמור, הרב גורן ראה בכניסת חברי הכנסת צעד של כיבוש ההר, וככל הנראה הבין שהוא הדין לכניסת יהודים אחרים. מדוע אם כן פרסם את ספרו כפסק הלכה המתיר אך ורק כניסה לאיזורים מוגבלים, ומדוע עסק כה רבות בשאלת סדרי הטהרה הנצרכים קודם לכניסה להר? מדוע לא התיר את הכניסה ככניסת הצנחנים במלחמת ששת הימים, ללא כל היטהרות מוקדמת?

לדידי, אין לנתק בין עמדתו של הרב גורן בשאלת הכניסה להר הבית, לבין ארועים שונים שהתרחשו בשנות השמונים, אותם ניתן לראות כתהליך של קיטוב בין ה"זרם המרכזי" של הציבוריות הישראלית לבין קבוצות קיצוניות במחנה הימין.

ביוני 1980 מולכדו מכוניותיהם של ראשי עיריות שכם ורמאללה, כנקמה על הריגתם של ששה מתושבי קריית-ארבע וחברון בפיגוע שביצע ארגון הפת"ח בחברון. הקבוצה שארגנה את הפעילות כונתה לימים "המחתרת היהודית". בשנת 1983 התנקשו בראשי הוועדה להכוונה לאומית, ובהמשך רצחו שלושה סטודנטים ערבים במכללה האסלאמית בחברון, כנקמה על רציחתו של אהרון גרוס. הזכרון הציבורי כולל גם את הצלחת השב"כ בניטרול חמישה אוטובוסים שמולכדו על ידי המחתרת.[עו]

בעקבות נסיון כושל זה נעצרו רבים מחברי "המחתרת", וביניהם אף דמויות שהיו מוכרות כמרכזיות בהתיישבות ביש"ע. במהלך חקירתם התברר כי בין תוכניותיהם היה מקום של כבוד לפיצוץ המסגדים שבהר הבית. הגינויים למעשי המחתרת היו רחבים. נשיא המדינה, חיים הרצוג, התייחס למעשיהם כאל "פרי טירוף הדעת של אנשים בלתי אחראיים ובלתי-שפויים", ובתקשורת התפרסמו מאמרים רבים המגנים את המחתרת ופעולותיה.[עז] לענייננו חשובה במיוחד העובדה שמעשי "המחתרת" זכו לגינויים חריפים בקרב הציבור הדתי-לאומי. הם נתפסו כמהפכנים חתרניים, כמי שמסכנים את מדינת ישראל, וכמי שנקטו באקטיביזם חסר גבולות אשר יביא בפועל לניתוק הזיקה הרגשית בין הציבור הישראלי להר הבית.[עח]

עה על הגבלת היתרים משיקול זה ומשיקולים נוספים ראו בפרק ח' בעבודתי, לעיל הע' א.

עו שרגאי, הר המריבה, 112-122.

עז דוגמאות שונות מובאות אצל סגל, אחים יקרים, עמ' 211-213.

עח הצגת שיטתו של עציון, תוך הצגת מעט מן הביקורת שנמתחה נגד פעילותו בעניין הר הבית ודיון באשר ליחס בין האקטיביזם שלו לזה של תנועת גוש אמונים מצוי אצל יוחאי ברוך

הפעילות למען הר-הבית התרחבה במהלך שנות השמונים וראשית התשעים, וחשובים לאיזכור מיוחד שלושה ארועים שמחוללם הוא ראש תנועת "נאמני הר הבית", גרשון סלומון. באוקטובר 1987 התפרסמה ידיעה עיתונאית, לפיה קיבל סלומון אישור מן המשטרה לקיים עם אנשי תנועתו תפילה בהר הבית. כשהגיעו סלומון ואנשיו לשער המוגרבים הם נתקלו בכאלפיים מוסלמים משולהבים. המשטרה ניסתה להרגיע את הרוחות, אך ללא הצלחה יתירה. אבנים הושלכו מהר הבית לעבר רחבת הכותל המערבי, וכוחות משטרה פרצו להר הבית. הארוע התפתח לכדי חטיפת שוטר, שחולץ על ידי חבריו, ללא נשקו שנותר בידי המוסלמים, אשר התבצרו בהר הבית.[עט]

ארוע נוסף התקיים בשנת 1989. גרשון סלומון הודיע על טקס "הנחת אבן הפינה למקדש". טקס זה גרר מהומות בקרב ערביי ירושלים, במהלכם נפצעו חמישה שוטרים וארבעים ערבים נעצרו.[פ] כשנה מאוחר יותר, בחול המועד סוכות תשנ"א, סלומון יזם טקס דומה, שהפעם התפתח לכדי מהומות בהן המתפרעים הערבים משליכים אבנים מהר הבית על ראשי המתפללים היהודים בכותל המערבי, וכוחות הבטחון שנזעקו להר הבית מצאו לפניהם מאות מוסלמים ובידיהם נשק קר. בהמשך, תקפו הפורעים את מטה המשטרה בהר הבית, ואף הציתו אותו על יושביו.[פא] בסיכום היום התברר כי המהומות גבו את חייהם של שבעה עשר מבין המתפרעים הערבים, לצד מאה פצועים ערבים ועשרות פצועים יהודים, בהם שוטרי משמר הגבול.[פב]

מאוחר יותר, יהודה עציון, חבר המחתרת שריצה את עונשו במלואו, עקב סירובו לבקש חנינה מנשיא המדינה, הקים בעזרת כמה חברים תנועה בשם "חי-וקיים", אשר חרתה על דיגלה את השאיפה לחידוש מלכות ישראל ולגאולת ישראל. בדבריהם שבו והבהירו כי האידיאולוגיה הציונית היא אשר מונעת מעם ישראל את גאולתו, הכרוכה בשיבה להר הבית. בכך יש ביטוי נוסף למרכזיות של הר הבית בקרב התנועות הרדיקליות שפעלו במפנה העשורים התשיעי והעשירי למאה העשרים.

רודיק, *ארץ גאולה: שורשים אידיאולוגיים של הציונות הדתית, גוש אמונים והמחתרת היהודית ומערכת יחסיהן לעולם החילוני במדינת ישראל*, ירושלים: המכון לחקר משנת ראי"ה קוק זצ"ל, תשמ"ט, עמ' 168-178. דוגמאות נוספות למחאה מצד מנהיגי הציבור של הציונות הדתית כנגד מעשי "המחתרת" מובאים אצל שרגאי, הר המריבה, עמ' 124-130, וכך גם אצל סגל, אחים יקרים, עמ' 213-218. עם זאת, כפי שציין מוטי ענברי, *פונדמנטליזם יהודי והר הבית*, ירושלים: מאגנס ומכון אשכול, תשס"ח, עמ' 85 (להלן: ענברי, פונדמנטליזם יהודי), על אף כל הביקורת הוא לא הודר חברתית, ואף זכה להערכה בקרב ציבורים מסויימים.

עט שרגאי, הר המריבה, עמ' 295.

פ שרגאי, הר המריבה, עמ' 345.

פא ראו באתר משטרת ישראל (נצפה בתאריך 9.3.2013): .http://www.police.gov.il/history/fullArticleText.aspx?aid=187

פב ארועי אוקטובר 1990, נסקרו באריכות אצל שרגאי, הר המריבה, עמ' 340-363.

האם יש קשר בין פעילותו של הרב גורן לעידוד יהודים לכניסה לאיזורים מוגבלים בהר הבית לבין פעילות תנועות אלה? מהי הזיקה בין פרסום ספרו של הרב גורן, בשנת 1992, לבין רצף הארועים המתואר כאן? האם היה הרב גורן פוסק רדיקלי שהיווה, בפועל, את הגב ההלכתי לפעולותיהם?[פג]

לדעתי, את מניע פרסום חיבורו של הרב גורן אין לראות כניסיון להתססה וכקריאה לשוב להר הבית, אלא כגורם שנועד להביע עמדה מתונה יחסית בשאלת הר-הבית, וזאת משתי בחינות. ראשית, השיח בספרו של הרב גורן הוא שיח הלכתי, מחושב, דקדקני, וככזה הוא פחות סוחף ונוטה להתפרצות. אולם, יתר על כן, בפני הרב גורן היו שתי אפשרויות תקפות מבחינה הלכתית: מתן היתר גורף לכניסה להר הבית, הדומה לזה שנתן לחברי הכנסת, או אישור כניסה מוגבלת, הן מבחינת אזורי הכניסה והן מבחינת סדרי הטהרה הנדרשים. לטעמי, הרב גורן חשש שהדגשה של האפשרות הראשונה עלולה להיות מובנת כהיתר לפעולות מלחמתיות נוסח "המחתרת היהודית". תמיכה שכזו אמנם יכולה להיחשב מוצדקת על ידי מי שאולי עודד את עוזי נרקיס לפוצץ את המסגדים, אולם משני טעמים היא תחשב לפסולה: ראשית, כאמור לעיל, הרב גורן טען שלא היתה תועלת בפיצוץ המסגדים בשנת 1967, מאחר שישראל היתה בונה אותם מחדש. אם הדבר היה נכון בשנת 67', בוודאי שהיה נכון בראשית שנות ה-90'. בנוסף, מאחר ופעילות "המחתרת" זכתה להד שלילי בציבוריות הישראלית, תמיכה בפעילות טרור ישראלית היתה עלולה להרחיק את הציבור הישראלי מהבעת זיקה וריבונות על הר הבית בפרט, ומתורת ישראל וההלכה בכלל. טעמים אלה הם שהכווינו את הרב גורן להצניע את האפשרות הראשונה, ולהציג בבולטות את האפשרות השניה, זו המוגבלת, ובכך הוא ריסן את התוקפנות שהיתה גלומה במתן היתר כללי וחסר גבולות. בהצגת עמדה זו הוא מצא את האיזון בין פעילות מעשית לחיזוקה של הריבונות בהר הבית לבין חציית קו שאותו, לפי הערכת הרב גורן, החברה הישראלית לא יכלה לשאת באותה העת.[פד]

פג קריאה מעין זו הציע מוטי ענברי במספר פרסומים. הוא הציג ארבע מגמות עיקריות במנהיגות הציונית דתית בשאלת היחס להר הבית. הזרם הרביעי, הקיצוני ביותר, הוא זה אליו משתייך הרב גורן, והוא זה הקורא לכניסה מיידית להר הבית, ראו: Motti Inbari, "Religious Zionism and the Temple Mount Dilemma—Key Trends", *Israel Studies* 12:2 (2007), p. 43; ibid, *Jewish Fundamentalism and the Temple Mount: Who Will Build the Third Temple?*, Albany: State University of New York, 2009, pp 28-29; הנ"ל, פונדמנטליזם יהודי, עמ' 36-37. לטעמי, הצגת הרב גורן כגורם הרדיקלי ביותר מפסידה את המימד השמרני שבפסיקתו.

פד חשש כזה, מפני האפשרות שמעשי המחתרת יפלגו את העם, הובעו בדברי הרב צבי טאו, המובאים אצל סגל, אחים יקרים, עמ' 215 (הוספתי הדגשה): "יש אנשים שטועים וחושבים שאם יוצאים בצורה חריפה נגד ה'מחתרת' ונגד אלה שעומדים רעיונית מאחוריה – עושים פירודים ומחלוקות בעם ישראל. צריך לדעת **שהדיון פה נועד למנוע את המחלוקת היותר גדולה שרק יכולה להיות, את התפוררות אחדות הציבור** [הישראלי] [...] העמידה נגד גורמי הרקבון הללו – זה לעשות שלום בישראל".

סיכום

רוב ימיו הבוגרים של הרב גורן עברו עליו כשהוא נושא בתפקידים ממלכתיים. הוא מונה לרב הצבאי הראשי כבר בהיותו כבן 30, ועזב את משרד הרב הראשי לישראל בהיותו כבן 65. למעשה, אף לאחר פרישתו מתפקידיו הממלכתיים, הוא המשיך להביע את עמדתו בבעיות הלכתיות וציבוריות שעמדו על הפרק.

כאחד מפוסקיה הבולטים של הציונות הדתית, נדרש הרב גורן במשך השנים לעשרות בעיות הלכתיות בעלות גוון ציבורי. בכל אלה הוא קירב וריחק מקורות שיכולים להיות רלוונטיים לסוגיה הנידונית, הוא עמד על פרשנויות שונות אפשריות, ומבין שלל האפשרויות הסבירות הוא בחר זו שנראתה לו ראויה.

במאמר זה הצגתי שלוש סוגיות בהן, להבנתי, פסיקתו של הרב גורן כעמדה אחת מבין הדעות ההלכתיות הסבירות, נעשתה תוך התייחסות לדעת הקהל בישראל. בפסקיו בקש הרב גורן להיות נאמן למסורת ההלכתית, ולפיכך התאמץ לעגן את פסקיו במקורות הלכתיים, אך מאידך בקש להציג פסקי הלכה אותם הציבור הישראלי – ובעיקר זה הרחוק משמירת תורה ומצוות – יוכל לעכל ולקבל כעמדה ראויה. בכך הוא מיצע בין שתי אהבות גדולות להן היה נאמן – המדינה והתורה.[פה]

לפי הניתוח הזה, הרב גורן הכיר בכך שלהלכה אין תשובה יחידה לשאלה, וכי במציאויות שונות תיתכנה תשובות שונות לבעיה דומה. מורכבות החיים דורשת מן ההלכה תשובות מורכבות, המספקות תוצאות שונות לפי תנאי הזמן והמקום בכלל, והתנאים החברתיים בפרט.

אך הצגה זו תהיה חסרה ללא הצבעה על תקוותו של הרב גורן לכך שבהתאמה לבחירתו באפיק ההלכתי המתאים לדמוקרטיה הישראלית, גם הדמוקרטיה הישראלית תבחר באפיקים התרבותיים שיכולים להיכלל תחת ההלכה. הרב גורן סבר שהאפשרות לאחד את עם ישראל עם תורת ישראל במדינת ישראל כרוכה בבחירה מתמדת של החברה הישראלית כולה להקדיש מאמצים לאיתור המרכיבים החופפים בין המסורת היהודית לבין המודרנה הדמוקרטית, וכה היו דבריו בהכתרתו למשרת הרב הראשי לתל-אביב-יפו:

[פה] במובן מסויים צודק אבי שגיא בטענתו שהרב גורן הציג דיכוטומיה בין דת ומדינה, ראו: הנ"ל, *המסע היהודי-ישראלי: שאלות של תרבות ושל זהות*, ירושלים: מכון שלום הרטמן, תשס"ו 2006, עמ' 171. ברם, הרב גורן ביקש לשבור את הדיכוטומיה בין השתיים, וטען לגמישותן של שתי המערכות. בכך עמדותיו אינן קשיחות כפי שהציגן שגיא.

אם ברצוננו לשמור על שלמות התורה ואחדות העם, עלינו להתמודד עם בעיות אלו, למצות כל אפשרות וכל רצון טוב מכל הצדדים כדי לפתור את הבעיות העומדות ברומו של עולמנו ואשר מהוות סכנה לקיומה, שלמותה ואחדותה של האומה.[פו]

ঞ

מאמר זה מבוסס על עבודת הדוקטורט שלי, אותה כתבתי בתמיכתן הנדיבה של "מילגת הנשיא לדוקטורנטים מצטיינים" שהעניקה לי אוניברסיטת בר-אילן, מילגת המכון הגבוה לתורה לדוקטורנטים מצטיינים, ומילגת מחקר של קרן הזיכרון לתרבות יהודית, ולהן נתונה תודתי והערכתי.

פו הרב שלמה גורן, "נאום הרב בהכתרתו לרב ראשי לתל-אביב", בתוך: יצחק אלפסי (עורך), *המעלות לשלמה: ספר זכרון בהלכה ובאגדה למרן הגאון האדיר שר התורה הרב ר' שלמה גורן זצוק"ל הרב הראשי לצה"ל ולמדינת ישראל ביום השנה להסתלקותו:* כ"ד במר חשון תשנ"ו, ירושלים: חש"מ, תשנ"ו, עמ' 151.

שיטת רבי יהודה הנשיא באיסור מלאכה בשבת ובמלאכת המשכן

מאת: משה צבי פולין

מקובל אצל רוב הלומדים של"ט המלאכות האסורות בשבת מבוססות על מלאכת המשכן. ברצוני לנתח את השקלא ותריא בכמה סוגיות במסכת שבת העוסקות בענין הזה ולהראות שרבי יהודה הנשיא דווקא דחה את הקשר בין המלאכות האסורות בשבת ומלאכת המשכן.

כתוב במשנה:

> אבות מלאכות ארבעים חסר אחת הזורע והחורש והקוצר והמעמר הדש והזורה הבורר הטוחן והמרקד והלש והאופה הגוזז את הצמר המלבנו והמנפצו והצובעו והטווה והמיסך והעושה שתי בתי נירין והאורג שני חוטין והפוצע ב' חוטין הקושר והמתיר והתופר שתי תפירות הקורע ע"מ לתפור שתי תפירות הצד צבי השוחטו והמפשיטו המולחו והמעבד את עורו והמוחקו והמחתכו הכותב שתי אותיות והמוחק על מנת לכתוב שתי אותיות הבונה והסותר המכבה והמבעיר המכה בפטיש המוציא מרשות לרשות הרי אלו אבות מלאכות ארבעים חסר אחת.[א]

האמוראים שאלו שתי שאלות על המספרים במשנה זו עד שהם ניתחו את רשימת המלאכות עצמן: האחת, במפורש, "מנינא למה לי"?[ב] והשניה בעקיפין, מנינא לאפוקי מאי?[ג]. על השאלה הראשונה תירץ "רבי יוחנן: שאם עשאן כולם בהעלם אחד - חייב על כל אחת ואחת".[ד] ועל השאלה השניה תירצה סתמא דגמרא:

> 'אלו אבות מלאכות' אלו לאפוקי מדרבי אליעזר, דמחייב על תולדה במקום אב. 'חסר אחת' לאפוקי מדרבי יהודה, דתניא: רבי יהודה מוסיף את השובט והמדקדק.

[א] שבת פ"ז מ"ב, ובגמ' בדף עג.

[ב] שם עג:

[ג] שם עה: השאלה לא נשאלה.

[ד] שם עג:

הרב משה צבי פולין הוסמך להוראה ע"י הרה"ג חיים קרייזווירטה ז"ל וראשי הישיבה בביהמ"ד לתורה בשיקאגו (היום בסקוקי). הוא שימש ברב בכמה קהילות בארה"ב ולבסוף במרכז היהודי קינגסוויי בברוקלין לעשרים וארבע שנים. הוא נבחר ע"י חבריו לנשיא הסתדרות הרבנים באמריקה. היום הוא גר בירושלים והוציא שלשה ספרים על הרמב"ם.

אמרו לו: שובט - הרי הוא בכלל מיסך, מדקדק - הרי הוא בכלל אורג.[ה]

עוד שאלה שאלו האמוראים על המשנה הזו, אולם היא לא נמצאת בסוגיא העוסקת במשנה אלא כמה פרקים קודם: "הדור יתבי וקמיבעיא להו: הא דתנן אבות מלאכות ארבעים חסר אחת כנגד מי?"[ו] ותירצו האמוראים: "אמר להו רבי חנינא בר חמא: כנגד עבודות המשכן".[ז] זהו המקור לקשר בין איסור ל"ט מלאכות בשבת ומלאכת המשכן. והאמורים המשיכו לחפש יסוד למקור הזה:

> אמר להו רבי יונתן ברבי אלעזר כך אמר רבי שמעון ברבי יוסי בן לקוניא: כנגד מלאכה מלאכתו ומלאכת שבתורה - ארבעים חסר אחת. בעי רב יוסף: (בראשית לט,יא) ויבא הביתה לעשות מלאכתו ממנינא הוא, או לא? - אמר ליה אביי: וליתי ספר תורה ולימני! מי לא אמר רבה בר בר חנה אמר רבי יוחנן: לא זזו משם, עד שהביאו ספר תורה ומנאום. אמר ליה: כי קא מספקא לי - משום דכתיב (שמות לו,ז) והמלאכה היתה דים ממנינא הוא, והא - כמאן דאמר לעשות צרכיו נכנס, או דילמא: ויבא הביתה לעשות מלאכתו ממנינא הוא, והאי והמלאכה היתה דים - הכי קאמר: דשלים ליה עבידתא? תיקו.[ח]

הדיון הזה תמוה. מה עניין מלאכה מלאכתו ומלאכת דווקא לעניין שבת? לכל הפחות, הדיון הזה מראה שהקשר בין מלאכה מלאכתו ומלאכת ואיסור מלאכה בשבת הוא קשר רדוד.

ועוד, יותר תמוה, המלים מלאכה מלאכתו ומלאכת אינן נמצאות בתורה שלושים ותשע פעמים. עיון במחשב מראה שהמילה מלאכה נמצאת שלושים וחמש פעמים, מלאכתו חמש פעמים, ומלאכת עשרים ושלוש פעמים. יש לציין שלמרות הצעת אביי: "וליתי ספר תורה ולימני! מי לא אמר רבה בר בר חנה אמר רבי יוחנן: לא זזו משם, עד שהביאו ספר תורה ומנאום," הגמרא לא אמרת שמנאום ומצאו מנין המלים ארבעים חסר אחת. אדרבא, מכיון שהמשיכו לשאול אם "ויבא הביתה לעשות מלאכתו" ועל "והמלאכה היתה דים" מנויים בסכום ארבעים חסר אחת מראה שלא מצאו מנין המלים בדיוק ארבעים חסר אחת.

אמנם, הסוגיא הזו ממשיכה לדון בקשר איסור מלאכות בשבת ומלאכת המשכן, הפעם בציטוט ברייתא:

> תניא כמאן דאמר כנגד עבודות המשכן, דתניא: אין חייבין אלא על מלאכה שכיוצא בה היתה במשכן, הם זרעו - ואתם לא תזרעו, הם קצרו - ואתם לא תקצרו, הם

[ה] שם עה:

[ו] שם מט:

[ז] שם.

[ח] שם.

העלו את הקרשים מקרקע לעגלה - ואתם לא תכניסו מרשות הרבים לרשות היחיד. הם הורידו את הקרשים מעגלה לקרקע - ואתם לא תוציאו מרשות היחיד לרשות הרבים, הם הוציאו מעגלה לעגלה - ואתם לא תוציאו מרשות היחיד לרשות היחיד. מרשות היחיד לרשות היחיד,[ט] מאי קא עביד? - אביי ורבא דאמרי תרוויהו, ואיתימא רב אדא בר אהבה: מרשות היחיד לרשות היחיד דרך רשות הרבים.[י]

יש לציין שההוכחה הזו היא מברייתא. הברייתות הן דברי תנאים שהוציא רבי יהודה הנשיא מן המשנה. כנראה, אם כן, רבי יהודה הנשיא לא קבל קשר בין איסור מלאכה בשבת ומלאכת המשכן. לקמן נראה שסוף כל סוף גם האמוראים הבינו שאין קשר בין איסור מלאכה בשבת ומלאכת המשכן.

בהמשך לתשובת רבי יוחנן לשאלה הראשונה על המשנה, מנינא למה לי, מצאנו הסבר בעוד מאמר בתחילת הפרק הזה:

חילוק מלאכות מנלן? אמר שמואל: אמר קרא (שמות לא,יד) מחלליה מות יומת - התורה רבתה מיתות הרבה על חילול אחד. האי במזיד כתיב! אם אינו ענין למזיד, דכתיב (שמות לה,ב) כל העשה [בו] מלאכה יומת - תנהו ענין לשוגג, ומאי יומת - יומת בממון. ותיפוק ליה חילוק מלאכות מהיכא דנפקא ליה לרבי נתן, דתניא, רבי נתן אומר: (שמות לה,ג) לא תבערו אש בכל משבתיכם ביום השבת, מה תלמוד לומר? לפי שנאמר (שמות לה,א) ויקהל משה את כל עדת בני ישראל אלה הדברים וגו' ששת ימים תעשה מלאכה. דברים, הדברים - אלה הדברים - אלו שלשים ותשע מלאכות שנאמרו למשה בסיני. יכול עשאן כולן בהעלם אחד אינו חייב אלא אחת - תלמוד לומר (שמות לד,כא) בחריש ובקציר תשבת. ועדיין אני אומר: על חרישה ועל הקצירה - חייב שתים, ועל כולן אינו חייב אלא אחת! תלמוד לומר: לא תבערו אש, הבערה בכלל היתה, ולמה יצאת - להקיש אליה, ולומר לך: מה הבערה שהיא אב מלאכה וחייבין עליה בפני עצמה - אף כל שהוא אב מלאכה חייבין עליה בפני עצמה.[יא]

דרך אגב, האמוראים הסבירו איך הגיעו חז"ל למנין ארבעים חסר אחת, דהיינו, סמכו על הדרשה אלה הדברים. לכל הפחות דרשה זו, בניגוד לדרשות מלאכה מלאכתו מלאכת,

---

[ט] לא מצאתי שום מקור לברייתא זו חוץ מן הגמרא שהבאנו.

[י] שם.

[יא] שם ע. וע"ע בחומש תורה תמימה שהביא את הירושלמי שבת פ"ז ה"ב [בדף ט טור ב]: אלה הדברים דבר דברי דברים מיכן לאבות ולתולדות ר' חנינא דציפורין בשם ר' אבהו אל"ף חד למ"ד תלתין ה"א חמשה דבר חד ודברי' תריי מיכן לארבעים חסר אחת מלאכות שכתוב בתורה רבנין דקיסרין אמרין מן אתרה לא חסרה כלום אל"ף חד למ"ד תלתין ח' תמניא לא מתמנעין רבנן דרשין בין ה"א לחי"ת. ההסבר הוא שאותיות גרוניות, אהח"ע, מתחלפות. ולכן ה"א וחי"ת מתחלפות.

נמצא על מקרא שמדבר בעניין שבת. אולם, גם דרשה זו מעוררת שאלה: האם באה הדרשה קודם וחז"ל טרחו למצוא שלושים ותשע מלאכות? או דילמא, חז"ל בדקו ומצאו שיש שלושים ותשע מלאכות וטרחו למצא דרשה לאשר את דבריהם?

סוף סוף, גם האמוראים בניתוחם את המשנה שלנו הבינו שאי אפשר למצוא קשר בין ל"ט המלאכות האסורות בשבת ומלאכת המשכן. כבר בניתוח הראשון נראה שאין קשר בין המשנה ומלאכת המשכן. הגמרא מבקרת את סדר המשנה:

> הזורע והחורש. מכדי, מכרב כרבי ברישא, ליתני חורש, והדר ליתני זורע! תנא בארץ ישראל קאי, דזרעי ברישא והדר כרבי.[יב]

לו היו למלאכות האסורות בשבת קשר עם מלאכת המשכן, לא הייתה סתמא דגמרא מתרץ "תנא בארץ ישראל קאי".

אותה סוג תשובה רואים אנחנו בעוד אחד מניתוחי המשנה:

> והלש והאופה. אמר רב פפא: שבק תנא דידן בישול סממנין דהוה במשכן, ונקט אופה! - תנא דידן - סידורא דפת נקט.[יג]

הגמרא הייתה יכולה לתרץ שמדובר באפיית לחם הפנים. מכיוון שלא תירצה כך משמע שמדובר בסתם אפייה שלא לצורך המשכן.

ובסוף הסוגיא מנתחים האמוראים את מלאכת שחיטה.

> והשוחטו. שוחט משום מאי חייב? רב אמר: משום צובע, ושמואל אמר: משום נטילת נשמה. משום צובע אין, משום נטילת נשמה לא? אימא: אף משום צובע. אמר רב: מילתא דאמרי - אימא בה מילתא, דלא ליתו דרי בתראי וליחכו עלי. צובע במאי ניחא ליה - ניחא דליתווס בית השחיטה דמא, כי היכי דליחזוה אינשי וליתו ליזבנו מיניה.[יד]

גם רש"י וגם התוספות דחקו לפרש כונת הקושיא שהרי שחיטה ממלאכות החשובות במשכן. לכן פירש רש"י, "למה לי בהו שחיטה, בחניקה נמי סגי".[טו] ולפי התוספות: "לאו אשוחט דמתני' קאי דההוא פשיטא דלא הוי אלא משום נטילת נשמה דצובע תנן בהדיא במתני' אלא אשוחט דעלמא קאי".[טז]

מכל אלה הקושיות והתירוצים בניתוח האמוראים את המשנה, רואים אנו איך הראו שלפי רבי יהודה הנשיא אין קשר בין מלאכת המשכן ובין רשימת המלאכות האסרות

[יב] שם עג:

[יג] שם עד:

[יד] שם עה.-:

[טו] רש"י בד"ה שוחט, שם עה.

[טז] תוד"ה שוחט, שם.

בשבת שבמשנה.

ואף דמצינו במשנה (שבת קג.) דהביא רבי דברי ר' יוסי דכן למד ממלאכת המשכן:

> הכותב--בין בימינו בין בשמאלו, בין משם אחד בין משני שמות, בין משני סמיונות, בכל לשון--חייב. אמר רבי יוסי, לא נתחייבו שתי אותות אלא משום רושם, **שכך היו רושמין על קרשי המשכן**, לידע איזה הוא בן זוגו.

עי' בפיה"מ לרמב"ם (שם) דזה דעת רבי ורבנן פליג עליה. וסתמא דמשנה דאין רושם אב בפני עצמה אלא תולדה וכן פסק הרמב"ם להלכה. (יא:יז)

אבל למלאכת מושיט היא סתמא דמשנה (צו.) דכן לומדים מהמשכן:

> כיצד: שתי כצוצריות זו כנגד זו ברשות הרבים, המושיט והזורק מזו לזו--פטור. היו שתיהן בדייטי אחת--המושיט חייב, והזורק פטור: **שכן הייתה עבודת הלויים**; שתי עגלות זו אחר זו ברשות הרבים--מושיטין את הקרשים מזו לזו, אבל לא זורקין. חולית הבור והסלע, שהן גבוהין עשרה ורוחבן ארבעה--הנוטל מהן והנותן על גבן, חייב; פחות מכן, פטור.

אבל הרי פסק הרמב"ם (יב:י) דאין מושיט אלא תולדה[יז] ולכן בכלל צ"ע הא דלמדו מעבודת הלוים. ועי' בפני יהושע (צו)

> יש לתמוה כיון דלמעלה מי' פשיטא לן טובא דמקום פטור הוא, אם כן מאי מהני האי טעמא דקאמר שכך היתה עבודת הלוים ומש"ה מחייב משום דהוה בעבודת המשכן, דאטו מי לא אשכחן נמי במשכן ענין הוצאה וזריקה מרה"י לרשות היחיד אחר או לכרמלית או למקום פטור וכה"ג במעביר אפ"ה פטור כיון דלא הוי מלאכה כלל בענין זה וא"כ ה"נ דכוותיה . וכתבתי שם **דשאני הכי במושיט כיון דלא אשכחן בעבודת הלוים בבני מררי שהיא מעבודת משא מלאכה אחרת כ"א מלאכת הושטת הקרשים מעגלה לבד אלמא דהושטה אקרי מלאכה** דלא דמי למוציא ומעביר דאמרינן דלמעלה מי' מקום פטור היא משום דעיקר תשמיש אדם ברה"ר בהוצאה והעברה אינו אלא למטה מעשרה כשמוציא ביד או בתוך חיקו מה שא"כ לענין הושטה היו אפכא דעיקר הושטה היינו ממקום גבוה למקום נמוך או אפכא.

ונראה על פי דבריו דהמשנה לא בא ללמד ממעשה הלוים אלא מה נחשב מעשה חשובה לכללה בתוך מלאכת הוצאה[יח] אבל לא למד רבי הל"ט מלאכות מהמשכן. ובזה מבואר גם כן דחייב רבי במשנה (צב.) אף המוציא בשמאל או על כתיפו "שכן משא בני קהת." ☙

[יז] וכן דעת תוס' ב. ד"ה פשט ועי' בתוספתא פרק א ופליג הרמב"ן (עג:) על פי הירושלמי ז:ב ויש מפרשים דמחלוקת בבלי וירושלמי היא

[יח] עי' ב"ק ב. ובתוס' שם ובתוס' שבת צו: בגרסאות על "דבמשכן חשיבי"